Strategic Electronic Marketing

Managing E-Business

Brad Alan Kleindl, Ph.D.

Missouri Southern State College
Joplin, Missouri

South-Western College Publishing
Thomson Learning™

Australia • Canada • Denmark • Japan • Mexico • New Zealand • Philippines
Puerto Rico • Singapore • South Africa • Spain • United Kingdom • United States

Strategic Electronic Marketing: Managing E-Business, by Brad Alan Kleindl

Publisher: Dave Shaut
Acquisitions Editor: Pamela M. Person
Developmental Editor: Mardell Toomey
Marketing Manager: Steve Scoble
Production Editor: Sandra Gangelhoff
Manufacturing Coordinator: Sandee Milewski
Internal Design: Joe Devine
Cover Illustration and Design: Tin Box Studio/Cincinnati, OH
Production House: Navta Associates, Inc.
Compositor: Navta Associates, Inc.
Printer: West Group

Printed in the United States of America
2 3 4 5 03 02 01 00

For more information contact South-Western College Publishing, 5101 Madison Road, Cincinnati, Ohio, 45227 or find us on the Internet at http://www.swcollege.com
For permission to use material from this text or product, contact us by
• telephone: **1-800-730-2214**
• fax: **1-800-730-2215**
• web: **http://www.thomsonrights.com**
Library of Congress Cataloging-in-Publication Data

Kleindl, Brad A.
    Strategic electronic marketing : managing e-business / by Brad A. Kleindl.
        p. cm.
    Includes bibliographical references and index.
    ISBN 0-324-01319-1 (alk. paper)
    1. Telemarketing. 2. Database marketing. I. Title.

HF5415.1265 .K44 2000
658.8′4--dc21

This book is printed on acid-free paper.

For Jane, Alex, Peter, Elizabeth, and John.

About the Author

Brad Alan Kleindl is an Associate Professor of Missouri Southern State College in Joplin, Missouri. He has been teaching computer technology to students since 1984. In 1994 he started a virtual marketing course which focused on using multimedia applications to create CD-ROM promotions. The course evolved with the growth of the World Wide Web to become an Internet marketing course with an e-business strategic emphasis.

Professor Kleindl's research and publication interests are related to entrepreneurship, innovation, strategy, and Internet marketing. He has a Ph.D. in Marketing from Oklahoma State University and an MBA from Southern Illinois University. Dr. Kleindl has consulted numerous businesses on Web page design, Web portal development, and developing business plans for Web business IPOs. He was the Director of the Center for Entrepreneurship at Missouri Southern. Dr. Kleindl is also a potter, showing his art in studios and galleries.

Brief Table of Contents

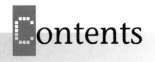

Contents

Preface

Over the last six years the Internet has evolved from communications medium to an epicenter of technological transformation in business models and processes. Businesses are adapting new technologies to improve their marketing strategies including not only the World Wide Web, but also databases, Extranets, customized production, customer relationship management software, Intranets, and other technologies, all discussed in this book. E-business practices are not only being used by "dot com" companies, but are also being adopted by established businesses. E-business is not just about new venture startups; it is also about transforming business to gain efficiencies. Students of marketing and business professionals must be prepared to enter into this new environment and understand the role that they will play in organizations. In academia we train marketing students to act as an interface between the customer and the company. There is not enough room in a traditional marketing curriculum to turn marketing students into network specialists, systems analysts, graphic designers, or web masters. Similarly, it is impractical for those already working in business to take on the in-depth study of all of these fields. The marketer's role, then, is to be able to devise strategies that enhance relationships with customers by working with technology specialists to implement strategies.

This text is targeted toward undergraduate, graduate students, and business professionals who will be undertaking the study of e-business development. While many pedagogical features have been built into the text for classroom use, these features, for the most part, are at the end of each chapter and will not interfere with the book's relevance and usefulness for professionals and others. The approach this textbook takes is to close a knowledge gap by introducing readers to the current "state of the art" in e-business practice. The references in the text are fairly exhaustive and represent e-business practice as of the year 2000. The heavy reliance on trade journals is due to the rapidly evolving business environment. Information in trade journals typically precedes material found in textbooks, journals, or academic papers. The text is designed to be academically sound by linking technology and techniques currently being used to established and emerging marketing and strategy theories. The text also takes an international perspective by reporting on changes occurring in nations and markets outside of the United States.

Organization of Text

The text is designed for all readers to build from their pre-existing familiarity with Marketing and e-business. Chapter 1 starts by building an overview of the e-business system. This is based on the major business functions and the economic flows that allow a business to meet customer's needs in a competitive environment. Chapter 2 is an infrastructure primer and is designed to give students a fundamental understanding of the technologies used to create e-businesses. This is not a computer systems design chapter; instead it allows the student to understand the Internet technology that underpins e-business communication. Chapter 3 covers the communication process in an e-business environment. This chapter is included early in the text because the Internet is primarily a communications medium. In addition, many of the assignments that instructors may wish to use will be focused around the creation of a Web page and so the fundamentals of Web page creation are covered early. Chapter 4 explores the changes in distribution that are impacting e-businesses. This chapter is more theoretical and covers the justification for business change. Chapter 5 outlines the major business models that are being used in the creation of e-businesses. Most businesses are using a combination of the models outlined in this chapter. Most e-businesses use a combination of these methods to develop relationships with customers and meet their needs. Once the student understands the possible e-business models, they investigate the diffusion process in Chapter 6. This chapter gives the student a perspective on who will accept these new business models and how quickly these new business models will diffuse. Chapter 7 investigates the use of information within e-businesses. This includes not only data collected on customers, but also how data is collected and turned into information to be used as a strategic tool. Chapter 8 ties together the preceding chapters by exploring e-business strategy. This chapter uses strategy theories and an analysis of the strategies e-businesses are currently using to give students a perspective on the competitive dynamics in the e-business environment. One of the skill areas marketing students need to have is the ability to aid in the process of transforming businesses. This internal marketing process is covered in Chapter 9. This chapter also includes organizational considerations that need to be addresses to allow businesses to structure themselves to be competitive. Chapter 10 covers the political, legal, and ethical considerations facing e-businesses in the United States and around the world.

Pedagogical Features

Professors are faced with two new challenges. The first challenge is that students today want to receive more than just a lecture over material they find in textbooks. They expect dynamic methods of teaching and presentation to better prepare them to compete and thrive in a rapidly changing, technological society. The second challenge is posed by distance learning. Web-based education should grow rapidly over the next decade. Professors must be able to provide a rich learning experience to hold students in a traditional classroom setting. This text follows an **active learning approach** to allow for a deep level of understanding. While reading a textbook is the first step in understanding a field of study, students learn by *doing* and *thinking* about course material. Each chapter supports an active learning approach with these features:

▶ An **opening vignette** is designed to illustrate the major issues found in each chapter with compelling real-world issues.

▶ **Thinking Strategically** sections following the opening vignettes and chapter cases provide thought-provoking questions and exercises which sharpen student's problem-solving abilities.

▶ **nSites** broaden students' understanding of issues by inviting them to think beyond the text material.

▶ **New terms and concepts** are defined in clear language right in the margins to facilitate learning.

▶ **Active Learning Exercises** found at the end of every chapter act as a basis for verbal analysis and discussion, allowing instructors to use their knowledge and experience to create a rich learning environment. These exercises are designed to have students actively work with ideas and concepts and perform written analysis. Some require a minimal amount of time to complete while others require students to move beyond the text and classroom to integrate the "real" world into the classroom.

▶ **Major terms and concepts** sections are included at the end of each chapter along with comments and questions for review.

▶ **Web Search—Looking Online** also found at the end of each chapter, provide immediate hands-on practice. Each chapter is followed by a series of Web page link suggestions. These were checked at end of 1999 to be sure that they all were operational and not linked to any sites that could be deemed offensive.

Support for the Instructor

Web Site *http://swcollege.kleindl.com*

All ancillary materials including instructor's manual, PowerPoint® presentation and sample syllabai are found at the site. In addition, there are Internet exercises with additional web listings, interactive quizzes, and hot topics. Finally, there is an example of an Internet marketing plan and also a complete product tour.

Instructor's Manual ISBN: 0-324-01320-5

The teaching manual for the text is developed by the author based on six years experience teaching an Internet marketing course. This is designed to support the text as well as act as a springboard for instructors to develop their own course. Included are:

- suggested syllabi
- project guides
- teaching aids
- lecture guide
- teaching suggestions
- Feedback guides for the cases and active learning exercises as well as additional active learning exercises, Web links, and additional reading suggestions.
- Community of instructors
- Web page development - multimedia development

There is also a complete **test bank** with over 50 multiple choice, true false, short answer, and essay questions for each chapter.

PowerPoint ® Slide Presentation, ISBN 0-324-01321-3

Over 300 slides featuring chapter outlines and all key concepts.

Acknowledgements

I would like to thank a large number of individuals who were instrumental in helping to get this text into the market. First of all I would like to thank William G. Zikmund of Oklahoma State University for recommending me to South-Western College Publishing. South-Western College Publishing has been very supportive in the development of the text. The Executive Marketing Director, Steve Scoble, originally helped in giving structure to the text. Since then I have been operating under the guidance of the developmental editor, Mardell Toomey. Her words of encouragement have been very helpful in keeping me focused. Sandra Gangelhoff, the production editor, has been essential in taking my raw material and turning it into a book. The entire team was able to take a basic set of ideas and turn it into a teaching tool.

I would like to thank the reviewers who carefully scrutinized the manuscript and made numerous suggestions:

John Bennett, Stephens College
Robert Galka, De Paul University
Albert Muniz, University of California at Berkeley
Shelley Rinehart, University of New Brunswick, New Brunswick, Canada
Ray Sola, University of Arizona

I think that the text is much stronger because of their questions, comments, criticisms, complaints, and suggestions. I would also like to thank my students, who for over seventeen years have taught me how to teach – especially those students who have taken my virtual marketing class and had to read articles from magazines, work with crashing Web browsers, and learn how to use Macromedia's Director. I really appreciate my Dean, Jim Gray, and his willingness to set up labs, purchase computers and software, and put up with me while I wrote this text. Without his support I wouldn't have a course or textbook.

I would thank my parents Jim Kleindl and Elaine Kleindl who are both retired teachers and who have taught me to love to learn and to teach. Their early lessons have given me the self-confidence to reach the goals that I have obtained. I would especially like to thank my wife, Jane Kleindl. She has put up with me though a Ph.D. program, house remodeling, and writing a textbook. Her support has been vital in all that I do. Finally, I would like to thank my children for making me realize that we all have a duty to make the world a better place. I hope that this textbook, in some small part, helps to accomplish that goal by aiding students and faculty in learning about the new and exciting world of e-business.

Chapter 1

Introduction to E-Business

Businesses are being forced to change in response to the rapid pace of technological change that has occurred over the last decade. A new competitive business model based on electronic business practices is evolving. The center of this e-business model focuses on changing the practice of marketing. The term e-business or electronic business refers to the process of conducting business using these new technologies. E-business includes using technology to enhance buying and selling online, improve customer service, and forge closer links with business partners. This includes the use of not only the Internet but other technology tools that are changing marketing and management practices.[1]

While the worldwide communications enhancements brought about by the Internet and the World Wide Web are very visible, there are also hidden aspects of this move toward e-business. Distribution systems are changing to lower costs and speed products to new markets. New product and pricing strategies are being developed. Behind the scenes, database marketing is being used to allow the targeting of a market-of-one. Firms are gathering data on people's behavior, demographics, and psychographic profiles. This is run through data warehouses and data mills to determine the individual customer's needs. Companies such as MCI use their databases to sift through more than 1 trillion bytes of customer data to fine-tune marketing campaigns.[2] Businesses are then able to individualize products, advertisements, and services to develop stronger relationships with customers. EDI (electronic data interchange) and extranets are linking suppliers with customers, allowing for reductions in inventory and costs, and an increase in responsiveness to the market.

This chapter gives an overview of the changes that businesses are implementing due to this new technology.

1. Explain what a business model is and how it is used.
2. List the technologies that are being used to foster e-business.
3. Describe the size of the Internet economy.
4. Recommend how a business can use e-business techniques to develop long-term marketing relationships.
5. Identify the components of a marketing system.
6. List the components of an e-business–based marketing system.
7. Explain how and why businesses need to evolve and change to maintain competitiveness.

Dell Computer Company

In 1983 Michael Dell assembled customer computers in his college dorm room. Dell's business grew when he pioneered the use of telephone direct sales for computers. In 1996 Dell started selling computers over the Internet; by 1998 sales to online customers had reached more than $5 million a day. Projections say that by year 2000 Dell will have close to 100 percent of its sales transacted online.

Selling over the Internet is only part of the reason that Dell's stock price rose 29,000 percent from 1990 to 1998. Dell's business was designed to be efficient. Major competitors, such as Compaq and IBM, built distribution networks that relied on resellers to sell their products. Switching to the Internet for e-commerce would have alienated their support. Dell was also able to meet the needs of its customers by customizing its computers. Dell preloaded required software so its computers could be unpacked and run. By gathering customer information, Dell was able to determine trends in the marketplace.

Source: www.dell.com

Supply chains are the suppliers, warehouses, shippers, distributors, and anyone else who may be involved in providing materials to a company.

Dell demanded that its suppliers locate their inventory 15 minutes outside of the Dell factory. Warehousing was outsourced to third parties that specialized in running **supply chains,** and all of the companies were linked electronically to speed information flow. Dell had no finished goods inventory and was therefore able to use the latest products and take advantage of dropping inventory costs. Rather than box and ship monitors with the computer, Dell had UPS store and deliver the specified monitor with the computer. Dell squeezed time out of every step in the business process. Dell's average sale turns into cash in less than 24 hours. Developing a more efficient marketing system gave Dell shareholders $1.54 in profits for every new dollar of capital investment in 1997, while Compaq returned only 59 cents and IBM, 47 cents.

Dell Computer identified areas of key competitive advantage and changed its business model to meet the customer's desire for speed of delivery, customized products, and low prices.[3] By 1997, Dell was able to receive orders at 9 a.m. on one day, build the computer, and deliver it by 9 a.m. the next day. This increase in speed allowed Dell to lower inventory costs and prices to its customers. A key to this strategy was using the Internet to link Dell to both its customers and its suppliers.[4]

Dell has expanded this sales model to other markets. Corporate customers are able to order directly from Dell using the Internet. Companies such as Pillsbury and Ford have designed their own internal Web pages that link to Dell's computer system to allow for online purchasing. This customization has saved corporate customers millions of dollars. Dell moved its business model overseas to allow for rapid delivery of computers in foreign markets. By 1997, 31 percent of Dell sales came from outside the United States.

Dell Computer is just one of the pioneers using information technology to change industries. Dell's business model consists of more than just selling over the Internet. It gains efficiency by developing links to suppliers. It collects information on customers to increase knowledge on market trends. By moving this highly efficient model around the world, Dell is forcing its competitors to change their business practices. Nations are reacting by developing the infrastructure necessary to allow their businesses to compete on the same global scale.[5]

Most computer buyers search for information before they buy. Dell's Web site allows those buyers to immediately move to areas that interest them. In 1997, Dell received one Web visit for every phone call inquiry; by 1998 there were 3.5 Web visits for every phone inquiry. Potential buyers visit the Web site 5 to 10 times to obtain information, have their questions answered, and determine prices before they buy. Because the Web visit is considerably less expensive, the cost savings are given back to the buyer.[6] Dell's business model is shown in Figure 1.1.

THINKING STRATEGICALLY

Determine if Dell has an advantage over traditional computer sales businesses. Decide if it has an advantage over other online sellers. Consider what you would want if you were to purchase a computer. Decide if you would feel it is necessary to talk to a person directly. Evaluate the Dell Web site *(www.dell.com)*. Determine if

Figure 1.1 Dell's Business Model

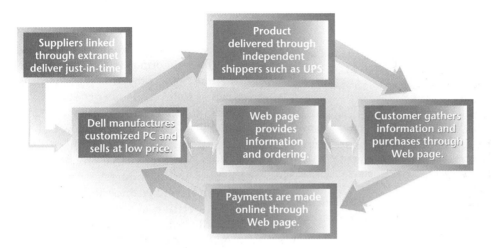

this site provides all the information necessary for you to buy. Determine the importance of the Dell brand name. Explain if the business system that Dell has developed will work for other types of businesses. Explore how Dell develops and maintains relationships with its customers.

....

"Asking how you make money on the Internet is a primitive question, like asking how you make money on the telephone."

Don Tapscott, Chairman
Alliance for Converging Technologies[7]

Information technology has fundamentally changed the nature of marketing. Today businesses collect data electronically at the point of sale and route that information from the retailer to the supplier and/or the manufacturer. Electronically linked distribution systems are speeding products through the channel of distribution and helping to forge strong relationships between firms. The World Wide Web is allowing businesses to reach customers around the world rather than just local markets. Information on customers' shopping behavior is being stored in databases to profile individuals for targeted promotions and customized products. The use of these new technologies in combination is creating a paradigm shift in how businesses need to compete.

Today, new information technologies are allowing businesses to redesign **business models** and change business practices. The Internet, which allows for almost instantaneous worldwide communication, is setting a new standard for

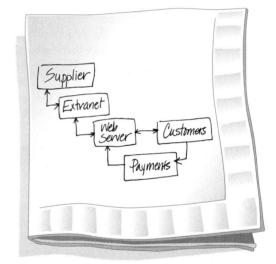

Compaq Computer's original business plan was drawn on a napkin.

A business model, or commerce model, is the basic process flow indicating how a business operates. It shows how business functions are linked together.

CASE 1.1

From Egghead to Egghead.com

At its 1992 peak, Egghead sold $700 million worth of computer software through 250 brick and mortar stores, but Egghead's competitive dynamics changed. Companies such as Dell preloaded software on the computers it sold. Office superstores entered the market and sold products at discount prices. By 1997 revenues were down to $361 million and losses had grown to $40 million.

The only growth area was Internet sales. Market estimates indicated that online sales of software would grow from $880 million in 1997 to $6.4 billion by 2003. In 1998 Egghead fired 750 of its 1,000 employees, closed all of its physical stores, and went totally online. By 1999 Egghead's Web site offered a superstore, discount software, a liquidation center, and online auctions.

This move has not yet brought Egghead back to profitability. Competitive pressure from brick and mortar companies and other online sellers has continued to depress Egghead's stock price.[9]

information flows. The World Wide Web is bringing global sellers into many customers' offices and living rooms. The Internet is standardizing how companies are linking themselves together online. Databases are being used to collect information and are enhancing the marketing process by allowing customized production of products and promotion. Internal communication, through the use of intranets, is allowing business to restructure to meet the needs of a rapidly evolving competitive environment. Businesses across industries are rapidly learning to leverage these technologies to gain competitive advantages. The Dell vignette illustrates how one company has been able to take advantage of this technological change.

Dell is not alone in changing its business model; Amazon.com, Ebay, and E*Trade have pioneered new business models to give them greater efficiency and competitive advantages, forcing their competitors to change or die. An Internet-based business model requires fewer hard assets (sometimes called **brick and mortar** assets), a direct distribution channel to the customer, less management hierarchy, and speed and flexibility in changing to meet market demands.[8]

Brick and mortar refers to tangible physical assets such as a factory, an office building, or a warehouse.

THINKING STRATEGICALLY

Consider the alternative outlets for software. Where would you look if you were going to purchase software? Determine what is most important to you—the store, the brand name, or the price. Evaluate the Egghead software site *(www.egghead. com)*. Determine if this is the type of company from which you would consider purchasing. Evaluate the Amazon.com site *(www.amazon.com)*. Decide if you would rather use this brand-name site. Determine why you would make that decision.

E-BUSINESS

Dell transformed its direct-marketing business model from telephone-based sales to an e-business–based model. **E-business,** or electronic business, systems use a number of information technology–based business practices to enhance relationships between the business and the customer. E-business includes changes in marketing communications, distribution systems, and business models. Implementing e-business practices requires an understanding of changes in customer behavior, using databases to build relationships, developing of strategies to respond to a

changing environment, as well as management techniques for new types of employees and new business practices, and legal and ethical concerns.[10]

The business practices, or techniques, illustrated in this text are used for both e-business and e-commerce applications. **E-commerce** is the practice of engaging in transactions online, but this does not fully explain the changes that business systems are facing. E-business is a broader concept and includes the use of **extranets,** which are Internet links between business suppliers and purchasers, and **intranets,** or Internets that operate inside a business. It also takes into consideration the changes in strategy and management practice needed to be successful in today's environment. Table 1.1 on the following page defines some of the current terminology used in this emerging field.

What Is the Impact of E-Business?

The Internet, and the World Wide Web, as a communications venue has received an enormous amount of media coverage. In 1998 the terms "Internet" and "Web" were used on average 285 times per day in press headlines[11]; 9 of the 10 top performing stocks in 1998 were related to the Internet. Amazon.com's stock share price alone increased over 850 percent in 1998.[12] In spite of the stock price declines

Table 1.1 E-Business Industry Terms

Name	Description
Internet	This is a global network of computer networks that use a common interface for communication. The World Wide Web uses graphically based Internet standards and has allowed easy access to information and communication around the world.
E-business	This is the process of using information technology (IT) to support a fuller operation of a business. This could include generating leads, providing sales support, integrating partners, and linking aspects of the business operation to suppliers and distributors through extranets, which are internal communications controlled through intranets.
E-commerce	E-commerce consists of using electronic information–based systems to engage in transactions or commerce online. This includes automating Web site purchases.
Extranet	An Internet-based connection between a business and its suppliers, distributors, and partners, an extranet is not open to the general public. These systems are replacing older electronic data interchange (EDI) systems.
Intranet	This is an internal private network that uses the same types of hardware, software, and connections as the Internet. It can link divisions of a business around the world into a unified communications network.

Sources: Terms compiled from: Techencyclopedia http://www.techweb.com/encyclopedia/; Chuck Martin, "Defining E-Business," *NewMedia*, July 1998, p. 26; and Gary A. Bolles, "Is E-Business Your Business?" *Sm@rt Reseller*, August 3, 1998, pp. 1–7.

in 1999, the stock market valuations of some businesses engaging in online commerce have reached unprecedented levels, even though they have not shown a profit. This has not prevented the business founders from becoming billionaires more rapidly than any time in history.[13]

How big is the Internet economy now, and how big will it grow? There is no simple answer to this question. A number of companies are using different research methodologies to estimate the number of users and to project commerce figures.[14] Table 1.2 compiles past and projected figures for Internet use and expected future growth.

It is difficult to predict the future with very little past history, but these figures indicate very rapid growth. In reaching a level of 50 million users, the Internet has grown faster than both radio and television.

THE E-BUSINESS-BASED MARKETING SYSTEM

According to an *Information Week* research poll, the areas of business practice that are facing the largest change due to technology include traditional marketing practices, customer service, and sales, all of which are part of a business marketing system. **Marketing** is the process of planning and executing the conception, pric-

Table 1.2 E-Business Growth and Projections

	1996	1999	Projected 2002–2003
Internet hosts (domains)	12.9 million	56.2 million	More than 100 million
Web users	28 million	65 million (U.S.) 163 million (worldwide)	83 million (U.S.) 175 million (worldwide)
Percent of users who buy goods or services	25%	39%	46%
Business-to-consumer Web commerce	$2.6 billion	$13 billion	$108 billion
Business-to-business Web commerce (includes transactions over extranets)	Less than $43 billion	$109 billion	$1.3 trillion (9% of U.S. sales)
Advertising revenue	$236.5 million	$2 billion	$7.7 billion

Sources: Network Wizards, "Over 43.2 Million Internet Hosts in January 1999," NUA Internet Surveys, September 7, 1999, <http://www.nua.ie/surveys/index.cgi?=VS&art_id=905354740&rel=true>; CIO Web Business, "Future Commodities," December 1, 1997, p. 24; Mel Duvall and Tom Steinert-Threlkeld, "B2B: Online and Off the Charts," Inter@ctive Week, December 7, 1998, p. 7; Mel Duvall, "Online Shopping: Big Sales, Snafus," Inter@ctive Week, January 4, 1999, p. 11; Mary Jones Thompson, "Crystal-Clear Crystal Balls," The Industry Standard, December 28, 1998–January 4, 1999, p. 52; Bob Tedeschi, "Real Force in E-Commerce Is Business-to-Business Sales," The New York Times on the Web, <http://www.nytimes.com/library/tech/99/01/cyber/commerce/05commerce.html>, January 5, 1999; Jim Kerstetter and Antone Gonsalves, "Online Selling Set to Snowball in '99," PC Week, January 4, 1999, p. 25; Laura Kujubu and Matthew Nelson, "The Return of the Shopping Mall," InfoWorld, February 1, 1999, pp. 1, 33, 36; and "Number of Internet Hosts," Internet Software Consortium, August 23, 1999, <http://www.isc.org/dsview.cgi?domainsurvey/host-count-history>.

ing, promotion, and distribution of ideas, goods, and services that create exchanges that satisfy individual and organizational needs.[15] Marketers must wear many hats in an organization. Marketers are involved not only in the purchasing and selling of goods and services but are instrumental in the designing, promoting, pricing, and distributing of products. A very important role for marketers is the development and maintenance of customer relationships. Customers can easily find alternative sources of supply, so marketers must use a **systems approach,** ensuring that all parts of a business system are focused on developing and maintaining long-term relationships between the marketer and the customer.

A **systems approach** helps decision makers look at how all aspects of a strategic business unit (SBU) interact with each other. Systems are also seen as being organic in that they must change in response to their environment or face the possibility of becoming extinct.

Relationship Development

Changes in information technology are both threatening and enhancing the ability of a business to develop long-term *relationships with its customers,* requiring **relationship marketing.** The Internet allows a customer to contact a business any time of the day or night from any location to gather information, to make purchases, or to obtain information on the status of accounts. This information

Relationship marketing refers to the strategies a business must undertake to hold desirable customers over a long time period.

can be personalized to the needs of the individual customer. The Internet allows buyers to easily find information on competitive products and services. This shifts the power to the customer. Companies can also more easily find new customers and serve existing customers by using databases to develop personal profiles and then target them with customized information that can meet specific needs. Amazon.com, for example, personalizes e-mail, customizes Web pages, and offers products based on a buyer's past purchases. The Internet is bringing about a hypercompetitive environment where IT is used as a vital part of marketing strategy and relationship development.[16]

A recent *Information Week* magazine survey of 300 IT executives indicated customer-centered companies are focusing on improving satisfaction by using customer data to gain a better knowledge of their customers to improve sales. Raising customer satisfaction levels is considered the number one priority of IT executives. This requires that businesses find a way to leverage their technological abilities to keep their customers happy.[17]

Information is also allowing businesses to estimate the lifetime value of customers. The **lifetime value of a customer (LVC)** is an estimate of the potential lifetime profit of a customer. If a customer's long-term value does not exceed the cost of maintaining that customer, the customer may be charged a higher price or dropped. Many individuals have seen an increase either in individual checking account charges or in additional charges to long-distance bills because they do not provide enough value to their bank or phone company. The ability to collect and use this type of information is refocusing companies; rather than just pursuing market share, which can result in high expenses, companies are deciding which customers to maintain over a lifetime. This allows companies to increase overall profits by dropping negatively valued customers.[18]

Developing an e-business system allows businesses to leverage information technology to develop and maintain relationships. Figure 1.2 represents the components of a traditional marketing system, including the traditional 4 Ps of marketing (product, price, place, and promotion). It also takes into consideration the customer as the targeted market, as well as the payment flow, and the information-gathering process undertaken by a business. Managers of these businesses must devise and execute a plan to reach organizational goals by considering the business's resources and the nature of the environment in which it operates.

All the components of a business must work in unison to allow the marketing system to operate in its environment. This system must organize itself and find an advantage over its competitors to ensure long-term sustainability. E-business systems are fostering a number of changes to the marketing system including[19]:

1. Customized products
2. Increased price pressure resulting in lower prices
3. Shorter channels of distribution dominated by facilitators
4. Nonlinear promotions

Lifetime value of a customer (LVC) is the sum of expected lifetime earnings minus the lifetime costs (acquisition costs, operating expenses, customer service) of a customer.

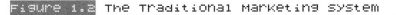

Figure 1.2 The Traditional Marketing System

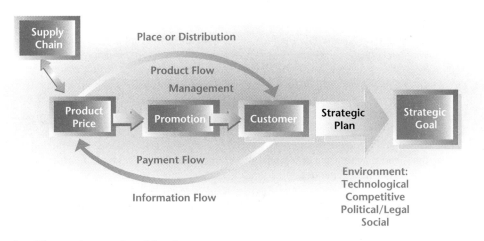

5. Electronic transfer of funds
6. Database information management systems

All of this is occurring in a dramatically changing environment requiring management to reorganize and develop new strategies. Figure 1.3 illustrates the new e-business system.

Figure 1.3 indicates that these e-business practices will allow for enhanced relationships by allowing a business to focus on its customers at an individualized level, or at a market-of-one level. Table 1.3, on the following page, outlines the chapters that will explore each of the components of the e-business system.

Figure 1.3 The E-Business-Based Marketing System

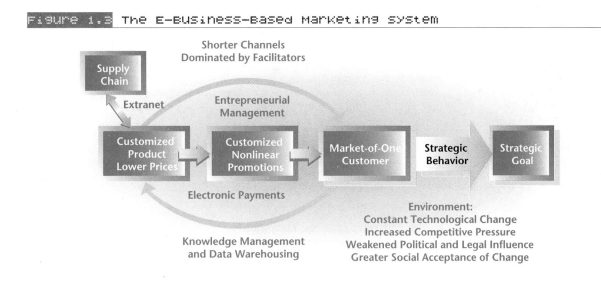

Table 1.3 Components of an E-Business System

Component	Chapter	Description
Technological environment	2	This chapter is a primer on the technology behind the Internet and the World Wide Web. It gives a perspective on how it works and where it is going.
Communication	3	This chapter looks at how communication is changing over the Internet. It includes not only advertising on the Web but also how communication is being structured for nonlinear communications systems.
Distribution	4	This chapter looks at the dynamics of change in distribution systems. By exploring the theories behind the development of channel systems, an understanding can be gained of current changes.
Value creation	5	This chapter explores the current business models that are being used on the Internet. This includes the use of extranets, e-commerce, auction systems, etc.
Diffusion process	6	To understand how quickly change will occur, the diffusion of innovations is explored. This includes exploring the diffusion process at the individual level and the diffusion process inside of businesses.
Information collection and use	7	This chapter looks at how firms are collecting and using information to gain competitive advantages. This includes the process of environmental scanning, data collecting, data warehousing, data mining, and knowledge management.
Strategy	8	The highly dynamic environment in which firms find themselves requires a more innovative approach to strategy. This chapter looks at how businesses are restructuring value chains to gain competitive advantages.
Management	9	This chapter explores the change in management that is required to operate in a dynamic and technical environment.
Political, legal, and ethical issues	10	This new industry is bringing about considerable change in the nature of relationships among businesses, individuals, and the government. Around the world, concerns are being raised about issues such as privacy, fraud, and pornography. In addition, the Internet offers the world the largest free-speech forum.

Source: John Deighton, "The Future of Interactive Marketing," *Harvard Business Review,* November–December 1996, pp. 4–16.

CHANGING BUSINESS MODELS

The field of marketing is at the center of change. Time and space are collapsing between the marketer and the customer.[20] The growth of the Internet and the World Wide Web is allowing individuals and businesses to gain information when and where it is convenient. Products from companies around the world can be discovered and compared with relative ease. Orders can be placed without the use of middlemen. Supply chains are being linked together allowing businesses to gain efficiencies. These new technologies are also allowing businesses to forge tighter relationships with their customers.

Business and marketing practices, and **theories of change,** have always modified in response to changes in environmental factors, but sometimes environmental change is more revolutionary.[21] The introduction of new technologies, such as the telephone, the television, and the computer, has created environments that dramatically altered the marketing process in the past. Customers have demonstrated that they will pursue their own best interest by shifting purchasing patterns to take advantage of offers of higher quality, greater variety, cheaper prices, more convenience, or other salient choice criteria. Customers make economic decisions to leave older business models behind when they find opportunities that match their needs, and businesses must evolve in order to keep up with these changes.

The main drivers of change in business practice come from advances in software, computers, and telecommunications. Perhaps the most visible aspect of this technology is the World Wide Web. Although there has been considerable press on the Web, the most important part of this phenomenon is not that the Web works; the Internet has been in place since the 1960s. Instead, the most impressive aspect is the level of business and organizational use and the level of consumer acceptance of Web-based technologies. This acceptance is based on computer systems that were not designed to deliver rich content and the use of data transfer lines that were not designed to allow large amounts of information to transfer to the individual home user. The Web is still in its infancy stage, just as were mechanical televisions, crank telephones, and crystal radio sets in the early years of their development. New telecommunications systems will allow full multimedia to be delivered through Web browsers directly to the individual user.

Theories of change: Change can be viewed as a constant process, such as the Darwinian evolutionary process. Many business systems [a system is a self-contained unit] have a tendency to remain stable until they are acted upon by some outside environmental force, at which time a large number of adaptations must occur, or the business system dies out. Businesses and consumers are currently facing such a dramatic change to their environment.

How Quickly Will These Changes Occur?

The 1998 Christmas shopping season was a watershed for retail e-commerce. Online sales were three times higher than expected, reaching close to $4 billion for the Christmas season. For the week of December 4–10, 55 percent of online shoppers were women, and 58 percent of all shoppers were purchasing online for the first time. By 1999 Christmas sales had grown to $7 billion and 90 percent of online customers indicated that they were satisfied with their shopping experience.[22]

These widely reported statistics have a tendency to overshadow a quieter evolution that is occurring across a broad spectrum of businesses involved in the business-to-business marketplace. Business-to-business transactions are expected to be close to 10 times higher than business-to-consumer sales. Eventually business-to-business transactions may impact 40 percent of all business transactions in the United States.

A driving force for the acceptance of e-business techniques is the attempt to lower costs through greater efficiency. CUC International, a discount retailer, found that its cost of servicing a customer over the Web is $2 to $3 per year versus $9 per year for catalog or telephone sales.[23] Companies that don't sell on the Web could face a 5 percent to 10 percent cost disadvantage.[24] Businesses are requiring suppliers to adapt online connections. General Electric, for example, is construct-

CASE 1.2

From Computers to Cars

A young entrepreneur named Scott Painter has started a business called CarsDirect.com (www.carsdirect.com). He modeled his business idea on Dell's computer sales system. Michael Dell's venture company also invested $10 million in this new business. CarsDirect.com plans to take the pain out of purchasing automobiles by selling them directly online. CarsDirect allows individuals to specify the car they want to purchase; then CarsDirect.com calls dealers to see if they will meet a price based on national sales averages. CarsDirect will also offer research, insurance, loans, and delivery. For a comparison of traditional and CarsDirect sales models, see Figure 1.4.

CarsDirect is competing against a number of other online auto brokers such as Microsoft's CarPoint.com *(www.carpoint.msn.com)*, Autoweb.com *(www.autoweb.com)*, and Autobytel.com *(www. autobytel.com)*. These brokers usually have an auto dealership make the sale. Dealerships and manufacturers are also moving information services and purchasing online.[28]

ing an extranet to have its suppliers transact $5 billion of business online. When Intel implemented its extranet, the online sales system took over $1 billion worth of transactions per month. Even the federal government is looking to use online efficiencies to reduce costs by lowering inventory requirements, reducing publishing costs, and forming tighter links to its customers.[25] The use of the Internet to increase efficiency is helping to keep U.S. inflation in check and may add as much as $40 billion to the U.S. economy through cost savings by the turn of the century.

Which Industries and How Far?

Will all industries face this evolutionary change? This question needs to be investigated from both an e-commerce and an e-business perspective. Internet-only–based businesses such as Amazon and Ebay have developed integrated e-business systems. Other businesses are making use of some of these system components by implementing promotionally based Web pages, fostering online customer inquiries and interactions, or providing limited online purchasing. The question of how many e-business system components a business will adopt—and

Figure 1.4   Two Car Sales Models

Traditional Car Sales Model	CarsDirect Sales Model
1. Auto manufacturer builds cars and sends cars to dealers' inventory and promotes brands.	**1.** Auto manufacturer builds cars and sends cars to dealers' inventory and promotes brands.
2. Dealer advertises locally to bring in the customer and attempts to close the sale. Car salespeople believe that if customers leave the dealership, they will most likely not buy there.	**2.** CarDirect uses Internet to provide information to customers and offers prices in the lowest 10% of national averages.
3. Customers endure sales pitches, salesperson talking to the manager and then must arrange insurance and financing if they wish to purchase.	**3.** Customers research cars and contact CarDirect online.
	4. CarDirect contacts dealers and attempts to negotiate sale on the phone. When price is obtained, CarDirect can arrange for insurance, financing, and delivery.

how quickly—will depend on the needs of the customer and how other constituencies are likely to behave. Businesses that require a person-to-person interface may take longer to adopt e-commerce.

In 1998 more than 2 million consumers used the Internet to research car purchases. This change in information power and sales patterns is having a strong impact on the entire automobile industry. More than 61 percent of auto dealers have their own Web sites and two-thirds of those have dedicated staff to maintain the site.[26] By 1999, 40 percent of U.S. car or truck consumers used the Net for information or to purchase vehicles.[27]

THINKING STRATEGICALLY

Would you rather purchase cars at a local dealership or online? Why should a dealership sell through CarsDirect.com and not some other online sales system? Why can't a local dealer sell online? What would happen if the auto manufacturers decided to sell online? Take a look at CarsDirect.com (www.carsdirect.com) and then GM's Buy Power site (www.buypower.com). From which site would you be most likely to purchase a car?

Why Is This Topic Important?

The material covered in this text is important for both students and managers. In 1996 the Internet spawned over 1.1 million jobs.[29] Businesses are in heavy competition to find employees who have the skills necessary to transform their businesses and compete in an e-business age. These skills go beyond the ability to develop Web pages; business students must understand this new competitive environment and know how to use and implement these techniques in current business models.

Today's managers face a new competitive environment. This text is a guide to this new world. The first step to changing a business model is to understand the new competitive dynamics. The tools and rules of business are changing. Managers who do not learn how to use these new tools may soon be out of the game.

KNOWLEDGE INTEGRATION

TERMS AND CONCEPTS

Brick and mortar 6	Intranet 7	Supply chains 4
Business model 5	Lifetime value of	Systems approach 9
E-business 6	customers 10	Theories of change 13
E-commerce 7	Marketing 8	World Wide Web 7
Extranet 7	Relationship	
Internet 8	marketing 9	

CONCEPTS AND QUESTIONS FOR REVIEW

1. Define a business model.
2. Describe the components of a business system and their changes.
3. Explain why a systems approach is important.
4. Define e-business.
5. Discuss how relationships are enhanced in an e-business environment.
6. Be able to calculate the lifetime value of a customer.
7. Determine how an e-business system is different from current business systems.
8. Explain which businesses are likely to be early adopters of change and which ones will adopt late. Justify why that is true.
9. Discuss why both students and managers need to know about the topics covered in this text.

ACTIVE LEARNING

Exercise 1.1: Imagining the Future

Imagine that the telephone and television were invented within the last 10 years. Decide how companies would need to change to use these new tools. Determine if they would be able to use the same techniques to promote and sell their products. Decide if they would use the same outlets to distribute goods and services. Speculate on whether the relationships between suppliers and producers would be handled in the same way. Decide if companies could be managed in the same manner.

Exercise 1.2: Checking Buyer Behavior

This exercise is designed to determine whether buyers will change their buying behavior and how e-business will impact established businesses. Most customers from developed countries have a great deal of shopping experience and have already developed purchasing patterns. Decide if you are likely to change your shopping behavior. Place in the first column five of the shopping activities that you engage in most often (examples are given but feel free to change them). Then rank-order the preferences for each of the shopping activities. Finally, indicate the number of local outlets.

Shopping Activity (Examples)	1: Like This the Most 5: Like This the Least	Number of Local Outlets
Shopping for specialty clothing		
Shopping for groceries		
Shopping for specialty items and gifts		
Shopping for computers and software		
Shopping for cars		

Explain how the e-business techniques outlined in this chapter would affect the shopping activities outlined above. Indicate how this would affect the way you would make your purchases. Determine if a smaller number of local outlets make it more likely that you would shop online. Decide which of these businesses are likely to have links to their suppliers. Explain which of these industries will face the greatest amount of change.

Exercise 1.3: Proposed E-Business Model

Draw a business model for a proposed business that would use the components of the e-business system indicated in this chapter. Use the Dell vignette as an example. Include the products and services you plan to offer and how they would be delivered. Then explain how your business model works to develop relationships with customers.

Exercise 1.4: Business Model

Outline a business model for an existing business. Indicate how it meets the needs of its customers, obtains its supplies, etc. Then draw a plan of how you think this business model should operate using the e-business techniques outlined in this chapter. Explain how you think the business could make the transition from the old business model to the new. Determine if there are any environmental drivers leading this business model to change. Decide what could hinder the move to e-business.

Exercise 1.5: Who Is Under Threat?

Not all businesses are ready to give up traditional models. The table below lists a number of businesses that may to be under threat if they do not change.

Industries Under Threat

▶ **Wholesaling:** Traditional wholesalers rely upon sales reps to maintain contact.

▶ **Travel agents:** Airlines are cutting commissions. Airlines are selling tickets directly and are expected to sell 62% of tickets by 2002.

▶ **Insurance:** Customers are able to obtain information online and will soon be able to compare prices. Insurance companies are reluctant to alienate their agent structure. It is projected that 92% of banks will begin to sell insurance online in the near future.

▶ **Car dealerships:** Customers are using the Internet to become informed about their car purchases. They are also using the Internet to purchase cars. At least one car company is bypassing the cost of establishing a dealer network and selling directly to the public.

▶ What businesses would you add?

Source: Nanete Byres and Paul C. Judge, "Internet Anxiety," *Business Week,* June 28, 1999, pp. 78–88; and Jeffrey Davis," 20 Industries That Must Change," *Business 2.0,* March 1999, pp. 44–54.

Create your own list of businesses and indicate why you think they are under threat.

WEB SEARCH – LOOKING ONLINE

SEARCH TERM: E-Business	First 6 out of 238,908

Amazon.com. Is one of the leaders of online shopping in books, music, and other types of products.
www.amazon.com

CDNOW. Is a competitor with Amazon.com in the music industry.
www.cdnow.com

Compaq. Is a close competitor of Dell in the same area of production.
www.compaq.com

Dell Computer. Is one of the top computer manufacturers in the world that sells computers and computer parts.
www.dell.com

Ebay. Is an online auction house that allows individuals to sell and buy just about anything.
www.ebay.com

IBM. Is a leader in the industry of business commerce and networking technology.
www.ibm.com

SEARCH TERM: Size of the Net	First 5 out of 23,890,844

Georgia Tech. Collects data on Internet use and has very good links to other Internet statistics Web sites.
www.gvu.gatech.edu/user_surveys

Internet Software Consortium. Is a nonprofit corporation dedicated to maintaining the Open Source, or standard interface Internet protocols.
www.isc.org

MIDS. Is an Internet monitoring service.
www.mids.org

NUA. Is an Irish-based Internet strategy and research and development agency that provides information on Internet statistics.
www.nua.ie

StatMarket. Provides raw data computed from daily Internet visitors to monitored Web sites.

www.statmarket.com

R E F E R E N C E S

1.   For more information on defining e-business, see: "e-business," whatis?com, *<http://whatis.com/>;* "What Is E-Business," IBM, August 23, 1999,*<http://www.ibm.com/ e-business/whatis.html>.*

2.   John W. Verity and Russell Mitchell, "A Trillion-Byte Weapon," *Business Week,* July 31, 1995, pp. 80–81.

3.   George Stalk, Jr., "Time—The Next Source of Competitive Advantage," *Harvard Business Review,* July–August 1988, pp. 39–60, in *Strategy, Seeking and Securing Competitive Advantage,* ed. Cynthia A. Montgomery and Michael E. Porter, *Harvard Business Review Book,* 1991; and Joseph T. Vesey, "The New Competitors Think in Terms of 'Speed-to-Market,'" *SAM Advanced Management Journal,* Autumn 1991, pp. 26–33.

4.   Gary McWilliams, "Whirlwind on the Web," *Business Week,* April 7, 1997, pp. 132–136.

5.   Gary McWilliams, "Whirlwind on the Web," *Business Week,* April 7, 1997, pp. 132–136; Saroja Girishankar, "Dell's Site Has Business in Crosshairs," *Internet Week,* April 13, 1998, pp. 1, 59; Andy Serwer, "Michael Dell Rocks," *Fortune,* May 11, 1998, pp. 58-70; and Lisa Dicarlo, "Dell Raises Bar on E-Commerce," *PC Week,* June 15, 1998, pp. 1, 16.

6.   Lisa Chadderdon, "How Dell Sells on the Web," *Fast Company,* September 1998, pp. 58–60.

7.   Clinton Wilder, Bruce Caldwell, and Gregory Dalton, "More Than Electronic Commerce," Information Week Online, December 15, 1997, <http://www.informationweek.com/ 661/61iuebz.htm>.

8.   Nanete Byres and Paul C. Judge, "Internet Anxiety," *Business Week,* June 28, 1999, pp. 78–88.

9.   James Ryan, "Egghead.com: Not Over, Not Easy," *Business 2.0,* September 1998, pp. 26–28; "Egghead.com Snapshot," Market Guide, *http://businesswire.marketguide.com/ mgi/snap/28800.html.*

10.   Bruce Caldwell and John Foley, "IBM Means E-Business," *Information Week,* February 8, 1998, pp. 18–20, 124–125.

11.   *The Industry Standard,* "'Internet' and 'Web' in Press Release Headlines," October 26, 1998, p. 45.

12.   Larry Barrett, "Net Fueled Frenzy in 1998," *PC Week,* January 4, 1999, p. 3.

13.   Thomas Easton and Scott Wolley, "The $20 Billion Crumb," *Forbes,* April 19, 1999, pp. 242–251.

14.   For an assessment of the major Internet research company methodologies, see: Jennifer Greenstein, "How Many? How Much? Who Knows?" *Brill's Content,* November 1998, pp. 54–58; Sari Kalin, "Reading Between the Lines," *CIO Web Business—Section 2,* April 1, 1998, pp. 43–48; and Daniel Roth, "My What Big Internet Numbers You Have!" *Fortune,* March 15, 1999, pp. 114–120.

15.   American Marketing Association definition, *Marketing News,* March 1, 1985, p. 1.

16.   Bill Blundon and Allen Bonde, "Beyond the Transaction," *Information Week,* November 16, 1998, pp. 5SS–6SS.

17.   Jeff Sweat, "Customer Centricity," *Information Week,* May 17, 1999, pp. 46–62.

18.   Adina Levin, "Relationship Management Critical to Web Success," *DM Review,* March 1999, pp. 20–24, 92.

[19] Frederick E. Webster, Jr., "The Changing Role of Marketing in the Corporation," *Journal of Marketing,* October 1992, pp. 1–7.

[20] For more on the impact of communications technology and its change on business practices, see: Frances Cairncross, *The Death of Distance. How the Communication Revolution Will Change Our Lives,* Harvard Business School Press, Boston, Massachusetts, 1997.

[21] For more information, see: Bruce D. Henderson, "The Origin of Strategy," *Harvard Business Review,* November–December, 1989, pp. 3–10; and Murray Brozinsky, "The Theory of Evolution," *Business 2.0,* December 1998, pp. 119–121.

[22] Compiled from: Jacob Ward, "Many Unhappy Returns," *The Industry Standard,* December 28, 1998–January 4, 1999, pp. 20–22; Sharon Machles, "Holiday Net Spree Encourages Retailers," *Computerworld,* January 11, 1999, p. 4; Matthew Nelson, "Post-Holiday Hangovers Afflict Sites," *Info World,* January 11, 1999, pp. 1, 23; and Jupiter Communications, "Online Holiday Sales Hit $7 Billion, Consumer Satisfaction Rising," January 13, 2000, <http://www.jup.com/company/pressrelease.jsp?doc=pr000113>.

[23] Nelson Wang, "Discount Retailer Makes a Strategic Move to the Net," *Web Week,* July 21, 1997, pp. 30–32.

[24] Sari Kalin, "Conflict Resolution," *CIO Web Business,* February 1, 1998, pp. 28–36; and Peter Coy, "You Ain't Seen Nothin Yet," *Business Week,* June 22, 1998, p. 130.

[25] Saroja Girishankar, "Feds Get Down to Business With Latest E-Commerce Push," *Internet Week,* November 3, 1997, pp. 18–20; John Evan Frook, "Buying Behemoth," *Internet Week,* August 17, 1998, pp. 1, 44; and Mitch Wagner, "Intel Sets Commerce Record," *Internet Week,* November 23, 1998, pp. 1, 48.

[26] Forrester Research, "Eight Million New-Car Purchases Will Be Influenced by the Internet in 2003," <http://www.forrester.com/Press/Releases?Standard?0,1184,127,00.html>, February 9, 1999.

[27] NUA Internet Surveys, "J.D. Power & Associates: 40 Percent of U.S. Car Buyers Shop Online," July 13, 1999.

[28] Susan Moran, "Tire Clickers," *Business 2.0,* September 1999, pp. 158–164.

[29] Kathleen Murphy, "Body of Research Builds on Net's Economic Impact," *Web Week,* March 31, 1997, p. 34.

Chapter 2

Understanding E-Business Technology

Making decisions about how to compete in an e-business world requires an understanding of the technology that underpins e-business. This includes looking at not only how the Internet works today but where it came from and where it is going. Business decision makers must understand this technology because they will be working with technical specialists to develop strategies on how to use e-business technologies for communication and the facilitation of commerce.

The World Wide Web is a major component of the Internet. It is the interface that most people use to access and transfer data. This is governed by a set of protocols. As the Internet and the World Wide Web evolve, new applications will be added to browsers. Linking the Internet to the end user's television and wireless phones will create considerable change.

This chapter is a primer designed to introduce the basic technological underpinning of e-business, the Internet, and the World Wide Web. Although some parts may seem technical, these ideas, terms, and concepts are the language of the Net.

1. Explain the importance of infrastructures.
2. Discuss how the Internet was developed.
3. Justify the importance of standards.
4. Describe how the Internet works.
5. Compare and contrast the last-mile connections to the Internet.
6. Discuss the role of an Internet service provider.
7. Provide the reasons for choosing an Internet service provider.
8. Define the World Wide Web.
9. Explain how the World Wide Web works.
10. Speculate on the future of the World Wide Web.

Developing Infrastructure

During the Cold War, the U.S. government aided in the development of an **infrastructure** designed to improve traffic flow and to cut costs. This new infrastructure bypassed older established systems, forcing businesses dependent on that old infrastructure to change or die. The public found this new infrastructure to be highly beneficial to their lives. It allowed individuals to move from city centers, to shop at locations far from their homes, and to visit family and friends much more easily than before. Businesses used this system to aid in the shipment of goods across the country, allowing for a more timely delivery. This new infrastructure transformed American society.

The infrastructure referred to above is the U.S. interstate highway system. Started in the 1950s and still under construction today, this road system helped to make the modern United States. Today a new infrastructure is developing that promises to have much the same impact. This new infrastructure allows for the movement of electronic information rather than physical products, but that may be more important in the long term.

Once a major highway, Route 66 is now a historic back road.

Infrastructure is the basic structure that allows a system to operate. For the Internet, this includes lines, browsers, computers, servers, etc.

THINKING STRATEGICALLY

Consider your national highway infrastructure. Speculate on how a consumer's life would be different if there was no national highway system. Speculate on how a business would have to operate differently if there was no national highway infrastructure. Determine what other infrastructures are important to a consumer's life and to business efficiency.

A transportation infrastructure allows an individual to travel from one location to another. This infrastructure includes small streets leading from the driveways of homes and the wider boulevards leading to highways. Ground transportation infrastructure includes the intersections, the stoplights, the traffic control systems, and even the pavement on which vehicles travel. If travelers are in a hurry, they may use the air transport infrastructure to move rapidly from one point to another.

The digital age is allowing the rapid movement of information around the globe on a digital superhighway, or I-way. Just as in the travel example above, digital information flows through a complicated and rapidly growing infrastructure. This telecommunications infrastructure consists of telephone lines and exchanges, cable TV lines and broadcasters, satellite and cellular broadcasters, and an Internet backbone. The Internet backbone consists of data lines, routers, switches, servers, and the local system used to send or view information at a user's site, such as a PC with a Web browser.

In the United States, no single entity owns the telecommunications infrastructure. The infrastructure that has developed was dependent on the type of information it was designed to carry. The telephone industry constructed a voice-switching infrastructure. The television cable industry developed a send-only video infrastructure. Companies such as MCI and UUNET specialize in the development and maintenance of data lines, routing, and switching for information using high-bandwidth Internet lines. Many smaller companies are providing access for the **last mile** of the telecommunications infrastructure by specializing in consumer premises equipment, such as the television set-top box or the PC online access to the Internet. Direct satellite and cellular systems bypass these landline-connected infrastructures. This allows electronic information to be delivered to remote areas around the world without the large expense of placing landlines.

The Internet is perhaps the best known of the digital telecommunications infrastructures. Originally just one of the many subsystems of the larger I-way, the Internet has set the standards that have allowed for the rapid growth of **e-mail** and the World Wide Web. It is estimated that by the year 2000 there will be 82.8 million e-mail users sending 6.6 trillion messages per year. The digital electronic signals that travel over the Internet can represent words, images, sounds,

The last mile is not literally a mile long. It represents the narrowest access to the user, which is usually the link from an exchange to an individual's home or business.

E-mail, or electronic mail, allows for the transfer of text-based content over the Internet. Current e-mail protocols allow for the sending of HTML code and attachments (additional files).

instructions, or anything else that a computer can produce or use. The more information that is needed to send, the larger the **bandwidth** needed to transport the information. Broad bandwidth is currently being delivered by a number of different companies.

THE INTERNET

"Sure we could build such a thing, but I don't see why anybody would want it."

> **Severo Ornstein,** one of the early developers of the Internet, when asked if it was possible to build an interconnected computer network.[1]

The **Internet** (or **Inter**connected **Net**work) started as a U.S. government–sponsored project to link computing systems. The ability to send packets of information between widely dispersed computer networks was seen as a means of lowering the cost of computing. The original 1969 project was called the ARPANET.[2] By the late 1980s, the National Science Foundation incorporated the ARPANET into its own network, the NSFNET.

The Internet allowed individual computer networks to interconnect with each other across common backbones. The NSF maintained the NSFNET backbone to which other local access systems connected. Each section of the backbone was rented from telecommunications companies. Universities using the Internet also developed and fostered **open standards,** or standardized means of sending and receiving electronic data.

Telecommunications Standards

Proprietary **computer networks** have existed for a long time on the information highway. Businesses have also used a variety of programming language systems to run networks and communications. Because the Internet was developed and used primarily by academics, it was based on a set of open standards, protocols of operation not owned by a single company. These open standards have allowed different computer systems (Windows, UNIX, Macintosh, etc.) to develop and read the same content. In essence, it is as if all systems were using the same language to communicate. Open standards such as Transport Control Protocols (TCP) and Internet Protocols (IP) (combined: **TCP/IP**) kept individuals, entrepreneurs, and businesses from being locked into one single company's communications system. The wide adoption of TCP/IP standards has fostered innovation, and its ease of use is leading businesses to adopt these standards for internal and external communication. Table 2.1 on the following page outlines the major standards used on the Internet.

Bandwidth indicates the amount of digital information that can be carried over a line. The basic rule in developing multimedia (combined text, images, sound) is that the richer the media, the larger the file, and therefore the higher the bandwidth needed to deliver the content in a given amount of time.

Open standards are basic sets of instructions, such as programs or programming methods, that are not owned by a single company and are free for others to use.

A **computer network** consists of a number of computers linked through a network server. The server controls the flow of information between the users.

Table 2.1 Internet Protocols

Term	Meaning	Used For
TCP/IP	Transport Control Protocol/Internet Protocol	It is a set of standards that are used on the Internet.
E-mail	Electronic mail	It allows the transport of text between users over the Internet.
Protocols below are now transparent, or unseen by the user, and are often integrated in other Internet applications.		
FTP	File Transfer Protocol	It allows computer files or software to be transferred online. This is most often used as an attachment with e-mail.
TELNET	Uses TCP/IP to exchange packets of data between computers	It allows a computer to connect into other computer systems, in essence becoming one of their terminals.
USENET	Standard for sites to share and forward discussion information	Like a chat room, it is a place for online discussions of areas of interest.
ARCHIE VERONICA WAIS	Mostly comic book characters	Search protocols for FTP sites, these Gopher menus allow for searching content on the Internet and file content searches. Most of these are now transparent to the user through a unified Web interface, such as a search engine.

The National Science Foundation withdrew from the governance of the Internet to speed the development of a private-sector Internet. Currently, the Internet's open standards are controlled by a number of not-for-profit groups, described in Table 2.2.

Infrastructure

Figure 2.1 illustrates the connected infrastructure of the Internet. Internet users must have some means of going online or linking to the Internet backbone (to find maps of telecommunications and Internet use, look at the Web search sites at the end of this chapter). This is accomplished through the use of an **Internet service provider (ISP).** The ISP could use a network access provider to link directly to the Internet backbone. The ISP can lease a certain amount of bandwidth access, allowing the setting of a fixed rate. The ISP is then able to charge its users a fixed rate, or a variable rate for bandwidth and time used. Business users also need an on-ramp to the Internet. They can use an ISP or, depending upon their size and capabilities, link to a network access provider.

If a business or an individual wants to access a Web site outside of a local network, it must be hosted on an Internet server with access to the Internet backbone.

Table 2.2 Internet Governing Organizations

Term	Meaning	Used For
ISO	International Standards Organization (www.iso.ch)	Is an international governing body located in Geneva
ANSI	American National Standards Institute (www.ansi.org)	Represents U.S. interests related to the Internet
IETF	Internet Engineering Task Force (www.ietf.org)	Is an open group that influences the standards set for the Internet
NIIT	National Information Infrastructure Task Force (iitf.doc.gov)	Was formed by the White House to help foster the development of the national infrastructure
W3C	World Wide Web Consortium (www.w3.org)	Governs the set of World Wide Web protocols

Source: Emily Leinfuss, "The New Politics of Standards," *InfoWorld,* June 24, 1996, pp. 1, 69–76.

Each server that is hooked up to the Internet is a **host.** When an individual logs on to the Internet from a home computer through a local area network server, he or she is not a host because other users do not have access to contents on the

Figure 2.1 How the I-Way Works

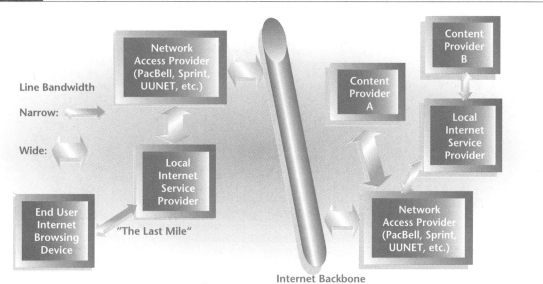

individual's computer. The number of host sites on the Internet is expected to increase from roughly 4 million host computers worldwide in 1995 to over 100 million hosts by 2001.

Bandwidth

Bandwidth indicates the size of pipe through which electronic information must move. Phone lines were originally designed to carry analog signals for voice. The thin copper, or **twisted pair,** wires that hook up to telephones were designed to carry this low-bandwidth signal. Computers use digital signals, or a series of ons (1) and offs (0). The more 1s and 0s that can to be sent over a given period of time, the higher the bandwidth needed to carry the signal. Different types of data lines and

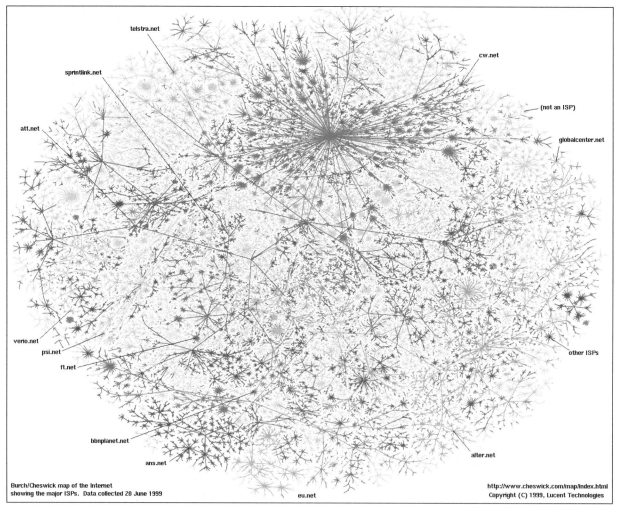

Bell Labs map of the major ISPs

methods of sending data allow for increased bandwidth and therefore greater amounts of information to be sent. Bandwidth is measured in **bits per second,** or **bps,** which are counted in thousands (kilobits per second: Kbps), millions (megabits per second: Mbps), and billions (gigabits per second: Gbps).

Backbone Speeds

In the early 1990s, a local ISP would be linked to the Internet backbone over T-1 lines at around 1.54 Mbps. Currently, companies are deploying new Internet backbones that can carry up to 2.5 Gbps. This is enough bandwidth to send the equivalent of 1,400 three-hundred-page books in seven seconds.

The **Internet2** is a new IP-based network designed to allow the transport of very high bandwidths of information. Universities and the federal government are once again spearheading this new infrastructure. This new network is being designed to send up to 9.6 Gbps, or billions of bits of data per second, across the Internet backbone. This will allow researchers at universities to share information from supercomputers. In addition, the new Internet is testing technology that will eventually move to the current Internet backbone.[3] The Internet2 is expected to allow for video and voice to travel over the Internet. Although these high-bandwidth lines allow for the delivery of large amounts of content, they still must be squeezed through the last mile to the individual's access device.

The Last-Mile Lines

Information must move through some type of pipeline to reach the end user. Business users are more likely to have wide bandwidth for their local area networks and high-bandwidth access to the Internet backbone. Individual home users are most likely to use the narrow bandwidth allowed by telephone twisted pair connections and a modem. The following list outlines the types of lines used to carry digital information:

Twisted pair. Two copper wires are used for analog telephones. This **analog signal** has traditionally needed to be turned into a **digital signal** for the computer by using a modem. In most cases, the lower-bandwidth capability of the twisted pair has limited the speed of phone modems to 56 Kbps. Currently new technology is allowing twisted pair lines to directly send digital signals. A digital subscriber line (DSL) allows higher-bandwidth connections but may require upgrading of older twisted pair wires.

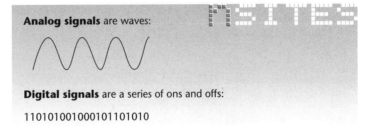

Analog signals are waves:

Digital signals are a series of ons and offs:

110101001000101101010

Phone companies have twisted pair lines running into most homes in the United States and have the ability to switch users around their network. Phone companies also have the ability to operate both **upstream** from the user to someone else and **downstream** to the user.

Upstream traffic is communication from the browser to the provider. This usually requires small amounts of data to be sent back to the provider, which may then send large files downstream to the browser.

Coaxial. Cable television systems most often use **coaxial** cables, which are designed to carry a higher-bandwidth analog signal to home users. Coaxial lines can also be made to operate with digital signals but require a cable modem for analog televisions. Cable companies can broadcast signals downstream to homes but, in most cases, do not have the ability to switch signals or to receive upstream signals; this needs to be done over phone lines.

Fiber-optic. Fiber-optic lines use light to carry digital signals. These pure digital lines carry very high bandwidth. Fiber-optic systems are used throughout the telecommunications backbone but are not widely installed in individual homes. Computers can use the digital signals they carry, but analog phones or analog televisions cannot use the digital signal.

Wireless. Wireless Internet access to home users can be provided over satellite broadcast systems and cellular telephone systems. Direct digital broadcast can send digital signals for Internet content using the same technology as is used for sending digital television signals from satellites to individual homes. This allows users in remote locations to receive high-bandwidth Internet access. For most satellite users, phones are still required for upstream signals, although this can be done over cellular phone networks. Some Internet service providers bypass Internet access providers by using satellite linkups that can be cheaper and easier to use than landlines.

Hughes Network Systems *(www.hns.com)* allows Internet users to bypass wire connections and receive signals from geostationary satellites at 400 Kbps. This system requires a phone line for upstream traffic. Craig McCaw, who sold McCaw Cellular Communications to AT&T, has started a new company, Teledesic *(www. teledesic.com),* which plans to place 840 satellites in low orbit. These satellites will broadcast to individual users who will receive the signal on dinner plate–sized receiving disks. This would allow for a 2-megabit connection to the Internet. It will also allow for two-way communication.[4] These ventures may or may not be successful enough to replace landlines, but wireless telecommunications connections are growing in countries where landlines do not exist or are too expensive to build.

Wireless cellular systems are also developing rapidly. Pagers, telephones, and handheld devices are linking to the Internet, giving access to e-mail and Web pages. Lack of standards has limited the growth of cellular access, but a new generation of cellular telephone standards called G3 has been set. This will be based on a digital communications system that will be able to send up to 2 megabits per second. This is enough bandwidth to allow cellular phones to provide videoconferencing.

Wireless cellular systems are rapidly developing around the world. Europe has standardized its cellular format, and the number of cellular users has increased tremendously. Norway has more cellular phones than landline-based phones. Wireless systems are allowing developing countries to avoid the costs of placing landlines and the use of older telecommunication systems.[5] It is expected that there will be over 830 million wireless subscribers worldwide by the end of 2003.[6]

Table 2.3 outlines current last-mile means of access methods for home users. Speed in seconds refers to sending 10 megabits of data (roughly 1 megabyte of

Table 2.3 Home User Internet Delivery Options

Term	Explanation	Speed in Seconds
Modem (14.4, 28.8, 56 Kbps)	Modulating/demodulating changes analog signals to digital and back. Used to connect to twisted pair phone lines.	@56 Kbps: 179 seconds
T1 or T3	T1 carrier line allows digital information to be sent. T3 line can have speeds of 44.7 Mbps.	T1 @ 1.5 Mbps: 6.6 seconds
DSL (ADSL: 1.54 Mbps)	Digital Subscriber Line allows digital signals on existing twisted pair phone lines. A DSL modem would connect to a PC and telephone. The number of DSL connections is expected to increase from 41,000 in 1998 to 2.56 million in 2001.	@ 1.5 Mbps: 6.6 seconds
Cable Modems (800 Kbps–3 Mbps)	Used with coaxial television cables, require a return line through a phone line.	3.3–20 seconds
Direct Broadcast Satellite (200–400 Kbps)	Data moved from Internet backbone to satellite gateway and then bounced off the satellite to small dish at user's location. Requires return line through phone line.	40–80 seconds
G3 Cellular Phones (projected 2 Mbps maximum)	Cellular phone format allows information to be sent digitally, allows broadband connection to any device that can access cellular network.	0.5–1 second

Source: Charles Waltner, "Bartering for Bandwidth," *Communication Week,* May 7, 1997, pp. S16–S18; and Roger O. Crockett, "Warp Speed Ahead," *Business Week,* February 16, 1998, pp. 80–83.

data, or one full screen of graphics). Business users may utilize high-bandwidth options such as T1 or T3 lines.

Digital Convergence

Digital convergence implies that multiple technologies will be used to access the Internet. For example, telephones will use IP standards to send and receive e-mail and Web page data, televisions will be able to access the Net, and computers will be accessible from other independent IP devices. Telecommunications companies are laying fiber-optic cables and placing satellites and cellular systems in an attempt to become the one-stop shop for Internet access. By 2001, the United States could have 80 times its 1999 telecommunications capacity with over 231,000 miles of long-distance telephone cable.[7]

For home users, a number of companies are aiming to be the primary source of Internet access. On June 24, 1998, the CEOs of AT&T *(www.att.com)* and TCI

CASE 2.1

Streaming Video

Broader-bandwidth information highways are fostering the use of Webcast video. **Webcast** video allows for streaming of video signals to an individual's Web-accessing device. This technology is being used to Webcast meetings between business locations and to deliver entertainment video content. There are problems in delivering streaming video. Plug-in players must be added to the Web browser. In addition, each time an individual requests a video, a great deal of data must move over the Internet. Broadcast.com attempted to host an online fashion show for Victoria's Secret, but the broadcast crashed because the demand was too high.

Streaming video content can be found at Broadcast.com *(http://broadcast.com/)*, RealNetworks *(www.realnetworks.com)*, SportsLine *(http://cbs.sportsline.com)*, and other media sites.[11]

(www.tci.com) announced a merger. This merger was designed to meld a TV cable company and a phone company to provide a wide variety of digital services through the last mile to the home user. TCI's cable will allow AT&T to access high bandwidth in 33 million homes. AT&T is also planning to use wireless technology to link homes outside the TCI area. This high bandwidth is designed to allow video to be sent with Web pages.[8] Microsoft is also positioning itself as a provider across platforms. In 1999 Microsoft spent over $7 billion to gain interest in AT&T, NTL *(www.ntli.com)* (a British company with phone and cable networks), and the wireless phone company Nextel *(www.nextel.com)*.[9]

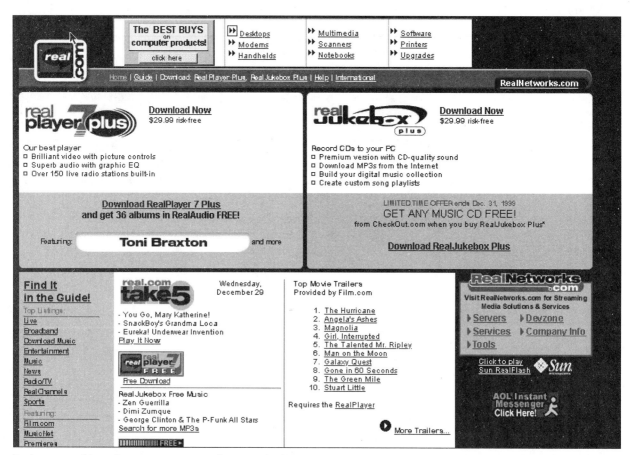

Real.com provides software to stream media across the Internet.

Western Europe is racing to bring IP access to homes and businesses. Competition has lowered the price of telecommunications services, and companies from around the globe are adding to the telecommunications backbone. Telephone, cable, and wireless services will provide home access to the Internet. To speed consumer acceptance of the Internet and to lock in customers, ISPs in Great Britain and Denmark are providing free ISP services.[10]

THINKING STRATEGICALLY

Consider the importance of streaming video. Determine how this will change the nature of communication over the Internet. Decide which types of devices will need to be used to maximize the use of streaming video. Explain how this will affect business and marketing practices.

THE ROLE OF AN INTERNET SERVICE PROVIDER

A business must decide if it will host its own Internet access or outsource the service. As shown in Figure 2.1 on page 27, a content provider can use its own computer network to access the Internet backbone through a network access provider, or it can host its site on a local ISP. Of the Fortune 1000 companies, 66 percent outsource some portion of their Internet access. This allows them to focus on their core competencies, and lets the access provider worry about the technological aspects of Internet connection.[12] Demands for bandwidth and access are expected to increase outsourcing revenue to more than $100 billion by the year 2003. UUNET offers international businesses the ability to have Web servers on numerous continents. This allows these corporations to have targeted information and to avoid sending content over ocean cables, which can bottleneck information flows. In addition, companies that specialize in Web access can meet peak demand periods. Over 100,000 people visited the 1997 Oscar site *(www.oscar.com)* in its first hour. By the end of the day, the

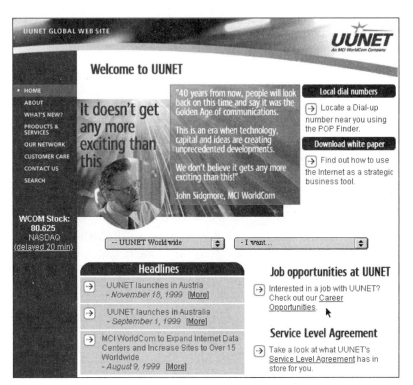

Source: www.uu.net

Table 2.4 Internet Delivery

Question	Outsource	In-house
Do you have the technology staff to develop and maintain a Web site?	No	Yes
Are you willing to pay the cost of continually upgrading the software and hardware necessary to maintain adequate resources?	No	Yes
Will you have a large number of hits in a short time?	Yes	No
Do you need high levels of security?	Yes	No
Will your technology needs change rapidly?	Yes	No
Do your users require round-the-clock access to support?	Yes	No

A **mirrored site** allows a Web site to be placed on more than one ISP, allowing less congestion and faster delivery of content.

site recorded over 1.5 million hits (visits to the site).[13] When NASA *(www. nasa.gov)* used the Internet to relay pictures from the Mars *Pathfinder,* it used 20 university and private **mirrored sites** for the content. This allowed NASA to handle the 46.9 million page visits it had on July 8, 1997. From July 1 to August 4, 1997, NASA had 566 million page visits.[14]

The use of ISPs can be advantageous for businesses that need extra services. Barnes and Noble *(www.BarnesandNoble.com)* uses MCI to host its servers and provide the bandwidth to the Web.[15] When a business is trying to decide if it is going to host its own site or use an ISP, it should answer the questions posed in Table 2.4.

ISP Choice

A recent survey of businesses indicated that 73 percent outsourced the hosting of their Web sites. The five most important considerations when choosing an ISP include:

1. **Connection availability.** How many users can access the site at one time?
2. **Network considerations.** How well does the ISP's network perform in terms of speed, lack of downtime, and capacity?
3. **Reputation for speed of repair.** If something goes down, how quickly can it be repaired?
4. **Price.** What are the prices for services, and are there fixed prices or pay-as-you-go flexibility?
5. **Service-level agreements.** What types of services are the ISPs offering?[16]

Five additional questions that businesses should consider when choosing an ISP include:

1. **Disk space.** What is the cost, and how much disk space does the business get?
2. **Programming support.** What capabilities does the ISP have to include database access, programming, or special design skills?
3. **E-commerce support.** Does the site allow for shopping carts, online transactions, and individualized marketing programs?
4. **E-mail services.** How many accounts can be provided, and how can they be accessed?
5. **Security.** Does the business have security for data transfer and for transactions conducted online?[17]

In 1998 small ISPs had 60 percent of the commercial customers. This is because the smaller ISPs are typically able to maintain tighter relationships with their accounts and are able to respond quickly to problems and needs.[18] Consolidation is occurring among small ISPs, allowing firms to gain efficiencies through size.[19] Projections estimate that the number of local ISPs could drop from around 4,500 in 1999 to around 2,600 by 2002.[20] This is assuming that these ISPs are able to meet the needs of the businesses.

security

Security of Web sites is an important consideration. This became even more obvious when the CIA's Web site was hacked or broken into and its Web page name changed from Central Intelligence Agency to "Central Stupidity Agency." **Firewalls** are security measures designed to prevent hackers from gaining access through a server to a Web site. For promotion-only sites, the most that may happen is that the page design could be changed, but when the Web site is the access point to an intranet, extranet, or e-commerce, the implications are much more grave.

Firewall software is designed to limit entry into a network to authorized users. This may be controlled through registrations and passwords. Firewalls by themselves may not be enough to prevent attacks because internal employees represent the greatest threat to networks. Internal employees are the individuals with access to security procedures and computer terminals, and they know what important types of data are stored.

CASE 2.2

The Race to Wire the World

In 1998 North America accounted for close to 55 percent of the 149 million Web users. By 2005, North America may only consitute 32 percent of the projected 716 million Web users. Western Europe is projected to have a 28 percent share and the Asia Pacific region would have close to 24 percent.[22] Growth in these areas will not necessarily be evenly distributed. In 1999 Northern Europe had Internet access at near equivalency to the United States while Southern Europe had little access. Only 2.9 percent of Greek citizens had access to the Internet.[23]

To meet the needs of these future Internet users, new backbone systems are being laid. Interoute Telecommunications Ltd. *(www.interoute.co.uk)* is one of the companies planning to build a high-capacity fiber-optic backbone across Europe. As more backbone is laid, prices will drop. In addition, cellular telephones in Europe operate off digital signals and will make a more rapid transition to the Internet. CTR Group has plans to develop an $8 billion, 100,000-mile network of undersea fiber-optic lines for Internet connections. Its project, called Project Oxygen *(www.projectoxygen.com)*, will connect 74 countries.[24]

Companies are positioning themselves to provide access to home users of the Internet. Microsoft has purchased cable companies in Europe, Canada, and South America. PSI Net *(www.psi.net)*, a large ISP, has purchased a number of Latin America's ISPs to take advantage of the expected 32 percent future growth in Internet use. AOL *(www.aol.co.uk)* has tried to increase its dominance in Europe but is facing stiff resistance from ISPs offering free Internet access. Free Internet access companies in Britain, Denmark, and other countries make money by obtaining part of the user's phone service fees, charging for advertising, and collecting commissions from e-commerce sales. Until Europeans are able to obtain flat rates for telephone use, their online time may be limited because of the per-minute charges paid for telephone access.[25]

THINKING STRATEGICALLY

Consider the growth of the Internet around the world. Determine how this will affect the content that is available online. If customers around the world are able to access the Internet, decide how important it is to have an Internet presence for a business. Consider what the language of the Web will be. Decide if a company needs to have Web sites designed for multiple languages. Speculate on the social impact of the Internet when the world is connected.

Another method of increasing security is the use of a **virtual private network (VPN).** A VPN can connect two businesses, such as a franchise and its headquarters, by using dedicated lines internally (communications lines that are not open to outside users) that are connected to ISPs. The ISPs then use the Internet for long-distance communication. This allows for higher levels of security between the local business and the ISP, making it less likely that outsiders can access corporate information. A VPN is cheaper than using dedicated lines for long-distance communication.[21]

THE WORLD WIDE WEB

The **World Wide Web (WWW or Web)** is a relatively new addition to the Internet. The Web uses the Internet backbone to send information from servers, or repositories of file information, to browsers, or software designed to display the files. The Web facilitates the transfer of hypermedia-based files, allowing links to other pages, places, or applications. By placing a hyperlink in a Web page, the user can be transferred to anyplace in the world through the Internet backbone.

Tim Berners-Lee developed the WWW in 1990 at the Particle Physics Laboratory in Geneva, Switzerland, as a means for helping particle physicists communicate worldwide. In 1998 Tim Berners-Lee was awarded a MacArthur Foundation fellowship grant for his work in developing the Web and the W3C. The Web architecture was designed to emulate the human brain by allowing the linkage of random associations.[26] The development of Web graphical browsers and the use of HyperText Transport Protocols (HTTP) have allowed easy access to data at remote locations. Just as the Internet has protocols to govern the use and transportation of data, the Web has a set of its own standards, outlined in Table 2.5.

The Browser

The growth of the Web is due to the GUI (graphical user interface) browsers that allow the user to access Web data without using UNIX- or DOS-based procedures. Mosaic, the first Web browser, could be downloaded free from the National Supercomputer Center. A number of companies licensed the technology to the browser. Netscape, Inc., allowed users to download its browser for free. This strategy allowed Netscape to grow rapidly and become a standard for the industry. Netscape used

Table 2.5 World Wide Web Protocols

Protocol	Title	Meaning
The Web	World Wide Web	Set of standards that allows hyperlinks and graphics to move through the Internet.
HTTP	HyperText Transport Protocol	Underlying protocol to the Web that allows linking to other sites and retrieving of information.
HTML	HyperText Markup Language	Text-based markup language, or set of codes that gives design (fonts, position, colors, etc.) to the Web page.
VRML	Virtual Reality Markup Language	Language that allows 3-D models to be displayed and rotated in a Web page.
CGI	Common Gateway Interface	Interface that provides links to other programs from Web servers, such as when a Web form is used to collect information.
URL	Universal Resource Locator Code	Address that is used to find a site at a server on the Web.
SET	Secure Electronic Transaction	Protocols that allow secure purchases on the Internet.

this leverage to help sell its server software to ISPs and content providers.[27] Netscape initially was able to capture 85 percent of the browser market. As competitors such as Spry's Air Mosaic, Netcom's Netcruiser, and others fell by the wayside, Microsoft introduced Microsoft Internet Explorer. By 1997 Netscape had only 50.5 percent of the browser market, with Microsoft's Internet Explorer at 22.8 percent, AOL with 16.1 percent and all others accounting for 10.6 percent.[28] In 1998 AOL purchased Netscape and took control of its browser division. By 1999 Internet Explorer had close to 74 percent of the market: AOL/Netscape's share was close to 25 percent.[29]

Browser Functions

The **browser** is the interface between the Web content and the user. The browser takes the information and codes and displays the requested design on the screen. For example, HTML code indicates color, location, size, hyperlinks, etc. When a hyperlink is clicked, the browser pulls up the associated file to "play" through the browser.

New versions of code are continually being developed for the Web. This requires new versions of browsers to be designed to read the latest codes such as Java script, DHTML, XML, and the most popular plug-ins. **Plug-ins** allow rich content files such as video, radio programs, and other multimedia content to play through browsers.

Table 2.6 Web Browser Languages and Plug-Ins

Code	Meaning	Use
HTML	HyperText Markup Language versions 3–4	Gives design (fonts, position, colors, etc.) to the Web page, using text-based markup language (a set of codes).
DHTML	Dynamic HTML	Allows movement and layering of text and images on a page, adding multimedia effects.
XML	Extendable markup language	Adds intelligence to Web pages.
JAVA	Programming language developed by Sun Microsystems	Allows Web developers to add programming applets to Web pages.
Plug-Ins (*Examples*)		
Video	Apple Computer's QuickTime	Downloads and plays video.
Video and Audio	RealNetworks' RealPlayer	Streams in video and audio.
Multimedia	Macromedia's Shockwave	Allows the streaming of multimedia and interactive games.
Chat	IChat Inc.s iChat	Allows real-time text conversations.
IP Telephony	Phone Calls	Allows phone calls to be placed over the Internet.

Figure 2.2 Server-Browser Interactions

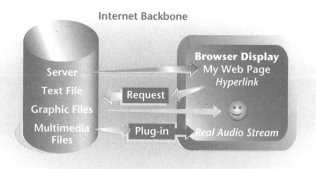

Table 2.6 lists the major browser languages and plug-ins. These are constantly evolving as new companies enter the market, as the W3C consortium adds flexibility to Web pages, and as the backbone grows allowing the transport of richer content. Fortunately for most Web developers, software exists to automatically insert these codes when Web pages are designed.

Some plug-ins allow the streaming of content. **Streaming** brings in a number of smaller packets of information to load and play. One packet can play while others are loading, which allows seamless media presentations. Figure 2.2 illustrates how the browser works.

Streaming allows digital information to be sent in packets, or small units. These packets can be played as they stream in. This allows large multimedia files to play without downloading the entire file at once.

Web Languages

An HTML tag, or code, is a command to the computer for setting fonts, formatting, locating, sizing, URL locations, etc. A Web page developer must program the code or use an editor to place the code. For example, to set up a hot spot, or hyperlink, on a page to allow a user to link to other sites, a locator code must be included to direct the browser to access information at the desired Web site. To access information at the local site, such as a different location on the current page or

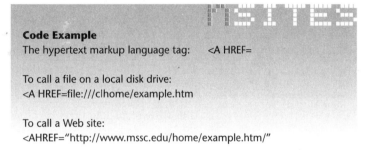

Code Example
The hypertext markup language tag: <A HREF=

To call a file on a local disk drive:
<A HREF=file:///c|home/example.htm

To call a Web site:
<AHREF="http://www.mssc.edu/home/example.htm/"

a file on a disk drive, a hyperlink must direct the browser to that targeted location. To access information elsewhere on the Web, the URL code address must be included.

The W3C is responsible for controlling the upgrades to the HTML. HTML 4 is the newest version of the code and allows greater flexibility in Web page design. Dynamic HTML (DHTML) allows movement and layering of text and images on a page and can add multimedia effects. XML is designed to add intelligence to Web pages. With XML, a Web page can act like a stand-alone program; for example, it could collect data and automatically send and verify the data without the additional action of the user. This can result in more efficient searches, higher degrees of personalization, more powerful Web applications, and links to databases.[30]

In order to read or create the newest code, browsers and editors must be updated. In addition, as the Web page becomes more sophisticated, the level of technical expertise of Web page designers must also be increased.

The Browser as an Operating System

Because a browser can display documents, play multimedia, and run programs, it acts as a de facto **operating system.** If a single browser was to become the industry standard for systems other than PCs, it could replace Windows as an operating system.[31] Microsoft could not sit by and let Netscape take over this important standard. Microsoft's Windows 98 is designed to integrate Internet features into the

An **operating system** is the program that controls the computer. Windows 95/98 is an operating system, as are Linux, OS2, Windows NT, and DOS.

operating system. It is optimized to run Microsoft's Internet Explorer and link to Microsoft Network (an ISP).[32] Microsoft has been accused of designing Internet Explorer so that it will play Microsoft's standards better than the open standards available on the Internet.[33]

Netscape, in turn, used Internet developers as a strategic tool to maintain its position. Netscape released its source code to developers. This allowed programmers to add enhancements to the browser.[34] The center of Netscape's strategy was to have its server software installed. Netscape's server software, in turn, competes against Apache, the number one server software for the Internet. Apache is a freeware supported by companies such as IBM.[35]

Web Site

In order for someone to visit a site, Internet addressing systems must be able to locate the IP address and domain name. The current IP address structure consists of four numbers separated by dots (.) or decimals (e.g., 111.222.333.4). The individual user does not need to know the numbers in order to access a site; instead the site uses a unique **domain name,** or name Web site, such as the domain for Missouri Southern State College: **www.mssc.edu.** The domain name is part of the URL (Universal Resource Locator) address. The format of the Missouri Southern URL is shown below.

InterNIC (Internet Network Information Center) was the original issuer of domain names. The InterNIC had received so many applications for names that the processing time increased, and the available names ran short. This required a change in the domain name structure. The U.S. government gave control of domain name registration to one company: Network Solutions *(www. networksolutions.com),* located in Virginia. At first, domain name registration was tax-supported and free. By August 1999, NSI had registered over 5.3 million domain names.

In October 1998, a nonprofit, private-sector corporation was formed to control the domain name system. The Internet Corporation for Assigned Names and

http://www.mssc.edu/pages/mssc.htm.

Hypertext Protocol	WWW	Page	Host	Group	File Path	File Name	Hypertext Markup File Type (HTML)
			DOMAIN NAME				

Numbers (ICANN) is a broad coalition of Internet businesses and technical and academic communities. ICANN authorizes businesses to register domain names. A current list of authorized companies can be found at: *http://www.icann.org/registrars/accredited-list.html.*

If a business decides to use an ISP to host its site, it is important that the business obtain its own domain name. That domain name can be transferred if the business wishes to switch to another ISP.

In order to obtain a domain name, the site must have a server linked to the Internet backbone. Seven new domain names have been recommended for the Internet. Table 2.7 outlines the old domain names and a list of newly recommended name extensions.

FUTURE OF THE WEB

The current Web runs on computers that are not designed to engage in the type of information transfer and display possible over the Internet. This is in part why multimedia systems are add-ons to computers. The PC is first a computer, then a multimedia player. Most people have a television, which is first a multimedia player that can be turned into a computer at one-tenth the cost.

Table 2.7 Web Domain Names

Old Domain Groups	Meaning	Proposed New Domain Groups	Meaning
.com	Commercial	.firm	Business/firm
.edu	Educational	.store	Goods for purchase
.gov	Government	.web	WWW-related activities
.org	Nonprofit organizations	.arts	Cultural/entertainment
.net	Network companies	.rec	Recreation/entertainment
	International	.info	Information services
.fr	France	.nom	Individual/personal
.de	Germany		
.ca	Canada		

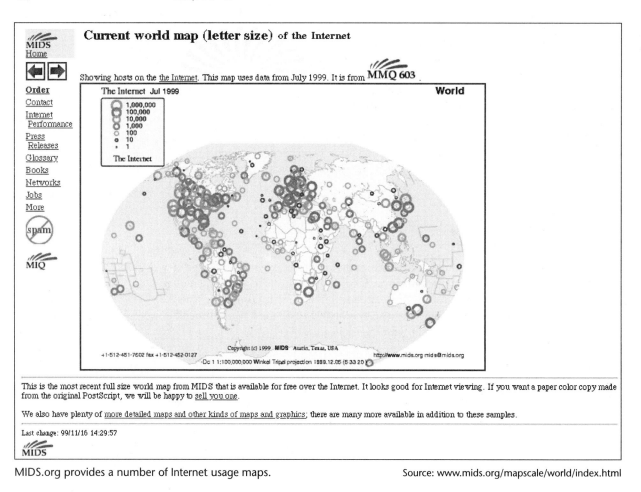

MIDS.org provides a number of Internet usage maps.   Source: www.mids.org/mapscale/world/index.html

High-Bandwidth Delivery

In 1998 only 40 percent of homes in the United States had computers, and only 25 percent were hooked up to the Internet. The remaining 60 percent that have televisions represent a very large and untapped market for interactivity. PC penetration is even lower in many other countries. Internet content can be delivered over a TV through set-top boxes or in TVs with built-in Internet connectivity. Often the price of the TV with Internet connection is lower than purchasing a PC just for Internet use.

There is no current open standard for how Web-based television will operate. Microsoft has a Windows CE interface it would like to see dominate the industry. Even though Microsoft has made a $1 billion investment in the cable company Comcast

The one-millionth registered domain name went to Bonny View Cottage Furniture in Petosky, MI (www.bonnyview.com).

Corporation *(www.comcast.com)*, other cable companies want to maintain open standards so competitive forces will deliver the lowest-cost system.[36] Microsoft purchased WebTV *(www.webtv.com)* for $425 million and faces competition from Worldgate *(www.wgate.com)* and @Home Network *(www.home.net)*. The lower resolution of TV-based Web pages requires that the pages be designed differently from computer-based pages. Simple designs and smaller pixel viewing areas are required. Light text with dark backgrounds improves text reading.[37]

The Holy Grail of Web browsing will be the delivery of high-bandwidth signals to a high-definition digital television (HDTV). The United States has lagged behind other countries in the development of HDTV. The Telecommunications Reform Act of 1996 has mandated that analog, or traditional, TVs can no longer be sold after the year 2006 if HDTV reaches a high enough acceptance level. HDTV sets are projected to be in 30 percent of American homes by the year 2006.[38] Computer makers designed hybrid PC/TV systems that allow TV and radio broadcasts in addition to other computer functions such as Web surfing, but these systems have not caught on with customers.

Web Appliances

As the Web becomes more ubiquitous, it is finding its way into more applications. Web-linked cellular phones and PDAs (personal digital assistants) allow salespeople to be linked through wireless backbones to a firm's intranet. PC-enhanced automobiles are being designed to read e-mail to the driver. Designers are even looking to add Web applications to appliances in an individual's home and business. This may some day allow a Web page to turn on a microwave oven in a home, control factory equipment at a business, and allow the electric utility company to monitor electricity use and charge higher rates during peak demand periods.[39]

TERMS AND CONCEPTS

KNOWLEDGE INTEGRATION

Bandwidth *25*
Berners-Lee, Tim *36*
Bits per second (bps) *29*
Browser *37*
Coaxial *30*
Domain name *40*
Fiber-optic lines *30*

Firewalls *35*
Internet2 *29*
Internet service provider (ISP) *26*
Last mile *24*
Open standards *25*
Plug-ins *37*

Streaming *39*
TCP/IP *25*
Twisted pair *28*
World Wide Web (WWW) (Web) *36*
W3C *27*

CONCEPTS AND QUESTIONS FOR REVIEW

1. Define infrastructure.
2. Discuss the major players developing the telecommunications infrastructure.
3. Explain what the Internet is and how the Internet came to be.
4. Describe the importance of telecommunications standards.
5. Explain how the Internet works.
6. Discuss the role of an ISP for an individual and a business.
7. Evaluate the alternatives that a home user has to go online.
8. Determine what a business should consider when deciding how to go online.
9. Explain the World Wide Web.
10. Differentiate the parts of a URL.
11. Explain the likely future of the World Wide Web.

ACTIVE LEARNING

Exercise 2.1: Chasing the Net Connection

Web users must have access to the Internet. Track that connection starting with an Internet device such as a PC or WebTV. What is used to connect to the last mile, a modem, coaxial, or fiber-optic cable? Describe how the speed of the connection influences how the Web is used. Determine how the last mile is connected to the backbone. Is it running through an ISP? Use the ISP's Web page, or call to investigate how it is linked online.

Exercise 2.2: Web Devices

Explore your home and determine what benefits there could be in connecting different appliances to the Net. Explain how an individual's life could be better if remote access to appliances was possible. Speculate on which companies, such as utility companies, could benefit by accessing information from a home or a business. Determine how these connections would be made.

Exercise 2.3: Choosing an ISP

Choosing an ISP for a business requires careful analysis. Investigate an ISP based on the criteria in the table on page 45. Discuss this with your classmates and determine which ISP would be the best to use. Explore both large and small ISPs.

ISP Evaluation Exercise

Criteria	Explanation	Site Evaluation
Connection availability	How many users can access the site at one time?	
Network considerations	How well does the ISP's network perform, based on speed, lack of downtime, and capacity?	
Reputation for speed of repair	If a component breaks down, how quickly can it be repaired?	
Price	What are the prices for services, and are there fixed prices or pay-as-you-go flexibility?	
Service level agreements	What types of services are the ISPs offering?	
Disk space	What is the cost, and how much disk space does the business get?	
Programming support	What capabilities does the ISP have to include database access, programming, or special design skills?	
E-commerce support	Does the site allow for shopping carts, online transactions, and individualized marketing programs?	
Available e-mail services	How many accounts can be provided, and how can they be accessed?	
Security	Does the business have security for data transfer and for transactions conducted online?	

WEB SEARCH — LOOKING ONLINE

SEARCH TERM:	Internet Maps	First 2 out of 1,999

Atlas of Cyberspaces. Provides a wide variety of maps showing Internet traffic flows and use.
http://www.geog.ucl.ac.uk/casa/martin/atlas/atlas.html

TeleGeography. Provides maps on telecommunications flows worldwide.
www.telegeography.com

SEARCH TERM:	Internet Service Providers	First 2 out of 115,808

MCI WorldCom USA. Is a global business telecommunications company that is a premier provider of local, long-distance, international, and Internet services.
www.mci.com

UUNET. Is the Internet service division for MCI.
www.uunet.com

SEARCH TERM:	Internet Regulation	First 9 out of 2,592

American National Standards Institute. Represents U.S. interests related to the Internet.
www.ansi.org

ARPANET. Is an Internet consultant that does Web page and site designing.
www.arpanet.com

International Standards Organization. Is an international governing body located in Geneva.
www.iso.ch

Internet Engineering Task Force. Is an open group that influences the standards set for the Internet.
www.ietf.org

Internet Service Providers' Consortium. Provides support services to other ISPs across the nation.
www.ispc.org

Internet2. Is a project to bring focus, energy, and resources to a new development of standards of teaching, research, and learning.
www.internet2.edu

InterNIC. Is a joint venture between the U.S. government and Network Solutions to help enlist sites with different domain names.
www.internic.net

National Information Infrastructure Task Force. Was formed by the White House to help foster the development of the national infrastructure.
www.niit.org

World Wide Web Consortium. Governs the set of World Wide Web protocols.
www.www3.org

SEARCH TERM:	Alternative Net Connections	First 2 out of 338,577

DirecPC. Uses a satellite system to allow quick Internet access nationwide.
www.direcpc.com

Teledesic. Is a company formed from AT&T telecommunications that enables low-orbit satellites to transmit information from person to person.
www.teledisc.com

SEARCH TERM:	Internet and Web Development	First 7 out of 217,588

America Online. Is an online company that distributes online services to people across the nation.
www.aol.com

CompuServe Internet Gateway. Is a division of AOL that distributes online services to the public.
www.compuserve.com

Microsoft. Is a major leader in software, that is positioning itself to be a major Internet access company over the Web with high bandwidth, and also distributes the most widely used browsers available, Internet Explorer.
www.microsoft.com

Netscape Communications. Is a division of AOL that produces one of the top-of-the-line browsers for computer connection to the Web.
www.netscape.com

Network Solutions. Is a domain name procurement Web site.
www.networksolutions.com

Opera. Is a new browser that is making some of the browsing quicker.
www.operasoftware.com

Sun Microsystems. Introduced Java and Jini technologies that are common-place for the Internet today.
www.sun.com

REFERENCES

1 Gary H. Anthes, "The History of the Future," *Computerworld,* October 3, 1994, p. 101.
2 Gary H. Anthes, "The History of the Future," *Computerworld,* October 3, 1994, pp. 101–105.
3 Barbara Grady, "New Super-Fast Net Being Built," *Internet World,* April 20, 1998, pp. 1, 57; and Brian Riggs, "Building a Better Net," *LANTIMES,* February 17, 1997, pp. 39–44.
4 Andrew Kupfer, "Craig McCaw Sees an Internet in the Sky," *Fortune,* May 27, 1996, pp. 62–72.
5 Steven V. Brull and Neil Gross, "Cell Phones: Europe Made the Right Call," *Business Week,* September 7, 1998, pp. 107–110; Blaise Zerega, "Crank Up the Broadband," *Red Herring,* August 1999, pp. 82–83; Blaise Zerega, "The 3G Force," *Red Herring,* August 1999, pp. 84–88; and Rick Overton, "Last-Mover Advantage," *Business 2.0,* August 1999, pp. 107–108.
6 SST MobileNet Systems, "Ericsson Presents New Cellular Subscriber Forecast—830 Million Subscribers by Year End 2003," September 1, 1999, *<http://mobile.softline.fi/sms-monthly/New/News_98044.htm>.*
7 Rachael King, "Too Much Long Distance," *Fortune,* March 15, 1999, pp. 106–110.
8 Peter Elstrom, "At Last, Telecom Unbound," *Business Week,* July 6, 1998, pp. 24–27.
9 Michael Mooler and Linda Mimelstain, "Who Do You Want to Buy Today?" *Business Week,* June 7, 1999, pp. 32–33.
10 Mary Lisbeth D'Amico, "Danish Providers Lure Users With Free Internet Access," *Infoworld,* May 17, 1999, p. 48H; Stephen Baker, Jack Ewing, and Kerry Capell, "The Race to Wire Europe," *Business Week,* June 7, 1999, pp. 48–50; and Paula Musich, "Bandwidth Boon for Europe?" *PC Week,* July 12, 1999, p. 86.
11 Neil Gross and Steven V. Brull, "The Net's Next Battle Royal," *Business Week,* June 28, 1999, pp. 108–112; Steven Vonder Haar, "High-Speed Net Access Has Got Game," *Inter@ctive Week,* June 7, 1999, p. 36; and Eric Brown, "Pipe Dreams," *New Media,* April 1999, pp. 34–43.
12 Kate Gerwig, "Easy Street?" *Internet Week,* June 8, 1998, pp. 67–71.
13 Brian Riggs, "Web Outsourcing Hits Big Time," *LANTIMES,* March 17, 1997, pp. 1, 24.
14 Todd Spangler, "Mars Attacks the Web," *Web Week,* August 18, 1997, pp. 27, 31.
15 Todd Spangler, "A Page-Turner on the Web," *Web Week,* November 3, 1997, pp. 27, 31.
16 TeleChoice, "Web Hosting Outsourcing Jumps to 73% of Firms Surveyed as Hosting Becomes More Strategic, TeleChoice Survey Says," July 26, 1999, *<http://www.telechoice.com/inthenews\telechoice\141.asp>;* Dennis Mendyk, "ISPs: The Rating Show," *Inter@ctive Week,* January 25, 1999, pp. 29–34; and Brian Caulfield, "What the Fortune 500 Want in Web Hosting," *Web Week,* September 22, 1997, p.35.
17 Nelson King, "Weighing Web Hosting Options for Electronic Commerce Sites," *Internet World,* March 16, 1998, pp. 34–35.

[18] Aaron Goldberg, "Local ISPs Rule," *Upside,* September 1998, p. 66.

[19] Brian Caulfield, "Dial-Up Industry Is Buyer's Market: Small ISPs Get Out, Telcos Move In," *Web Week,* November 10, 1997, p. 34.

[20] E Marketer, "Net Market Size and Growth: Internet Service Providers," September 2, 1999, *<http://www.emarketer.com/estats/nmsg_isps.htm>;* and Jeff Sweat, "ISPs Step Out," *Information Week,* January 19, 1998, pp. 73, 80.

[21] Kristina B. Sullivan, "VPN Market Tide Rises High," *PC Week,* March 22, 1999, p. 128; and Derek Slater, "What Is a VPN?" *CIO Enterprise—Section 2,* July 15, 1999, p. 74.

[22] Elizabeth Gardner, "Net Is Advancing Quickly Toward Mass-Media Status in United States," *Internet World,* April 19, 1999, pp. 13–14.

[23] Elizabeth de Bony, "Internet Use Doubles, But Still Low in Europe," *Infoworld,* August 23, 1999, p. 50B; Stephen Baker, Jack Ewing, and Kerry Capell, "The Race to Wire Europe," *Business Week,* June 7, 1999, pp. 48–50.

[24] Michael Grebb, "20,000 Gigabits Under the Sea," *Business 2.0,* September 1998, pp. 100–102.

[25] Mary Lisbeth D'Amico, "Danish Providers Lure Users With Free Internet Access," *Infoworld,* May 17, 1999, p. 48H; Catherine Yang, Kerry Capell, Jack Ewing, and Marsha Johnson, "I Claim This Land . . . Whoops!" *Business Week,* June 14, 1999, pp. 115–119; and Richard Tomlinson, "Internet Free Europe," *Fortune,* September 6, 1999, pp. 165–172.

[26] Process Software Corporation, "Understanding the Internet and the World Wide Web," Supplement to *Internet World,* 1995.

[27] Robert D. Hof, "From the Man Who Brought You Silicon Graphic . . . ," *Business Week,* October 24, 1994, p. 90.

[28] James C. Luh, "Is the Browser War Irrelevant?" *Internet World,* June 29, 1998, p. 5.

[29] StatMarket, "Web Browser Trends," *<http://www.statmarket.com/SM?c=Browsers>,* August 26, 1999.

[30] Joe Paone, "XML to Power Smart Web Pages," *LANTIMES,* January 19, 1998, pp. 1, 26.

[31] J. William Gurley, "The Browser *Is* the Operating System," *Fortune,* February 16, 1998, pp. 128–130.

[32] Bill Roberts, "Windows 98 Hits the Web—But Who's Buying?" *Internet World,* June 29, 1998, p. 26.

[33] David Fiedler, "Casting a Developer's Eye on Internet Explorer 5.0," *Internet World,* June 29, 1998, pp. 26, 28.

[34] Joe Paone, "Developers Browsing Netscape's Freeware," *LANTIMES,* April 27, 1998, pp. 1, 28.

[35] Amy Cortese and Ira Sager, "A Feather in Apache's Cap," *Business Week,* June 29, 1998, p. 42.

[36] Edward W. Desmond, "Malone Again," *Fortune,* February 16, 1998, pp. 66–69; and Andrew Kupfer, "How Hot Is Calbe, Really?" *Fortune,* February 16, 1998, pp. 70–76.

[37] Joseph T. Sinclair, "WebTV Forcing Sites to Revamp Design," *Internet World,* December 1997, p. 22.

[38] Susan Miller, "Consumers Want HDTV CEMA Study Finds," *AV Video Multimedia Producer,* April 1998, p. 22.

[39] Susan Moran, "Step by Step 'Internet Anywhere' Approaches," *Internet World,* April 12, 1999, pp. 1,10.

chapter 3

10001000010010111111
11111110000000000001
00001111100000000000
11111111111111111111
00000000000000000000
10101010101010101010
1110001110011010100111001010011
10101001010110011000000
101010101010100100

<marketing>

E-Business Communication

This chapter looks at using the Internet as a communications medium. The Internet, through the World Wide Web and e-mail, has become a dominant means of communicating for businesses, reaching both internal and external audiences. Web sites are acting as the public "face" of companies providing information to customers, employees, and the general public. Web sites are also hosting advertising for third parties and facilitating a customer's ability to take actions such as purchasing. It is important for business students to know how to use the Internet as an effective communications vehicle.

1. List the audiences with whom an e-business would need to communicate.
2. Compare and contrast a one-to-many and a many-to-many communications model.
3. Explain how the communications process works.
4. Describe the role involvement plays in Web site design.
5. Relate hypermedia's role in gaining audience attention.
6. Outline what should be done with a Web site to gain audience interest.
7. Explain how an e-business can develop desire from its target audience.
8. List what is important in motivating an audience to take action.
9. Explain how e-business communication can be used in industrial markets.
10. Contrast the strengths and weaknesses of using the Internet as an advertising medium.

Amazing Amazon.com

Jeff Bezos started Amazon.com *(www.amazon.com)* in his garage in 1994. Sales have increased from $1 million in 1994 to $100 million in 1997 and $610 million in 1998. To achieve this tremendous growth, Amazon.com developed a marketing strategy to strengthen its brand name, increase customer traffic to its Web site, build customer loyalty, and encourage repeat purchases. In 1998, Amazon.com spent $60.2 million on a variety of promotional strategies to reach its goals. Amazon.com employed public relations activities along with online and traditional advertising such as radio, television, and print media. Amazon.com's Associates Program allows the associates to encourage their members to purchase from Amazon.com, which then returns to them a percentage of the sales.[1] In 1998, associates signed up over 200,000 Web sites and newsletters.

Customers can visit Amazon.com directly, or they may link to the site from numerous other Web sites. For example, when an individual requests information on a topic, a search engine may display a button that links to suggested book titles at Amazon.com's Web site. In 1997, Amazon.com spent $50 million to purchase banner ads on the three most visited sites on the Web: Yahoo!, Excite, and America Online's home page.[2]

Amazon.com maintains relationships with its book-buying customers by offering a large number of book titles, databases that may be accessed by titles or topics, online discussions with book authors, and e-mail notification of new titles; book buyers can rate books so individuals using Amazon.com's Web site can see others' comments before they buy. Purchases are added to a customer profile database, and this information is then used in e-mail broadcasts that suggest related titles the buyer may wish to purchase. Amazon.com also customizes its home page to the individual user based on his or her past interaction with the site.

Amazon.com has moved beyond selling books and is now using this communications model to help promote music CDs, merchandise, and auctions online. Customers who have an interest in a CD can often listen to clips of the music to see if they want to purchase the music online. Buyers are notified by e-mail when the order is to be

shipped and again to update order status. Amazon.com has designed its site to act as a communications interface to take the customer from interest through desire and on to the action of purchasing.

THINKING STRATEGICALLY

Make a short list of what you know about Amazon.com. Decide how much of that information comes from its paid advertising, how much from publicity seen on news programs and in the press, and how much from interacting with the Web site. Use an Internet search engine to see if there is a button linking to the Amazon.com Web site. Visit the Amazon.com Web site. Evaluate the design of the Web site. Determine what is in the Web site design that would encourage you to purchase.

The Internet is used to communicate to constituencies or audiences both external and internal to the e-business. **External audiences** include customers, stockholders, the general public, and other specifically targeted audiences. **Internal audiences** can include both employees and suppliers. Employees such as field salespeople, staff, and others use intranets to access internal information and training. Suppliers communicate with e-businesses through extranets checking on inventory shipments, parts availability, service bulletins, or other information. This multiple use of Internet and Web page interfaces requires an understanding of how to use these tools to reach specific communications goals.

Traditionally, businesses use a variety of methods of **linear communication** with their various constituencies: broadcasts such as television and radio; print such as newspapers, magazines, and newsletters; direct marketing such as direct mail and telephone sales; and other specialized types of media. The Internet and the World Wide Web are fostering a hypermedia environment that allows companies to deliver targeted messages to specific audiences. According to Hoffman and Novak, two researchers from Vanderbilt University, a **hypermedia** environment is one in which a distributed network allows **nonlinear communication** that uses hyperlinks and search and retrieval processes to collect information.[3] The best current example of this process is the World Wide Web, but this hypermedia environment is also projected to exist for interactive television, interactive Web-based cellular telephones, and other portable devices.

Linear communication follows a scripted flow. Nonlinear communication allows a free flow and exchange of information. Most conversations individuals have with others are nonlinear. Good sales presentations are free flows of communication.

According to Hoffman and Novak, traditional media often follow a **one-to-many communication model** in which a single promotion, such as a print ad or television commercial, is sent by one source and seen by many without the opportunity for immediate feedback. For example, when a television ad is being developed, the concept is often storyboarded to structure a sequence of scenes designed to reach narrow and specific goals by taking the targeted audience through a linear sequence of words, images, or events. Interactivity and hyperlinks allow for a type of two-way communication between the e-business and its audience. Hypermedia allow the communications process to act more like a salesperson than a linear advertisement. A salesperson is able to follow a nonlinear communications process and provide relevant information for any query a customer may have. Just as a salesperson closes a sale, current hypermedia also allow direct links to e-commerce for closing the sale with the customer.

Many firms are using hypermedia, such as the Web, to communicate to the public. Bristol-Myers questioned whether the Web would be a useful medium to target customers. During a tax season, it placed ads with financial Web sites. When people clicked through a banner ad and entered their name and address, the company offered a free sample of Excedrin. The results exceeded Bristol-Myers's expectations with more than 1,000 hits per day, which enabled it to add 30,000 new names to its database.[4]

Total expenditures for Internet advertising have been growing, with 1996 ad revenue at $267 million, 1997 exceeding $907 million, and 1999 reaching $4.4 billion.[5] This is less than 1 percent of 1998 total advertising media spending, but the Internet spending figure includes the placement of paid advertising only and does not include the related costs of Web page development and design for internal and external audiences. The Internet offers unique advantages when combined with traditional media. When hypermedia are linked to a database, messages can be developed that change the relationship between the e-business and its constituencies. The e-business can customize promotions to fit an individual customer's interests, target market profile, and past behavior. Relationships between advertising agencies and the marketer are changing as well. The marketing field has a well-developed framework for understanding how businesses communicate with their constituencies. This promotional framework will be used to illustrate how a hypermedia environment can enhance the communications process between an e-business and its audiences.

WHAT IS PROMOTION?

Promotion is a communications process consisting of advertising, publicity, sales promotion, and salesmanship. The development of a promotional strategy is guided by the communications system outlined in Figure 3.1.

The sender, a person or business, wishes to communicate to the target audience. The message, the specific information the sender wishes to get across, is carried by a media source such as print, broadcast, direct marketing, or hypermedia. When a message is sent, the receiver may not always understand the intended message. The sender must encode the message or design the promotion in a way that will be decoded as desired by the targeted receiver. Each individual receiver interprets the message based on his or her own perceptions about the product, spokesperson, theme of the ad, and other factors that are unique to the individual. The promotion carrying the message must overcome any background noise or interference that keeps the message from being understood.

 **Figure 3.1** The Communications System

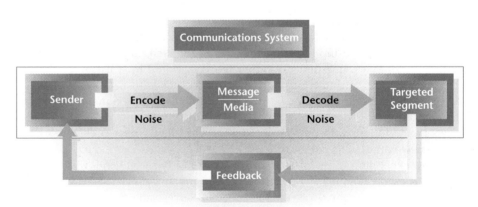

Traditional media vehicles such as broadcast (TV or radio) and print (newspapers, magazines) flow one way, from the sender to the receiver (within the dotted box shown in Figure 3.1). In most traditional advertising, the message will be carried by the media without face-to-face communication and with no means of immediate feedback.

Many-to-Many Model

The **many-to-many model** places the hypermedia in the center of the communication process; hypermedia become a meeting place where anyone can communicate with anyone else. Figure 3.2 illustrates the many-to-many model in which firms (F) and customers (C) can both obtain and deliver content.

The many-to-many model allows feedback from others involved in the communications channel. All customers can communicate with each other as well as with the firms. This communication is not time dependent as is face-to-face communication; a customer can create a Web site or post a message and leave it for others to see. The Amazon.com vignette at the beginning of the chapter illustrates how this model allows customers to communicate with many others. Individual consumers can leave comments on books and records and engage in online conversations with the authors and artists. The many-to-many model is also evident in the use of **chat** or **threaded discussion lists** at Web sites. These give individuals the ability to directly engage with others who have a shared interest. The individuals could be customers who discuss a product or company; persons who are members of an online course or training session; or coworkers who use an intranet to discuss strategy, sales techniques, new products, or any other topics of interest.

A chat online involves a number of individuals who leave messages for others to see. These can be placed in a repository or chat room for viewing at later times or could be "live," with individuals writing to others in real time.

Threaded discussion lists allow individuals to add to an initial message with successive messages. This allows a newsgroup user to add to a thread, or single conversation, by indicating a response to the prior message. Messages are available for others to read and are indented under topic headings:
Initial Post
 First response
  Second response, etc.

Figure 3.2 Many-to-Many Model

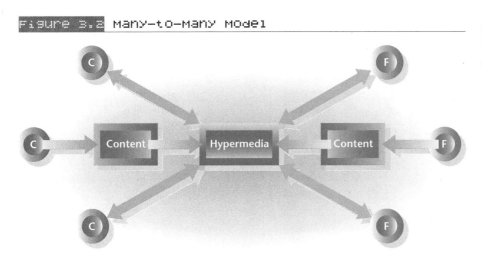

Source: Adapted from Donna L. Hoffman and Thomas P. Novak, "Marketing in Hypermedia Computer-Mediated Environments: Conceptual Foundations," *Journal of Marketing,* July 1996, vol. 60, p. 53.

Talk City *(www.talkcity.com)* has fostered thousands of chat groups at its Web site. In March 1999, Talk City had approximately 2.6 million unique visitors and generated over 6.6 million hours of conversations. In the early evening hours, Talk City can have as many as 18,000 users simultaneously chatting or engaging in other interactive activities.[6] Talk City is just one of thousands of Web sites that offer online chat or threaded discussion lists.

Traditional media's one-way flow requires that the communication be designed to reach narrower goals. To reach these goals, the message must be designed or encoded to allow the media vehicle to have some specific impact on the viewer's knowledge, attitudes, desires, etc. For television, the proposed message is laid out as a storyboard. Each part of the message must flow into the next to tell the story. This same linear flow holds for radio commercials. Print messages are developed to create a story as well. The headline, the illustration, and the body copy should convey the same message as the subheading. The movement of the eye is controlled by the layout, with all elements enhancing the image of the company and product. The same logic holds true for longer print materials such as brochures or other collateral sales materials. Figure 3.3 illustrates **thumbnails** for a TV storyboard and print advertisement layout.

A thumbnail is a quick sketch of a communications concept. This allows the developer to create a large number of ideas in a short time period.

The nonlinearity of a hypermedia site allows the designer to tailor the message to multiple audiences. A Web page can be designed to allow a visitor to find specific areas of interest. Figure 3.4, for example, shows how visitors to the home page can move to commercial content, end-user content, commercial content by type, and end user by interest. Each page of the Web site can be designed to meet individual needs.

Figure 3.3 Communications Thumbnails

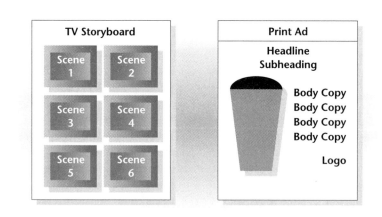

Figure 3.4 Hypermedia Connections to Multiple Pages

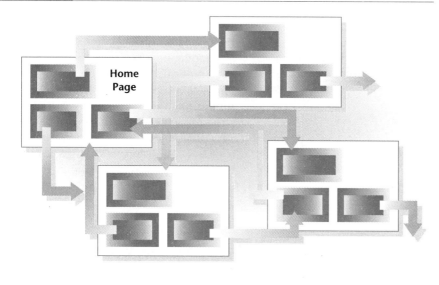

HYPERMEDIA COMMUNICATIONS GOALS

When communicating to external audiences, promotional campaigns are designed to reach specific goals. These can include informing, persuading, or reminding the external audience of a company's image, new products, business locations, etc. These communications goals should be specified by the marketing department, be based on an analysis of the target audience, and be in support of the organization's marketing strategies. The use of hypermedia can enhance a business's ability to inform, persuade, and remind a market, as well as allow for final action to be taken. Integrating hypermedia into promotional campaigns allows a business to reach specific objectives such as driving visitors to the hypermedia site, obtaining sales leads, collecting user data, or closing a sale.[7]

A Web site can provide a little or lot of information for a site visitor. A single site can be designed for goal-directed buyers as well as for those who are Net surfing and are looking only to experience the site. For **high-involvement** visitors, the Web site can be designed to allow links to other individuals who share the same interests. Customers can also interact with authors, artists, brewmasters, chefs, and many others who are normally unattainable through traditional media. Involvement levels of individuals can be high when they are goal-directed, such as attempting to gather information to make a purchase. Individuals can also have high **enduring involvement** with products or product categories and engage in Net surfing to obtain high levels of interactivity with sites.[8] As Web sites gain bandwidth to match other multimedia delivery systems such as CD-ROMs and interactive kiosks, they will allow even richer visitor experiences.

Individuals with high involvement are likely to see a topic as interesting or important. These individuals attend to information more, are more likely to comprehend complex messages, and may be willing to spend more time with a Web site.

Enduring involvement exists when an individual has a high-level interest in a topic over an extended time period.

Web Sites and Company Image

Some individuals have set up Web sites that attack a company's image. To prevent this, a number of companies have registered domain names that could be seen as offensive to the company so others cannot use them. Charles Schwab & Co. has registered !#%*schwab.com and schwab!#%*.com. Other companies that have registered domain names to prevent attack include:

▶ Bell Atlantic: Bigyellow!#%*.com
▶ Chase Manhattan Bank: Chase!#%*.com
▶ Cox Communications, Inc.: Cox!#%*.com
▶ Vail Resorts: vailresorts!#%*.com
▶ Volvo Cars of North America: volvo!#%*.com
▶ Playboy Enterprises: Playboy!#%*.com

!#%* represents a deleted offending word.

From Public Relations to Supporting Relationships

Hypermedia also allow for the development and maintenance of relationships by providing in-depth information for customers. These rich information sites can help consumers engage in ongoing searches or pre-purchase searches. Web sites can be designed with differing levels of communications complexity. The simplest sites are often **brochure sites** that engage in advertising or public relations. Brochure sites may contain the same information as a business's print material. These sites are designed to make visitors aware of and informed about a business's image or products. This can be seen as a simple extension of traditional media campaigns. Brochure sites should be designed to enhance the overall promotional campaign.

Web sites are often the public face of a business. For non–brick and mortar pure-play Internet businesses, the Web page may be the only chance a customer has to interact with the business. The Web page must project and protect the **image** of the company. Protecting a company's image is a concern on the Internet. EWatch *(www.ewatch.com)* provides a service to other companies by searching the Internet for any comments related to corporate clients. To protect a public image, some companies are registering domain names that could be seen as negative to prevent others from using them.[9]

Relationship sites often target individuals who may have higher levels of information involvement. Some large corporate beer companies offer sites that are designed for individuals with high levels of enduring involvement. They often contain games, chat groups, or other interactive components to maintain relationships with customers. Individuals who see microbrewery beer as a specialty product may visit the sites of smaller specialty beer companies for information on the products and manufacturing.

Web sites can be designed to take their customers from a stage with little information through the process of engaging in online transactions.[10] Wells Fargo, for example, developed a brochure site in November 1994. By 1995 a survey indicated that its customers desired to engage in financial transactions online. Wells Fargo then became the first bank to offer online account balance information.[11] Experienced salespeople are key in developing a relationship site. They are able to identify the needs of their sales prospect and are then able to tailor, or encode, their communication to meet the prospect's information needs and to answer any questions the prospect may have.

THINKING STRATEGICALLY

Visit the BMW Web site. Determine if the site is designed just for current BMW owners, or if it is targeting potential owners as well. Decide if this site appeals to individuals with high or low levels of automotive involvement. Visit another Web site for a single automobile or manufacturer. Determine if that site is designed to appeal to high or low automotive involvement levels.

CASE 3.1

In the Web Driving Seat

Hypermedia are ideal for maintaining relationships between an e-business and its customers. The Web allows for relationship development through its ability to almost instantaneously transfer information between parties. As early as 1977, BMW of North America hosted over 150,000 hits a day at its Web site. BMW's site allowed current or prospective customers to use virtual reality technology to take a drive behind the wheel of a BMW. Images of BMWs are morphed or changed to show new models. For BMW owners, chat rooms allowed individuals to talk about their cars. Feedback links allowed car designers to gather information about new features and accessories that potential customers may desire. Public relations specialists responded to inquiries and answered questions without time-consuming phone calls.[12]

Upgrades to the BMW site *(www.bmw.com)* have increased the content, allowing interested individuals to find information on the many products that BMW offers as well as to communicate with its engineers.

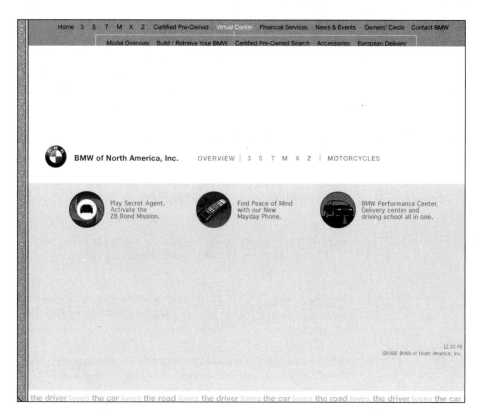

THE AIDA MODEL

Web sites are currently the dominant hypermedia and will be the focus of communications strategy development in this chapter. The AIDA model will be used as a framework for understanding how to use Web sites to reach communication goals. The **AIDA process** indicates that the audience's **attention** must first be gained, **interest** created in the product or service, **desire** generated, and finally some **action** taken by the targeted audience. The AIDA process is based on attitude models in which the audience first thinks about an object (cognition), then develops feelings (affect), and then engages in some type of behavior (conative).[13] A single communication will, in most cases, not move an audience through every stage of the AIDA process. A combination of promotional methods is often more efficient in reaching desired goals. Table 3.1 outlines the attitude components of the AIDA process and relates these to the effect on e-business communications strategy.

A promotional mix includes the use of public relations and publicity, advertising, personal selling, sales promotions, and hypermedia such as Web sites.

Figure 3.5 on the following page matches the components of a **promotional mix,** including hypermedia (a Web site), with the four stages of the AIDA process. The darker the area on the table, the stronger is the influence the promotional element has on the AIDA process.

Figure 3.5 shows that each part of the promotional mix plays a different role. Public relations and advertising are effective in obtaining attention, interest, and desire in the promotional campaign. Personal sales, as two-way person-to-person communication, are not highly efficient in creating attention due to the high costs of fielding a sales force to make cold calls. Personal sales are more effective at creating desire and closing the sale. Sales promotion (such as couponing or point-of-purchase displays) is most effective in obtaining action. A Web site is strongest in the areas of interest and desire but can also be used to create attention and facilitate actions such as sales. From this figure, it can be seen that Web sites are a vital

Table 3.1 AIDA Process

Attitude Model	AIDA Process	E-Business Communications Strategy
Cognition (thinking)	**Attention**	Use offline media to attract the audience's attention to the Web site. Use search engines to allow a Web site to be found in searches. Use other Web sites as media for advertising a Web site.
Affect (feeling)	**Interest**	Use customization and personalization techniques to meet the individual's needs. Use targeted e-mail and permission marketing. Use push to send information to the audience.
Conation (behavior)	**Desire**	Develop content and design that appeal to the target audience. Include relationship development components that will keep the audience at the site.
	Action	Use promotions to entice actions.

Figure 3.5 Promotional Strategy Matrix

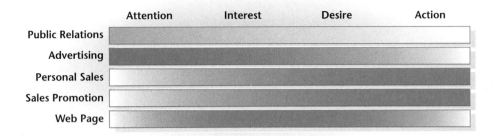

component of a media mix because they can enhance the AIDA process, but they may not be able to reach all promotional goals. The following sections will cover the strategic use of Web sites to aid in reaching AIDA goals.

Attention

A target audience may be unaware of a business's facets. Audience members may be unaware of the existence of an e-business or its Web site. They may be unaware of what a business does or the products it sells. In order to make the audience aware of this information, attention must be gained. Traditional media gain attention by designing messages with enough impact to attract and hold the audience; the messages can be repeated numerous times. A Web site differs from traditional media in that the receiver must actually use the Internet to link to Web page content. An individual will not be exposed to the message unless actively viewing a Web site.

The first step to gain the audience's attention is to include a site's URL or address in other media. The Web address should be included in advertising copy and layouts, business cards, banner ads located in other Web sites, direct e-mail, and other directed media. The use of URLs in print ads has increased from about 10 percent of ads in 1995 to more than 90 percent by 1998.[14] Traditional media have much wider exposure than the Internet. Using these media can help to create site preference. Autobytel.com broke new ground when it spent $1 million on Super Bowl advertising to promote Autobytel.com's site. Other companies, such as E*Trade, Excite, Yahoo!, and Eblast, are using traditional media to promote their sites and services. Internet companies spent $1.4 billion in offline advertising for the first three quarters of 1999.[15]

Search engines should also be used so the business's Web address will appear when the Web user searches for related topics. Search engines are a cost-effective means of making people aware of a site, but they do not guarantee that a viewer will choose or remember the site. The Amazon.com vignette illustrates that Amazon.com uses search engines to link to its Web site. When an individual uses a

Search engines come in three types:

Search directories require that Web sites be submitted for cataloging. They often list the most relevant and popular sites but have limited listings.

Search engines use **Web spiders** or Web bots to collect information from sites. These sites will find information for narrowly targeted searches but can return a very large number of hits (e.g., 1,256,890).

Metacrawlers use the databases of multiple major search engines. These are good for power searches, but combining multiple results can lead to repetitive hits.

Web spiders are bots, or software robots, that "crawl" through the Internet looking at Web sites. They collect site information and send it back to the search engine database, allowing the information to be retrieved.

It is important to have key terms placed into the HTML meta tags indicating the reference heading for a page.

Spam is the process of broadcasting unsolicited content to a large number of individuals over the Internet. Like the edible Spam, taste is often in the eyes of the beholder.

search engine to look up a topic, the Amazon.com link will present books related to the Yahoo! search topic. Search engines, in turn, are using television as part of their campaign to drive traffic to their sites. Yahoo!'s specific goal has been to obtain top-of-mind awareness as "the" search engine for the Internet.[16] **Search engines** are attempting to "collect eyeballs" (obtain a large number of visitors to increase the audience reach for the advertisers on their sites).

Directories such as Yahoo! *(www.yahoo.om)* and search engines such as WebCrawler *(www.webcrawler.com)* and AltaVista *(www.altavista.com)* contain large databases of information related to Web sites. When a Web site is posted to a server, information about that site can be placed with the directory or search engine by filling out an electronic form at each search engine. A new Web site could wait for a **Web spider** to find it, but the new site may not have control over the search topics used in the search engine. To ensure that Web spiders find the proper search term, a site designer should include specific search criteria in the home page's meta tags, which are located in the heading HTML of the Web page. Although meta tags do not guarantee proper searches, they are the best means of having Web spiders find content. A directory such as Yahoo! uses a human interface to place a site into categories. If a business tries to **spam** a search engine by submitting multiple listings, it may be kicked to the bottom of a list of 2,000,000 hits and never be seen by an audience.

A business should not rely on search engines to make a potential visitor aware of the site. Search engines use rules to place URLs at the **top of the search**, or at the beginning of a search list. Those rules can include how often a site is updated, the number of times it has been hit, and other criteria that are known only to the management of the search engine.[17] On average, search engines only index about 6 percent of all Web content. Those sites that do make it to the top of searches are often from large U.S.-based businesses. In 1998 there were over 800 million pages to search through; by 2002 there may be over 7 billion. New search engines base their results on the number of Web site links as well as the number of users who visit sites and how long they stay there. Researchers have found that any Web site in the world is separated from all others by at most 19 to 21 hyperlinks.[18]

HYPERMEDIA HYPERLINKS. It is possible to use another party's Web site as a means of gaining attention. In 1998, the most common method used to advertise on a Web page was through banner ads, which accounted for 52 percent of all advertising dollars spent on the Web. The popularity of banner ads is dropping because they have not been highly effective in achieving **click-through**, or having an individual click on a linked banner to link to other sites. **Banner ads** are usually small rectangular block messages. Banners are becoming more active with the inclusion of animation, JAVA programming, and multimedia. Banner ads may be more effective in attracting attention to a product or brand than having individuals click through the banner to another site. By 2002, banner ads are expected to account for only 26 percent of advertising dollars.[19] Figure 3.6 indicates the major types of advertising found on Web sites.

Other Web ad types include **sponsorship,** or co-branded ads integrating a company's brand to the editorial content of the Web site. For example, a firm may sponsor a news site or a community bulletin board. Sponsorship's share of advertising dollars is expected to increase from 40 percent in 1998 to 58 percent by 2002. **Interstitials** automatically load and display content as a Web site is brought up. This includes the use of **daughter windows** that pop up and freely float to display ad content. Interstitials that cannot be closed have not received wide use because when viewers must watch 5- to 30-second ads over a Web site, they often get angry at the lack of control. By the year 2002, interstitials are expected to account for about 6 percent of advertising dollars spent.[20] New types of advertising are expected to emerge. New software is allowing the cursor to act as an advertisement. For example, Comet Systems *(www.cometsystems.com)* has developed a plug-in for browsers that will turn the cursor into a logo or another symbol to promote an image. When an individual surfs to a site, the cursor would change automatically for that site.

When using a hypermedia site to obtain objectives related to attention, the site designer must consider the technology likely to be used by the audience. Interactive banners allow for a higher level of impact but may be effective only if the user has a high-bandwidth line. A study by the Internet Advertising Bureau indicated that banner ads were effective in creating awareness of products and in communicating information about them. Banner ads had a smaller impact on

Figure 3.6 Major Types of Web Advertising

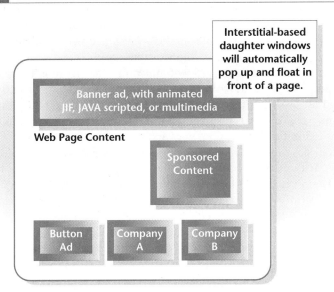

intent to purchase. The resulting increase in awareness was from exposure to the ads and was not related to click-through rates. Seeing a banner ad once had a greater effect on memory than a single exposure to a television ad, but less than exposure to print ads.[21]

Interest

Before individuals are likely to take action, they must first have a positive predisposition to act. This requires the ability to create a positive feeling or interest in the company, product, or service offered. Web sites must offer the site visitor some compelling reason to stay at the Web site. The site designer must take into consideration the goal of the Web site, the nature of the audience, and the level of technology the user will be employing. This means that Web sites need to be constantly upgraded as the Internet backbone rapidly adds bandwidth and as each new version of browsers adds multimedia players.

When the targeted audience members see a Web page, they will make a decision in the first few seconds whether or not to explore the site. The **home page,** or the first page that a visitor sees at a site, becomes very important in this respect. If a visitor has specifically tried to find the Web site or has high involvement with the company or product, the visitor may wait for the page to load and spend time watching and interacting with the site. If, on the other hand, visitors are only browsing, they may zap the site and move on if it takes too long to download or is not interesting.[22] Speed of download is an important consideration. The longer the individual must wait for a site to download, the more negatively the individual rates the Web site.[23] A number of sites have been redesigned to allow their home page to load faster.

With so many Web sites and so little space to display information on a home page, Web site designs can start to look generic. This is in part due to limited creativity in design. The use of frames, banners, animated GIF files, Java script, sound, etc., is allowing for more creativity, but it can increase the bandwidth needed to display content. Some sites are developed with a home page that offers multiple types of visits such as high or low graphics, nonframed and **Flash** or **Shockwave** sites, and high- or low-bandwidth sites. As high bandwidth becomes more dominant and download speeds increase, Web sites will need to add increased levels of multimedia to interest audiences. Some businesses may have their employees' browsers disabled for plug-ins and other heavy-bandwidth design elements to limit traffic use on a network.[24]

A Web site should give a compelling reason for the viewer to stay and explore the page. If there is too much text, the viewer may not continue into the document.[25] Design considerations are also important. For some Net surfers, the overall look and feel of the site may be as important as the content of the site. Ease of navigation should be considered when laying out the page.

When the site designer is developing the page, he or she can control the display and also how the user interfaces with the page. The viewer must be able to interact with the site and should not be expected to have to figure out how the site

Flash and Shockwave platforms allow multimedia (sound, videos, animation, etc.) to be played on Web pages. More on Flash and Shockwave can be found at the Macromedia Web site (www.macromedia.com).

Welcome to Six Flags Great America!

Source: www.sixflags.com/greatamerica/

works. The visitor should find information easily. The site should have an easy-to-use interface that appeals to the target audience. For example, children's sites are likely to be very rich in animation and graphics. Sites for news hounds such as CNN *(www.cnn.com)* are often more text-driven.

THINKING STRATEGICALLY

Consider which types of design elements would be of interest to Six Flags' customers. Visit the Six Flags Web site. Determine the types of plug-ins that are required to use the site. Decide how important having high bandwidth is for users of this site. Evaluate the design elements. Determine what this site has that will get its target audience to visit more than once.

A Web site should accomplish two goals: communicate the firm's message and foster the development of relationships. If the

CASE 3.2

Ride the Wild Mouse

Six Flags *(www.sixflags.com)* amusement parks have a strong teen appeal, but it is the parents of the teens who pay the bills. For parents, information on hours, locations, and rides are important considerations. When targeting the teens, Six Flags subdivided the market into influencers, followers, and independents. For the teens, the goal of the Web site design is to have a Web page that has the excitement of taking rides through the park. This is achieved by using color, action (through the use of flash plug-ins), video, and Shockwave games. The Web site attempts to collect information from individuals by offering a promotional incentive with a chance to win free tickets.[26]

Table 3.2 Web Site Design Resource

Site	Address	Comments
Communication Arts	www.commarts.com/index.html	Site for identifying design trends and learning what works and what doesn't on the Internet
Web Pages That Suck	www.webpagesthatsuck.com	Examples of good and poor Web page design
NewMedia Invision Awards	www.invisionawards.com	Good examples of Web page and multimedia design and past award winners

Source: Jeff Frentzen, " 'Flat' Web Sites Are Out; Sites That 'Pop' Are In," *PC Week,* February 3, 1997, p. 141.

business is using the site as a brochure site or for public relations, the compelling reasons for the visitor to remember and return to the site should be communicated. If the firm wants the targeted audience to take some type of action, the communication should be focused around the unique selling proposition of the firm or the advantage of the product over competitive products. For high-involvement users, large amounts of information should be refreshed often, if not daily, to keep individuals returning to the site. There is little incentive for a visitor to return to a site if the information is not updated. Table 3.2 outlines a number of Web sites dedicated to giving information on Web site creation and design.

Desire

A Web site's goal may be to move the audience toward some type of behavior or action. To reach this goal, the site must generate desire. This is typically designed into the promotional message, enhanced through sales promotion, and/or acted on by a salesperson. New Internet-based techniques are beginning to create higher levels of desire. These include the use of targeted e-mail, permission marketing, push, and personalization.

The cost of obtaining a new Web customer averages $34, so when a customer is found, an e-business has an incentive to keep that customer's interest and desire to return. This can be accomplished by effective message design and communications strategies. Direct marketers practice the art of creating desire. This starts with having a narrowly defined target audience and then providing a message designed to generate interest and desire before the direct marketer asks for action. Direct marketers have often employed professional salespeople to develop sales presentations. Sales representatives then use this presentation as well as shift the flow, depending on the customer's questions or objections. The better a direct marketer is able to assess the needs of the customer, the more that salesperson is able to fine-tune the presentation to help create desire in the customer.

The nonlinear design of multimedia presentations allows for linking to various parts of the message based on the customer's information needs. If visitors to the site want to know more about a topic or product, they should only be a click away from that information. This can be accomplished by using the **sales force**'s internal knowledge of a firm. This knowledge can be tapped to outline the information flows. If a business is using the Web page as a promotional tool, the sales force can assess the most effective communications method and the types of objections and questions customers are likely to raise so the site can be developed to present that information.

This process is not problem-free. The **sales force** must be drawn into the process but should not see the Web site as a threat to their job. Salespeople live by their ability to make a sale. When asked to give up this information, they may see the process as sowing the seeds of their own destruction.

This process is not problem-free. The sales force must be drawn into the process but should not see the Web site as a threat to their job. Salespeople live by their ability to make a sale. When asked to give up this information, they may see the process as sowing the seeds of their own destruction.

A company's Web page should include a means of obtaining feedback from customers facilitated by e-mail links or comment sections on the Web page. An FAQ, or frequently asked question, section can be developed for the Web site and should be taken into consideration when designing the site. A Web server can use tracking software to look at where people go on the site and how long they stay at a particular point. This gives the Webmaster a plan of the dead areas as well as the most active areas on the site.

National Semiconductor tapped into three sources of information to enhance the sales of its products: traditional sales and order information, data from its Web-tracking software, and questions obtained from e-mail. This information was used to develop a push platform through Pointcast to send information directly to interested customers' PCs.[27]

Targeted E-Mail. Businesses can contact individuals directly through **targeted e-mail.** Marketers rate this as the most effective means of directing individuals to Web sites. Most e-mail systems allow individuals to click on a hyperlinked URL and call up the Web site. E-mail is the most used Internet application. In 1998, 107 billion pieces of first-class post office mail weighing 2.7 billion pounds were delivered while over the same time period 3.4 trillion e-mail messages (weighing zero pounds) were delivered.[28]

Targeted e-mail works best with individuals who have already given their permission to receive messages. **Permission marketing** allows firms to target only those individuals who have expressed an interest and helps to avoid spamming and privacy concerns. Permission-based e-mail may be a $2.1 billion business by 2002. Permission marketing works best when the goal of the communication is to create desire or move the individual to a Web site, and not to sell.[29] ECommercial.com *(www.ecommercial.com)* acts as a service bureau sending e-mail to targeted audiences. Interested parties then view mini Web pages with links that allow the downloading of larger multimedia advertisements.[30]

Permission marketing is when the customer ops in, or signs in, at a Web site and agrees to receive e-mail based on direct marketing.

Push and Personalization. Direct marketing has relied on computer databases to develop personalized media. This **personalization** has allowed direct marketers to send targeted messages directly to a prospective customer. Hypermedia-based promotion is following this lead by developing personalized messages and then sending them to the individual via push technology. Internet users can customize the home pages of Web search engines (e.g., Microsoft Network, Yahoo!, Altavista, Netscape, and Go) by submitting lifestyle information such as activities, general and specific interests, and other segmentation information. Sites such as Amazon also collect past behavior data and customize their Web pages to the user. These Web sites tailor their messages and page design **on the fly,** or as they are sent, to match the individual user's profile, enhancing the relationship experience.[31]

Webcasting allows users to have information delivered to their "doorway" or browser without requesting or searching for information. For example, if the target individual has an interest in football, a push system will deliver that information to the individual's computer. Webcasting also occurs when an individual visits a Web site. The Web server can look at the individual's **cookies** and then use a database to design and push the Web site for the individual. Web sites use software to "read" the behavior of the visitor by keeping track of the Web pages the visitor sees, how long they are viewed, what is passed over, what is placed in a shopping basket, and what is removed. This suggests the type of information the user may be interested in.[32]

PointCast *(www.pointcast.com)* pioneered the push delivery of content to Web users. The electronic wallet company Launchpad Technologies purchased PointCast in May 1999 to add to its EntryPoint Web access sytem *(www.entrypoint.com).* This type of push system has the user fill out a profile of interests. Based on this profile, narrowly targeted information is delivered. Mentadent has used PointCast's system to find out the dental-hygiene habits of PointCast users. Based on its findings, Mentadent targeted a banner ad that resulted in twice the normal click-through rate.[33]

A **cookie** is a small code left on the user's computer that is used to look up information on an e-business's database. This code retrieves information such as past actions, search interests, or past purchases, which can be used to personalize the site.

Figure 3.7 Using Webcasting Technology

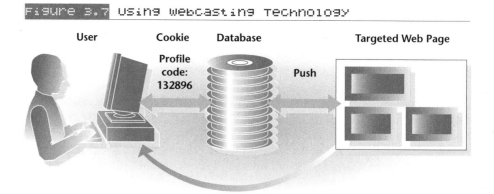

User	Cookie	Database		Targeted Web Page
	Profile code: 132896		Push	

Figure 3.7 illustrates how this process works. The user gives a profile to the Web site database; the Web site places a cookie, or record, of the individual's activity on the user's computer, or the Web site tracks the user's interest and tailors the site to the user's browsing interest. The database then creates the Web site on the fly for the user to browse or Webcast it for the user to view.

Two companies using personalization to target their customers are American Airlines *(www.aa.com)* and Dell Computer Corp. American Airlines has designed a system using 56 interactive applications with over 200 decision rules to personalize its site for the more than 31 million members of American's frequent-flyer program. Dell has personalized its sites by using 3,000 different page designs for its clients.[34]

Action

The action stage of the AIDA process does not necessarily imply that a purchase needs to be made. The action could be to have individuals visit a Web site, provide information for databases, obtain information for future purchases, or make online purchases. To encourage these actions, promotional incentives, including coupons, frequent-buyer programs, loyalty programs, and special offers, are often provided.[35]

Online Incentives. According to a Forrester Research study of 8,600 households, a key to holding and enticing viewers to action is providing strong content and an easy-to-use site that has quick download. Figure 3.8, on the following page, outlines the reasons that individuals return to favorite sites.

As Figure 3.8 shows, the most important concerns for the user are ease of use and updated content. E-businesses must consider relationship development as one of the keys to successful selling over the Internet. Many commercial sites are adding information content and improving design to entice users to return.[36] Sites often offer incentives, such as chances to win prizes, to view ads or to play games. While these promotions may attract individuals to specific sites to play games or sign up for contests, they do not ensure return use or loyalty.

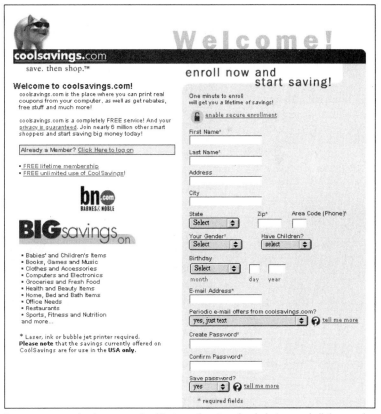

Source: www.coolsavings.com. CoolSavings, the piggy bank design, and all the purple and gold color schemes are trademarks of coolsavings.com inc.

Figure 3.8 Reasons for Using Favorite Sites

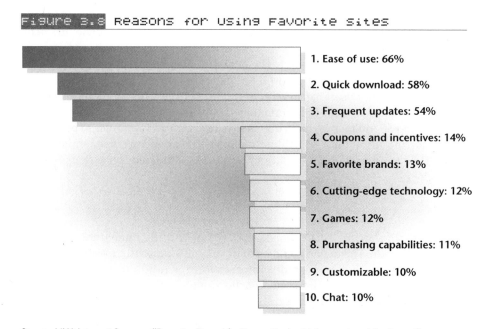

1. Ease of use: 66%

2. Quick download: 58%

3. Frequent updates: 54%

4. Coupons and incentives: 14%

5. Favorite brands: 13%

6. Cutting-edge technology: 12%

7. Games: 12%

8. Purchasing capabilities: 11%

9. Customizable: 10%

10. Chat: 10%

Source: NUA Internet Surveys, "Forrester Research: Strong Content Means a Loyal Audience," *<http://www.nua.ie/surveys/index.cgi?f=VS&art_id=905354655&rel=true>*, January 27, 1999.

Disney *(www.disney.com)* has designed a site with multiple activities for children and families and has been very effective in converting browsers to buyers. Disney's site allows personalization, product customization, push promotions,and automated order processing to achieve sales. In 1998, an estimated 50 percent of site visitors purchased from the site, with average orders double those at retail sites and triple those of catalogs. To foster the development of relationships, Disney personalized Web pages for repeat visitors and offered promotional incentives, such as free gifts, for repeat purchases.[37]

Impulse purchases can be facilitated at Web sites through the use of banner ads. For example, an individual may see a promotional special for flowers or candy and can then order by clicking on the banner without going to the selling company's site. Web sites can also be used to offer coupons for online and offline purchases. CoolSavings *(www.coolsavings.com)* has developed a business model in which it offers personalized coupons for more than 130 national retailers. By March 2000 it had more than 6 million registered households. The coupons, rebates, and free samples offered to members are based on registration information, shopping habits, and previous clicks on the site. The coupons carry special bar codes to track use. Companies that use CoolSavings's service track the effectiveness of their offers, which helps to shape one-to-one relationships with their customers.[38]

THINKING STRATEGICALLY

Decide who the target market was for *The Blair Witch Project*. Determine what this target market would be interested in seeing at a Web site. Visit the Web site. Evaluate the content developed for the site. Determine what is the most compelling for individuals interested in this movie. Consider what should be changed to keep individuals returning to the site. Visit other movie Web sites. Determine their target markets and how they develop relationships with their audiences.

CASE 3.3

Which Media Helped the Witch?

At a time when most movies cost over $25 million, *The Blair Witch Project* cost just over $30,000. To promote the film, the producers developed a Web site *(www.blairwitch.com)* in June 1998. They included content such as fake police reports and newspaper clippings that appeared to make what happened in the film a "real" occurrence. The Web site was refreshed often to provide a constantly changing and episodic experience for the visitor. Other media were used to build hype for the film. Trailers appeared on the *SciFi* network and *MTV,* as well as before the *Star Wars* movie. The weekend the movie opened, a full-page advertisement was placed in *Variety*. The ad read: "Blairwitch.com, 21,222,589 hits to date." In its first week of release, *Blair Witch* earned $50 million.[39]

INDUSTRIAL MARKETS

Whereas consumer markets have been centered on advertising, industrial markets have traditionally relied more on personal sales for communication. Figure 3.9 indicates the relative use of promotional elements for each of these markets. It may not be surprising that many of the current Web sites and much of e-commerce are currently targeting business markets.

Industrial markets are also heavy users of Internet-based communication through the use of extranets and intranets. The Web interface is becoming the standard for this intrafirm and interfirm communication. In addition, sales representatives are using sales force automation tools to enhance their ability to sell to business markets.

Extranets and Intranets

Web sites must be designed to enhance the communications process within and between firms. Extranets and intranets use the common IP interface and have the same communications considerations as Internet-based Web communication. It is important to consider issues such as ease of use and content delivery for all extranet users. Applications such as push technology are used to enhance

Figure 3.9　Consumer vs. Industrial Markets

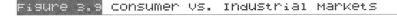
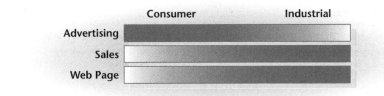

communication. For example, distributors and T-shirt designers receive updated inventory information when they log on to Fruit of the Loom's extranet site. Push technology can be used to deliver information over a firm's intranet as well.[40]

Internet standards and practices have moved to internal, private intranet networks. Like the Internet, intranets use browsers, servers, and Internet protocols but are not open to unauthorized users. The relative ease of development, lower costs, and higher levels of user experience have caused tremendous growth in organizational intranets. Intranets open up and speed communication, helping to facilitate change inside organizations. Over 95 percent of Fortune 1000 companies use intranets to disseminate information such as policies and procedures, as well as share documents, offer phone directories, provide human resources information, give online training, and conduct information searches.[41]

Often the bandwidth available inside an organization is higher than that available to access the Internet; this gives the potential for higher-bandwidth applications such as voice, video, and conferencing online. Businesses are using intranets for a variety of strategic purposes. Some businesses are using intranets as the hub of communication and collaboration; others are offering narrower information services. By linking extranets, intranets, and the Internet, businesses are developing a dynamic information hub, changing organizational cultures and allowing rapid response to environmental change.[42]

Sales Force Automation

Sales force automation (SFA) uses the information power of interactive media to enhance selling efforts. Colgate-Palmolive's sales force used a CD-ROM and Web site combination to enhance its ability to sell its new gingivitis and gum disease–fighting Total toothpaste.[43] Sales force automation empowers salespeople by allowing them to link to vital information from the company's Web site. This can provide inventory data or price information and can aid in the sales presentation. The focus of sales force automation is on using Web-based technology to aid in the sales process. Altus Biologics *(www.altus.com)* produces drug catalysts for industrial use. In 1999 it had a small sales force of twelve people who supported more than 100 customers each. Altus used its sales force automation system to keep track of customer types, products, product stage of development, inquiries, e-mail messages, and anything else that could help in developing sales. For example, if a new catalyst was developed, the information could be used to target customers who would be interested in those products.[44]

ADVERTISING

The Internet has promised a number of benefits to advertisers: The Web allows direct communication and interaction with customers, it tracks customers' media use, it can develop customized ads and placement, and it facilitates actions such as purchasing. However, because content providers on the Internet have not been able to keep these promises, per-company spending on Internet advertising dropped from 1997 to 1998 even though total advertising spending is increasing.[45]

The Internet is a new and evolving medium being judged by standards developed for more mature industries. Larger advertisers are not ignoring the promise of the Net. In August 1998, Procter & Gamble *(www.pg.com)* sponsored a Future of Advertising Stakeholders, or FAST, summit *(www.fastinfo.org)*. In attendance were 150 large advertisers who were looking to increase media spending on the Internet. These advertisers see the potential of the Internet as well as its current problems and are committed to making the new medium a viable communications vehicle.[46]

The Internet has made inroads into traditional media. When asked about which activity they were likely to give up when they surfed, Web Surfers shifted away from television watching. The Internet is the fastest-growing medium, taking only 5 years to reach 50 million users compared to radio's 38 years, television's 13 years, and cable's 10 years.[47] The use of the Internet and the Web as advertising media offers some unique advantages and problems. The Web allows tracking of individual behavior, including measuring the actual exposure to a message rather than estimating advertisement exposure. In response, advertisers are demanding a change in how they pay for Web ad placement.

Relationships among the media, the advertising agency, and the business client are changing with this new promotional medium. New vendors are entering the market offering content development, Web page hosting, media buying, and targeting services. The use of hypermedia is also affecting the timing of campaigns, and payments, as well as the traditional measurements of effectiveness and reach.

Agencies

In the promotional process, advertising **agencies** act as intermediaries by providing the talent to help set promotional objectives, create the content, place the promotion in the media, and provide feedback on the results of the campaign to the client. Advertising executives are still debating the future of Internet advertising. Although it is clearly a multibillion-dollar advertising medium that has surpassed outdoor advertising in dollar sales, it may never reach the size of television, newspapers, or magazines. Problems include narrow target markets, privacy concerns, limited bandwidth, no effective measures of success, and hard-to-prove returns on investments. In addition, if offline media advertising and targeted e-mail are more effective in getting audiences to visit a Web site, then online advertising is not needed. Advertisers may begin to use Web sites as centers of complex communication and use other media to drive the audience to the Web site.[48]

Traditional agencies were slow to respond to the changes brought about by hypermedia. At first, many agencies did not understand the technology or how to use hypermedia in a campaign. This left the door open for new firms to specialize in digital advertising. New York, home to Madison Avenue, has given rise to a new Silicon Alley, a digital advertising center with over 100 agencies, venture firms, content developers, and support businesses. In Los Angeles, another interactive services center, called the Digital Coast, has started.

High growth in the industry and larger clients have led firms such as DoubleClick *(www.doubleclick.com)*, USWeb *(www.usweb.com)*, and Razorfish *(www.razorfish.com)* to grow and obtain new talent by purchasing other firms. As advertisers come to realize that Web pages should be used in conjunction with larger media campaigns, they are relying on more traditional agencies to provide interactive content.

Timing

Traditional promotional campaigns use a mix of media to reach all the AIDA goals. This could be a combination of broadcast and print over differing time periods. The Web allows advertisers to develop sites that the target audience can visit whenever they want and as often as they like. **Timing** is important; Web sites should be refreshed to encourage the users to return. Some sites, such as CNN, do this minute by minute as the news changes. Unlike other media, the advertiser does not need to wait for the media cycle to allow new print or broadcast placements. Placement and access to new information can be instantaneous.

FlyCast Communications Corporation *(www.flycast.com)* allows advertisers to use agent technology to make ad placements in three to five minutes. Reporting features allow advertisers to see which ads are working and which aren't and then to make adjustments.[49]

Measurement of Effectiveness

Measurement of traditional media's impact is an inexact science. While an advertisement may reach the intended audience, the ad may not receive any attention. Also, just because the audience members are exposed to the ad does not mean that they will remember any of the messages. Most evaluations of advertising campaigns come after the advertisements are placed. Starch reports *(www.roper.inter.net)*, for example, allow advertisers to see the number of people who have noted an ad and who remember the headline, illustration, body copy, etc. Broadcast media may be evaluated through diaries or other monitoring devices.

Internet advertising has the potential to allow the advertiser to collect information such as who sees which ad and for how long. Web servers can track every time an individual moves from one linked page to another. Dead pages, or pages no one visits, can be updated or deleted. This data can be collected from both the

Table 3.3   Measurement of Hypermedia Advertising

Measurement Method	Definition	Comments
Hit count	Measures the number of times a page is requested but not necessarily seen or displayed at the user's browser	Provides information on actual hits, but there could be multiple hits counted for every click of the mouse or page refresh. Records activity regardless of the viewer's location, such as workplaces, homes, schools, or other countries. Provides no information on users.
Page view	Tracks the number of individual pages sent to Web viewers	Gives no indication of how many users receive or view pages and no profile data on users.
Click-through	Tracks the number of times an online ad is clicked on	Gives no information about the customers. Customers who click through may dump a page before it loads.
Unique visitors	Allow tracking by the IP address of the viewer	Many people use the same IP address to access a site.
Reach	Measures sampled group's visits (if 25% of sample has visited site, reach obtained 25%)	Requires the use of panels or surveys. This can pair information on the individual's background with individual behavior. These panels may be narrow in scope and not account for all Web surfers, such as those at work or from other countries.
New measures	Include linking individuals by demographic data, loyalty, site behavior, and other measures	May allow online, constant measures of who visits a site and how long they stay at a site.

Source: Fast Principles of Online "Media Audience Measurement," FastInfo.org, <*http://www.fastinfo.org/measurement/pages/index.cgi/ audiencemeasurement*>, September 22, 1999; and Steven Vonder Haar, "Web Metrics: Go Figure," *Business 2.0*, June 1999, pp. 46–47.

sending server and the user's PC. Data from cookies may even provide a profile of the user.

Industrial standards measuring online advertising are evolving. Table 3.3 outlines the measurement standards used for Internet advertising.

Measurements that are based on server data require the media hosts to do the reporting. This could be a conflict of interest; therefore, measurements should be audited. There is also a lack of standards and comparability between measurements. To overcome these weaknesses, third-party ad-serving companies such as FlyCast place ads on multiple Web sites and provide measurement statistics. Again, there could be a conflict of interest because these ad-serving companies may represent the Web sites. These problems are not unique to the Web. Other media have rating problems as well, but the Internet may provide stronger measurement data as companies agree on standardized rating systems.[50]

Ad Blocking

The shift in power from businesses to consumers is also aided by **ad blocking**, when consumers filter, or block, ads from Web sites. These filters look at the HTML code and check files and file types against a filter list to block ads, interstitials, or animated banners. A stronger interest in this type of technology exists inside companies where ad blocking can improve speed and network performance. Some advertisers have retaliated by blocking users who use ad-blocking software.[51]

Ad Payment

There has been a shift in the payment method used for Internet advertising. In the first quarter of 1999, 43 percent of campaigns used cost per thousand, 6 percent used performance-based measures, and 51 percent used a combination of measures.[52]

Cost per thousand or **CPM,** is the traditional payment measure used by advertisers. This is based on the number of people who see the ad. CPM also can act as a standard of comparison across media outlets. For example, if multiple media outlets target the same market, the advertiser can purchase a lower cost medium if the CPM rate is lower. For traditional media, the number of thousands that each medium reports is most often based on an audited source such as Nielsen *(www.nielsen.com)* or Arbitron *(www.arbitron.com)* rating service. Web CPM rates can vary from a few dollars to $70 or more depending on the outlet used and the audience reached. These rates may be higher than other media such as radio and TV, but the ability to reach the desired market can make the Web more cost-effective.

The ability to track users also allows charges based on click-throughs. Interactive Imaginations, a game site on the Web, charged 75 cents for a click-through from a banner ad and 15 cents for each full-page ad pulled up on its content site.[53]

Table 3.4 Web Site Ratings Indicators

Payment Method	Meaning	Comments
CPM	Cost per thousand	Typical method used to compare across media
CPC	Cost per click	Cost of clicking through from a hypermedia page
Pay per action Pay per performance	Per sales lead, per download, per purchase, etc.	Variable cost by company

Source: Compiled from Jeff Frentzen, "'Flat' Web Sites Are Out; Sites That 'Pop' Are In," *PC Week,* February 3, 1997, p. 141.

A new method of paying for advertisements is emerging on the Web. **Pay for performance** occurs when an ad actually leads to a sale. Amazon has 35,000 affiliate sites that receive 15 percent of book sales when purchases are made after linking from the affiliate site. This model shifts the risk of advertising to the media.[54] Table 3.4 outlines the major rating systems used for Web advertising.

TERMS AND CONCEPTS

KNOWLEDGE INTEGRATION

Action *60*
Ad blocking *76*
Agencies *73*
Attention *60*
Banner ads *62*
Brochure sites *58*
Chat *55*
Click-through *62*
Cookies *68*
Cost per thousand (CPM) *76*
Daughter window *63*
Desire *60*
External audiences *53*

Hypermedia *53*
Interest *60*
Internal audiences *53*
Interstitial *63*
Involvement *57*
Linear communication *53*
Many-to-many model *55*
Measurement *74*
One-to-many communication model *53*
On the fly *68*
Pay for performance *77*

Permission marketing *67*
Personalization *68*
Promotion *54*
Sales force automation (SFA) *72*
Search engines *62*
Targeted e-mail *67*
Threaded discussion lists *55*
Thumbnail *56*
Timing *74*
Top of the search *62*

CONCEPTS AND QUESTIONS FOR REVIEW

1. Explain the role promotion plays in the marketing system.
2. Define hypermedia.
3. Describe how the communications process works.
4. Contrast a many-to-many model with a one-to-many model.
5. What is nonlinear communication?
6. Explain how relationship development is achieved in a hypermedia environment.
7. What is the AIDA process?
    a. How is attention gained using hypermedia?
    b. How is interest created using hypermedia?
    c. How is desire generated using hypermedia?
    d. How is action encouraged using hypermedia?
8. Describe the role of hypermedia for industrial markets.
9. Explain how media relationships are changing.
10. List the major means of measuring online advertising effectiveness.
11. Describe the major standards for paying for online advertising.

A C T I V E   L E A R N I N G

Exercise 3.1: Evaluate Web Sites

Web sites should be designed to reach specific communications goals. Visit a Web site and evaluate what you believe to be its communications goals. Create a table like the one on the following page and answer the questions related to the AIDA process.

Exercise 3.2: Determining Advertising Rates

It is relatively easy to find pricing information on advertising rates from media kits at Web sites. For example, go to DoubleClick's Business Rate Card *(www. doubleclick.com/advertisers/business/rate_card.htm)*. Evaluate how DoubleClick assigns its charges. Visit another site and find its advertising rates. How do these compare to DoubleClick's? Compare the target markets of the two Web sites. Determine which Web site is the better value.

Exercise 3.3: Charting a Thumbnail

Traditional media create linear flows in their advertising. Create a thumbnail of a TV ad by charting the flow of the major scenes. Draw a rough sketch of each scene in a storyboard format as shown below. Find a Web site for that product or a similar product. Draw a thumbnail of the Web site with its associated links, going down two or three layers into the interactive design. Don't follow every link; within 21 links, you will have mapped the entire Internet.

Contrast the differences in information flow. Consider which approach works best in moving the audience through the AIDA process. Determine how each medium could support the other in reaching communications goals.

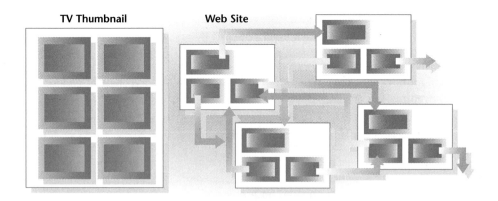

TV Thumbnail   **Web Site**

Web Site Evaluation

AIDA Process	E-Business Communications Strategy
Attention	Describe how offline media make the audience aware of the Web site. Use a search engine to see which search terms allow the Web site to be found. How far is this business from the top of the list? Determine if other Web sites are used as media advertising this Web site.
Interest	Decide whether this site uses customization and/or personalization techniques to meet an individual's needs.
Desire	Describe how content is designed to appeal to the target audience. How does this site attempt to develop relationships with its audience?
Action	Decide which types of actions the site attempts to achieve. Determine if the site uses promotions to entice actions.

Exercise 3.4: Soft Drink Design

A few large manufacturers dominate the soft drink market, but competition is increasing from smaller specialty drink manufacturers. For small soft drink companies, it is important to develop a relationship with customers so they will buy the product when it gets to the store shelf; ideally, customers will request the product from the retailer. Your job is to design a Web site for a new soft drink. In developing this site, you will need to consider each of the following areas:

▸ What is the nature of the target market? (You are free to choose the market segment that you would like to target.)

▸ What is the main selling point you want to use to create a relationship with the customer? (To do this, place yourself in the role of the seller or buyer. What questions would you ask and answer about the product?)

▸ How do you think the target market will decode the message? (Are members familiar with using the Web? Do they like graphics? What type of system will they use?)

▸ What other media will you use to tie in with this site as part of a campaign?

▸ How will you encode that message? (What are the main message components, and how will they be linked?)

▸ How will the site be designed? (You must develop a thumbnail of a site indicating the links.)

When you are finished, use the Web to look at existing soft drink sites. Determine how your Web design compares to existing sites. Determine how these larger companies develop relationships with their target audiences.

WEB SEARCH – LOOKING ONLINE

| SEARCH TERM: Search Engines | First 5 out of 1,111,913 |

Altavista. Is an online search engine that searches one of the largest databases of Web sites.
www.altavista.com

Excite.com. Is a search engine that provides searches as well as other information.
www.excite.com

Statmarket. Displays the relative search share for the major search engines.
http://www.statmarket.com/SM?c=Search_Engines

WebCrawler. Is another search engine that is popularly used to gain more information.
www.webcrawler.com

Yahoo.com. Is an online directory–based search engine.
www.yahoo.com

| SEARCH TERM: Communication Technology | First 2 out of 22,906 |

Macromedia. Is a company that produces software to bring multimedia to the Internet.
www.macromedia.com

Webcast. Is a company that allows video transmission of data.
www.webcastcentral.com

| SEARCH TERM: Online Advertising Support | First 4 out of 449,213 |

Ad Resource. Provides a library of advertising and marketing links.
www.adresource.com

Flycast Network. Is one of the world's leading Web advertising networks.
www.flycast.com

Razorfish. Is an online firm that helps companies with digital advertising.
www.razorfish.com

USWeb. Is an online firm that helps companies with digital advertising.
www.usweb.com

REFERENCES

1. SEC's Edgar Database, "Amazon Form 10K,"<*http://edgar.sec.gov/Archives/edgar/data/1018724/0000891020-99-000375.txt*>, September 8, 1999.
2. Elizabeth Gardner, "Amazon.com Spends Millions on High-Profile Ads," *Web Week,* July 14, 1997, p. 5.
3. Donna L. Hoffman and Thomas P. Novak, "Marketing in Hypermedia Computer-Mediated Environments: Conceptual Foundations," *Journal of Marketing,* July 1996, vol. 60, pp. 50–68.
4. Linda Himelstein, Ellen Neuborne, and Paul M. Eng, "Web Ads Start to Click," *Business Week,* October 6, 1997, pp. 128–138.
5. CIO Web Business, "Where the Money Goes," *CIO Web Business,* December 1, 1997, p. 18; and Brian Caufield, "Report Says Ad Spending Inched Up in Q1 to S351M$," *Internet World,* June 29, 1998, p. 56.
6. Talk City Corporate Site, "Our Story," <*http://www.talkcity.com/corp/story.htmpl*>, September 14, 1999.
7. Joelle Klein, "Anatomy of an Interactive Campaign," *Silicon Alley Report,* Summer 1998, pp. 12–14, 80.
8. Donna L. Hoffman and Thomas P. Novak, "Marketing in Hypermedia Computer-Mediated Environments: Conceptual Foundations," *Journal of Marketing,* July 1996, vol. 60, pp. 62–63.
9. Andrew Marlatt, "Who's Owner of Chasesucks.com and Chasestinks? Three Guesses," *Internet World,* June 15, 1998, p. 52.
10. Tracy Emerick, "Media and Marketing Strategies for the Internet," pp. 93–110, in ed. Gegina Brady, Edward Forrest, and Richard Mizerski, *Cybermarketing,* NTC Business Books, Lincolnwood, Illinois, 1997.
11. Michael Nolan, "Building Corporate Identities is Tricky on Net, But Payoff Can Be Great," *Web Week,* April 28, 1997, p. 31.
12. Ruth Greenberg, "The Road to Interactivity," *CIO Web Business,* November 1, 1997, p.70.
13. The AIDA process is only one of the hierarchy of effect models in advertising. For more on this topic, see: Demetrios Vakratsas and Tim Ambler, "How Advertising Works: What Do We Really Know?" *Journal of Marketing,* January 1999, pp. 26–43.
14. Steve Bennett, "Get the Message," *Small Business Computing,* September 1999, pp. 49–50; and Insane Stats, "URL Ubiquity," *Business 2.0,* February 1999, p. 8.
15. Joshua Ozarsky, "Offline, on Message," *Business 2.0,* August 1999, pp. 50–64 and CyberAtlas, "Offline Spending by Internet Brands Passes $1 Billion," <*http://cyberatlas.internet.com/markets/advertising/article/0,1323,5941_259071,00.html*>, December 14, 1999.
16. Nelson Wang, "Web TV Takes on a New Definition," *Web Week,* July 21, 1997, p. 14.
17. Al Berg, "Go to the Top of the Hit List," *LANTIMES,* November 10, 1997, p. 101; Jim Sterne, "Stacking the Deck," *CIO Web Business,* December 1, 1997, pp. 36–37; and David Haskin, "Power Search," *Internet World,* December 1997, pp. 78–92.

[18] Matthew Fordahl, "The Web's 19 Degress of Separation," *Mercury Center*, <*http://www.sjmercury.com/svtech/news/breaking/merc/docs/008115.htm*>, September 9, 1999; and Sean Donahue, "Smarter Returns," *Business 2.0*, August 1999, pp. 46–48.

[19] Internet.com, "Banners on the Decline,"<*http://cyberatlas.internet.com/markets/advertising/print/0,1323,5941_154461,00.html*>, April 22, 1999.

[20] Nelson Wang, "Sponsored Content Interstitials Emerge as New Rivals to Banners," *Web Week*, October 6, 1997, pp. 15, 21.

[21] Nelson Wang, "Researchers Find Banners Boost Product Awareness," *Web Week*, September 29, 1997, p. 6.

[22] See: Carol Nelson and Rocky James, "Creative Strategy for Interactive Marketing," in *Interactive Marketing*, eds. Edward Forrest and Richard Mizerski, American Marketing Association, Chicago, Illinois, NTC/Contemporary Publishing Company, Lincolnwood, Illinois, 1996, pp. 215–227.

[23] Jonetta Delaine Mosley-Matchett, "The Effects of Presentation Latency on Proficient and Nonproficient Users of Internet-Based Marketing Presentations," *Proceedings of the 1998 AMA Winter Educator's Conference*, American Marketing Association, Chicago, Illinois, pp. 399–400.

[24] Elizabeth Gardner, "ANALYSIS: What's Behind the Flurry of Redesigns," *Internet World*, June 8, 1998, pp. 1–53.

[25] See: Herschell Gordon Lewis, "Copywriting for Interactive Media," in *Interactive Marketing*, eds. Edward Forrest and Richard Mizerski, American Marketing Association, Chicago, Illinois, NTC/Contemporary Publishing Company, Lincolnwood, Illinois, 1996, pp. 229–239.

[26] Andrew Marlatt, "The Web as Thrill Ride," *Internet World*, March 30, 1998, pp. 20, 22.

[27] Mary J. Cronin, "Using the Web to Push Key Data to Decision Makers," *Fortune*, September 29, 1997, p. 254.

[28] Insane Stats, "E-Mealstrom: Snail vs. Email," *Business 2.0*, April 1999, p. 11.

[29] Doug Uptmor, "Make Them Want It," *NewMedia*, July 1999, p.66.

[30] John Moore, "Get Ready For E-Commercials," *Sm@rt Reseller*, August 23, 1999, p. 16; Steven Vonder Haar, "Infomercials Coming to E-mail," *Inter@ctive Week*, July 19, 1999, p. 40; Whit Andrews, "E-mail Marketing Is Stumbling Forward," *Internet World*, March 8, 1999, pp. 13–14; and Roberta Fusaro, "Groups Eye Model for E-mail Ads," *Computerworld*, December 21, 1998, pp. 47–48.

[31] Jeff Sweat and Rick Whiting, "Instant Marketing," *Information Week*, August 2, 1999, pp. 18–20.

[32] Justin Hibbard, "Getting Personal," *Red Herring*, September 1999, p. 128; Rivka Tadjer, "Giving Content a Push," *Communication Week*, June 2, 1997, pp. 73–78; and Dan Richman, "Let Your Agent Handle It," *Information Week*, April 17, 1995, pp. 44–56.

[33] Linda Himelstein, Ellen Neuborne and Paul M. Eng, "Web Ads Start to Click," *Business Week*, October 6, 1997, pp. 128–138.

[34] Julia King, "Web Success Boosts Customer Expectation," *Computerworld*, August 16, 1999, p. 40; and John Evan Frook, "Future Trend: Getting Personal With Customers," *Internet Week*, June 22, 1998, p. 11.

[35] Sharon Machlis, "Web Retailers Try to Keep Their Hits Up," *Computerworld*, February 8, 1999, p. 48; and "Right On Target," *Silicon Alley Report*, vol. 3, no. 3, pp. 66–72, 126–127.

[36] Sharon Machlis, "Web Sites Add Content to Boost Sales," *Computerworld*, September 28, 1998, pp. 1, 98.

[37] John Evan Frook, "Disney Tempts Web Visitors to Buy," *Internet Week*, March 23, 1998, pp. 19–20.

[38] Elizabeth Gardner, "Finding a Niche as the Web's Coupon Source," *Internet World,* March 23, 1998, pp. 13, 16; and CoolSavings, "About CoolSavings," *<http://www9.coolsavings. com/scripts/frame_enter.asp?OpType=intro&SessionID=1594218253&RefURL=http//www.cool-savings.com>,* September 21, 1999.

[39] John Leland, "The Blair Witch Cult," *Newsweek,* August 16, 1999, pp. 44–49; David Ansen and Corie Brown, "A Hex Upon Hollywood," *Newsweek,* August 16, 1999, pp. 50–51; Tim Carvell, "How *The Blair Witch Project* Built Up So Much Buzz," *Fortune,* August 16, 1999, pp. 32–34; and Richard Corliss, "Blair Witch Craft," *Time,* August 16, 1999, pp. 58–64.

[40] Clinton Wilder and Justin Hibbard,"Pushing Outside the Enterprise," *Information Week,* August 4, 1997, pp. 20–22.

[41] Amy Cortese, "Here Comes the Intranet," *Business Week,* February 26, 1996, pp. 76–84; and Eric Chabrow, "Instruments of Growth," *Information Week,* October 5, 1998, pp. 4SS–5SS.

[42] Lew McCreary, "The Birth of the Do's," *CIO Web Business—Section 2,* July 1, 1998, pp. 45–47.

[43] Tita Theodora Beal, "Tooth in Advertising," *AV Video Multimedia Producer,* January 1998, pp. 31, 144.

[44] Bill Roberts, "Net Helps Company Organize Complex Sales Cycle," *Web Week,* December 15, 1997, p. 21.

[45] Association of National Advertisers, "Third Annual ANA Web Site Study Indicates Emphasis on Web Marketing; Increases in Online Advertising Expected," *<http://www.ana. net/about/ananews/05_04_99.htm>,* May 4, 1999; Internet Advertising Bureau, "Internet Advertising Revenues More Than Double in 1998," *<http://www.iab.net>,* September 8, 1999; and Megan Santosus, "Bang for the Buck?" *CIO Enterprise—Section 2,* May 15, 1998, p. 74.

[46] Elizabeth Gardner, "Meeting of Big Advertisers Points Up Web's Problems," *Internet World,* August 24, 1998, pp. 1, 57.

[47] Tom Hyland, "Why Internet Advertising?" *AIB Advertising ABC's, <http://www.iab.net/ advertise/content/adcontent.html>,* September 16, 1999.

[48] Nelson Wang, "Ad Execs Predict Continued Growth, See Need for Sensitivity on Privacy," *Internet World,* June 7, 1999, pp. 1, 16–17; and "The Round Table," *Silicon Alley Reporter,* vol. 3, no. 6, pp. 102–121.

[49] Richard Karpinski, "Ad Sales Go Real-Time," *Internet Week,* December 1, 1997, p. 19.

[50] Elizabeth Gardner, "But Who's Counting? Ratings Under Fire," *Internet World,* July 13, 1998, pp. 1, 10; and Nelson Wang, "Ratings Firms Face Questions About Data Collection and Projections," *Internet World,* July 13, 1998, p. 10.

[51] "Fiction Site Spurns Surfers Who Use Ad-Blocking Apps," *Computerworld,* June 12, 1999, p. 28; Charles Babcok, "Dollarwise, Ad Blockers Add Up," *Inter@ctive Week,* April 5, 1999, p. 24; and David Ball, "Online Marketing and Its Discontents," *Silicon Alley Reporter,* vol. 3, no. 6, pp. 94–100.

[52] Internet Advertising Bureau, "First Quarter 1999 Internet Advertising Revenues Double Over First Quarter 1998 for the First Time," *<http://www.iab.net>,* August 17, 1999.

[53] Nelson Wang, "Click-Through Pricing Plan Gains," *Web Week,* March 3, 1997, p. 26.

[54] J. William Gurley, "Ginsu Comes to the Web," *Fortune,* May 11, 1998, pp. 170–172.

chapter 4
E-Business Distribution Systems

Channels of distribution evolve over time in response to changes in the environment. The new technology-based information environment is transforming channel structure and relationships between intermediaries and those who facilitate the transport of goods. Channel functions are being taken over by cybermediaries. Power is shifting from manufacturers and retailers to customers. Conflicts are arising between channel members as traditional middlemen are facing disintermediation, or the loss of their intermediary function.

Students working for businesses operating in today's electronic environment will be involved in transforming enterprises. It is vital to understand the reasons that channels are evolving in order to understand how to construct e-business–based marketing distribution systems.

The Car-Buying Game

"The customer is going to grab control of the process, and we're all going to salute smartly and do exactly what the customer tells us if we want to stay in business."

Robert Eaton

Chrysler Corporation Chairman [1]

Eaton's remark was made to the National Automobile Dealers Association in response to the changing power relationship between the dealer and the consumer in an automotive purchase. By 1997 the number of auto buyers who were willing to purchase a car without a test drive rose from 5 percent to 10 percent. Consumers now have greater amounts of information, dealer choice, and bargaining power. The growth of the World Wide Web is a driving force of this change; in 1998 44 percent of potential car buyers had Internet access, and one-third of that group has used the Web for car-buying information. By 1999, 40 percent of U.S. consumers who purchased a car or truck used the Internet to aid in the shopping process.[2]

Until the advent of online sales, car purchasing had not fundamentally changed since the early part of the 20th century. Back then, car companies did not have the resources to develop manufacturer-owned dealerships and so relied upon independent businesspeople to offer sales and service. The manufacturers distributed cars to these dealers who, in turn, provided service and sold to the customer. Once the dealer network established itself, sales techniques were slow to change. Car salespeople worked on commissions and, thus, had an incentive to close the sale. When the prospective buyer entered the dealership, the salesperson's goal was to keep the prospect there and close the sale. The salesperson acted as a gatekeeper of information on the product and attempted to control the sales price of the product.[3]

In 1998, about 2 million people (25 percent of buyers) armed themselves with information from the Internet before they attempted to purchase a car. By 2003, that number is expected to increase to nearly 8 million, with over one-half million closing the deal online.[4] Companies such as Dealernet.com *(www.dealernet. com)* provide information for auto comparisons, links to dealers, and information on auto financing. Carprices.com *(www.carprices.com)* provides information on dealer list prices for the car and all chosen options. Autobytel.com *(www.autobytel.com)* has a network of dealers that will supply a car at a predetermined price. Auto dealers will bid against each other to make the sale. By 1999, Autobytel had 2,700 participating dealers and 100,000 purchase requests, and it helped close over 28 percent of the sales. Both the auto dealers and the customers benefit from this relationship. The dealer's marketing and commission costs are lower, but this is offset by increased sales.[5]

Microsoft has set up its Internet Explorer browser to allow linking to Microsoft Network and then to Carpoint *(www.carpoint.msn.com)*. This auto-purchase site charges dealers fees for being included in the network and also charges for listing used cars. Carpoint alone claims to generate over $200 million in sales per month for its dealers. Both customers and dealers benefit from this system. When customers post more than three complaints about a dealer, the dealer is dropped from the system. Although dealers agree to set a minimum markup over the invoice price, they increase the volume of cars sold.[6]

Auto manufacturers and dealerships have been forced to respond to the changes in how consumers use Internet information. GM and Ford have developed Web sites to support dealers' sales. The GM BuyPower site *(www.gmbuypower.com)* allows the buyer to shop from home and obtain detailed information on a car model and on competitive autos. The site also helps to determine which dealer has the car the customer desires. The prospective buyer can see the dealer's price for the car, arrange for a test drive, and order the car over the Web. Dealers who choose not to become a member of the network are at a competitive disadvantage.[7] Ford *(www.fordvehicles.com)* also has a number of sites supporting new and used car sales, and other manufacturers are following with their own sales sites.

Both Ford and GM are using the Internet to develop extranet links to their suppliers. These companies are developing central Web sites for their suppliers to collect information. Ford's Web site will personalize for each supplier.[8] A number of manufacturers are planning to sell used cars online. GM found that implementing its strategy has some roadblocks. The Texas Department of Transportation denied GM a license to sell used cars in Texas because the manufacturer would compete with local car dealers.[9]

THINKING STRATEGICALLY

Decide how important a test drive is before choosing a car model to purchase. Evaluate whether the test car has to be the same car the buyer would take home, or if a standard test-drive model would work. There is a belief among car salespeople that when customers come into a dealership, they have to be "sold to" before they leave or the sale is lost. Investigate the way people make decisions to purchase a car. Determine when they start thinking about the model to purchase. Investigate the type of information they gather before they buy. Speculate on how the Web could help in their decision process.

Source: www.gmbuypower.com

The shift in power from the seller to the customer illustrated in the above vignette is not the only distribution issue facing the automobile market. All businesses are striving to become more competitive by making changes in their business systems, especially in their logistical and distribution systems. Currently the development of extranets is allowing suppliers, manufacturers, and dealers to link together. Middlemen, who are threatened with disintermediation as a way to reduce transaction costs, are attempting to hold onto their positions by offering greater value. Channel conflicts are brewing as firms develop multiple distribution channels, and the dynamics of marketing relationships are changing as power shifts from manufacturers to new intermediaries and customers.

The automobile is not the only industry facing restructuring due to these changes. Industries as varied as music, grocery, and real-estate sales are being challenged by newly emerging distribution systems. Businesses are receiving returns on their e-commerce investments, and small firms are using third-party intermediaries to offer online commerce for as low as $100 a month.[10] This chapter will cover the theory behind the development and structure of marketing channels and explore the new distribution relationships that are emerging. The next chapter will outline the new retail and distribution business models.

Channels of distribution provide a standard of living for customers by moving products from producers to users in the most cost-efficient manner possible. In traditional markets, this has included producers and intermediaries such as wholesalers and/or retailers. Marketing systems are constantly trying to lower the overall cost of distribution channels while striving to improve relationships between channel members. This requires that the system evolve in response to changes in the environment.[11] These new e-business–based distribution systems differ from traditional channel systems. They are characterized by:

- Greater reliance on cybermediaries and facilitators
- Reduction in the number of traditional middlemen
- Reduced inventory and shorter inventory cycles
- Tighter relationships between trade sellers and buyers
- Power shifts from producers and retailers to customers
- Lower prices and greater variety for the consumer
- Greater responsiveness to the customer

Projections say the development of e-business channels will affect not only retailer channels selling to the ultimate customer but also the business's supply chain. It is projected that Internet-based business-to-consumer markets will increase from around $5 billion in 1998 to over $108 billion by the year 2000. Although this figure may seem substantial, Wal-Mart alone had sales over $100 billion in 1998. What these commerce figures do not represent is the much larger estimate of the overall savings and number of supply-chain transactions that are restructuring marketing channels and adding efficiencies to business practices. Wal-Mart, for example, has required its suppliers to use extranets to link with Wal-Mart's inventory system to reduce its costs and speed inventory delivery.

Evolution of Distribution Channels

Channels of distribution have always evolved as new infrastructures and consumer shopping patterns developed. In the 1800s, Sears took advantage of newly developed rail systems to build a retail empire by using catalogs to offer customers products that were not available locally. Sears's purchasing power allowed a greater variety of products, increasing its negotiation power and forcing down the prices offered to its customers. In the second half of the 1900s, customers took advantage of improved highway systems to move to the suburbs; Kmart followed and built a discount empire. The growth of suburbs led to retail concentrations in malls, which, in turn, fostered a shift in consumer purchasing patterns. The growth of national franchises and malls helped lead to the decline in retail sales in central business districts. Consumer acceptance of credit-card use and 1-800 phone numbers has allowed a multitude of catalog companies to offer niche products to customers and deliver directly to their homes.

The growth of large retail outlets such as Wal-Mart has shifted power from manufacturers to retailers. **Just-in-time (JIT) inventory** systems allow firms to respond to competitive pressures by forcing lower overall costs and increasing quality and efficiency. Electronic data interchange (EDI) systems allow channel members to transfer transaction and inventory data electronically. Currently Internet protocols are being used for the same types of data transfer, lowering the cost of linking suppliers, producers, the sales force, and customers.

WHAT IS DISTRIBUTION?

Intermediaries and facilitators enable a transaction to take place between producers and customers. **Intermediaries,** such as wholesalers and retailers, split large production runs into small amounts (this is called **breaking bulk**), **creating an assortment** of products to offer a customer. **Facilitators** help the flow of the transaction by physically moving the product, information, or funds through the distribution channel. Figure 4.1 outlines a distribution system.

Distribution systems attempt to establish a level of coordination and control in hopes of developing the most efficient system at the lowest cost.[12] Channel members will spin off functions to other intermediaries or facilitators if they can perform the function more efficiently. For example, if a firm had its own trucking service and decided it would be less expensive to have an independent trucking company ship its product, it would most likely close down its own operation and use the independent service.

Manufacturers break their large production runs into smaller units to sell to wholesalers. Wholesalers create an assortment for the retailer, which, in turn, breaks the wholesaler's bulk into smaller units. Customers visit the retailer because it has created an assortment of products for them. The overall system is more efficient; it reduces the total number of transactions because the customer doesn't need to visit every manufacturer to obtain the desired products. If a channel can-

Figure 4.1 Distribution System

not establish an efficient means of distribution to a market, it will be left unserved. Small towns, for example, often don't have the same access to goods and services as larger communities. Figure 4.2 illustrates how intermediaries break bulk and create assortments to serve markets.

Figure 4.2 indicates that the overall number of transactions is reduced for the manufacturers, retailers, and customers. The manufacturer can produce larger production runs because it can move inventory and does not need to sell to each customer on an individual basis. The retailer and consumer, in turn, can go to a single source to purchase products. In the example below, a market (customers D and E) is left unserved because it is not efficient for the channel to sell at that location.

The channel members must perform a number of **channel functions:**

▸ **Physical possession.** The good or service must be transferred to the customer. This includes the warehousing process and the physical movement of the product from the producer to the customer.
▸ **Title or ownership flow.** When the customer purchases or receives the product, title or ownership must be transferred.
▸ **Promotion.** Communication between the channel members is essential for promotion.
▸ **Ordering system.** The channel member must also structure an ordering system. This could be through a paper-and-pencil system, or through electronically controlled data interchanges.
▸ **Payment flows.** A system for payment must be developed for goods when they are transferred. A customer may pay cash or use credit from other channel members by postponing payments (e.g., due in 30 to 60 days). The customer

Figure 4.2 Breaking Bulk and Creating Assortments

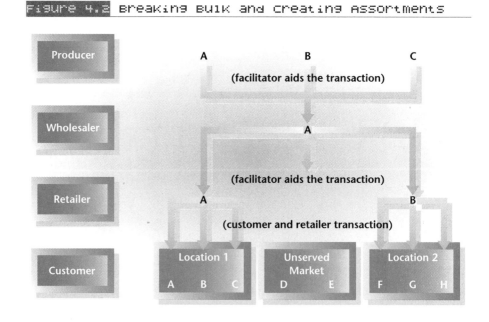

may also finance the purchase with a credit card or a store's charge card. This process implies risk on the part of the supplier if the customer does not pay. There is also risk on the purchaser's side in that the product may not perform as required.

The direction of flow for each of these functions is outlined in Figure 4.3.

Each of the channel functions outlined in Figure 4.3 can occur between producers (such as raw material suppliers and manufacturers) and intermediaries (wholesalers, agents, and retailers) as well as between intermediaries and consumers. For example, a traditional retailer may receive products, promotion support, and financing from a distributor, which has received its products from another distributor or manufacturer. The retailer would then promote to the consumer (end user) and distribute the product. The retailer would forward its payments back through the channel to the distributor from funds received from its customers. Some of these functions may be delegated to a facilitator, such as a trucking company. Promotional flows could use advertising facilitators that provide communications services for channel members. Credit-card companies also act as facilitators of payment and credit flows.

Channel systems evolve and attempt to become more efficient. The systems that grow and dominate offer a wider assortment of product choices to the customer, speed up delivery of goods and services, communicate more efficiently, lower the risk to the seller and the purchaser, ease the ordering process, and speed up payment flows. In addition, if the new distribution channel can lower costs by eliminating unneeded intermediaries and facilitators, it can gain cost advantages.

Figure 4.3 Traditional Channel Intermediary Flows

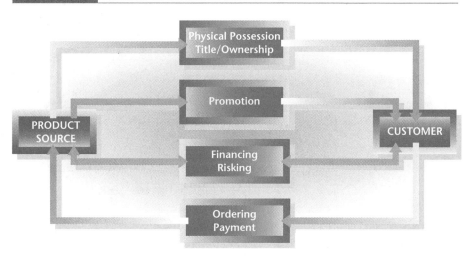

Souce: Adapted from Roland S. Vaile, E.T. Grether, and Reavis Cox, "Channels of Distribution," *Marketing in the American Economy,* Ronald Press Co., New York, 1952; and Louis W. Stern and Adel I. El-Ansary, *Marketing Channels,* Prentice Hall, Engelwood Cliffs, New Jersey, 1992.

E-BUSINESS CHANNEL SYSTEMS

E-business is changing the traditional channel structure. Electronic linkages through e-commerce and extranets are lowering the overall transaction costs associated with channel functions.[13] When customers can efficiently choose from a number of different suppliers of products or services at a low cost, they do not need to have a retailer create an assortment. In addition, the manufacturer does not need an intermediary to find customers. If a manufacturer's strategy includes **mass customization** of products for the customer, there is a strong incentive to sell directly to the end user and no reason to break bulk.

Mass customization is the process of producing individualized products at mass-production speeds and efficiencies.

Figure 4.4 illustrates how an e-business uses extranets and cybermediaries to facilitate transactions. One channel has an e-business–based retailer that uses extranets and the Internet to facilitate the transaction and to reach customers who order online. This can save on the retailer's costs because it does not need to structure a brick and mortar site to reach consumers. If, on the other hand, the producer finds that its overall transaction costs are lower, it is possible for the producer to sell directly to the end user by bypassing its traditional intermediary.

The **cybermediaries** shown in Figure 4.4 are organizations that operate in electronic markets to facilitate the exchange process.[14] These facilitators are taking a more commanding role and are restructuring the channel system. Facilitators support the functions required in marketing channels. Examples of facilitators that help move the physical product include trucking companies and overnight shippers. Facilitators that help payment flows include credit-card companies and banking institutions. Facilitators that help the communications process include advertising companies and host ISPs that develop promotional content.

An e-business needs to determine the most cost-effective means of achieving coordination and control between the cybermediaries and the customer. The

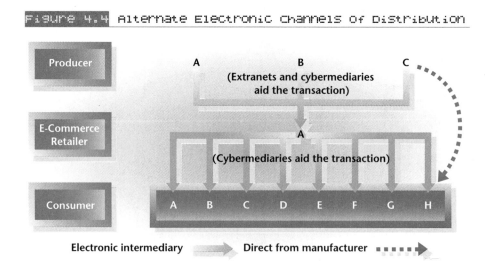

Figure 4.4 Alternate Electronic Channels of Distribution

e-business could coordinate the Web site to communicate information about the product or service directly to the consumer. When the consumer places an order, the payment could be routed through credit-card companies or banking institutions. The e-business could arrange to have the product shipped to the customer, utilizing an overnight shipper or another shipping system. Additional inventory could be controlled online over extranets. Figure 4.5 illustrates how channel functions are performed in an e-business distribution system.

An e-business distribution system can be a large investment. Costs are estimated to run between $50,000 and $5 million to set up an e-commerce site from scratch. In addition, changes in staffing and culture are often required. New e-business facilitators have set themselves up to act as commerce service providers, or coordinators of the exchange process, for firms that do not desire to set up their own e-commerce sites. These commerce service providers charge a fee and/or percentage of the sales for these services. It should be no surprise that Microsoft, IBM, AT&T, and other firms are attempting to move into this position.

E-Business Distribution Development

The e-business shown in Figure 4.5 is positioned to become the electronic channel captain. A **channel captain** is an intermediary that organizes and controls the channel. Any company that can gain this position can obtain power over other members, allowing it to take a higher percentage of the overall transaction costs.

Figure 4.5 E-Business Distribution System

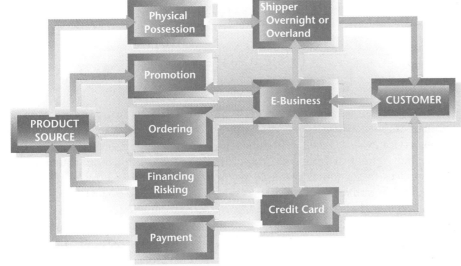

Source: Based on Brad Kleindl, "Virtual Marketing," *Southern Business and Economic Review,* Spring 1996, pp. 10–15.

Internet malls were the original models for e-channel captains. Internet malls act as host and coordinator for a number of individual businesses. The customer can find multiple vendors and browse the mall for products. Both the business and the mall benefit from each other's cooperation: The individual business does not have to set up and maintain Internet access and e-commerce servers; the mall takes fees and a percentage of sales for the service. If the seller wants its customers to be able to purchase products at its site, it must advertise the mall's Web address. Once the investment has been made to make the market aware of a site's address, changing to a lower-cost mall site would mean incurring additional transaction costs. To lower this dependency, the seller should consider having its own IP address and host its site on an ISP that can provide commerce functions. The downside is that the business loses the mall's drawing power.

A large number of companies have started to position themselves as e-channel captains. For example, NetMarket *(www.netmarket.com)* has set itself up as an intermediary for discounted products and shoppers' services, including Shopper's Advantage, TravelersAdvantage, and AutoAdvantage. NetMarket is reported to have sales of over $100 million a month to its more than 400,000 members, each of whom pays a yearly membership fee.[15] Microsoft, AT&T, IBM, and even search engines such as Yahoo! and Excite have been attempting to position themselves as the e-channel captain in the distribution process.[16] By helping to develop e-commerce sites and hosting those businesses, e-channel captains are able to gain power in the distribution channel and retain a percentage of the sales.

The speed with which current channels move toward an e-business distribution system outlined in Figure 4.5 depends on how efficient this system is over current systems. To understand this change, each of the functions of the e-business distribution system is outlined below.

CHANNEL FUNCTIONS

Physical Possession

Physical possession requires physically moving products from one location to another. Shippers, such as Federal Express Corporation *(www.FedEx.com),* United Parcel Service *(www.ups.com),* and others, have developed logistical systems to efficiently move products from one site to another. These shippers have expanded their services to customers through technological integration. All of the major transportation and delivery companies offer online tracking of packages. FedEx is expanding to include the pickup, transport, warehousing, and delivery of finished goods. FedEx is handling all the logistical operations and warehousing for a number of companies including National Semiconductor Corporation. Integration between FedEx and these companies is so tight that customers can order FedEx services directly from a product vendor.[17] FedEx is spending $1 billion annually to develop services that allow the receiving customer the ability to track a package and specify where a package should be picked up.[18] UPS, Ryder Corporation, and others are positioning themselves to offer the same services as FedEx.

Businesses that do not wish to be locked into a single transportation facilitator can use information intermediaries to provide efficiency to the channel. TanData Corporation *(www.tandata.com)* has set up a service that allows a business to do price comparisons on shippers. For a low setup charge of $250 and a $1-per-transaction cost, a business can determine the lowest-cost shipper for its product delivery.[19]

Communication Linkages

Communication between the firm and the customer can be facilitated over the Internet through the design of Web pages, as outlined in Chapter 3. Extranets are used to link businesses together, enabling communication between companies and allowing for transactions. Wal-Mart's extranet invites buyers and suppliers to access terabytes (trillions of bytes) of data on sales figures, product sales, and even individual customers' sales. The data is used to help determine customer shopping patterns. This has allowed Wal-Mart to reduce store inventories and speed up its supply chain. For example, Wal-Mart currently receives three to five shipments of Christmas seasonal items when it used to receive only one. This permits Wal-Mart to limit losses from excess inventory.[20]

Extranets are becoming the basis for this information flow. As these changes move more strongly toward the Web, customers, shippers, producers, and others will be able to access the status of orders, products, and processes online. This will speed communication and help limit gatekeepers' ability to control information.

Payment Flows, Financing, and Risk Taking

One of the major considerations cited as hindering the growth of e-commerce is the consumer's perceptions of the risk of making payments over the Internet. There are actually four parties at risk in electronic transfers: the customer (end user), the seller (business-to-business or retailer), the producer, and the transfer agent (credit-card companies or banking institutions). An example of the type of electronic flow of funds between these parties is shown in Figure 4.6 on the following page.

The flow outlined in Figure 4.6 is very similar to the traditional credit payments process. In an e-commerce purchase, all the payment flows can be handled electronically. The vendor must receive approval for the purchase made by the customer. The customer's exposure to loss is much more limited than the seller's. Although a credit-card holder may be liable for a limited amount, such as $50, the vendor may be the victim of fraud and liable for the entire amount of the purchase. Because these payments are made electronically, the seller must be sure that the customer is an authorized purchaser. If the vendor acts on an unauthorized payment, it may be at risk for the loss of product and funds.[21]

The payment processor attempts to lower the overall risk involved in the purchase by limiting fraud. Criminals who attempt to use credit-card numbers do not have to physically steal a credit card to use it. Some criminals use computers to

Figure 4.6   Transfer of Electronic Payments (E-Payments)

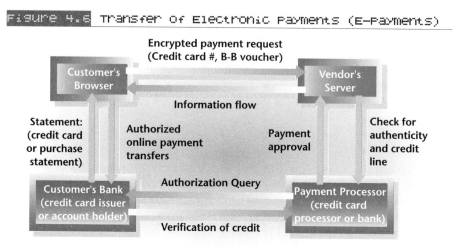

Source: Adapted from Ravi Kalakotoa and Andrew B.Whinston, *Frontiers of Electronic Commerce,* Addison-Wesley Publishing Company, Reading, Massachusetts, 1996, p. 319. Netscape Developer's Edge Archived Conference Materials, "Commerce & Security Credit Card Processing Using the Netscape Server Platform", *http://developer.netscape.com/misc/developer/conference/proceedings/cs4/sld008. html>,* January 14, 2000; and Harry Tennant and Associates, "5 Payment Models on the Internet," *<http://www.htennant.com/hta/askus/5models.htm>,* 1997.

randomly generate card numbers until they find one that is active. The credit-card companies, in turn, attempt to block unauthorized use by accessing their data-bases to look for any purchasing behavior that falls out of the norm for the card-holder. For example, if it looks as if the cardholder never buys products in Hong Kong, the cardholder may receive a call from the card company to verify a Hong Kong sale.

Electronic Credit

In 1998, 90 percent of payments for online sales were made with credit cards, but ordering online can be a hassle. Up to 27 percent of online buyers cancel transactions when filling out forms.[22] To enhance the security of online payments and to make purchases easier, new standards for consumer credit payments are being set for the Web; for instance, **secure electronic transaction (SET)** allows for the encryption of all transaction data. Merchants never see the credit-card number so it cannot be stolen from them, and they cannot fraudulently use the number. The cardholder is required to set up an account with the credit-card processor to use this system. This technology has received greater acceptance in Europe and Asia but has not yet received wide support from U.S.-based merchants.[23]

One company, eCharge *(www.echarge.com),* uses an online credit system that bypasses credit-card payment systems. The merchant sets up an eCharge button for customers to pay for merchandise. The buyer opens a credit account with eCharge and then uses a name and password when clicking on a merchant's eCharge button. There are no credit-card numbers to enter, and the card numbers do not need to clear the credit-card company. The buyer receives one bill from all of his or her eCharge online purchasing.[24]

Many merchants would like to sell products or services online that would cost pennies rather than dollars: Music companies would like to be able to sell individual songs online; information sources such as newspapers, magazines, dictionaries, and encyclopedias would like to sell content on a per-use basis. **Micropayments** are a means of paying for these small Web transactions. The transaction cost of making payments with credit cards or voucher checks can be high for these small purchases. Micropayment systems can be set up with digital wallets or be charged to an individual's credit card. A **software wallet** requires that a buyer set up an online account. This allows an amount of money to be added to a Web browser's wallet. When a microtransaction is undertaken, the wallet is debited or has money taken out. This system works much the same way as a smart card.[25]

Smart cards or **e-cash** (electronic cash) allow individuals to purchase without paper dollars. Smart cards have been in use in much of the world except for the United States, where magnetic-strip cards have dominated. Many Americans are currently using debit cards for making purchases that authorize payments from their bank accounts. Smart cards use a micro-controller chip embedded in a card. A number of devices, such as parking meters, newsstands, vending machines, and pay phones, can read the cards for payment. The cards can be purchased and reloaded from a bank account using an ATM-style machine. Information on individual purchases can be collected from the cards for the marketer's database. This technology is becoming predominant because it reduces the overall transaction expense for businesses.[26] Smart cards are being adapted for use on the Web. Gemplus *(www.gemplus.fr)* is the French firm that developed the smart card, which allows purchases to be made over France's telecommunications network. Gemplus is designing a system to allow its smart cards to be used in PCs. Adoption of these cards in the United States has been slow, but the rapid growth of phone cards, which are smart cards used for phone calls, indicates that consumers will accept this type of technology. Smart cards are being developed that will use fingerprint recognition of the owner, allowing only one authorized individual to use the card.[27]

Online payments can reduce the cost of processing checks. The federal government has mandated that businesses start to make their tax payments to the federal government through online systems. In addition, the federal government is pushing the electronic transfer of checks rather than issuing paper. The cost savings to the government are substantial. In 1996, 63 billion consumer and commercial paper checks were written. Processing costs for electronic transactions are 25 cents versus the check processing costs of $1. Having businesses engage in electronic transfers can lower fraud and check-processing costs. It is estimated that costs for all parties can be reduced by $300 billion.[28]

Electronic Billing

Electronic billing, or sending bills and making payments over the Internet, would greatly reduce transaction costs for companies. Not only do the bills need to be printed and envelopes stuffed and posted, but there must be a human interface to record when the payments are made by check. This can result in a cost to the company of up to $1.75 per bill. Online billing can cut that cost to around 25 cents to 30 cents per bill. Online billing-consolidation companies such as CheckFree *(www.checkfree.com)* and Transpoint *(www.transpoint.com)* will consolidate individuals' bills, allowing them to make one payment online. These consolidators also get the public to visit their sites many times in one month, facilitating advertising.[29]

Business-to-business markets are taking advantage of electronic payment systems. This includes making small transactions such as travel reimbursement payments, online parts and supplies payments, and large transactions payments between firms.[30]

E-commerce security

E-commerce security is a major concern for businesses conducting online transactions; as stated in Chapter 2, online security is controlled through firewalls. E-commerce security represents some unique considerations. E-commerce sites are at the top of a hacker's hit list. Some of these hackers may be looking only for information on how the site is maintained. Of greater concern is credit-card theft. Individuals attempting to use fraudulent card numbers can be detected by artificial intelligence software that looks at a number of factors to flag suspicious behavior. When CyberSource *(www.cybersource.com)* first sold software over the Internet, it was overwhelmed by fraud. In response, it developed a software package that looks at over 30 variables and a database of 75,000 past offenders to flag suspicious orders. CyberSource has sold this service to other online venders, allowing them to reduce fraud to as low as .5 percent of all orders.[31]

RELATIONSHIP DEVELOPMENT

The search for channel members is a time-consuming and expensive undertaking for a business. Once these relationships are established, firms have an incentive to attempt to maintain the best possible relationship. Yet each channel member must balance its needs with those of its fellow channel members. To make this balancing act work, a firm must take into consideration the behavioral aspects of channel **relationship development.** These include factors such as dependence, cooperation, conflict, power and power bases, satisfaction, and relational issues.

Extranet supply-chain management allows firms to keep inventory levels low. Dell uses its extranet to maintain 8 days of inventory, and has plans to move the level down to 4 days. Dell's nonintegrated competitors could carry up to 20 or 30 days of inventory. Although this lowers the cost to Dell, it also makes Dell dependent on other firms. This dependency can exist throughout the entire distribution system. The 1997 UPS strike demonstrated the reliance that many firms have on a single distribution facilitator; many firms found that they were unable to receive raw materials or to ship products.

The electronic marketplace is changing how marketing relationships develop. New business models are increasing the power of some facilitators while removing other intermediaries. The following sections will investigate each of the behavioral dimensions of channel relationships.

Power

Part of the total **power** of a channel member is due to the dependency of one channel member on the other; a channel member is dependent if it does not have alternatives to provide the same channel functions. In e-business channel relationships, the dependency of one member upon another can be lessened when partnerships are no longer limited to geographic convenience. **Transaction cost analysis** has typically governed how much effort would be used to keep channel members as partners. If the cost of finding alternative sources was too high, then alternatives would not be pursued. The Internet allows businesses to find intermediaries and facilitators easily and offers the possibility of bypassing some channel members, causing a reduction in the **power dependency** of some channel members.

CASE 4.1

Fighting for the Middle Position

Ingram Micro, Inc. *(www.ingrammicro.com)* is the world's largest warehouser and distributor of software and computer products. It has positioned itself as the back warehouse for over 100,000 corporate resellers in more than 120 countries. Ingram acts as a company's warehouse, facilitating frictionless inventory delivery. Information moves online from a buyer through the reseller's site to Ingram for assembly or delivery. Information then flows back to the material suppliers over the firm's extranet system indicating delivery times and conditions.

The reason that Ingram remains in the channel is because it manages a number of distribution functions in an effective way. This includes providing a large assortment of different products from different vendors. Ingram will undertake credit checks and extend credit. Ingram will **drop-ship** the product directly to the buyer. This increases the power of Ingram in the distribution channel, but it also allows niche businesses to start with little capital or without a brick and mortar physical location by using Ingram's system.

Ingram does not see itself as becoming the e-channel captain. The companies it serves undertake the research and development (R&D) necessary to develop new products, create pull-through promotion, and interface with the market. Ingram has extended its power by hosting or partially funding branded Web transaction sites for its customers. In this process Ingram can ship and invoice a product so that it looks as if it came from any retailer. This allows a retailer to exist with no back-end or supply-chain functions. This also gives Ingram the first chance to fulfill orders and to offer a direct link to inventory.[32]

To **drop-ship** means a manufacturer or wholesaler ships directly to the customer at the request of the seller (retailer or broker).

Transaction cost analysis is the process of assessing the overall cost of maintaining and finding new relationships. A firm will stay with a current partner if the cost of finding a new partner outweighs the benefits that can be obtained.

THINKING STRATEGICALLY

Consider the position of Ingram Micro, Inc. Explain why it exists in the channel by looking at the benefits it provides to the seller and the buyer. Determine the long-term viability of Ingram. Consider whether the manufacturers of software and hardware could bypass Ingram. Consider Ingram's customers. Recommend to Ingram whether or not it should start selling directly to the end user.

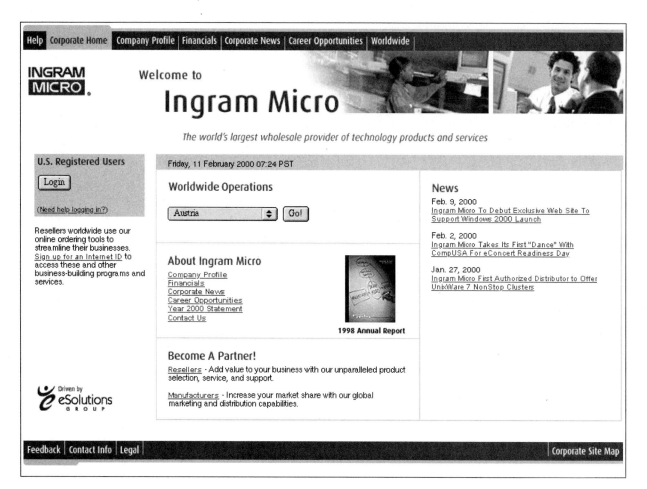

consumers' power

The consumer, or end user, is perhaps the biggest winner in the e-business distribution channel. Many consumers have limited alternative sources of supply because they are not geographically centered in large market areas. The Internet's ability to provide information increases the customer's power because the customer can become aware of a wider variety of providers. In addition, customers are able to voice their opinions on businesses and products at discussion sites and business sites. At Amazon, for example, customers can make comments on a book so others can see the "common man's" opinion.

A consumer in a local market area may wish to purchase a specific brand of automobile. That individual has traditionally been locked into using the local dealer, or dealers who are within a limited driving area. Now with Web-based searching systems and online sales systems, the local customer can shop the entire country (or world) for that automobile. There may be additional costs of having the auto shipped from one location to another, but lower prices (due to increases in negotiation power by the customer) will more than make up for the additional cost. The buyer can also obtain information, such as invoice costs, dealer costs, complaints, and repair notices for the brand of car, to aid in the purchase.

THINKING STRATEGICALLY

Visit Accompany's and Mercata's Web sites. Explain how these companies increase customer power. Find a product you would consider purchasing; compare this price with other Web sites. Decide if these sites give the purchasers a better price. Consider whether you would contact your friends and ask them to make a similar purchase to lower the price.

Channel Conflicts

A **channel conflict** exists when a company sells products to the same market through more than one distribution system. In some cases, manufacturers have refused to supply online sales businesses due to fear of channel conflicts. To avoid these conflicts, some manufacturers have set up e-commerce sites that offer different products online. Wal-Mart *(www.wal-mart.com)*, for example, sells products through its traditional stores, Sam's Clubs, and online. Each outlet carries different product lines to minimize cannibalization of other outlets.

Companies are undertaking a number of strategies to handle channel conflict problems.[34] Some companies will not take the risk of selling online and alienating their resellers. VF Corporation *(www.vfc.com)*, a maker of clothing products such as Lee and Wrangler jeans, decided that the $5 to $10 million it could make over e-commerce was not worth the risk of alienating the $5 billion in business it obtains through traditional channels of distribution. VF's Web sites are designed as destination sites offering information and entertainment. When customers want to buy, they are pushed to a vendor site.

A second approach is to offer products at the same price as retail outlets and then adding a shipping fee. This raises the price of distribution but allows the seller to reach a wider audience than would be available through the retail outlet alone. A third alternative is to press ahead with a commerce site. Many firms are offering product lines and services that distributors do not carry.

CASE 4.2

More Means Less

Customers can use e-businesses to gain power and lower prices. Accompany *(www.accompany.com)* and Mercata *(www.mercata.com)* have developed business models that allow consumers to pool their buying power to lower prices. The way these businesses operate is to offer a number of items for sale at volume discount prices. The closing date for the purchase is indicated, but as more people commit to buy, the price drops. If the potential buyers entice others to buy, they can actually help to lower the price. When the buying cycle is over, buyers receive an e-mail notifying them of the final price, which can never be higher than the price to which they first committed.[33]

CASE 4.3

Buying the Bug Online

Volkswagen Corporation is unsure how the Internet will impact sales of its car parts and accessories. Customers can go to the VW *(www.vw.com)* or Audi *(www.audi.com)* site to order luggage racks, wheel covers, and other accessories. VW has had to assure their dealers that they will not be cut out of the distribution chain. To decrease conflicts with its dealers, VW allows the local dealers to fulfill the order and be credited with the sale. VW also is setting up dealer Web pages.

VW and its dealerships consider a large percentage of their customers to be do-it-yourselfers. These individuals will use the Web site as an online catalog to order parts. Between August 1995 and January 1997, VW could trace 300 car sales to contacts made over the Web. This was second only to television advertising.[35]

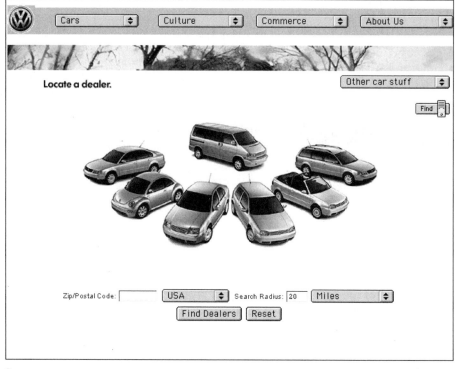

Source: www.vw.com

THINKING STRATEGICALLY

Consider the position of the car dealer. Determine why it should remain in the channel by looking at the benefits it offers manufacturers and customers. Recommend to Volkswagen whether or not to sell cars online. Decide whether or not the dealers should continue to receive credit. Speculate on the future, and determine the benefits the car dealers will need to provide in the future.

DEATH OF THE MIDDLEMAN

Disintermediation is the process of eliminating the middleman from the exchange process.

Middlemen are facing **disintermediation,** or elimination, of their role between the producer and the customer. This is having a strong impact on the traditional middleman. Many salespersons have made their living by leveraging both their knowledge of customers' needs and their access to goods and services. For some industries, new commerce models have the potential to replace salespeople. Industries as varied as real estate, stock brokerage, insurance sales, travel agencies, automotive sales, and order-taking sales could face extinction if they do not find a way to add value to the exchange process.[36]

The Middleman's New Role

The middlemen most likely to be hurt are those who do not add value to the exchange but are only go-betweens, information brokers, or order takers. Middlemen concerned about their careers should offer value to the exchange process. If they are only acting as a go-between for the buyer and the seller or only providing information to the client, they are in danger of being disintermediated. VARs, or value-added resellers, must make use of new technologies to shorten lead times and create greater efficiency.[37] Without adding value, information gatekeeping is not enough for survival.

TERMS AND CONCEPTS

KNOWLEDGE INTEGRATION

Breaking bulk *89*
Channel captain *93*
Channel conflict *101*
Channel functions *90*
Channels of
 distribution *88*
Creating an
 assortment *89*

Cybermediaries *92*
Disintermediation *102*
E-commerce security *98*
Facilitators *89*
Intermediaries *89*
Just-in-time (JIT)
 inventory *89*
Power *99*
Power dependency *99*

Relationship
 development *98*
Secure electronic
 transaction (SET) *96*
Smart cards *97*
Software wallet *97*
Transaction cost
 analysis *99*

CONCEPTS AND QUESTIONS FOR REVIEW

1. Explain what distribution channels do.
2. Describe why distribution channels evolve.
3. List the distribution channel functions, and explain why they must be performed.
4. Explain how e-business distribution functions operate.
5. Describe how the behavioral dimensions of channel functions differ under an e-business environment.
6. Consider relationship development in an e-business channel. Explain who loses power and who gains power.
7. Outline how channel conflicts can be controlled in an e-business channel.
8. Explain what disintermediation is and who will feel this effect.
9. Recommend what middlemen need to do to keep their job.

ACTIVE LEARNING

Exercise 4.1: Lassoing Jeans Online

Lee Jeans *(www.leejeans.com)* and Wrangler Jeans *(www.wrangler.com)* both push purchasing to other vendors. Arizona Jeans *(www.arizonajeans.com)* and Bugle Boy

Jeans *(www.bugleboy.com)* allow sales online. Levi Strauss *(http://store.us.levi. com/store/home.asp)* also allowed sales online, but then pulled back from this strategy. Visit each of the sites listed. Decide why these brands have adopted different strategies for using the Web in aiding distribution. Consider who owns the brands and how that may make a difference in the chosen strategy. Determine why Levi Stauss follows its strategy.

Exercise 4.2: Outlining a Distribution System

Use the Web to find a business that is engaging in e-commerce. Diagram its distribution process as shown below. Determine how each of its distribution functions is being performed.

1. Describe the role of the e-business in the distribution model.
2. Explain how each function is performed.
3. Determine if the cost of the product offered is different from the cost of the product available locally.
4. Do you see any channel conflicts that may occur with this system?

Exercise 4.3: Searching for E-Business Help

Some businesses may find it is more efficient to allow others to control some aspect of their distribution functions. These businesses may turn to commerce service providers for support. Evaluate each of the following commerce service providers and determine which would be best at providing support. Also determine whether or not each of the following companies facilitates the distribution function.

Example of an E-Business Distribution System

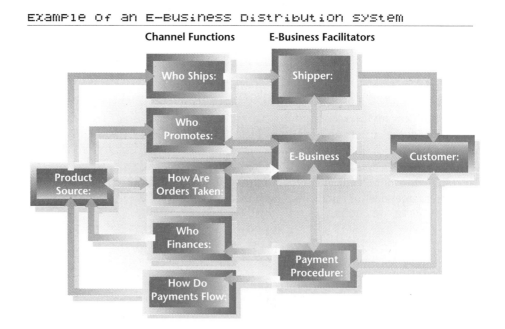

AT&T *(www.ipservices.att.com/products/index.html)*

IBM *(www.ibm.com/e-business)*

Microsoft *(www.microsoft.com/biz/solutions/ecommerce.htm)*

Yahoo! *(http://store.yahoo.com)*

WEB SEARCH — LOOKING ONLINE

SEARCH TERM:	Online Auto Sales	First 6 out of 449,213

Autobytel.com. Is a site where dealers bid to sell cars to individuals.
www.autobytel.com

AutoNation, Inc. Links new and used car dealers with car buyers. When potential buyers go to the AutoNation site, their information is sent to the dealer. AutoNation can provide services such as insurance and financing.
www.autonationdirect.com

Carprices.com. Provides pricing of options for vehicles.
www.carprices.com

Dealernet.com. Allows the comparison of auto prices between dealers.
www.dealernet.com

General Motors. Gives buyers the chance to find the vehicle they want and be able to check its availability through local dealer lots.
www.gmbuypower.com

Online Car Guide. Provides advice to car buyers on how to purchase automobiles over the Internet. Ford supports this site.
www.onlinecarguide.com

SEARCH TERM:	Shipping Companies	First 3 out of 267,342

FedEx. Is a popular shipping company that allows customers to track the items sent via tracking numbers.
www.fedex.com

United Parcel Service of America. Allows tracking of items that are sent via a tracking number.
www.ups.com

United States Postal Service. Provides special delivery items with a tracking number that is accessible via the Internet.
www.usps.com

SEARCH TERM:	Electronic Payments	First 7 out of 6,342

CyberCash Inc. Provides a new way to pay bills out of an individual's checking account.
www.cybercash.com

1Clickcharge. Describes a single click payment system for Internet purchases.
www.1clickcharge.com

Qpass. Allows the setting of digital wallets to facilitate purchases.
www.qpass.com

SET. Is the organization home page for the SET security protocols.
www.setco.org

Tellan Software. Is encrypted software that helps process credit-card transactions online.
www.tellan.com

Trivnet Inc. Allows purchases to be charged to the user's ISP bill.
www.trivnet.com/html/prod.html

VeriSign. Is a secure server system that ensures safety of online transactions.
www.verisign.com

REFERENCES

[1] Clinton Wilder, "Online Auto Sales Pick Up, Transforming an Industry," *Information Week,* February 9, 1998, p. 73.
[2] Clinton Wilder, "Online Auto Sales Pick Up, Transforming an Industry," *Information Week,* February 9, 1998, p. 73. and NUA Internet Surveys, "J.D. Power & Associates: 40 Percent of U.S. Car Buyers Shop Online," *<http://www.nua.ie/surveys/index.cgi?f=VS&art_id=905355022&rel=true>,* July 13, 1999.
[3] Alex Taylor III, "How to Buy a Car on the Internet," *Fortune,* March 4, 1996, pp. 164–168.
[4] Bob Wallace, "Car-Buying Site Could Help Put GM on the Road Again," *Computerworld,* March 8, 1999, p. 43.
[5] Robert McCarvey, "In the Driver's Seat," *Upside,* April 1999, pp. 66–72.
[6] Brian Caulfield, "Microsoft Has Muscle, But Car War Is Tough," *Internet World,* July 27, 1998, pp. 17, 20.
[7] Sari Kalin, "No Haggling, No Money Down," *CIO Web Business,* February 1, 1998, p. 12.

8 David Joachim, "Ford Rebuilds Extranet as Supplier Portal," *Internet Week,* May 17, 1999, pp. 1, 47; and Julia King, "GM Races Toward Internet Payoff," *Computerworld,* August 16, 1999, pp. 1, 89.

9 Brian S. Akre, "Carmakers Profit Selling Off-Lease On-Line," *Marketing News,* March 15, 1999, p. 11; and Bob Wallace, "GM Hits Bump in Used Car Sales," *Computerworld,* July 12, 1999, pp. 1, 16.

10 Karen Epper Hoffman, "Some Big Firms Elect to Add Commerce to Their Sites," *Internet World,* July 27, 1998, pp. 17, 20.

11 For a further discussion of transaction cost on channel evolution and development, see: Oliver E. Williamson, "The Economics of Organizations: The Transactional Cost Approach," *American Journal of Sociology,* vol. 87, no.3, 1981, pp. 548–577.

12 Wroe Alderson, "Factors Governing the Development of Marketing Channels," *Marketing Channels for Manufactured Products,* ed. Richard M. Clewett, Richard D. Irwin, Homewood, Illinois, 1954.

13 Robert Benjamin and Rolf Wigand, "Electronic Markets and Virtual Value Chains on the Information Superhighway," *Sloan Management Review,* Winter 1995, pp. 62–72.

14 Matrabarun Sarkar, Brian Butler, and Charles Steinfield, "Cybermediaries in Electronic Marketspace: Toward Theory Building," *Journal of Business Research,* vol. 41, 1998, pp. 215–221.

15 Clinton Wilder, "NetMarket Set to Grow," *Information Week,* December 8, 1997, p. 108.

16 Whit Andrews, "Online Malls Revisited: New Names, Strategies," *Web Week,* October 6, 1997, pp. 15, 21.

17 Monua Janah and Clinton Wilder, "Special Delivery," *Information Week,* October 27, 1997, pp. 42–60; and Warren Karlenzig and Steve Barth, "Will FedEx Reposition as Supply Chain Manager?" *Knowledge Management,* February 1999, p. 10.

18 John Evan Frook, "FedEx Extranet App Customizes Tracking," *Internet Week,* June 29, 1998, pp. 25–26.

19 John Evan Frook, "APIs Could Open Up Shipping Options for Web Storefronts," *Internet Week,* February 9, 1998, p. 9.

20 Clinton Wilder, "Chief of the Year," *Information Week,* December 22, 1997, pp. 43–48.

21 For more on this topic, see: Gene Koprowski, "Cache and Carry," *Business 2.0,* October 1998, pp. 24–26; and Amy K. Larsen, "Virtual Cash Gets Real," *Information Week,* May 31, 1999, pp. 46–58.

22 Christy Walker, "Digital Wallets," *Computerworld,* July 5, 1999, p. 65; and Patricia B. Seybold, "Wrap Up Your E-Wallets for the Holidays," *Business 2.0,* September 1999, p. 58.

23 For more information, see: Lydia Lee, "Getting SET for Electronic Commerce," *NewMedia,* September 22, 1997, p. 22; Lincoln D. Stein, "SET—Who Needs It?" *Web Techniques,* August 1998, pp. 10–14; Connie Guglielmo, "Set Ready to Go—Again," *Inter@ctive Week,* May 17, 1999, p. 8; and Ellen Messmer, "MasterCard, Visa Trade Strong Security for Ease of Use," *Network World,* March 22, 1999, p. 18.

24 Greg Dalton, "Online Payment Options Open Up for Asia," *Information Week,* August 16, 1999, p. 28; and Kimberly Weisul, "ECharge Takes a Run at MasterCard, Visa," *Inter@ctive Week,* August 16, 1999, p. 9.

25 For more information, see: Eric Brown, "Micropayments: No Small Change," *NewMedia,* June 23, 1997, pp. 30–37; Russ Jones, "Small Change," *Web Techniques,* August 1998, pp. 51–56; Whit Andrews, "Microsoft Bets $15M on Maker of Micropayment Technology," *Internet World,* March 15, 1999, pp. 13, 15; and Jim Kerstetter, "Micropayments Rebound," *PC Week,* March 22, 1999, p. 22.

[26] Janet Guyon, "Smart Plastic," *Fortune,* October 13, 1997, p. 56.

[27] Amy Leung, "Smart Cards Seem a Sure Bet," *InfoWorld,* March 8, 1999, pp. 37–38; Jim Kerstetter and Scott Berinato, "Smart Cards Get Hand," *PC Week,* September 1999, p. 6.

[28] Julekha Dash, "Uncle Sam Wants You! to Stop Writing Those Checks," *Software Magazine,* October 1997, pp. 69–71.

[29] Alan S. Kay, "Pay Dirt," *CIO Web Business,* November 1, 1998, pp. 36–45.

[30] Gregory Dalton, "E-Bills Arrive," *Information Week,* April 19, 1999, p. 18.

[31] Todd Spangler, "Stopping Digital Thieves in Real Time," *Web Week,* December 8, 1997, pp. 1, 44.

[32] Richard L. Brandt, "Ingram Micro: The Tech World's Warehouse," *Upside,* August 1998, pp. 94–98, 142–146; and John Evan Frook, "Serving Up E-Commerce," *Internet Week,* July 13, 1998, pp. 1, 52.

[33] Jennifer Tanaka, "The Never-Ending Search for the Lowest Price," *Newsweek,* June 7, 1999, p. 86; and Michael Grebb, "Riding the Buy Cycle," *Business 2.0,* July 1999, pp. 122–130.

[34] Sari Kalin, "Conflict Resolution," *CIO Web Business,* February 1, 1998, pp. 28–36.

[35] Bill Roberts, "Volkswagen Walks a Fine Line as It Prepares Commerce Site," *Web Week,* January 20, 1997, pp. 27, 29.

[36] For more information, see: E. B. Baatz, "Will the Web Eat Your Job?" *Webmaster,* May/June, 1996, pp. 40–45; and John Berry, "Death of a Middleman," *Internet World,* March 1997, pp. 39–41.

[37] Howard Anderson, "http://www.you're_fired.com," *Sales & Field Force Automation,* April 1997, pp. 38–46; and Clinton Wilder, "Middlemen Beware?" *Information Week,* October 20, 1997, pp. 94–95.

Chapter 5

E-Business Value Strategies

This chapter explores seven e-business strategies that are creating value for customers. Implementing these new strategies in business models requires more than simply applying technology to the business system; it also implies new ways of developing relationships with customers, employees, and suppliers.

Increased competition and consumer access to information are having a major impact on the ability of businesses to maintain prices. Consumers use the Internet to gather information about products and to find alternative suppliers. While reducing prices to customers, this is placing pressure on older business models. Many businesses see the Internet as an alternative channel for serving customers. Businesses attempting to add these new strategies to their business models must determine whether they will develop their own e-business systems or use commerce service providers as facilitators of value creation. Future competitiveness depends on how efficiently businesses can deliver utility to their customers. E-commerce is growing overseas, but structural problems exist that must be overcome in order for these new business models to develop.

1. Explain the seven strategies e-businesses are using to create value for customers.
2. Compare and contrast how e-commerce is being used as a strategic tool by e-retailers and traditional retailers.
3. Perform a benefit analysis of alternative sales channels.
4. Discuss how digital communication adds value to a business.
5. Describe how the delivery of services is changing because of new technologies.
6. Explain how the business process is changing through the use of the Internet, extranets, and EDI systems.
7. Discuss how a market-of-one strategy will impact businesses.
8. Outline how auctions are used to facilitate commerce.
9. Describe the impact of e-business strategies on pricing.
10. Explain the determinants of hosting the technology required to implement the e-business strategies.
11. List the limitations to international e-commerce.

What's Old Is New Again in Grocery Shopping

Once upon a time, small grocery stores could be found conveniently down the street from most homes. Homemakers would call the grocer, who would then prepare groceries for pickup. Butchers would pack meats to the buyer's specifications. If needed, the delivery boy would place the groceries in his bicycle basket and deliver them directly to a home. Most of these small grocers closed when supermarkets opened and offered greater variety at lower prices. Improved roads, multicar homes, larger refrigerators and freezers, and a growing assortment of prepackaged food enticed homemakers to shop at these supermarkets. Today grocery shoppers have many alternatives, including hypermarkets and convenience stores. The World Wide Web is offering opportunity for change in this industry by offering access to more products than found in grocery stores, while allowing the shopper to order from home and have products delivered. Consumers, who have considerable experience shopping for package goods, are reacting to offers of greater convenience, lower prices, and faster service.[1]

Most consumers do not see the changes occurring behind the checkout counter, but information technology is having a major impact on the overall food industry. Scanner data is used to track the profiles of shoppers to create databases of information to meet consumers' needs. Extranets link sellers with suppliers by providing constant inventory data online.

Peapod (www.peapod.com) works with local grocers to develop a business model that offers groceries to online shoppers. Peapod allows the buyer to select groceries online, which are then pulled from local grocery stores and delivered to the buyer's home. The benefits to the customer include convenience, selection, and time savings. In 1997 Peapod had over 20,000 users in two cities. By 1999 it had 100,000 users in eight cities.

Webvan *(www.webvan.com)* has adopted a different sales model. It offers a full-service online grocery and drugstore with free delivery. Webvan is lowering the cost of grocery delivery by developing distribution centers that are as large as 18 conventional grocery stores. These act as hubs for home delivery. Webvan's San Francisco Bay service offers more than 350 types of cheese, 700 different wines, more than 300 varieties of fresh fruits and vegetables, and locally produced goods, as well as traditional packaged goods. Prices average 5 percent less than those in local grocery stores. Customers create personalized lists that allow shoppers to complete their grocery shopping in just a few minutes. Webvan can create and deliver chef-prepared meals. Its personnel is trained to provide a high level of customer service. Webvan is developing 26 new distribution centers across the United States.[2]

Priceline's *(www.priceline.com)* WebHouse Club allows grocery shoppers to name their own prices before they shop at participating supermarkets and grocery stores. Independent grocers, such as Schnucks Markets *(www.schnucks.com/home_shopping)* in St. Louis, are being forced to compete by developing their own Web sites to foster customer relationships and increase sales.[3]

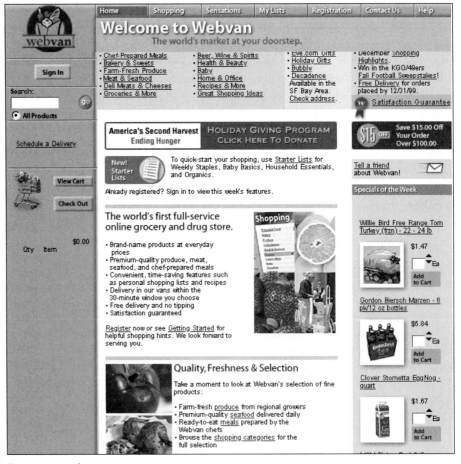

Source: www.webvan.com

The grocery industry in the United States has realized that new business models are threatening current practices. The Grocery Manufacturers of America *(www.gmabrands. com)* is working on an extranet-based trading network to cut costs and lower errors when handling the association's $450 billion worth of transactions.[4]

THINKING STRATEGICALLY

Evaluate your grocery shopping habits. Determine how often you purchase the same products. Consider if you would trust a grocer to pick out your meats, fruits, and vegetables. On your next visit to a brick and mortar grocery, determine which aspects of grocery shopping could be automated. Evaluate the business model for a traditional grocery and determine where its competitive advantage lies. Estimate the expenses that a business can save by moving grocery shopping online.

....

"The newest innovations, which we label information technologies, have begun to alter the manner in which we do business and create value, often in ways not readily foreseeable even five years ago."

Alan Greenspan, Chairman, Federal Reserve Board
May 6, 1999[5]

CREATING VALUE

Businesses create value for their customers by providing quality goods and services at acceptable prices.[6] A **business model** that provides more benefits to its customers and/or sells at a lower price will take market share away from competitors. Information technology–based e-businesses are leveraging new technologies to gain competitive advantages. Seven strategies have emerged that help e-businesses use technology to develop business models that provide value to customers:

> A commerce or business model is the basic process by which a business obtains its inventory, produces its good or service, and delivers to its customer.

1. **Online purchasing strategy.** Allows buying and selling of products and information on the Internet and other online services.
2. **Digital communications strategy.** Allows the delivery of digital information, products, services, or payments online.
3. **Service strategy.** Allows reduced cost of services, improves quality of services, and increases speed of services.
4. **Business process strategy.** Allows automation of business transactions and workflows.
5. **Market-of-one strategy.** Allows developing of products for a single customer with close to the same costs as mass production.
6. **Auction strategy.** Allows automation of bidding for products or customers online.
7. **Pricing strategy.** Allows businesses to pursue market share by selling at low prices or giving away products and services for free.[7]

Many businesses combine a number of these strategies in developing business models. Figure 5.1 illustrates how Amazon used all of these business model strategies at its site.

These new strategies are forcing industries to restructure past practices to maintain competitiveness. The Internet is emerging as an alternative sales strategy. Pure-play Internet companies are gaining advantages in cost, but brick and mortar businesses that move online may have advantages in brand name and the ability to service accounts. Creating value requires an understanding of what customers consider important when they purchase a product. Research by

Figure 5.1 Amazon's Site

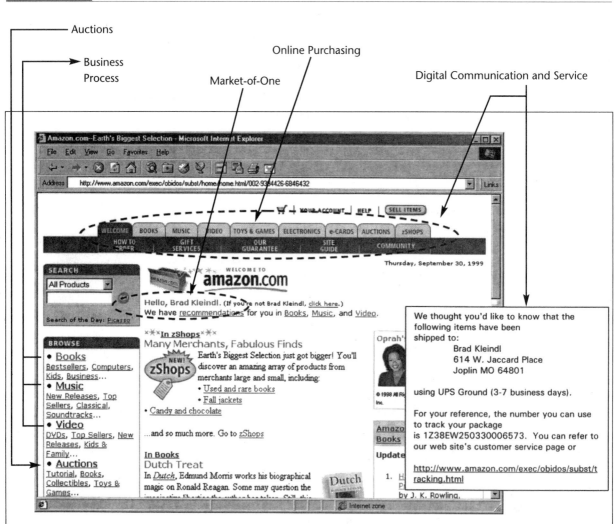

Nielsen/NetRatings indicates that when individuals purchase online, speed, quality, and value are more important than low prices. Personalized sites are also better at influencing individuals to buy.[8] As customers realize additional value to purchasing online, sales shift from traditional channels to electronic channels. The change in competitive business models for many industries has been much more rapid than was expected, and the amount of sales created through the use of these new models may well exceed expectations.

ONLINE PURCHASING STRATEGY

E-commerce is the process of allowing Web-based technologies to facilitate commerce or trade. E-commerce can be retail, it can be between an e-business and an end user, or it can be used for business-to-business transactions; all of these are **online purchasing strategies.** An e-business could be the producer of the product, as in the case of Dell, or an intermediary that coordinates the distribution process, such as Peapod.com. These distinctions are becoming blurred as manufacturers bypass established distributors and retailers and sell directly to the end users.

E-Retailing

In 1998 retail e-commerce **(e-retailing)** reached $7.8 billion, accounting for only around 0.5 percent of total retail sales. By 1999 online retail sales were over $20 billion; this figure is expected to reach $108 billion by 2003, but this will still be only about 6 percent of retail sales. Consumer retail purchases entail a rich and complex buying process. Consumers will often spend considerable time evaluating information, touching or sampling products, evaluating services, and asking friends and/or opinion leaders about what and where to purchase. The introduction of e-retailing will not necessarily result in an increase in overall retail sales; instead, sales are likely to shift among various alternative **sales channels.** Traditional retailers, as well as pure-play Internet retailers, see that consumers are using the Internet to collect information, compare prices, and discuss products through e-mail or online chat and discussion groups. Developing an e-retail presence is becoming important to traditional retailers because of how much the Internet is used as a channel for information collection and purchase.[9]

Sales channels are the models that businesses use to sell to their customers. These could include brick and mortar outlets, catalogs, direct marketing, or e-commerce.

A number of brick and mortar retailers are using the Internet to enhance their present business models. Sears is currently selling appliances online. Its Web site *(www2.sears.com)* allows customers to collect information and make purchases. In 1999, the site received over 1 million visitors a month; many customers used the site for collecting information and then visited a physical store to purchase. In 1999, Sears had problems with returns; customers could not return online purchases because individual store managers had those returns counted against their overall sales. The Web site also allows vendors to check product sales and inventory levels.[10]

Other retailers such as the Gap *(www.gap.com)*, Macy's *(www.macys.com)*, Home Depot *(www.homedepot.com)*, Office Depot *(www.officedepot.com)*, and Wal-Mart *(www.wal-mart.com)* are selling online. Catalog retailers such as L.L. Bean *(www.llbean.com)* and Land's End *(www.landsend.com)* use the Internet to increase their catalog sales. Land's End enhanced its services by offering its phone services linked to Web page use. Williams-Sonoma operates both the Williams-Sonoma *(www.williamssonoma.com)* and Pottery Barn *(www.potterybarn.com)* stores. Williams-Sonoma's stores receive 50 million visits a year, and it has a database of 19 million customers. These well-known brand names are leveraging their existing supply chain and purchasing power to compete online. This is placing pressure on pure-play Internet businesses.[11]

By 1999, 97 percent of large businesses were connected to the Internet in some way; only 21 percent of smaller businesses were. Of those, 33 percent of large corporations conducted sales over the Net while only 4 percent of small businesses were selling online.[12] Venator Group *(www.venatorgroup.com)* did not want to sit back and wait so it had commerce sites developed for its Foot Locker, Kids Foot Locker, Lady Foot Locker, Champs Sports, and Eastbay stores. The goal of these sites was not just to engage in sales but to also create **destination sites.** These sites include interactive games, consumer surveys, contests, online chats with professional athletes, feature articles, and a full array of athletic products.[13]

A destination site is a Web site that is designed to entice the visitor to return over and over. This requires including extras, such as games, chats, contents, or new information, and any other content that the targeted audience may desire.

Pure-Play Internet Businesses

According to a 1999 study by the National Retail Federation *(www.nrf.com)*, the top 10 retail e-commerce sites were eBay, Amazon.com, Dell, Buy.com, Onsale.com, Gateway.com, Egghead.com, Barnesandnoble.com, CDNow, and AOL. Travel sites and financial services were not evaluated. Of the top 100 e-commerce sites, 50 used the Internet as their primary sales channel, 21 were traditional retailers, and 21 were catalog/mail-order retailers. The most successful sites had established offline brands and had proven ability to provide customer service.[14]

The National Retail Federation study indicated that the top five online sellers were pure-play Internet retailers. Although the auction business eBay moved the greatest amount of product, eBay only acted as an agent in the sales process. Amazon.com is perhaps the best-recognized example of a pure-play Internet-based retailer. Amazon.com's founder chose books as his initial product because he believed they were a product that individuals did not need to see, feel, and touch before purchasing. Amazon.com has added product lines that consumers feel comfortable shopping for without having physical interaction. Customer acceptance of Amazon.com's online shopping model will depend on the value that Amazon.com can deliver to its customers. Table 5.1 outlines the benefits that consumers can find with online bookstores versus other booksellers, and indicates the competitiveness of the online seller.

A bookstore such as Amazon.com is not designed to replace more traditional booksellers or superstores such as Barnes & Noble. A customer shopping in a brick

Table 5.1 Benefit Analysis for Amazon.com

Benefits	Amazon.com	Mall Bookstore (e.g., Waldons, B. Daltons)	Superstores (e.g., Barnes & Noble, Borders)
Number of books	2.5 million +	70,000	175,000+
Discounts on books	Percent off all titles (customer pays shipping)	Discounts on selected titles	
Ability to browse by topics	Online databases with links to topic areas	Books placed in topic sections	
Consumers' access to books	Average 2–3 days	Immediate	
Access to information about books	Immediate—online	Consumers browsing or asking for help	
Ability to converse with authors	Online through discussion groups or e-mail	Rarely, except for book signings	
Shipping of gift books	Handled online	Done by customers	
Other relationship development tools	Personalization Database recommendations based on past purchases E-mail comments	Other stores for customers to visit	Coffee shops
Interaction with customers	E-mail links to service personnel Chat rooms with other customers	Face-to-face sales representatives	Face-to-face sales representatives

Source: Anthony Bianco, "Virtual Bookstores Start to Get Real," *Business Week,* October 27, 1997, pp. 146–148.

and mortar store may be looking for a different type of shopping experience, but this alternative sales channel pressured a number of book retailers to follow Amazon.com's example. Barnes & Noble *(www.barnesandnoble.com)* launched its own Web site offering many of the same advantages as Amazon.

E-commerce has already had a major impact on a number of consumer and business-to-business industries. The largest category for sales is currently in the PC hardware and software industry. In 1999 online sales exceeded $52 billion, and are expected to reach $410 billion by 2003. Hardware and software buyers may be the first adopters in the purchase process, but as individuals become more familiar and comfortable with purchasing online, other product categories will grow. For example, travel-related sales, such as airline tickets and car and hotel reservations, reached over $12 billion in 1999 and are expected to top $67.4 billion by the year 2003.[15]

E-retailing is expanding around the world. A Japanese study by Fujitsu Research indicated that 65 percent of respondents that use the Internet had experience purchasing online. The reasons given for making online purchases included access to a wide range of products, lower prices, knowledge of the store, and seller-provided ordering and confirmation information. Books and magazines were popular with both men and women. Men purchased more software and computer goods; women purchased food, beverages, and clothing.[16] Across the rest of Asia, e-commerce sales are expected to reach $1.3 billion by 2003.[17]

Table 5.2 Niche E-Retailers

Business	Site	Target Market	Product Offering
Tavolo	www.tavolo.com	Individuals who desire gourmet and specialty cooking items and information	This site offers an extensive line of specialty cooking items, gourmet chef advice, and recipes.
Violet	www.violet.com	Busy, professional women and men who are ages 25 to 55	This site lists six categories of gifts: house, office, identity, thanks, kids, and bath. The items are considered to be "authentic chic."[a]
Justballs	www.justballs.com	Individuals and institutions that need unique or specialty balls and ball-related items	This site carries a narrowly focused line of products. It has a comprehensive assortment of balls and ball-related products. It also offers expertise and information on all types of balls.[b]
Another Universe	www.anotheruniverse.com	Males with an average age of 28 who have higher-than-average incomes	This site emphasizes information on television, movies, comic books, and collectibles to hold viewers' interest.[c]

Sources: [a] Evantheia Schibsted, "Nouveau Riche Media," *Business 2.0,* July 1999, pp. 25–26.
[b] Andrew Marlatt, "Web Merchant Gets the Ball Rolling," *Internet World,* March 1, 1999, pp. 10–11.
[c] Rachel K. Perez, "Tapping a Market Driven by Mania," *Internet World,* July 13, 1999, pp. 17, 26.

Niche E-Retailers

Given that established retailers and brand-name e-retailers have advantages in e-commerce, is there room for smaller e-retailers? Many small e-retailers have set up shop on the Internet. These e-retailers typically target narrow market segments with clearly differentiated offerings. Table 5.2 lists four e-retailing sites, their target markets, and their product offerings.

Successful **niche e-retailers** can offer an extensive product line and add expertise and advice that cannot be found in traditional stores. However, they need to develop brand names and establish credibility with their customers if they are to succeed.[18]

CASE 5.1

A Prescription for Success?

Pharmacy sales may seem like an ideal market for retail e-commerce. An aging baby-boomer population and a more health-conscious marketplace are expected to push retail and prescription pharmaceutical sales to over $170 billion in the United States and over $406 billion worldwide by 2002. Online pharmacies promise e-mail contact with pharmacists **24/7/52.** They will provide information on products and drug interactions. They can deliver products overnight and can provide anonymity for individuals who may be embarrassed to purchase in a regular pharmacy. To generate profits, online pharmacies must be able to sell prescriptions and over-the-counter drugs.

There are a number of problems that pure-play Internet pharmacies must overcome. Pharmaceutical sales regulations differ among countries and states. Large offline competitors can engage in deep discounts because they have diverse product lines to maintain overall profits. Brick and mortar competitors such as Rite Aid and Walgreen have established brand names and existing customer databases and are offering online e-commerce and services.[19]

THINKING STRATEGICALLY

Consider the types of products that individuals usually purchase at a pharmacy. Determine the importance of receiving that product immediately versus waiting until the next day. Decide how important it is to talk to a pharmacist about products purchased at a pharmacy. Visit an online pharmacy. Compare the services it offers to what can be found at a brick and mortar store. Determine whether consumers' purchasing patterns would differ if they were buying products on a continuing basis. For example, if an individual was permanently on a heart medicine, would he/she order that online and have it delivered to his or her home? Speculate on the future of online pharmacies.

24/7/52 or 24/7 indicates that the business is open 24 hours a day, 7 days a week, 52 weeks a year.

DIGITAL COMMUNICATIONS STRATEGY

Individuals may use the Internet to collect information about a product before making a purchase, but the Internet, using a **digital communications strategy,** can also deliver information-based products directly to the customer. **Digital products** such as multimedia entertainment, programs, online information services, published information, music, video, or any other digital content can be transferred over the Internet. A number of businesses are currently taking advan-

Source: www.drugstore.com

tage of the Internet's ability to transfer digital content by setting up online versions of newspapers, magazines, or other media sites.

Perhaps the greatest advantage of online content is the lower cost involved in transfer and delivery. Just like online advertising, electronic content allows for a publish-once, read-many-times environment. This allows existing content developers to reach a wider audience and opens the door to smaller firms that provide content at low start-up costs. If sold, digital content is usually purchased on a per-time-period subscription or per-use basis. Pay content sites generally target individuals who have a high need for information. *The Wall Street Journal Interactive Edition (www.wsj.com)* has been able to sign paying subscribers to its services. At *The Wall Street Journal* site, subscribers access large amounts of infomation by company and industry. Other online publishers, such as *Business Week (www.businessweek.com),* or online-only electronic magazines (or e-zines), such as *Slate (www.slate.com),* have followed the subscriber model.[20]

Not all digital communications sites require payments. Newspapers, such as the *New York Times (www.nytimes.com),* and information sites, such as CNN *(www.CNN.com),* MSNBC *(www.MSNBC.com),* and ABC-News *(www.ABC-News.com),* offer digital content on an ongoing basis. These sites follow radio and broadcast television models and obtain revenue through advertising. They also play a role in supporting and enhancing the associated traditional media.[21]

Business-to-business sales of digital content also exist online. Lawyers in small offices who can't afford to purchase legal reference books or CD-ROMs can obtain the same information online from legal publisher Matthew Bender *(www.bender.com).* Lawyers pay a subscription fee or pay-per-view. The system also used push technology to send summaries of requested content to the lawyer's office.[22]

Some products that have traditionally been purchased as tangible products, such as music CDs, are available as digital content. As early as 1997, Todd Rundgren sold directly to his customers over the Web. For $25 a year, fans could down-

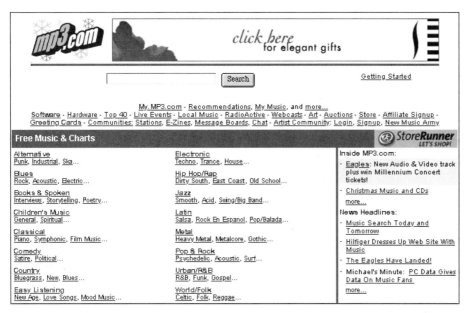

Source: www.mp3.com

load music files; for $40 a year, they obtained music files, news, and two hard CDs.[23] Sending music digitally over the Internet is currently available using an MP3 format.

THINKING STRATEGICALLY

Determine the advantages and disadvantages of using MP3 for the consumer. Consider the advantages and disadvantages of this format for the music industry. Compare and contrast those advantages and disadvantages, and speculate on the future of MP3. It is projected that within the next 5 years an entire movie will be downloaded in 20 minutes or less. Speculate on how this will affect the movie and video rental industries.

SERVICE STRATEGY

The **service strategy** impacts two areas. The first is in supporting individuals or businesses that specialize in providing services to the customer, including educational

CASE 5.2

The Market Wants Its MP3

MP3 is becoming the de facto standard for music delivery over the Internet. The music recording industry sees this delivery system as a threat to copyrighted sales. The Recording Industry Association of America *(www.riaa.com)* lost a lawsuit against Diamond's Multimedia's *(www.diamondmm.com)* Rio portable MP3 player. With portable devices such as the Rio, individuals can download music over the Web for later playback. This process has allowed unknown bands and musicians to use Web sites such as MP3.com *(www.mp3.com)* to reach audiences. Sales of playback devices are expected to exceed 32 million units by 2003.

The music industry has conceded that it must be able to deliver music online. One plan is to allow individuals to purchase and record information online, then limit their ability to transfer the music to other persons or computers. Another procedure will place codes that prevent copying into the music files. Sales of music online are projected to be over $1.1 billion by 2003.[24]

institutions, physicians, banks, realtors, insurance agents, and many others. The second service strategy includes enhancing the service component of a business by meeting customer service needs before, during, and after the sale. This might include answering questions about a product and how it is used or how it fits a specific purpose. Very importantly, it also includes handling any problems that may occur after the sale.

Service Industries

Use of traditional business models by service industry businesses is being threatened. Service businesses are typically characterized as having:

▶ **Intangibility.** It is often difficult to see or feel what a service business does. For example, the education that an individual receives is intangible. After years of college or university education, a student sees only a diploma.

▶ **Perishability.** Services often cannot be placed in inventory or stored. If a movie theater shows a film to empty seats, it loses the chance to receive revenue from that showing.

▶ **Inseparability.** A service cannot be easily separated from its provider. Medical services typically require that the patient be in direct contact with the physician.

▶ **Variability.** Services can often vary in their quality of delivery because of the human interface that is required.

A number of service industries are changing business models to take advantage of e-business practices. This is allowing these services to meet customers' needs more efficiently. Table 5.3 outlines the characteristics of services and how technology can be used to change service delivery.

The banking industry is in the process of changing new business models. In May 1995, Wells Fargo *(www.wellsfargo.com)* became the first bank to allow its customers to access account information over the Web. Wells Fargo added to its services by allowing customers to check balances, transfer funds, stop payments on checks, receive low balance warnings, and access information from the bank's economists.[25] By 1999, Wells Fargo had over 1 million customers using online services. [26]

Online-only banks can obtain a national presence without the cost of brick and mortar. They are also able to reduce operating costs because they do not have large staffing requirements. Bank transaction costs that require tellers can cost $1; online transactions cost as low as 1 cent. NetBank *(www.netbank.com)*, an online-only bank, offers many of the same services as physical banks, such as checking, money market deposits, CDs, home and business loans, and investing. Because of its reduced overhead, it attempts to provide higher returns on deposits and lower fees for services.

Many brick and mortar banks have embraced e-business to overcome the threats posed by online-only banks. Citigroup *(www.citigroup.com)* has set a **stretch goal** of increasing its customer base from 100 million customers in five

Stretch goals are goals that may seem impossible to reach. A stretch goal focuses a business on what it would like to achieve and motivates employees to be creative.

Table 5.3 Technology's Impact on Service

Service Characteristic	Technology Leveraging	Industry Example
Intangibility	The Internet enables buyers to directly compare products and services offered online, allowing them to search for the greatest value.	HSH Associates *(www.hsh.com)* offers information on mortgage rates. Quotesmith *(www.quotesmith.com)* and 4Insurance.com *(www.4insurance.com)* allow individuals to obtain quotes from multiple carriers.
Perishability	Digital information can be stored and delivered as needed. Online services do not perish; they can be created as needed by the user. Online sales systems also can fill unused capacity for transport companies such as airlines.	National Public Radio *(www.npr.org)* stores its radio programs for individuals to download and play at their leisure. Priceline.com *(www.priceline.com)* sells excess capacity for airlines.
Inseparability	Real estate buyers can use the Web to view homes and take virtual walkthroughs. The medical industry is using the Web to deliver services directly to the user's home computer. Retailers are providing shopping services online.	WebMD *(www.webmd.com)* provides information on medical issues. Nordstrom *(www.nordstrom.com)* has a personal shopper to suggest products for customers.
Variability	Databases and standardized procedures can remove the variability of service delivery.	Amazon, Dell, and many other companies use e-mail, FAQs, and other technology to standardize services.

states and 57 countries to 1 billion customers by 2012. To reach this goal, it plans to use the Internet for Citibank *(www.citibank.com)* online banking and use e-commerce services for other financial services such as insurance, brokerage services, and investment banking.[27] Small- and medium-sized banks are responding to the threat from online-only banks and large banks with vast resources by leveraging e-business technologies. From 1998 to 1999, the number of banks offering online services increased by more than 100 percent in eight countries in Western Europe. Most of this growth was caused by smaller banks placing their services online to compete with larger banks. [28]

Banks provide a number of services that are being targeted by niche businesses. Companies such as CheckFree *(www.checkfree.com)* allow businesses to post their bills online and have customers make transfers without writing a check. The benefits to customers include taking less time to pay their bills and having their businesses receive reduced transaction costs by not handling checks.[29] Banks are following this lead by providing their own online bill-paying services.

All types of loans—auto, student, installment, mortgage—are moving online. Online mortgage companies are already impacting the lending industry. In 1998, $4.2 billion in mortgage loans were transacted online. This was a small percent of the $1.5 trillion mortgage market, but by 2003 it is expected that one in four mortgage loans will be secured online. The majority of these loans may be through institutions such as banks that have large employee bases to handle the complex loan applications. [30]

Customer Relationship Management

Customer relationship management systems combine software and management practices to serve the customer from order through delivery and after-sales service. Enhancing customer service is rated by IT managers as the number one method to gain competitive advantage, followed by improving internal business processes.[31] The ability of the Internet to offer almost instant access to information makes it an ideal solution for offering product support services, with the advantage of reducing costs. A typical service transaction with a live call agent can cost $5, a voice response system can cost 50 cents, and a web-based system can cost only a few pennies. Technologies to serve customers include e-mail, knowledge bases on customers' service needs, personalization of automated responses, wizards that allow individuals to ask questions, and auto-response e-mail. Web-based consumer service systems can also track individuals' actions online and offer help if it appears that someone is having a problem. Cisco *(www.cisco.com)* has estimated that it saved $550 million in its customer care division and increased customer satisfaction by leveraging the Internet. Cisco allows its customers to engage in real-time question-and-answer sessions with intelligence agents. It personalizes information for its customers, and customers can use Internet telephony systems to interact with live customer representatives.[32] Companies such as Michelin of North America *(www.michelin.com)* have deployed extranets to serve the same function as sales support staff. Michelin's 280 dealerships are able to look up inventory, order tires, check order status, and obtain answers to questions.[33] National Semiconductor *(www.national.com)* posted detailed descriptions for over 30,000 products, allowing its customers access to information 24 hours a day.[34] Table 5.4 outlines the best practices being used by businesses that focus on customer relationship management.

Although some companies are leveraging technology to deliver service online, many e-commerce companies are negligent at online contact and response. The American Customer Satisfaction Index *(www.bus.umich.edu/research/nqrc/ acsi.html)* dropped 4.4 percent in the United States from 1994 to 1997 even though spending on customer service applications increased from $200 million to $1.1 billion.[35]

BUSINESS PROCESS STRATEGY

Using **business process strategies,** business-to-business transactions, including one-time transactions using e-commerce systems or auctions, use the same techniques as business-to-consumer e-businesses. The transaction costs for businesses to find appropriate buyers and sellers can be high, and businesses often have an

Table 5.4 Providing Service Online

Best Practice	Site	Technology Leverage
Respond quickly	Be able to respond to customers within 6 hours if possible (but definitely within 24 hours).	Knowledge bases and intelligence agents can provide instant feedback.
Provide link to inventory	Be sure products are available for delivery.	Use extranets and inventory databases linked to e-commerce software.
Use automatic order confirmation	Automatically send confirmations through e-mail to customers, giving confirmation numbers and routing numbers.	Confirmation can be sent from databases through automated e-mail systems.
Furnish information	Provide product, security, and shipping information.	Information delivery can be designed into the Web site. The use of FAQs (frequently asked questions) allows self-service.
Provide alternative means of contact	800-number phone lines allow customers to place orders, inquire about orders, or receive service information as an alternative to Internet use.	Chat systems can be a lower-cost alternative to phone systems. IP telephony can also be used if customers possess the technology.
Avoid extra fees	If offline businesses do not charge for service support or gift wrapping, these should not be charged online.	Lower costs available through the Internet should allow services to be delivered at low or no cost.
Use customer response specialists	Use "live" individuals to support automated service transactions.	Customer response can be facilitated by chats or through the use of intelligence agents or wizards.

Source: Aileen Crowley, "Order? What Order?" *PC Week,* March 8, 1999, pp. 82–86; and Justin Hibbard, "Web Service: Ready or Not," *Information Week,* November 16, 1998, pp. 18–20.

incentive to develop long-term relationships. To lower the costs of these relationships, businesses are being linked through extranets and supply-chain management systems. The Gartner Group has projected that the value of worldwide Internet-based business-to-business transactions will be greater than $7 trillion by 2004.[36] Table 5.5, on the next page, indicates projected business-to-business sales.

Business-to-Business E-Commerce

The business-to-business model of e-commerce allows businesses to sell to other businesses online. The Internet also enables businesses in narrowly defined vertical markets to engage in e-commerce. VerticalNet, Inc. *(www.verticalnet.com)* offers a

Table 5.5 Projected Business-to-Business Sales

Category	1999 Sales (billions of U.S. dollars)	Projected for 2003 (billions of U.S. dollars)
Computers and electronics	50	395
Utilities	15	170
Petrochemicals	10	178
Motor vehicles	9	213
Aerospace and defense	7	38
Paper and office products	3	65
Shipping and warehousing	3	62
Food and agriculture	3	54
Consumer products	3	52
Other	5	105

Source: Zorawar Biri Singh, "Super Markets," *Business 2.0,* March 1999, pp. 80–85.

Web site that facilitates vertical trading communities. VerticalNet allows buyers and sellers from around the world to find Web sites that match business and professional interests.[37]

The office supply industry has rapidly moved to business-to-business e-commerce. Large suppliers such as Office Depot *(www.officedepot.com),* Office Max *(www.officemax.com),* and Staples *(www.staples.com)* are facing a number of **pure-play** Internet-based companies. Office supplies are small and easy to ship, and buyers often know what they want before they buy. Businesses are expected to place more than 30 percent of their office supply purchases online because of the convenience and lower costs of ordering.[38]

Mack Tilling moved from waiting on tables to building a food service intermediary e-business. The business he started, Instill Corporation *(www.instill.com),* brings together restaurants and restaurant suppliers. Restaurants can order supplies from aprons to food products. In December 1997, the business processed over $21 million in orders. Growth was so rapid that this privately held company was expected to reach sales of $1 billion for 1998. By 1999 the company served over

6,900 businesses. Instill Corporation, as the middleman, takes a percentage of the sales. Restaurants typically work with a number of different suppliers and must track orders through paper-and-pencil systems. With Instill, customers control their ordering system and save order-processing time by 50 percent with increased inventory control.[39]

Supply-Chain Management and Extranets

Information technology can be used to link a firm and the members of its **supply chain** to facilitate the flow of purchasing. This increases efficiency in the logistical process, sales and marketing, manufacturing, and finance, as well as to other parties inside or outside the firm involved in the distribution chain, product development, or manufacturing. A study by Giga Information Group *(www.gigaweb.com)* projected that worldwide savings could reach $1.25 trillion from using extranets and other IP-based communications systems used to streamline business processes.[40] Extranet supply-chain management systems link vendors to facilitate ordering; provide marketing and product information; automate inventory supply processes and enable **JIT (just-in-time)** inventory and automated restocking systems; and allow for interbusiness communication. JIT is a business process strategy that minimizes inventory requirements by delivering products just in time for use. Businesses that are best-in-class in using this technology can gain a 45 percent cost advantage over their median competitors. A $500 million company can receive savings of between $15 million and $35 million in supply-chain costs by controlling inventory levels and materials costs. It is also able to meet customers' delivery dates better than competitors. Oracle *(www.oracle.com)* restructured its business process to automate its supply chain, link with suppliers, and provide online sales help. Oracle expected to cut $1 billion from the company's operating expenses and increase gross margins from 20 percent to 30 percent within 18 months.[41]

Supply-chain management is a strategic tool for a firm's competitiveness because it allows the firm to lower costs, serve customers better, and speed up cycle times. By implementing supply-chain management systems, industry leaders are able to outperform their rivals in a number of measures. Some businesses have been able to cut the average number of days inventory is held by 60 percent. Businesses linked through extranets have increased production rates by 20 percent in less than two weeks; nonintegrated firms have needed months. Efficient businesses can meet customers' delivery dates 96 percent of the time versus 83 percent for inefficient businesses.[42] General Electric *(www.ge.com)* has required its suppliers to go online. This has increased GE's productivity, allowing its purchasing agents an extra week each month for strategic planning; reduced overall material costs by 5 percent to 20 percent (depending on category and vendor); reduced order-processing time from seven days to one day; and reduced cycle time by 50 percent to 60 percent.[43]

The root of **electronic supply-chain management** is found in **electronic data interchange (EDI)** systems. EDI technology that allows information to

> The **supply chain** is the network of suppliers and customers for goods, services, or information used from the point of origin to final consumption.

flow over telecommunications lines is more than 20 years old. EDI systems were adopted by a small percentage of larger businesses, but they were often based on proprietary software and network systems. This usually resulted in higher overall costs. The growth of the Internet and its open platform have led a larger number of companies to offer data interchange systems over the Internet backbone. Wal-Mart *(www.wal-mart.com)* expected to have its more than 2,000 trading partners linked through Internet-based EDI systems by the end of 1999.[44]

Extranets use IP standards to route information between a business and its external partners. This allows for more than just controlling the supply chain. The largest push for extranets inside corporations comes from marketers and their customers because it is seen as a means of tightening relationships between firms by improving communication.[45] Harley-Davidson *(www.harleydavidson.com)* uses its extranet to allow its more than 1,000 dealers to service warranties, obtain engine diagrams, and order parts.[46]

MARKET-OF-ONE STRATEGY

Many companies are using personalized Web sites to form tighter relationships with their customers, but a market-of-one strategy also goes beyond this process. Dell Computer Company's business model allows buyers to place custom orders directly over the telephone or the Internet. The computer is then designed to meet the specifications of the buyer. Dell's ability to customize production is due to the development of the **digital factory,** an automation process in which software and computer networks are more important than production machines. When this digital manufacturing process is combined with the human worker, the resulting "soft manufacturing process" brings flexibility to production and allows manufacturers to produce individualized products at mass production speeds. For example, Motorola *(www.motorola.com)* manufactures pagers using flexible production techniques. Resellers and salespeople deliver orders to the factory specifying colors, tones, and other details. These specifications are relayed to pick and place robots that deliver the parts and orders to the assembly line. The finished product can be shipped the same day the order came in.[47]

This build-to-order business model is also called **mass customization** and is a market-of-one process. Don Peppers and Martha Rogers's book *The One to One Future (www.1to1.com)* expands on how this process allows marketers to develop tight customer relationships.[48] The Internet is bringing mass customization to a wide range of products. Companies are now allowing customers to design golf clubs, bicycles, fishing rods, and CDs; Levi Strauss *(www.levi.com/originalspin/)* is making built-to-order blue jeans. Smaller firms may use mass customization to gain competitive advantages, but larger firms are using the process to lower costs. Building to order cuts down on inventory costs that can amount to 10 percent of sales per year for some companies.[49] A **market-of-one** means that the firm must develop strong relationships with its customers and understand their individualized needs. Using the Internet for communication can facilitate this relationship development process. Once the relationship is established, customers are less likely to leave as long as their needs are being met.

Technology is also used in-store to facilitate purchases. Eyewear manufacturer Paris Miki *(www.paris-miki.com.au)* takes a digital picture of an individual's face. The customer then enters self-image and lifestyle information (such as intelligent, sexy, distinctive) into a computer. The customer is shown a 3-D representation of his or her face with lenses and frames on a computer screen. The custom frames are ordered, with no extra charge for using the computer system.[50] Once a company has acquired the data on a customer's requirements, there may be little incentive for the individual to switch to another provider.

AUCTION STRATEGY

Two types of **auction** sites are being developed over the Internet: **Sales auction** sites allow individuals and businesses to sell products online and have potential customers bid on the product; **buyer-driven commerce** sites allow customers to specify how much they are willing to pay for a product or service and then let the providers bid for customers. These auction sites are changing the pricing structures traditionally controlled by businesses. Auctions can shift power from a business to the customer. Auction sites also allow businesses to use pricing strategies to reduce unwanted or unused inventory.[51]

Sales auctions allow parties to place bids during a specific time period for products that are for sale. Sales auctions can be business-to-consumer, business-to-business, or consumer-to-consumer; they can also be facilitated through exchanges. Although consumer-to-consumer auction revenue was twice that of business-to-consumer revenue in 1998, by 2003 business-to-consumer auction revenue is expected to be close to twice that of consumer-to-consumer revenue.[52] Business-to-consumer sites, such as the Universal Studios interactive auction house *(www.universalstudios.com/files/pages/auctions)*, carry exclusive celebrity memorabilia and collectibles. Buyers can find one-of-a-kind pieces for collecting. Bids can be placed on everything from signed posters to movie props and are in specified dollar increments. A wide variety of products, including computers, books, salvaged cars, and industrial raw materials and products, are offered over a number of different auction sites.

Businesses are using auction sites to sell new products and excess inventory. Weirton Steel Corp. *(www.weirton.com)* used a business-to-business online auction site to sell $50 million in excess steel. Business-to-business auction sites were expected to produce sales of $8.7 billion in 1998.[53] USBid *(www.usbid.com)* and TradeOut *(www.tradeout.com)* offer businesses auction services to move excess inventory. Other companies are matching buyers and sellers for highly perishable inventories such as meat and poultry [FoodUSA *(www.foodusa.com)*], frozen seafoods [Gofish *(www.gofish.com)*], and fruits and vegetables [ProduceWorld *(www.produceworld.com)*].[54]

The consumer-to-consumer Web site at eBay *(www.ebay.com)* allows individuals to post products for sale. Sellers post information at the site, and bidders place their bids online. Once the preset time expires, the seller pays eBay a commission and consummates the deal offline. In 1998, eBay had over 150,000 items for sale and estimated sales of over $100 million a year; by 1999, eBay had over 3 million items and estimated sales of over $1.3 billion.[55] Consumer-to-consumer auctions have been subject to buyer and seller fraud (more on fraud in Chapter 10). Third parties are moving into auctions to help guarantee merchandise, confirm sales, and collect money.

Exchanges use a third party that acts as an agent facilitating the sale, most often based on a commission. Sotheby's *(www.sothebys.amazon.com)* formed an alliance with Amazon.com to offer online auctions. This allows sellers to use Sotheby's as an agent to sell the products, collect the money, and move the merchandise. eBay purchased Butterfield & Butterfield, the third-largest auction house in the United States, to act as one of the exchange agents for its great collections site *(www.ebaygreatcollections.com)*.[56]

Sellers can use **reverse auctions** that allow individuals and companies to have sellers bid for the purchase. Businesses that use reverse auctions can have bidding companies check the status of the lowest bid (with the bidding company's name withheld) and then add their bid.[57]

The buyer-driven business Priceline.com *(www.priceline.com)* offers individuals the opportunity to name their own price for airline tickets and automobiles. It offers additional consumer services such as home mortgages, insurance, personal computers, telecommunications, hotels, cruises, and credit cards. Priceline.com receives the bid price from the purchaser and then submits the bid to companies that accept or decline the offer to purchase. The purchaser must be very flexible when purchasing airline tickets because airlines will sell excess capacity at less-than-ideal travel times. When this name-your-own-price business model moves to other products that are not time-dependent, the customer may see greater benefits.[58]

PRICING STRATEGIES

The e-business environment is impacting pricing strategies in a number of different ways. As has already been stated in this chapter, some businesses are becoming more efficient and are therefore able to sell with lower overall costs. Cost savings can be found in lower fixed costs because of minimized use of brick and mortar assets, and lower variable costs due to reduced staffing requirements. EMarketer *(www.emarketer.com)* reports that businesses that sell online have an economic advantage in the lower marginal costs needed to reach and serve additional customers. Table 5.6 outlines comparative costs of traditional transactions versus online transactions.

Table 5.6 Transaction Cost Comparisons

Traditional Method	Average Amount	Internet	Average Amount
Telephone transaction cost plus related customer service charges	$5.00	Automated Internet transaction cost	$0.01
Bank transaction cost	$1.07	Bank transaction on the Web	$0.01
Airline ticket transaction cost	$8.00	Airline ticket transaction on the the Web	$1.00

Source: EMarketer, "1998 eCommerce Report Indicates: Consumer eCommerce Segment will Grow to $26 Billion by 2002," October 20, 1999, <http://www.emarketer.com/eservices/000099_eacommrpt.

The Internet also allows a customer to obtain information and prices from a larger number of alternative sources of supply. This has a tendency to make the demand curve for products more elastic. Businesses are forced to bid against each other, lowering the price. Customers are using buying agents and shopping services to obtain price information. The Internet's ability to offer pricing information to all buyers and sellers at any place at any time is leading to a dynamic pricing market. **Dynamic pricing** implies that products will sell for something other than list prices. Prices are set dynamically based on market demand for that product. This can lead to higher or lower prices, depending on how the market bids for the product.[59]

Product Pricing Information

Intelligent shopping agents are software-based search systems that return product and pricing information from multiple vendors. To use these systems, the customer specifies the product or other criteria, such as a price range for a product category. The agent then returns information on sales outlets, prices, and availability. When Web agents were first used, many merchant sites blocked them from receiving pricing information. Now merchants see agents as a means of delivering customers to sites. Although this forces price competition, merchants can use service, brand names, or means other than the lowest price to obtain the sale. Shopping agents currently used by consumers include MySimon *(www.mysimon.com)* and Yahoo! Shopping *(www.shopping.yahoo.com)*.[60]

Shopping agents are useful for products that have multiple vendors and are easily compared. For more complicated purchases, a number of businesses are acting as shopping services for customers. **Shopping services** such as Respond.com *(www.respond.com)* and Imandi.com *(www.imandi.com)* allow individuals to submit requests for products; "live" agents at these sites then solicit bids for the requested products and services.[61]

Pricing Strategies

Two broad strategies are used to set prices: skimming and penetration. **Skimming pricing** sets high initial prices to skim off payments from individuals who are willing to purchase products when they first come to market. **Penetration pricing** sets prices lower in an attempt to capture market share for a product. In the e-business competitive marketplace, firms are attempting to capture market share, often by selling at very low prices or even below cost. If a firm has an overriding goal of attaining market share, it may even give products away for free. Low product prices and free products may mask ulterior motives. Netscape *(www.netscape.com)* gave away its browser for free to build loyalty and then sold server software to support the growing number of users. This model has been copied by companies such as RealNetworks *(www.realnetworks.com)* and Adobe *(www.adobe.com)*, both of which have given away players for their proprietary media formats. Adobe's software packages must be purchased to create the PDF files that are sent over the Internet.[62] In 1999, Blue Mountain Arts Publishing Co. *(www.bluemountain.com)* received as high as 12.6 million unique visitors to its free electronic greeting cards site. Excite at Home *(www.home.com)* paid $1.06 billion for Blue Mountain Arts in order to gain the opportunity to engage in e-commerce with this customer base.[63]

To build market share, ISPs started giving away free e-mail accounts; now some ISPs are giving away free connection services both in the United States and around the world. Freeserve *(www.freeserve.co.uk)* is just one of the over 200 free ISPs in the United Kingdom. In the United States, AltaVista Co. *(www.altavista.com)* offers free Internet access for customers willing to be targeted with directed advertisements.[64]

A number of companies have developed marketing strategies to give away free PCs or reduce the price through rebates. To receive these low prices, customers must give up personal information for targeted advertising and agree to purchase up to three years of ISP service. The "free" computer is a promotional incentive to build market share for ISPs, which then hope to recover costs through advertising.[65]

HOW QUICKLY CAN BUSINESS MODELS CHANGE?

"It was easier for me to do it and more convenient."

John Steffens,
Vice Chairman of Merrill Lynch & Company,
on online trading.[66]

Example of Changing Business Models: Stock Brokerage

The stock brokerage industry has adopted a number of value strategies to develop new models of exchange. What happened in this industry may be a precursor of what other industries will face. The brokerage industry's traditional business

Figure 5.2 Traditional Brokerage System

model has been shaken by the speed of change since 1997 because online trading offers many advantages over the traditional model of stock investing.

The traditional business model for stock sales is outlined in Figure 5.2. A firm issues stock through an underwriting company. The underwriting company issues this stock through an exchange where stockbrokers sell the stock to individual purchasers. Each of these intermediaries has traditionally received a commission because they all have had access to some part of the exchange process. Stockbrokers interfaced with the investor because they could buy or sell stock and had access to information on the company issuing the stock as well as the current sales price.

The Internet brings both information and brokerage services to the investor. Investors can access information on stocks from the exchange; they can also obtain information through a number of businesses designed to offer information and advice without the sales pressure of traditional brokers.[67] E*Trade launched a $100 million advertising campaign in 1998 to promote its free stock-trading information site. The goal of this campaign was to add 1 million new accounts to its already 500,000 active accounts.[68] Table 5.7 outlines the advantages of the new brokerage business models.

Table 5.7 Benefit Analysis for Online Brokerage

Benefits	Traditional Brokers	Online Brokers
Purchaser's cost for transaction	Depends on broker and amount of stock	Costs one-third to one-tenth of traditional brokers' cost
Information on companies and quotes	Requires that broker act as gatekeeper between corporate information and customer, and receive quotes	Uses online data to obtain information and stock quotes immediately
Speed and convenience	Requires customer-broker interface for information and trades	Obtains immediate information at customers' convenience and places trades instantly
Expertise of advice	Depends on broker	Depends on buyer

Source: John Thackray, "Defining Moment: Online Stock Sales," *Information Week,* October 20, 1997, pp. 115–122.

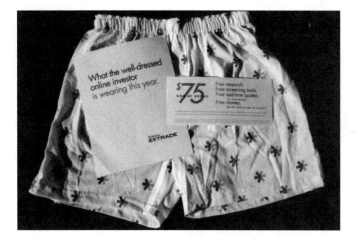

Online investing is expected to increase from less than 2 million accounts in 1996 to more than 24.7 million accounts by the year 2002. U.S. online brokerage revenues are expected to exceed $5.3 billion by 2002. The major reasons that individuals choose to use online brokerages include lower commissions, ability to research investments online, convenience, and control of the transaction process.[69] By the year 2002, it is projected that online accounts will hold nearly $700 billion in assets and account for 30 percent of all stock trading.[70] Charles Schwab placed about 35 percent of its trades over the Internet in 1996. By 1999, online trading accounted for 65 percent of Schwab's retail trades.[71]

Figure 5.3 outlines the results of the competitive dynamics during 1997 as online trading moved from a niche business to over 90 million trades per day; prices dropped over this time period. In 1997, Web Street charged $0 for trades of at least 1,000 shares on the NASDAQ exchange. These companies also make money on margins and holding investors' cash between trades. Online investors also trade more than other investors, increasing the overall commissions paid. By 1998, Internet trades reached 340,000 trades per day; by 1999, average online commissions had stabilized at around $15 per trade.[72]

Figure 5.3 Online Brokerage Prices and Volume

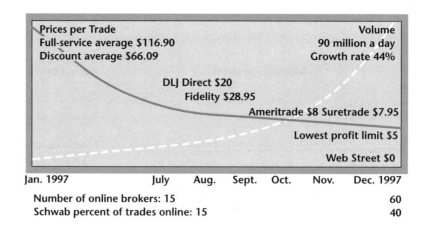

Prices per Trade	Volume
Full-service average $116.90	90 million a day
Discount average $66.09	Growth rate 44%

DLJ Direct $20
Fidelity $28.95

Ameritrade $8 Suretrade $7.95

Lowest profit limit $5

Web Street $0

Jan. 1997   July   Aug.   Sept.   Oct.   Nov.   Dec. 1997

Number of online brokers: 15   60
Schwab percent of trades online: 15   40

Source: Suzanne Woolley, "Do I Hear Two Bits a Trade?" *Business Week,* December 8, 1997, pp. 112–113.

To survive this challenge, full-service brokers have been forced to find new ways of adding value to their services. Electronic trading has put such pressure on traditional exchange models that the price of a seat on the Chicago stock exchange dropped 50 percent in value; the growth of electronic exchange has lessened its value. Old-line brokers have moved slowly toward online trading. In 1999, Merrill Lynch decided to offer online trading at $29.95 for 1,000 shares, an 80 percent decrease from its normal $210 fee. Merrill Lynch's brand name put direct pressure on other online traders, although Merrill Lynch's late move had allowed online firms to capture market share. Merrill's 14,000 brokers have not adjusted well to this change; facing lower commissions, some of Merrill's brokers left for other full-service firms.[73]

Alternate Channels

The shortest brokerage channel would be sales from the brokerage directly to the investor. NASDAQ investigated a new exchange model wherein it would sell directly to the investor and bypass the broker.[74] Other exchanges are also moving to electronic trading, forcing brokers to reconsider their role in the exchange process.[75]

The broker may be bypassed altogether for some issuing companies and stock buyers or sellers. The broker has been used as an intermediary between a company issuing stock and the investor because the broker had access to the stock purchasers and could sell the stock more efficiently than the issuing company. By selling stock online, a company can bypass the broker, keeping more of the money raised in the stock issue. This process is used for both buying and selling of previously issued stock and for **IPOs.** Instinet *(www.instinet.com)* allows buyers and sellers to post their prices directly to each other. Instinet has been offering this service to large traders such as pension funds and insurance companies but will join a number of other electronic trading networks already selling to the individual customer. These electronic trading networks cut out the broker, allow 24/7 trading, and decrease transaction costs.[76]

A company has an IPO (initial public offering) of stock when it first offers shares to the public.

Issuing or purchasing IPOs is a more complicated transaction, and many businesses use brokerages to help them through the process. Some firms are willing to offer their stock directly to the public through the Internet, either directly from the company or through online facilitators such as Direct IPO *(www.directipo.com).* This could mean that buyers have increased risks because they become responsible for all the evaluation of the business before they buy and may not have the same expertise in stock evaluation as a broker. [77] OpenIPO *(www.openipo.com)* uses **Dutch auctions** to bring buyers to a stock offering. When potential buyers bid enough to reach the amount of money the company planned to raise, the stock is issued with a low commission.

A **Dutch auction** works by having the seller lower the price continuously until a buyer decides to purchase at the stated price.

HOSTING THE TECHNOLOGY

Marshall Industries *(www.marshall.com)*, an electronics supplier, started changing its business model in 1994 before the first Mosaic browser was released. Marshall's investment in information technology allowed its customers to visit its suppliers using a split screen so customers didn't have to leave Marshall's site. This allowed buyers to obtain instant pricing information. Through Marshall's site, customers can currently receive online product sales presentations. Customers can also order products through software agents; customers click an order button, and the agent goes to Marshall's site. Customers' credit is verified through Wells Fargo, and products are shipped via UPS. By entering an order number, customers can check orders or shipping status.[78] Close to 80 percent of global CEOs believe that e-commerce will reshape competition in their industries; 20 percent think that it will reshape how they do business.[79]

The cost of implementing new business models based on the strategies outlined in this chapter depends on the goals the company sets for itself. A number of large and small businesses would like to use the Internet as a sales channel but don't know how to start, nor can they afford setup costs. This has opened the door to a number of e-business facilitators.

Commerce service providers (CSPs) are companies that facilitate commerce for other businesses. Businesses can form an alliance with hosting sites such as ISPs, banks, distributors, or online malls. IBM, for example, offers a hosting service providing security, content management, and order management on a fee basis. A number of companies, including AT&T and IBM, developed one of the first models for online commerce: online malls. (They later dropped these projects.) Other companies have set up malls for individual merchants to sell products. Stumpworld Systems, Inc., has a mall called BuyItOnline *(www.buyitonline.com)*; individual merchants pay a per-month fee plus a percentage of the transaction.[80] Yahoo! offers a service to host online transactions. Businesses can use Yahoo!'s merchant server system to set up their own e-commerce site, allowing buyers to use shopping carts to pick products, determine the total charges and shipping costs, and acquire credit-card information for the merchants to use to place the order. In September 1999, Amazon.com opened its zShops site, allowing any retailer to sell online. To give retailers access to Amazon.com's 12 million customers, Amazon.com charges $9.99 a month plus 1.25 to 5 percent of sales. Amazon.com allows these retailers access to its auction site. Customers can use an "All Products Search" to search the Web for items they cannot find at Amazon.com's site.[81]

The low-cost entry of a CSP is very attractive to merchants. They must still market their site as they would any other business, but they do not have the brick and mortar costs and can reach the entire world with the e-commerce site. Table 5.8 outlines the advantages of using a stand-alone versus a CSP site.

Table 5.8 Advantages of Selling with Stand-Alone vs. CSP Sites

Issue	Stand-Alones	Commerce Service Providers
Costs	No fees paid to CSP Higher costs in personnel, hardware, software, and development	Lower cost for maintaining technology to support site
Control	Can control all their policies related to selling If mall closes, may lose past customers	May need to comply with mall's sales, credit, and return policies
Customers	Must get customers to their site by themselves through promotion	Can pull in larger number of shoppers
Quality of traffic	May have higher-quality traffic that is more likely to buy	May attract individuals who browse one day but who may turn into shoppers at another time

Sources: James R. Borck, "Building Your Site from Scratch," *InfoWorld,* October 4, 1999, pp. 65–66; Lori Mitchell, "Using an I-Commerce Service Provider," *InfoWorld,* October 4, 1999, pp. 68–70; and Nick Wreden, "Retailers Seek to Capture Fly-By-'Net Traffic," *Communications Week,* November 25, 1996, p. 56.

INTERNATIONAL E-COMMERCE

The seven strategies outlined in this chapter are reshaping the way businesses interact with their customers, supply chains, distributors, and competitors. In order to implement these new business models, four factors must be in place. First, the technical infrastructure must allow the flow of information. Second, flexibility of channel relationships is required. In countries such as Japan where long distribution channels are maintained through personal relationships, disintermediation and restructuring will be much more difficult. Third, the political and legal structure must allow for the use of e-commerce. The ability to ship products without tariff restrictions and the free flow of capital are requirements. Finally, although the Internet is the facilitator for this change, it is the willingness of businesses and customers to change their business and purchasing habits that allows the change to move forward.

While the United States is expected to see substantial e-commerce growth in the near future, Europe is also a growth market. Roughly 25 percent (65 million) of the U.S. population had Internet access in 1998 versus only 6.2 percent (23 million) in Europe. Europe's business-to-consumer market is expected to grow from $126 million in 1997 to more than $5 billion by 2002. Business-to-business sales are expected to grow from $1 billion in 1997 to more than $30 billion by 2001.[82]

Infrastructure

The percentage of use for the Internet in the European Community (EC) varies, with the United Kingdom and Germany ahead of other EC countries. Germany is expected to grow from 7.5 million Web users in 1998, with 14 percent shopping, to 27.4 million Web users by 2002, with 40 percent shopping.[83] In Central and Eastern Europe, the telecommunications infrastructure is not as advanced as in more developed countries. In 1994, Hungary only had 1.2 million phones, with a waiting list of 800,000. It was projected that it would take 20 years to hook up all the phone lines. In Brazil's largest city, São Paulo, 400,000 people were waiting for telephone installation in 1997. Wireless communications may foster more rapid growth in these markets.[84]

Political and Legal Problems

There are a number of legal problems hindering the implementation of e-commerce across borders. Table 5.9 outlines some of these problem areas.

Other problems can develop over the free flow of information. Russia's Federal Security Agency is extending its practice of listening to private phone calls to include intercepting and reading e-mail.[85]

Table 5.9 Political and Legal Problems

Problem	Examples
Advertising and competition	**France:** By law, all Web sites aimed at French customers must be in French. **Germany:** Some promotions, such as two-for-one or promotional tie-ins, may be illegal. Land's End was forced to drop its "Money Back Guarantee, No Matter What" promise in Germany because it was seen as anticompetitive. The Land's End German Web site will link to other Land's End Web sites that show the guarantee.[a] **Sweden:** Toy advertising may not be directed at children.
Payments	Credit-card payments can be used, but because of differing currencies customers may not know the exact price until the currency exchange is made. The development of the Euro should allow smoother payments.
Delivery	The cost of shipping a product 30 miles across a border can be more expensive than 300 miles within the borders of a country.
Legal issues	Return policies may not be the same for all countries. Setting liability for faulty products may be unclear. It may be difficult to determine how value-added taxes are assessed. Privacy laws in Europe are more stringent than in the United States.[b]

Sources: [a] Ann Therese Palmer, "Land's End's End Run," *Business Week,* October 18, 1999, p. 8.
[b] Martha Bennett, "The Worldwide Sell," *CIO—Section 1,* July 15, 1998, pp. 60–63; and Henry Heilbrunn, "Interactive Marketing in Europe," *Direct Marketing,* March 1998, pp. 56–59.

Acceptance

Close to 80 percent of Web sites are in English. To foster international growth, a number of companies have developed multilingual Web sites and extranets. In addition, countries are setting up search engines that will search sites by country and language.[86]

As with any type of international cross-cultural communication, careful translation of words, symbols, and images is important. Web sites should be carefully screened by native speakers, and cross-translations (translating back to the original language) should be undertaken. Symbols and imagery should be screened to avoid anything offensive. For example, the meaning behind hand gestures differs from one culture to another. Yahoo! changes the colors of its buttons for different markets. For Ireland, the buttons are colorful, but for Germany and France they are more subdued. For some Asian cultures, traditional pictographs require two bytes of information instead of one, which requires that language-specific browsers be developed.[87]

TERMS AND CONCEPTS

KNOWLEDGE INTEGRATION

24/7/52 *119*
Auction strategy *113*
Business model *113*
Business process strategy *113*
Buyer-driven commerce *129*
Commerce service provider (CSP) *136*
Customer relationship management *124*
Destination site *116*
Digital communications strategy *113*

Digital factory *128*
Digital product *119*
Dynamic pricing *131*
E-commerce *115*
E-retailing *115*
Electronic data interchange (EDI) *127*
Exchange *130*
Intelligent shopping agent *131*
IPO (Initial public offering) *135*
JIT (just-in-time) *127*

Market-of-one strategy *113*
Mass customization *128*
Niche e-retailer *119*
Online purchasing strategy *113*
Penetration pricing *132*
Reverse auction *130*
Service strategy *113*
Shopping services *131*
Skimming pricing *132*
Stretch goal *122*
Supply chain *127*

CONCEPTS AND QUESTIONS FOR REVIEW

1. List the seven strategies e-businesses are adopting to gain competitive advantages.
2. Describe how online purchasing is used strategically for traditional retailers and e-retailers.
3. List the types of digital products offered by e-businesses.
4. Explain how service businesses are being impacted by e-businesses.

5. Explain how customer relationship management techniques can improve the overall value offered to customers.
6. Determine how the business process is changing because of EDI and extranets.
7. List and explain the techniques businesses are using to engage in commerce with other businesses.
8. Define the market-of-one process. Explain how this impacts the way companies deliver products.
9. List and describe the various types of auctions being used online.
10. Justify how a business can "give away" products for free or at a low price.
11. Evaluate why a business would want to use a commerce service provider (CSP).
12. List some companies that are positioning themselves as CSPs.
13. Describe some problems that are involved in setting up international e-commerce.

A C T I V E   L E A R N I N G

Exercise 5.1: Business Model Strategies

Use the Web to evaluate different business models. Determine how many of the strategies outlined in this chapter are used at the Web sites you visit. Explain how those strategies are used to create value for the business.

Exercise 5.2: Evaluating Business Models

Use the following matrix to compare an e-business against traditional business models. Determine the benefits the business provides to its customers. Decide how these benefits compare to traditional models. Determine what the online business would need to do to get you to purchase online. Explain what the traditional model will need to do to keep you buying at its site.

Benefits	Online Model	Traditional Model

Exercise 5.3: Niche Retailers

Use the Web to find narrowly targeted niche retailers. Determine the target market for the e-retailer. Describe how these e-retailers target their market. Explain how they are differentiated from other competitors.

Niche E-Retailers

Business	Site	Target Market	Product Offering

Exercise 5.4: Business Model Building

Pick a business-to-consumer or business-to-business industry where you would be interested in working. Determine the best business model for meeting your customers' needs. Decide which of the strategies outlined in this chapter would be beneficial in providing value to customers. Use the following matrix to determine whether a business should host the technology or use a commerce service provider (CSP).

Advantages of Selling With Stand-Alone vs. CSP Sites

Issue	Stand-Alone	Commerce Service Provider
Costs		
Control		
Customers		
Quality of traffic		

WEB SEARCH — LOOKING ONLINE

SEARCH TERM:	E-Commerce Support	First 6 out of 3,800,001

CommerceNet. Is an industry site providing research, news, promotional information, and support for developing e-commerce.
www.commerce.net

E-Commerce Times. Is an online Webzine related to e-commerce issues.
www.ecommercetimes.com

eMarketer. Provides reports, statistics, and consulting for businesses engaging in e-commerce.
www.emarketer.com

National Retail Federation. Is the world's largest retail trade association's Web site for supporting e-retailing.
www.nrf.com/ecommerce/ecommerce.htm

New York Times. Offers a special section on e-commerce. Individuals must register to log on to this free service.
www.nytimes.com

Shop.org. Is an online retailers' support site offering forums, research, news, and other industry support.
www.shop.org

SEARCH TERM:	Niche Lists	First 3 out of 32,787,323

BotSpot. Lists the bots, or software agents, that are available on the Internet.
www.botspot.com

c|Net Web Host List. Is a list Web host that allows for comparison of services.
webhostlist.internetlist.com

Soprano.com. Offers lists of sites that provide information, services, and free stuff. The free stuff list:
www.soprano.com/frees.html

SEARCH TERM:	International Support	First 5 out of 4,949,671

AsiaBizTech. Is a source on technology business information for Japan and Asia.
www.nikkeibp.asiabiztech.com

Asia Source. Is an online resource developed by the Asia Society to provide information on events across Asia.
www.asiasource.org

Electronic Commerce Europe. Is an association that promotes, coordinates, and assists the development of electronic commerce in Europe.
www.ec-europe.org

Electronic Commerce and the European Union. Was developed by European experts on electronic commerce with the goal of ensuring that the European

Union remains at the forefront of electronic commerce.
www.ispo.cec.be/ecommerce

Electronic Commerce Association of South Africa. Promotes the use of electronic commerce to improve South Africa's commercial, industrial, and government business efficiency.
www.ecasa.org.za

REFERENCES

1 For more on changes in the grocery industry, see: Barbara E. Kahn and Leigh McAlister, *Grocery Revolution,* Addison-Wesley, Reading, Massachusetts, 1997.

2 Robert Lenzer, "Bagging Groceries," *Forbes,* October 18, 1999, p. 80; and WebVan, "Company Information," October 5, 1999, <*http://www21.webvan.com/default.asp*>.

3 "Schnucks Sells Groceries Online," *Business Geographics,* October 1997, p. 54.

4 Charles Walter, "New Recipe for IT Implementation," *Information Week,* September, 27, 1999, pp. 169–174.

5 U.S. Department of Commerce, "The Emerging Digital Economy II," June 1999, Chapter 1, <*http://www.ecommerce.gov/ede/chapter1.html*>.

6 For more on the concept of perceived value, see: Valerie A. Zeithaml, "Consumer Perceptions of Price, Quality, and Value: A Means-End Model and Synthesis of Evidence," *Journal of Marketing,* July 1988, pp. 2–22.

7 Ravi Kalakota and Andrew B. Whinston, *Electronic Commerce, A Manager's Strategy*, Addison-Wesley, Reading, Massachusetts, 1997.

8 Paul A. Greenberg, "Nielsen Reports on Keys to Online Sales Success," *E-Commerce Times,* October 19, 1999, <*http://www.ecommercetimes.com/news/articles/991019-2.shtml*>.

9 Blaise Zerega, "Online Shopping Gets Real," *Red Herring,* September 1999, pp. 112–113.

10 Clinton Wilder, "Retail Turns to Clicks and Mortar," *Information Week,* September 27, 1999, pp. 257–263; and Edward Cone, "Sears' Vendors Pay Via the Web," *Inter@ctive Week,* August 30, 1999, p. 22.

11 Blaise Zerega, "Getting Virtual," *Red Herring,* September 1999, pp. 122–126; and Brian Caulfield, "Offline Retailers Size Up Net Strategies," *Internet World,* June 21, 1999, p. 4.

12 EMarketer, "1998 eCommerce Report Indicates," October 20, 1999, <*http://www.emarketer.com/eservices/000099_eacommrpt.html*>.

13 Jeff Sengstack, "Foot Locker's Big Play for E-Commerce," *NewMedia,* July 1998, pp. 66–67.

14 Nua Internet Surveys, "National Retail Federation: Report Identifies the Web's Top 100 Retailers," October 5, 1999, <*http://www.nua.ie/surveys/index.cgi?f=VS&art_id= 905355319&rel=true*>.

15 Kathleen Kerwin, Peter Borrows, and Diane Brady, "A New Era of Bright Hopes and Terrible Fears," *Business Week,* October 4, 1999, pp. 84–98; and Heather Green, Gail Degeroge, and Amy Barrett, "The Virtual Mall Gets Real," *Business Week,* January 26, 1998, pp. 90–91.

16 AsiaBizTech, "Sixty Pct. of Internet Users in Japan Shop Online, Fujitsu Research Says," September 21, 1999, <*http://www.nikkeibp.asiabiztech.com/wcs/leaf?CID=onair/ asabt/cover/82488*>.

[17] IDC.com, "Asia's Internet Ecommerce Applications Markets to Top US$1.3 Billion by 2003, Says IDC," July 13, 1999, *<http://www.idc.com/data/asiapacific/content/ap071399pr. htm>*.

[18] Lynda Radosevich and Dylan Tweney, "Retooling Retail," *InfoWorld,* March 22, 1999, pp. 1, 62–63.

[19] Connie Guglielmo, "Drugstore Wars: Web Remedy," *Inter@ctive Week,* September 13, 1999, p. 40; Saroja Girishankar, "Walgreen Hustles to Close Online Gap," *Internet Week,* July 19, 1999, pp. 1, 53; Elizabeth Gardner, "If This Were a Test, Drugstore.com Would Get a 'C'," *Internet World,* April 12, 1999, pp. 1, 73; Evantheia Schibsted, "Prescription for Profits," *Business 2.0,* March 1999, pp. 58–62; and Brad Stone, "Nothing to Sneeze At," *Newsweek,* February 15, 1999, p. 60.

[20] Sharon Machlis, "Journal Finds Quality Pays Off," *Computerworld,* May 18, 1998, pp. 41, 44.

[21] Anna Maria Virzi, "News Sites Are Coming of Age," *Internet World,* September 14, 1998, p. 13.

[22] David F. Carr, "Enabling 'By the Slice' Sales of Site Content," *Internet World,* February 9, 1998, pp. 25–27.

[23] Peter Fabris, "Funky Music," *CIO Web Business—Section 2,* December 1, 1997, pp. 68–76.

[24] Steven V. Brull, "Are Music Companies Blinded by Fright?" *Business Week,* June 28, 1999, pp. 67–68; James C. Luh, "Going Public with MP3," *Internet World,* June 7, 1999, p. 46; and Ann Harrison, "U.S. Music Biz Accepts MP3, Global Publishers Rebel," *Computerworld,* March 29, 1999, p. 43.

[25] Clinton Wilder, "Wells Fargo Opens Cyberbank," *Information Week,* June 5, 1995, p. 90; and Tom Duffy, "Wells Fargo Cashes In on Intranet," *Communications Week,* May 26, 1997, p. 44.

[26] Kimberly Weisul, "Online Banks: Mixed Messages," *Inter@ctive Week,* September 20, 1999, p. 53.

[27] Bob Violino, "Banking on E-Business," *Information Week,* May 3, 1999, pp. 44–52.

[28] Bluesky International Marketing, "The Number of Retail Internet Banks in Europe Doubles in 6 Months," July 12, 1999, *<http://www.blueskyinc.com/pressreleasejune99.htm>*.

[29] Jennifer Lach, "Point, Click and Pay," *Newsweek,* August 17, 1998, pp. 66–67.

[30] Kimberly Weisul, "What Price Online Mortgages?" *Inter@ctive Week,* July 19, 1999, p. 62; Robert L. Scheier, "Online Mortgage Less Than Meets the Eye," *Computerworld,* January 11, 1999, pp. 52–54; and Karen Epper Hoffman, "Online Loans Pick Up Momentum," *Internet World,* October 12, 1998, p. 46.

[31] Kathy Chin Leong, "Customer Service Gets Royal Treatment," *Internet Week,* September 14, 1998, pp. 32–34.

[32] Martin LaMonica, "Untangling Online Customer Service," *InfoWorld,* January 11, 1999, pp. 75–76; and Tom Stein, "Service On The Net," *Internet Week,* December 21–28, 1998, pp. 76–80.

[33] Justin Hibbard, Gregory Dalton, and Mary E. Thyfault, "Web-Based Customer Care," *Information Week,* June 1, 1998, pp. 18–20.

[34] Cate T. Corcoran, "National Semiconductor Uses Web to Ease Support Services," *InfoWorld,* July 22, 1996, p. 62.

[35] Jeff Sweat and Justin Hibbard, "Customer Disservice," *Information Week,* June 21, 1999, pp. 65–78.

[36] Klaus Etzel, "The Changing EC Landscape," *EC World,* August 1999, pp. 42–45.

[37] VerticleNet, "Welcome," October 19, 1999, *<http://www.verticalnet.com/>*.

[38] Natalie Engler, "Supply in Demand," *Business 2.0,* November 1999, pp. 56–60; Elizabeth Goodridge, "Staples of E-Commerce," *Information Week,* September 20, 1999, p. 16; and Karen Epper Hoffman, "A Cyber Source for Office Supplies," *Internet World,* October 19, 1998, pp. 15–16.

[39] John Evan Frook, "Taking Orders off E-Commerce Menu," *Internet Week,* January 19, 1998, pp. 1, 73.

[40] NewsFront, "Costs Savings from EC to Reach $1.25 Trillion," *EC World,* October 1999, p. 12.

[41] Sean Donahue, "Nothing But Net," *Business 2.0,* November 1999, pp. 241–244; and Edward Cone, "Oracle Cost-Cutters Spin Web," *Inter@ctive Week,* October 11, 1999, p. 34.

[42] Tom Stein, "Orders from Chaos," *Information Week,* June 23, 1997, pp. 44–52.

[43] Julie Bort, "Big Money Behind EDI," *Client/Server Computing,* June 1997, pp. 44–47.

[44] John Evan Frook, "Wal-Mart Opens Its Arms to Internet EDI," *Internet Week,* June 22, 1998, p. 16.

[45] Alan S. Horowitz, "Year of the Extranet At Last?" *Information Week,* January 5, 1998, pp. 67–74.

[46] Sari Kalin, "The Fast Lane," *CIO Web Business—Section 2,* April 1, 1998, pp. 28–35.

[47] Jacqueline Emigh, "Agile Manufacturing," *Computerworld,* August 30, 1999, p. 56; and Gene Bylinsky, "The Digital Factory," *Fortune,* November 14, 1994, pp. 92–110.

[48] Don Peppers and Martha Rogers, *The One to One Future,* Doubleday, New York, 1996.

[49] Candee Wilde, "Personal Business," *Information Week,* August 9, 1999, pp. 76–80; Elizabeth Gardner, "'Build It Yourself' Is Motto of Sites Selling Everything from Golf Clubs to CDs to Bicycles," *Internet World,* March 2, 1998, pp. 13, 15; and Larry Marion and Emily Kay, "Customer of One, the Next Market Paradigm," *Software Magazine,* November 1997, pp. 38–50.

[50] Eric Torbenson, "As You Like It," *CIO Enterprise—Section 2,* February 15, 1998, pp. 61–64.

[51] Amy E. Cortese and Marcia Stepanek, "Good-Bye to Fixed Pricing?" *Business Week,* May 4, 1998, pp. 70–84.

[52] Paul Keegan, "Online Auctions: From Seedy Flea Markets to Big Business," *Upside,* July 1999, pp. 70–81.

[53] Sharon Machlis, "Online Auction Services Thriving," *Computerworld,* June 15, 1998, pp. 1, 17.

[54] Mark Halper, "Sell It," *Business 2.0,* November 1999, pp. 172–180.

[55] Phil Hood, "Seller's Market," *NewMedia,* February 10, 1998, p. 61.

[56] Paul Klebnokov, "Art's Big Bang," *Forbes,* August 9, 1999, pp. 92–96.

[57] Gregory Dalton, "Going, Going, Gone!" *Yahoo! Internet Life,* October 4, 1999, pp. 44–50.

[58] Peter Elkind, "The Hype Is Big, Really Big at Priceline," *Fortune,* September 6, 1999, pp. 193–202; David Leonhardt, "Make a Bid, But Don't Pack Your Bags," *Business Week,* June 1, 1998, p. 164; and Priceline.com, September 17, 1998, *<http://www.priceline.com>*.

[59] Robert D. Hof, Heather Green, and Paul Judge, "Going, Going, Gone," *Business Week,* April 12, 1999, pp. 30–32; and Amy E. Cortees and Marcia Stepaneck, "Good-Bye to Fixed Pricing?" *Business Week,* May 4, 1998, pp. 70–84.

[60] Alan Majer and Mike Dover, "License to Bill," *NewMedia,* January 1999, p. 11; Clinton Wilder, "Call Your Agent for Online Shopping," *Information Week,* December 7, 1998, pp. 126–28; and Clinton Wilder, "Agents Go Price Shopping," *Internet Week,* December 7, 1998, p. 23.

[61] Niall McKay, "Human Touch," *Red Herring,* September 1999, pp. 142–143; and Michelle V. Rafter, "Cheap, Cheaper, Cheapest," *The Industry Standard,* January 11–18, 1999, pp. 50–51.

[62] George Anders, "Eager to Boost Traffic, More Internet Firms Give Away Services," *The Wall Street Journal,* July 28, 1999, pp. A1, A8; and David Cowles, "The Best Things in Life Are Free," *Fast Company,* April–May 1998, pp. 38–40.

[63] Kara Swisher, "Excite at Home to Purchase Greeting Card Web-Site Firm," *The Wall Street Journal,* October 26, 1999, p. B4.

[64] Julia King, "AltaVista Plans Free Net Access," *Computerworld,* July 19, 1999, pp. 1, 101; Richard Tomlinson, "Internet Free Europe," *Fortune,* September 6, 1999, pp. 165–172; Kaitlin Quistgaard, "Free for All," *Business 2.0,* March 1999, pp. 20–22; and Mark Dolley, "It's Free, Baby," *Business 2.0,* March 1999, pp. 74–78.

[65] Megan Santosus, "The Price Is Right," *CIO Enterprise—Section 2,* June 15, 1999, p. 24; and John G. Sponner, "Free PCs: Future or Fad?" *PC Week,* July 19, 1999, pp. 1, 24.

[66] Carol Marie Cropper, "Online Trading Changes Landscape for Old-Line Brokerage Firms," *The New York Times,* September 22, 1999, *<http://www.nytimes.com/library/tech/99/09/biztech/technology/22crop.html>.*

[67] Amy Dunkin, "For Investors of All Stripes, A Cornucopia on the Net," *Business Week,* December 22, 1997, pp. 104–106.

[68] Susan Moran, "A Plan to Spend $100M to Lure New Online Traders," *Internet World,* September 14, 1998, p. 6.

[69] Business 2.0 Numbers, "Internet at a Glance," *Business 2.0,* February 1999, p. 102; Nelson Wang, "E-Brokerages in Bruising Fight," *Web Week,* January 12, 1998, pp. 38–41; and Gregory Dalton, "Nasdaq, Online Brokerages Crack Under Trade Volume," *Information Week,* November 3, 1997, p. 28.

[70] Mark Halper, "(Almost) Making Money on the Web," *CIO Enterprise,* January 15, 1998, pp. 57–62; and David Whitford, "Trade Fast, Trade Cheap," *Fortune,* February 2, 1998, pp. 108–114.

[71] Bronwyn Fryer, "Trading Push," *Information Week,* April 13, 1998, pp. 97–100; Gideon Sasson, "E-Commerce Success Story: Charles Schwab.Com," *E-Commerce Times,* December 6, 1999, *<http://www.ecommercetimes.com/success_stories/success_schwab.shtml>.*

[72] Leah Nathans Spiro and Edward C. Baig, "Who Needs a Broker?" *Business Week,* February 22, 1999, pp. 113–118; and Maryann Jones Thompson, "Online Trading," *The Industry Standard,* February 8, 1999, *<http://www.thestandard.com/metrics/display/0,1283,840,00.html>.*

[73] Megan Barnett, "Merrill Talks, Brokers Walk," *The Industry Standard,* October 11, 1999, *<http://www.thestandard.com/articles/0,1449,6845,00.html?1447>;* Leah Nathans Spiro, Timothy J. Mullaney, and Louise Lee, "Bullish on the Internet," *Business Week,* June 14, 1999, pp. 45–46; and Thomas Hoffman, "Merrill Lynch Bows to Low-Cost Net Trading," *Computerworld,* June 7, 1999, p. 20.

[74] Tim Wilson, "Nasdaq Puts Stock in Web," *Internet Week,* July 6, 1998, pp. 1, 48.

[75] Paula Dwyer, Andrew Osterland, Kerry Capell, and Sharon Reier, "The 21st Century Stock Market," *Business Week,* August 10, 1998, pp. 66–72.

[76] Brenon Daly, "Stock Around the Clock," *Business 2.0,* November 1999, pp. 297–300.

[77] Stephanie T. Gates, "The IPO Tease," *Red Herring,* August 1999, pp. 140–148; Randall Smith, "So Far, 'E-Underwriting' Gets a Slow Start," *The Wall Street Journal,* August 13, 1999, pp. C1, C10; and Eileen P. Gunn, "Back to the Future: From the Curb to the Web," *Fortune,* May 13, 1996, p. 30.

[78] Tim Wilson, "Wholesale Shift to the Web," *Internet Week,* June 20, 1998, pp. 1, 61.

[79] "Electronic CEOs," *CIO Enterprise—Section 2,* June 15, 1998, p. 16.

[80] Jim Kerstetter, "Online Mall Thinks Big," *PC Week,* September 7, 1998, p. 25.

81 Robert D. Hof and Steve Hamm, "Amazon.com Throws Open the Doors," *Business Week,* October 11, 1999, p. 44; and Connie Guglielmo, "Amazon.com Shopping Portal Opens for E-Biz," *Inter@ctive Week,* October 4, 1999, p. 12.

82 Martha Bennett, "The Worldwide Sell," *CIO—Section 1,* July 15, 1998, pp. 60–63.

83 Kevin Jones, "Web Retailers Court Euro-Dollars," *Inter@ctive Week,* August 24, 1998, p. 34.

84 Alice LaPlante, "Eastern Europe's Virtual Curtain," *Computerworld,* September 12, 1994, pp. 73–79; and Peter Fabris, "Going South," *Webmaster,* April 1997, pp. 22–24.

85 "You Call This *Glasnost?" Business Week,* August 17, 1998, p. 12.

86 Michael J. Mandel, "A World Wide Web for Tout le Monde," *Business Week,* April 1, 1996, p. 36.

87 Lynda Radosevich, "Local Color," *CIO Web Business—Section 2,* December 1, 1997, pp. 56–64.

Chapter 6

The Individual and the Diffusion of Innovations

Change is the nature of today's competitive environment. Technological change related to the Internet and the World Wide Web is forcing businesses to take into consideration the diffusion of innovations process in order to design products and develop strategies. The diffusion process helps to explain what is considered to be a new product and what can be done about the innovation to make it more acceptable to the target audience. The adoption curve indicates that innovators will purchase first and influence the later adopters. These same basic principles operate inside a firm. In order to respond to the environmental change, firms must allow change agents to develop coalitions and build consensus. This chapter will examine these concepts as they are related to current e-business practice and relationship development.

1. Define an innovation.
2. Discuss how to speed the acceptance of an innovation.
3. Outline how the individual adoption process works.
4. Explain what a product life cycle is and how this concept relates to new and older technologies.
5. Describe how online communities are targeting individuals and what it takes to make a successful online community.
6. Discuss why some cultures may be slow to accept technological change and the associated implications.
7. Explain how innovations diffuse in a business and what role change agents play in that process.

Getting the Message Across

In the late 1700s, the French developed a communications system to send messages more than 80 miles in three minutes. This was accomplished through a series of towers that displayed large wooden signs to relay codes. One of the main uses of the signaling system was to send winning national lottery numbers around France. In 1837, the U.S. Senate called for proposals for a similar system in the United States. Instead, Samuel Morse submitted a proposal for an alternative signaling process that would rely on electricity to relay messages. Government support of Morse's proposal gave birth to the telecommunications industry.

After a slow start, demand for the telegraph grew to provide information on winning lottery numbers, stock prices, and other data vital for businesses. In 1847, the United States had 30,000 miles of telegraph lines; by 1880, the United States sent more than 32 million messages over 291,000 miles of cable. Telegraph use peaked in 1945 with 236 million messages; by 1990, the telegraph system had all but vanished. The main reason for the decline of the telegraph was the introduction of the telephone, as well as the gradual improvement of long-distance telephone lines.

After Alexander Graham Bell's 1876 invention, the growth of the telephone was rapid. Initially the phone was used like a telegraph to send messages one way. Businesses saw the benefits and reorganized around the telephone. Salespeople reported in by phone, and manufacturing plants separated from headquarters. Although first discouraged by the phone companies, the telephone expanded into the frivolous use of social chatting. Then the telephone began to transform society. Housewives used the telephone to place purchase orders. People interacted over the phone lines and avoided the more formal social conventions involved in a face-to-face visit. By 1980, there were over 1 billion miles of phone lines, with over 750 million calls being made every day.[1] Figure 6.1 represents the relative growth, maturity, and decline of the telegraph and the growth of the telephone system.

Figure 6.1 Life Cycles of the Telegraph and Telephone

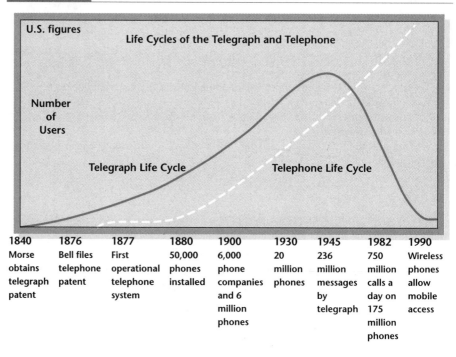

1840	1876	1877	1880	1900	1930	1945	1982	1990
Morse obtains telegraph patent	Bell files telephone patent	First operational telephone system	50,000 phones installed	6,000 phone companies and 6 million phones	20 million phones	236 million messages by telegraph	750 million calls a day on 175 million phones	Wireless phones allow mobile access

Source: Steven Lumbar, *InfoCulture,* Houghton Mifflin Company, New York, 1993; and Joseph McKendrick, "IDC Charts the World Wide Web," *Midrange Systems,* February 16, 1997, pp. 36, 42.

THINKING STRATEGICALLY

Figure 6.1 illustrates the relative life cycles of two communications technologies. Determine why the telephone was not more rapidly accepted. Explain why the telephone has grown and the telegraph has declined. Speculate on whether the telephone will ever decline in use as the telegraph has. Consider how the telephone has evolved, and speculate on how the telephone may be different in 10 years.

Explaining how individuals react to and interact with innovations is key to understanding the growth of e-business. These innovations include the use of the Internet as a communications vehicle, as a means of engaging in commerce, and as a way of delivering services. This is true not only for individual buyer behaviors but also for business purchases. Understanding how change is accepted is also vital for implementing intrafirm change. It is the individual who adopts innovative products or processes for personal or business use by changing his or her behavior and influencing others to change. E-businesses and designers of Internet sites need to develop business models and Web sites with interfaces that are easy to understand and appealing for new users. For example, of the $5 million start-up costs, MetalSite *(www.metalsite.com),* an online e-commerce market for excess steel, spent $2 million on a study exploring the exchange process between steel producers and their customers. It then spent another $1 million on a study investigating how to develop an interface for online commerce.[2] MetalSite's goal was to lower the barriers to exchange by making the online experience as familiar as the traditional process.

This chapter will explore how innovations are adopted by using the diffusion of innovations framework. The diffusion of innovations model will provide insight into how and why the Web is becoming a tool for communication and commerce and how rapidly it will grow. It will also outline how newer technologies can be designed to increase the speed of adoption and reach specific target markets to help shape new communities. Finally, it helps to explain how new ideas are introduced into a firm to foster change and transform businesses.

THE DIFFUSION OF INNOVATIONS PROCESS

The major theoretical model used to understand how new ideas and new technology spread over time is the **diffusion of innovations process.**[3] Gatignon and Robertson[4] have outlined a model of the diffusion process that can give marketers an understanding of

1. The concept of an **innovation**
   The acceptance process for new products
2. The adoption process
   a. The personal influence process and opinion leadership
   b. The role of the innovator
3. The spread of new ideas inside organizations
4. The impact of both the social system on diffusion and diffusion on the social system
5. The role of marketers as change agents
6. The role of competitive actions

Diffusion of innovations theories date back to 1903 when Gabriel Tarde observed that, of 100 new ideas, 10 will succeed and 90 will be forgotten. By 1987, over 1,840 empirical studies on diffusion had been published.

A simple definition of an innovation is a new idea, product, or process.

Figure 6.2 on the following page outlines a model of the diffusion process. This figure illustrates that a number of factors influence how quickly, if at all, innovations spread in a social system.

The model in Figure 6.2 shows that five factors influence the rate of individual adoption, which in turn influences how quickly the innovation diffuses or moves through a society. The individual adoption process influences how quickly an innovation is accepted within a society. This model can be better understood in the context of the growth of the World Wide Web. Prior to 1994, the Internet existed in relative obscurity. The ease of use of the Web's graphical interface has changed the nature of the Internet as a product, speeding acceptance of the technology. Netscape and Microsoft spurred growth by giving away their browsers and promoting the advantages of the Web as a communications medium. The press also aided

Figure 6.2 The Diffusion Of Innovations Model

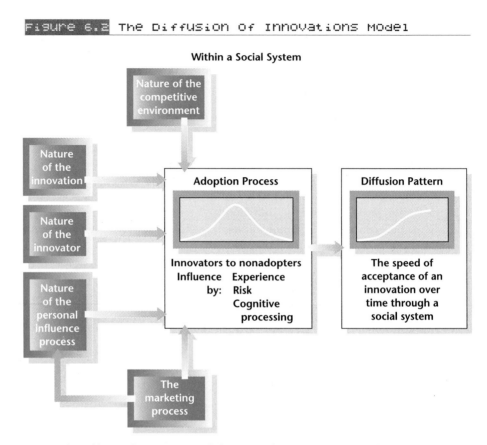

Source: Adapted from Hubert Gatignon and Thomas S. Robertson, "A Propositional Inventory for New Diffusion Research," *Journal of Consumer Research,* vol. 11, March 1985, p. 850.

in the marketing process by heavily promoting this new technology and its uses. Figure 6.3 indicates the worldwide growth of the Web.[5]

The growth of the Web has been quite strong in the United States as well as in selected countries in Europe and Asia. From 1997 to 1999, the number of Internet users worldwide grew by over 300 percent and total revenue generated on the Internet grew 900 percent.[6] In the United States and Canada, the Web has penetrated about 40 percent of the market, but as new hypermedia innovations such as interactive television and Internet cellular phones move through their diffusion process, larger percentages of the overall population will have access to the Internet. As this chapter will illustrate, increased ease of Web use is a key to increasing the penetration of the Internet into homes worldwide.[7]

Figure 6.3 Growth of the Internet and World Wide Web

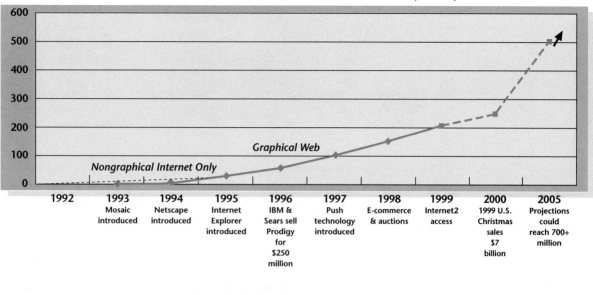

Growth of the Internet and World Wide Web in Users (millions)

THE NATURE OF THE INNOVATION

Not all innovations are totally new to the world; most are variations of older technologies. How new an individual perceives an innovation is dependent on two aspects: The first is how much the user must change behavior in order to use the innovation; the second is how new the technology is to the user and, therefore, how much the user has to learn or unlearn to make use of the innovation. The more the potential adopters must change their behavior and adjust to new technologies, the less likely they are to accept the innovation. Innovations can be categorized on a continuum of newness as illustrated in Figure 6.4, on the following page.

At one end of the continuum are the new-to-the-world products, classified as **discontinuous innovations,** which may arise through changes in technology or a recombination of existing technologies. Discontinuous innovations require high levels of behavioral change on the part of the user. At the other end of the spectrum are **continuous innovations,** which are often variations of existing products. Past experience with similar products or product categories allows continuous innovations to be accepted more rapidly because they do not require major behavioral change by the user. Between these two extremes are **dynamically continuous innovations.** Not all target markets will perceive the same levels of newness

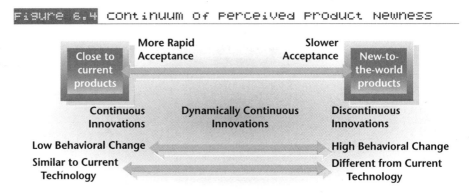

Figure 6.4 Continuum of Perceived Product Newness

for a single innovation; some markets may have greater levels of experience with a product or product category and therefore may not have to change behavior as much to accept a new technology. For example, individuals who have had experience with computers and software would make an easier transition to using the Web because they face a smaller behavioral change in order to use computer-based Web technology.

THINKING STRATEGICALLY

Consider the World Wide Web when it was first introduced: Was it a discontinuous innovation, a dynamically continuous innovation, or a continuous innovation? Discuss whether your answer will differ for different market segments. Explain whether an individual's past experience with computers and technology would have required less behavioral change and technology learning when accepting PC-based Web browsing. Evaluate what new interfaces such as Web TV mean for the future growth of the Internet and for those who do not own or use PCs.

CASE 6.1

Surfing the Net—Discontinuous or Continuous Innovation?

The introduction of the Mosaic World Wide Web graphical browser in 1994 enticed many individuals to try the Internet for the first time. All that the new user had to do to surf the Net was load the browser onto a PC, configure the browser to interact with the operating system, purchase a modem, find an ISP, load and make functional the ISP's log-on software, and then learn how to interface with the browser and Web pages.

Currently individuals can use devices such as Web TV to surf the Net. The system works with an existing television and does not require additional software interfaces. Individuals can surf using a wireless keyboard and/or a push-button remote control.

A key to speeding up the acceptance of discontinuous innovations is to incorporate into the new-to-the-world products **transparent technology** for the user. This decreases the level of behavior change needed by the market and helps to make discontinuous innovations seem like continuous innovations. This is in part the reason for the growth of the Web. It was possible to use the Web in a nongraphical mode, which required that the user be familiar with nongraphical interfaces often based on mainframe computer operating systems. It is not surprising that the Web and the Internet remained mainly a tool for academics for a long time. Graphical Web browsers made the linking and searching technology more transparent, enticing more individuals to access the Internet and Web content.

Transparent technology for a browser-based Web may exist only for those who are familiar with graphically based computers. By 1998, this was slightly less than 50 percent of the U.S. population. The growth of Web access over a Web-based TV will allow users who have less expertise with computers to use tools that they are already familiar with for Web browsing. For millions of potential Web users, the ability to use a TV remote control to access content through their televisions will require a minimum of behavioral change. In addition, increasing populations of young people have received computer training in schools, and their expertise with PCs and the Web is considerably higher than that of their parents or older brothers and sisters.[8]

Just because an innovation requires little behavioral change does not guarantee that it will be accepted quickly. Innovations must offer significant advantages over older ideas and products to gain acceptance. Table 6.1 outlines the five factors that can speed up an innovation's acceptance.[9]

Transparent technology implies that the user does not need to be familiar with any of the technical aspects to use the product. Windows 95 went a long way toward achieving transparency when it provided plug-and-play technology, allowing an individual to add components to a PC without any technical skills. With Apple's iMac, users only need to plug the computer into an electrical socket and phone plug to use the computer and go online.

Table 6.1 Relative Advantages Influencing Internet Technology Acceptance

Utility	Web as a Communications Tool	E-Commerce
Form (Nature of finished goods and services)	The Web allows an individual to find and access vast amounts of information. Push technology can meet customized information needs.	E-commerce allows individuals access to many alternative vendors. A market-of-one model allows an individual to have custom-made products.
Time (Available when the market wants them)	Communication over the Web is close to instantaneous. E-mail allows written messages to be delivered and stored, speeding communication. Finding information or products online is aided by the use of search engines.	Online purchasing allows time savings because of the number of vendors that can be evaluated in a in a short time. Delivery can also be on an overnight basis. Businesses can use online supply-chain management to ensure JIT delivery of goods.
Place (Available where the market wants them)	Communication over the Web can be directed to one's business or home. As wireless access becomes more common, access may be universal across locations.	Goods can be delivered directly to an individual's home or business. Portable Web devices allow individuals to compare prices and make purchases from any location.
Ownership (Transfer of ownership)	Information is transferred over the Web. Copyright laws cover ownership of information.	E-commerce enhances one's ability to receive title by facilitating both financing and payment flows.

1. **Relative advantage.** The innovation must offer greater utility (form, time, place, and possession) or more usefulness than existing products.
2. **Compatibility.** The innovation should be compatible with the market's lifestyle (social system and norms).
3. **Complexity.** The less the perceived complexity of an innovation, the faster is its acceptance.
4. **Trialability.** The easier it is for the market to experience the innovation and receive the benefits, the more quickly it will be accepted.
5. **Observability.** The easier it is for the market to see others receive benefits from using the innovation, the more quickly it will be accepted.

The killer application (killer app) is the software product that entices a user to adopt a larger technology. Spreadsheets were the killer apps for PCs. E-mail is the killer app for the Internet.

Snail mail is mail delivered through a postal service.

Relative Advantage

The acceptance of the Internet as a communications and commerce tool will rely heavily on the advantages offered. These advantages can be viewed in terms of the **economic utility** (the total level of satisfaction received from a good or service consisting of form, time, place, and ownership utility) offered. Table 6.1, on the previous page, indicates how total economic utility can be increased using the Internet. This will affect the Web as a communications tool and as a means of purchasing through e-commerce.

The information in Table 6.1 is backed by research data that indicates the reasons why people use e-commerce: convenience (66%), avoiding crowds (44%), prices (42%), items not available locally (39%), selection (26%), and speed and delivery (19%).[10]

CASE 6.2

The Rise of the Killer App

E-mail is considered to be the **killer application** on the Internet. In 1999, e-mail replaced research as the number one reason that people in the United States went online; e-mail is also a dominant reason that businesses add Internet access. The U.S. Postal Service (USPS) has projected that e-mail and e-billing will dramatically impact first-class mailing. First-class mail is expected to peak in 2002 and decrease 2.5 percent until the year 2008.[11]

To compete with e-mail, Sweden and Finland have deregulated postal services. Sweden's competitive postal system hosts a commerce site *(www.torget.se)*. Finland Post takes e-mail messages from individuals, prints them, and then delivers them to postal addresses. The USPS has developed plans to take advantage of the Internet. It has considered a service like Finland Post's. It is considering both Internet-based purchasing for shipping labels and for transmitting secure documents.[12]

Instant messaging services allow an individual to know when a buddy goes online. Individuals can create buddy lists so they can engage in real-time communication over the Internet. This technology is of interest not only to individuals who want to communicate but also to businesses that can use this to know when a prospective customer goes online. This technology could allow individuals to videoconference with friends over high-bandwidth communications lines. It could also allow targeted ads to be sent to an individual's home PC or Web TV.[13]

THINKING STRATEGICALLY

Consider why individuals may be shifting from postal letters to e-mail. Determine what utility e-mail offers over **snail mail.** If e-mail is the current killer app for the Internet, determine which other technologies would be adopted after the individual's use of e-mail. Speculate on whether or not instant messaging will be the next killer application. Consider which technologies would be threatened by the use of instant messaging.

COMPatibility and COMPlexity

Changes in technology **interface** design are undertaken to increase the rate of adoption. It is easier for users to access information when technology uses real-life **metaphors** as an interface to computer-mediated information. For computers, this has been tried with interfaces such as Microsoft's Bob and Packard Bell's Navigator living room.[14] These products had a tendency to slow computers down and were not widely accepted or used. Microsoft's Windows 95 environment uses the metaphors of a desktop, folders, and files. Apple's iMac was designed to make the computer and its interface very simple for home users.[15] As individuals gain experience with Web sites, they develop **mental models** of how to navigate the site. Amazon's Web site design has set the look and feel for millions of people whose first shopping experience was with Amazon. Many other sites have copied Amazon's file tab interface. Amazon has developed a one-click payment technology that allows repeat buyers to purchase with just one button click. To maintain the ease-of-use advantage, Amazon filed a patent infringement suit against its rival Barnes & Noble's *(www.barnesandnoble.com)* one-button technology.

Two computer interface consultants recommend that technology designers change the way they develop products. Dr. Clare-Marie Karat of IBM's Thomas J. Watson Research Center recommends that **computer engineers** understand that the user is always right. If the system doesn't work, it is the technology's fault, not the user's. Donald Norman, a consultant for Apple Computer, believes that technology must become idiot-proof by hiding the technology and bringing out the benefits.[17]

Interfaces are being designed to make it easier for individuals to use the Web for communication, training, and data searching. Tripod *(www.tripod.com)* redesigned its site to meet the needs of both savvy users and potential new users. The firm used a number of sources of input, including user focus groups, members of its premium fee-based program, a marketing research firm, its employees, and its management, to aid in designing its site. The newer Tripod site removed old clutter and used four stacked bars to allow users to easily find the four main services offered: *Build* for building a home page, *Explore* for browsing Tripod pages, *Interact* for accessing chat and message boards, and *Buy/Sell* for linking to Tripod's commerce partners. The site was reduced in size from over 50 Kbytes to less than 28 Kbytes, allowing faster download.[18]

Bankers Trust, a New York corporation, uses game-based interfaces over its intranet to aid corporate training. The corporation has designed games called Sexual Harassment Solitaire and Straight Shooter for learning new rules related to derivative trading. Bankers Trust has a young workforce, and the training was designed to meet their learning styles. For individuals who do not like a game type of interface, straight ques-

An **interface** links the user to the technology. An ideal interface does not require any behavioral change on the part of the user.

"Surfing the net" is a **metaphor**. It implies that one slides from place to place. Metaphors allow one to understand a new idea by relating it to previously understood concepts

A **mental model** is a set of relationships that one keeps in mind to understand how the world, or a piece of it, operates.

nsites

Computer engineers and technologically trained individuals often have a different world-view from marketers. Their higher levels of experience and expertise in using the Internet and the Web can lead to designs that are not intuitive for the general user. Differences in beliefs between technologically trained individuals and marketers will be further explored in Chapter 9.

tion-and-answer training is available. The game is linked to a database that keeps track of the users' scores.[19]

A **hyperbolic tree** allows users to visually navigate hierarchies of hundreds or thousands of objects. Each level of the hierarchical structure is linked to other subcategories.

The viewing of Web content is changing as well. **Hyperbolic tree** browsing allows an individual to see a topic of interest in the middle of a search area with associated branches, like the spokes of a wheel, to linked data. Xerox's Palo Alto Research Center researched computer/human interfaces to develop software drive hyperbolic trees. Xerox started Inxight Company *(www.inxight.com)* in 1997 to market this interface. A Web site mapped with a hyperbolic tree allows individuals to see the higher-level pages with all the associated links. When a related page or topic is clicked on, it brings that topic and related branches to the center of the search. It is hoped that this nonlist search system will speed a user's ability to retrieve data.[20]

Cartia Inc. *(www.cartia.com)* has an interface that uses a topographic map metaphor to allow individuals to find links to related words or concepts.[21] Ask Jeeves *(www.askjeeves.com)* is a natural language–based search engine. The interface metaphor is a butler. Users can ask questions in plain English; Ask Jeeves combines a natural language engine with a proprietary knowledge base that processes the meaning and grammar questions in plain English and then provides intelligent responses for the user. The knowledge base gets more intelligent the more Ask Jeeves is used. Ask Jeeves has been licensed by a number of businesses to allow individuals to ask natural language questions. Figure 6.5 indicates the growth in millions of questions that Ask Jeeves has answered from August 1998 to May 1999.[22]

The download time, or the amount of time a Web page takes to load and display on a computer, can also have an effect on users' willingness to view pages and shop at sites. Zona Research *(www.zonaresearch.com)* has determined that up to one-third of individuals will leave Web sites if the average download time is longer than eight seconds. This could result in potential e-commerce losses of up to $4.35 billion a year.[23] A 1998 study by Zona Research found that even experienced Internet users often found it difficult to navigate online commerce sites. These shoppers will often not purchase the product, and will turn to brick and mortar or catalog stores, or try another Web site.[24]

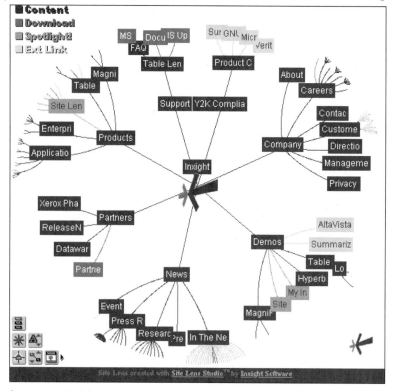

Source: www.inxight.com

Figure 6.5 Ask Jeeves Growth (in millions of questions)

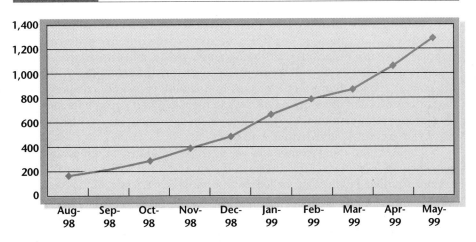

Interface design is a moving target. Markets vary in their levels of experience and knowledge, and their current preferences for interfaces may be based on past experiences. Preferences change as individuals gain experience. Companies should test Web interface designs often to be sure they are acceptable to the market.[25]

Trialability and Observability

By trial and observation, individuals lower the risk of adopting a new innovation. Consumers face a number of risks in purchasing over the Internet. One study found the concerns that individuals have about using the Internet for commerce include (in order of importance): security (fear of being robbed by hackers), lack of selection, unknown quality of the merchandise (inability to touch), and privacy issues.[26]

As consumers gain greater experience with online commerce, they are increasing their amount of purchasing online. Table 6.2 indicates how the market is shifting its purchase patterns, moving from information search and purchasing offline to greater amounts of purchasing online. This table may indicate that individuals

Table 6.2 Shifting Online-Influenced Purchasing (billions of dollars)

	Browsed Online, Purchased Offline	Ordered Online, Paid Offline	Paid Online
1997	$44.8	$10.2	$ 5.2
1998	50.8	15.5	11.0
1999	103.0	23.5	19.2

Source: Adapted from Connie Guglielmo, "If Amazon Ruled the World," *Inter@ctive Week,* October 11, 1999, p. 45.

gain trial experiences by using the Internet for information purposes first and then move to purchasing online as their comfort level grows.

Companies are attempting to lower the perceived risks involved in using the Web for communication or purchases. Security is the primary concern, and a number of security measures are being employed to make transactions more secure (see Chapter 2). In reality, security of credit-card information over the Internet may be higher than other forms of transactions. A security company found that it took 50,000 CPUs working 39 days to break a 59-bit encryption code. Most companies use more than 59 bits, making them even more secure, but consumer perception can carry more weight than reality.[27]

One tactic that many companies use to entice customers to use the Web is to give away free products. This has been the standard for Web browsers but also extends to other products as well. Free information services such as free e-mail have helped to establish the Web as a communications tool. Companies are also using incentives to entice individuals to purchase over the Internet. These include earning points or credit based on the number of purchases that individuals undertake, which can be redeemed for gift certificates, frequent-flyer miles, or cash.[28]

THE INDIVIDUAL ADOPTION PROCESS

The individual **adoption curve** indicates how individuals react to innovations over time. The adoption process places adopters into categories and explores how the earlier adopters influence later adopters. Marketers can use this information to segment markets and design promotional campaigns.

Adoption Curve

The adoption curve is used as a model to understand both who is likely to be an innovator and how interpersonal influence passes to later adopters of innovations. Figure 6.6 outlines this process by placing individuals into adopter categories based on how quickly they adopt innovations over time.

Innovators are the first to adopt; they are seen as having personal characteristics that make them different from later adopters. Innovators are reported to have higher income and higher educational levels, to be younger and more socially integrated, and to have a higher risk tolerance.[29] These characteristics are somewhat reflected in the profiles of early Web and e-commerce users, as illustrated in Table 6.3.

Innovators with these characteristics are likely to have greater experience with technology and its uses. They may be able to see advantages that others do not see in using the Web for information or purchases. Using technology may be more compatible with their lifestyles and considered less complex. These knowledge advantages, along with higher incomes and more risk tolerance, may allow innovators to perceive the Web differently from later adopters.

Figure 6.6 The Adoption Process

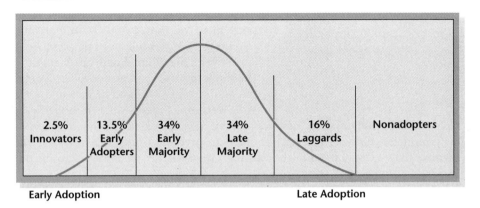

2.5% Innovators	13.5% Early Adopters	34% Early Majority	34% Late Majority	16% Laggards	Nonadopters

Early Adoption   Late Adoption

Personal Influence Process

Once individuals gain experience with the product, they may act as **opinion leaders** and communicate with others about their experience. The interaction of an **early adopter** (the second adopter category, following innovator) with an innovator lowers perceived risk. Once early adopters gain experience, they communicate to the **early majority** (the third group of adopters). This process continues down through the fourth adopting category, the **laggards.** Some companies are taking advantage of this word-of-mouth system to attract new

Table 6.3 Web Users, Demographic Profiles (1996–1997)

Profiling Factor	Web as a Communications Tool	E-Commerce
Age	U.S.: 35 (increasing over time) Europe: range 21–30	U.S.: 33
Gender	U.S.: 61.3% male, 38.7% female Europe: 83.7% male, 16.3% female (Note that number of females increasing over time)	In U.S., varies by product category: Sex sites: 98% male, 2% female Amazon.com: 57% male, 42.8% female Specialty gifts: 31% male, 69% female
Income	$52,000	Average: $59,000
Education	Some college: 80.9% At least one degree: 50.1%	College degree: 57%

Source: Information compiled from *GVU's 9th WWW User Survey,* Georgia Tech Research Corporation, 1996, <*http://www.cc.gatech.edu/gvu/user_surveys/survey-1998-04/*> (note that Georgia Tech updates its survey data on a regular basis); James E. Pitkow and Colleen M. Kehoe, "Emerging Trends in the WWW User Population," *Communications of the ACM,* June 1996, vol. 39, no. 6, pp. 106–108; and David Batstone and Eric Hellweg, "Cash on the Line, Introducing the Internet Consumer," *Business 2.0,* 1998 premiere issue, pp. 28–29.

Luddite is a name given to individuals who reject technology. The Luddites were Scottish weavers who destroyed automated weaving machines in an attempt to keep technology out of their industry. The lasting impact of their action was that their name became part of our vocabulary.

Viral marketing occurs when a customer promotes something through use of a product or service such as a Web site or e-mail.

customers by engaging in **viral marketing.** Hotmail's free e-mail service has captured more than 40 million subscribers. The company spent less than $500,000 on marketing to gain this share while its major competitor spent over $20 million on advertising. Part of Hotmail's marketing plan was to use a tag at the end of every sent e-mail message—"Get Your Private, Free E-Mail at *http://www. hotmail.com*"—making every sent message an advertisement. Friends who received an e-mail message from a user could gain greater confidence in the service because they know someone who has used the service.[30] In 1999, Microsoft purchased Hotmail for $450 million.

Nonadopters will never accept the innovation; this could be due to lack of access or lack of interest, or the individual could be a **Luddite** and have disdain for technology. Nonadopters of computer-based Web access may become adopters of television-based Web access. The number of users already accepting television as a one-way communication device is close to 100 percent of U.S. homes.

THE PRODUCT LIFE CYCLE

The **product life cycle** is a representation of the cumulative adoption of an innovation by a society over time. This is generally viewed in terms of a product category, such as the use of the Internet or Web, and may not accurately represent a single product. Single products usually enter an industry at some point in the industry life cycle. The product life cycle uses a metaphor that indicates that products are developed, are introduced, grow, mature, and decline. The rate at which products have been moving through their life cycles has been decreasing over time; in many high-tech industries, life cycles for products can run from 6 to 18 months. Figure 6.7 illustrates the basic product life cycle.

Figure 6.7 indicates that the number of users of a product increases over time, the growth eventually peaks, and then the number of users declines. The development of the new product results in an initial cost. As the product moves into its growth stage, profits grow. These profits can draw competition, which in turn drives down the price of the product and eventually reduces the profitability of the product. As new technologies emerge, they replace the older product, resulting in a decline in the number of users. Eventually competitors shift away from the product; the only purchasers who remain are those who are loyal to the product or technology, allowing prices to increase and possibly return profits to the few remaining companies. Some products, such as the telephone, saturate potential markets. These products may then evolve through continuous innovations. Dial-tone telephones have given way to Touch-Tone phones, and landline phones are giving way to cellular systems.

Analog television has moved through a life cycle. It has been a mature product since the introduction of color television in the 1960s. New digital television

Figure 6.7 Product Life Cycle

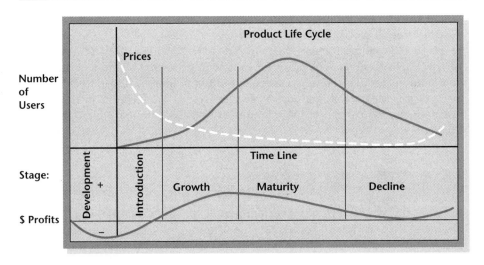

standards are being introduced, and viewing of television is down 15 percent in homes that have Web access.[31]

Web-Based Television

Web-based television and computer-based television are current mass-market options for Internet access. The growth of these television alternatives is dependent on the value they offer. Bringing the Web to SDTV (standard definition television) results in poor-quality images and text. Downloads present problems because most systems use the telephone line for the last-mile connection. Personal computers can be enhanced with TV cards that allow television broadcasts to be played through the computer monitor. This adds utility to the computer but creates an expensive stand-alone television.

Digital television has many advantages over standard analog television. Its high-definition picture (HDTV) holds 1,080 horizontal and 1,920 vertical lines, three times the current U.S. standard, which result in a sharper image. At close to $6,000, prices at the beginning of the HDTV life cycle are high. The early buyers of HDTV were individuals who are considered to be innovators in the product category. By the end of 1999, less than 50,000 homes across the United States had HDTVs, and only 30 out of 1,600 TV stations had digital signals carried over cable lines. Lack of copyright protection has limited release of HDTV programs, and there is still a conflict over the HDTV format that will be used.[32] By 2002, broadcasters are expected to increase their digital broadcasts by 50 percent. Digital signals require more bandwidth than analog, and cable companies may not transmit digital signals as quickly. The HDTV life cycle will grow over time; analog broadcasting may cease altogether if and when digital television becomes the standard.[33] Another advantage of digital HDTV is that it can be combined with computer processing power to become the interface access to the Web, allowing for fast download over cable, satellite, or broadcast signals. HDTV will be the battleground for all companies looking to capture "eyeballs," including television broadcasters and Web sites.[34]

Figure 6.8 outlines the projected life cycle of HDTV and analog TV. Analog, or current U.S. TV formats, took off after World War II. In 1998, digital television was introduced in San Diego; set prices were initially very high. As the market matures, prices are expected to fall, and sales of sets are expected to increase. If HDTV penetration reaches 85 percent of the U.S. market by 2006, sales of analog televisions will cease.

ELECTRONIC COMMUNITIES

Online communities are groups of individuals who share common interests and use the Internet to foster their communities by accessing the same Web sites for communication, commerce, or support.

Although the Web allows the development of one-to-one marketing, it is also being used to target broader market segments through the creation of online communities. **Online communities** are created to provide mutual support or to drive Web users with shared interests, opinions, or activities to a site. Businesses develop online communities to appeal to groups of users who will use the site's products or who can be targeted by advertisers through the site. Online communities drive traffic to sites and have grown faster than general Internet use. Individuals also stay longer at community sites. Online communities allow narrow targeting for advertising and e-commerce offers; these sites can also generate support for social causes.[35]

Figure 6.8 Projected Digital Television Life Cycle (U.S.)

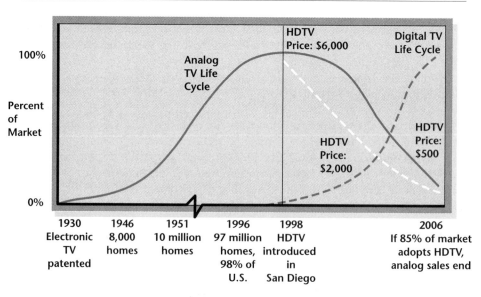

A number of new online communities are being developed for **Netizens,** or Internet citizens. AOL may have set the first model for Net communities, but a number of other companies are developing and fostering communities online. Yahoo! has a club section *(www.clubs.yahoo.com)* on its site to allow individuals to create their own communities. This includes setting up message boards, chats, e-mails, online photo albums, and other community information. These can be listed publicly or kept private. Yahoo! also purchased GeoCities *(http://geocities. yahoo.com),* which has 41 different "neighborhoods" where any of the subscribers can interact.[36] XOOM.com *(www.xoom.com)* is an e-commerce site that entices users by offering a hosting service whereby individuals can build their own home pages and set up chat rooms, message boards, and other community tools. To use the site, individuals must submit their e-mail address and personal data for targeted e-mail advertising.

Firms wishing to expand their markets online must do more than just offer products; they must develop tight relationships with their target markets. This section will explore a number of market segments and their use of the Web both as a communications and shopping source and as a means of creating community.

Online Market Segmentation Process

Markets can be segmented on a number of characteristics. Many widely reported statistics of Internet use are based on demographic factors such as gender, age, and income. The results generally indicate that younger males with higher incomes dominate the Internet. Businesses also use **psychographics** to segment markets, which entails identifying lifestyle criteria of markets. Table 6.4, on the following page, outlines two marketing research companies' psychographic profiles of Web shoppers. BMRB International is a United Kingdom–based marketing research firm; it identified six categories of shoppers, all related to the amount of experience that individuals have with online shopping. McKinsey & Company also looked at online shoppers and identified four groups that differed in their surfing and shopping behavior.

Psychographics (lifestyle criteria) generally profile individuals based on their preferred activities, interests, and opinions.

Psychographics and demographics can be used with other behavioral data to draw profiles of Internet users. Just as magazines target markets by these profiles, community sites attempt to draw markets based on shared lifestyle activities, interests, and opinions.

Female Markets

Males have been the major users of Internet technologies, but the gap between males and females has been diminishing over time. In 1994, almost 95 percent of Web users were male; by 1998, only 61 percent were male. In addition, 1998 marked the first year that females outnumbered males in users who were online for less than one year (51.7% female, 48.3% male).[37] Media Metrix *(www. mediametrix.com)* reported that women and men used the Internet in equal numbers in 1999. Some researchers are projecting that women will outnumber men

Table 6.4 Industry Psychographic Profiles

BMRB International[a]	McKinsey[b]
Confident Brand Shoppers (more than two years' experience; 16% of the market, spend 20% more than average): Confident about e-commerce, this group searches for a cheaper price for well-known brands. This group will shop around.	**Directed Settlers:** These individuals settle on a site and buy directly.
Carefree Spenders (more than two years' experience; 15% of the market, spend 55% more than average): This group is carefree when approaching purchasing online. This group will buy from unknown companies and purchase lesser-known brands even without seeing them first.	**Direct Wanderers:** They use the Web to surf from site to site. They like to gather their own information and make up their own minds.
Realistic Enthusiasts (more than two years' experience; 15% of the market): Enthusiastic about e-commerce, they are willing to purchase products from an unknown company. Convenience of online shopping is more important than price. Ideally, they would like to see the product in real life before making a a purchase. They also consider that finding the product to purchase is a difficult process.	**Fickle Settlers:** These individuals learn how to use a site and do not like to move if the site learns their buying habits.
Bargain Hunters (one to two years' experience; 16% of the market): They will spend very little online, mainly based on low prices.	**Fickle Wanderers:** These individuals like to surf the Net but like to have informediaries, such as agents or search engines, do the searching for them.
Cautious Shoppers (less than one year's experience; 20% of the market): Very cautious about e-commerce, they are not likely to use an online auction. They are concerned about product quality and would like to see products before making a purchase.	
Unfulfilled (less than one year's experience; 17% of the market): This group finds shopping online to be an unfulfilling experience. It is too difficult to find the products online, and they want to see the products first and purchase from a known company. They will not purchase from an online auction and want products delivered quickly.	

Source: [a] BMRB International, Internet Monitor, "E-Commerce—An attitudinal evolution," BMRB International Press Release, April, 1999, <http://www.bmrb.co.uk>, with [b] Jim Sterne, "Promote and Deliver," *CIO Web Business—Section 2,* December 1, 1998, pp. 66–68.

online by the year 2002. The online market may grow to reflect the U.S. mass market in which women account for 54 percent of the population and influence 85 percent of purchase decisions.[38]

Women are responsible for more than 70 percent of traditional retail purchases and must become a vital component of e-commerce. In order to target this segment, Web sites must offer benefits that women look for, including savings of time and money; in addition, Web sites must also develop a sense of community. A number of sites have been developed to specifically foster Web communities for women. Traffic at the top four women's sites grew 200 percent to 300 percent in 1997. In 1998, 51 percent of America Online's 13 million subscribers were women, up from 16 percent in 1994. iVillage is a community Web site that allows women to obtain information, engage in chats, and share expertise. At one time, iVillage had 1,400 discussion boards. iVillage also allows links to shopping sites that target women and run classified ads targeted to women.[39]

Women's sites are adding interactive components that act as personal shoppers. Bloomingdale's gives fashion and shopping advice; shoppers can fill out a profile and receive customized advice. Bloomingdale's doesn't want its users to worry about technology; just click and use. Clinique invites users to its Web site to build a profile of their skin type. It also provides information on skin care and how to use the Internet for saving time and money.[40]

Source: www.ivillage.com

CASE 6.3

It Takes an iVillage to Start a Trend

iVillage is a community site for women between the ages of 25 and 40. The site provides access to experts in different content areas, chat rooms, news, and many other information areas of interest to the women's market. iVillage started in 1995 and by 1999 received over 3 million unique visitors a month. Each visitor viewed an average of 25.6 pages and stayed at the site an average of 8.5 minutes. On the first day of iVillage's initial public offering, the stock price increased from $22 to over $95. By the end of 1999, the stock price had dropped back into the $20 range. This could be due to the large number of other women's sites that have grown online, including Hearst Communication's HomeArts network *(www.homearts.com)* and Women.com *(www.women.com)*, Microsoft's WomenCentral *(http://women.msn.com/women/),* and specialty women's sites such as Martha Stewart's *(www.marthastewart.com).*[41]

THINKING STATEGICALLY

iVillage's stock price may indicate the market's beliefs about the viability of community sites such as iVillage. Visit the iVillage site *(www.ivillage.com)*. Decide if this site is too general or has too broad an appeal to entice individuals to return. Visit the competitive site Women.com *(www.women.com)*. Determine how this site is different from iVillage. Identify some specific interests that women may have. Search the Internet for Web sites that may provide support for those narrower interests.

Children and Youth Markets

The number of U.S. children who have Internet access through school or home is expected to increase from 10.5 million in 1998 to more than 30.4 million by 2002. Worldwide, there may be 77 million under the age of 18 online. The youth market has lagged behind the adult market in part due to safety issues. The Web can allow access to pornographic, violent, or suggestive material. Advertisers are also concerned with issues of manipulative advertising; advertising on children's TV shows is highly regulated through governmental and industry policies. Regardless of these constraints, a number of firms are looking to develop online children's communities.[42]

When using online services, adults spend on average one hour online; children will spend up to three hours online. The children's market is expected to spend $1.8 billion on e-commerce by 2002. America Online *(www.aol.com)* offers a kid-only section on its electronic service. Other media companies are targeting this market as an additional service. Yahoo! offers a Yahooligans *(www.yahooligans.com)* search for children to find kid-friendly sites. Disney *(www.disney.com)*, Fox TV *(www.fox.com)*, and Nickelodeon *(www.nickelodeon.com)* have set up sites to entertain and promote other products and services offered by these companies. MaMaMedia *(www.mamamedia.com)* allows children to surf kid-friendly sites, play games, and personalize a Web page. By 1998, the site had 90,000 registered users who created over 60,000 multimedia projects.[43]

Older youth segments spend the most time on the Internet. Individuals between the ages 18 and 29 spend an average of 9.3 hours a week on the Internet. These older markets are often targeted on a more segmented basis.[44]

Niche Markets

Niche sites are designed to target a market's psychographics by focusing on narrow activities and interests. The ability to tailor information and to target these narrow markets makes the Web an ideal medium to develop niche communities.

Sport sites offer enthusiasts the ability to interact with their favorite sports leagues or teams, including not only the large national sport teams but also niche sports as well. In 1998, ESPN.com *(www.espn.com)* received over 66.5 million page views per week. Visitors can not only follow major teams but can link to sites that cover tennis, hockey, soccer, etc.[45] Companies are developing strategies around these narrow niche sports. InterZine *(www.interzine.com)* develops sites for skiing, biking, snowboarding, golfing, etc. InterZine was purchased by Times Mirror to enhance its print material.[46]

The over-50 user market is expected to exceed 115 million in the United States over the next 25 years. This Internet-user segment is one of the fastest growing and purchases online at rates higher than other segments. In 1998, over 13 million U.S. adults over the age of 50 had Internet access; the highest uses were for e-mail, research, and investment information. Of this group, 92 percent had window-shopped online, and 78 percent had made online purchases. Those over age 65 see the Internet as a means of improving their lives with the ability to connect to others online. Marketers have started to see this segment as a very important growth market. The AARP *(www.aarp.org)* and ThirdAge *(www.thirdage.com)* are Web sites for this mature market. They offer information, guides, support, and shopping targeted to this growing market.[47]

Many Web sites target very narrow Web communities. Individual TV shows such as *Drew Carey,* rock groups such as the Rolling Stones, individual support groups for diseases, and many more types of sites offer unique benefits to their users. As these communities become more widely known, they help to expand the reach of the Internet.

Development of Online Communities

Online communities are designed to not only target markets within the general population but also to be used by both extranet communities within vertical industries and intranet communities within organizations. A study by Arthur Andersen LLP *(www.arthurandersen.com)* identified seven key principles that are critical for successful online community development; these are outlined in Table 6.5 on the following page.[48]

Virtual Communities' Effect on Society

Sociologist Sherry Turkle argues that the Web is redefining the sense of community. The Web is seen as a medium that allows individuals to explore different sides of

Table 6.5 Seven Principles of Success for Online Communities

Principle	Description
Focus on design.	Find activities and designs that will increase the targeted market's participation in the site.
Focus on the needs of members.	Design the site around the needs of members, such as the work they do, the hobbies they have, or the interests they share. Use individuals from the community to help with the design.
Do not attempt to control.	Attempting to control the flow of information may drive users away. Some sites may want to suggest guidelines; other sites may offer free open forums along with controlled forums.
Do not assume the forum is self-sustaining.	A champion of the site may be needed to keep the site up-to-date and vibrant.
Evaluate the community's culture.	Consider how the targeted community shares information. A community that shares information will require a different site than one that likes to receive but not give information.
Allow communications growth outside local discussions.	Any growth in communication or interaction should be facilitated on the site. Use tools such as e-mail, discussion lists, and buddy lists.
Use facilitators.	Find and support members who can act as facilitators. These individuals could encourage others to visit, lead discussions, provoke controversy, and raise issues.

Source: Adapted from Daintry Duffy, "The Seven Principles of Community Success," *CIO Enterprise—Section 2*, October 15, 1999, p. 38.

their personalities by adopting online personae. Persons can communicate globally but are forming "local" communities with individuals who share targeted interests. Individuals are also tinkering with technology and integrating it into their lives.[49]

Web communities and Web use have been criticized. A study funded by the National Science Foundation through Carnegie-Mellon University found that using the Internet had a weak but significant relationship to feelings of social isolation, depression, and loneliness. The results of this one study have been disputed, and further research is recommended.

Speed of Adoption Based on Relationships

The rate of adoption of Web-based communication and commerce will depend on how much additional benefit the marketer can offer through this medium. Customers are more willing to adopt when their needs are met. Once a firm establishes this relationship, it has an incentive to maintain that relationship over a long time period. The catalog clothing store Land's End prides itself on how well it maintains relationships with its customers. Land's End sees the Internet as a tool and wants its customers to have the same experience online as they would have over the phone or with the catalog. Its Web site mirrors the catalog by having in-depth information on products; however, the Web site can carry more in-depth and up-to-date information than the catalog. Shoppers can see how various items look together to create a coordinated outfit by placing ties over shirts and shirts with pants. Out-of-stock items are not displayed so customers are not disappointed. On Wednesdays, the site allows individuals to purchase overstocked items. Prices are reduced every hour until they sell out.[50] Land's End is developing a virtual community of shoppers who maintain their loyalty.

CROSS-CULTURAL ACCEPTANCE

Alexis de Tocqueville visited the United States in the 1830s and noticed that Americans were building sailing ships of much poorer quality than those built in Europe. When he inquired as to the reason, he found a logical explanation. The American builders realized that sailing technology was changing so quickly that it didn't make sense to build a boat to last any longer than the technology would be current. To do so would be a waste of resources; it would also lock the owner into technology that would be out-of-date but too expensive to get rid of. What De Tocqueville realized was that American society was willing to let go of past practices and accept innovation in product and process.

Acceptance of the Internet as a communications and commerce tool is dependent on the infrastructure that is in place for the transport of high-bandwidth data, as outlined in Chapter 2. For Web use, individuals must have access to the Internet through computers or Web-enabled televisions. Businesses and the population of a country must also be willing to develop content and to use Internet services. This is somewhat dependent on a culture's willingness to abandon old practices and accept new ones.

Lionel Dersot, a French national living in Japan, has noted that the Japanese do not readily accept the Web as a communications medium. This is in part due to the low level of computer penetration in Japan (15 percent of homes) and a cumbersome telephone system. Dersot also sees the problem of acceptance related to the nature of Japanese culture: Japanese don't readily express their opinions to others. The Internet is, at its heart, a communications medium. The Japanese desire for consensus restricts discussion, argument, and debate, limiting the Internet's usefulness as a tool.[51]

Acceptance of the Internet varies across countries. Table 6.6 on the following page indicates the measure of acceptance by showing the number of domains per capita for several countries. This is a reflection of how heavily the Internet has penetrated those societies.

Table 6.6 shows that acceptance rates by domain are highest in the United States, followed by countries in Western Europe. Japan lags behind considerably.

Table 6.6 Relative Acceptance of the Internet (1998 figures)

Country	Number of Domains (in thousands)	Population of Country (in millions)	Index (individuals per domain)
United States	3,680	268.0	73
Denmark	66	5.3	80
Australia	55	8.0	145
Sweden	59	8.9	151
United Kingdom	172	58.6	341
Germany	219	84.0	384
Taiwan	17	21.5	1,265
France	26	58.5	2,250
Japan	47	125.0	2,660
Brazil	29	165.0	5,690

Source: Statistics are taken from DomainStats.com, part of the NetNames Domain Name Information Service, October 14, 1998.

Table 6.7 on the following page indicates projections of worldwide and regional Internet use by the number of individuals.

Each culture determines its acceptance of technological change. Countries that are laggards in the acceptance of Internet-based technologies will not face the disruption caused by these new communications tools. However, they are also less likely to receive the benefits of open communication and more efficient business markets. A study by David Altig and Peter Rupert, reported in the *Economic Commentary of the Federal Reserve Bank of Cleveland,* found that there was a significant relationship between Internet use and economic growth. The relationship indicates that 100 percent Internet usage would be associated with 4 percentage points in economic growth. The researchers concluded that the adoption of the Internet actually measures a society's willingness to adopt technology innovations. Some societies have reduced the structural barriers to adoption by deregulation and fostering of Internet connections. In addition, a society's willingness to accept technology innovations results in higher growth rates.[52]

Table 6.7 Internet Users by Region

Internet Statistics	1995	1998	2000	2005
Worldwide Internet users (in thousands)	39,479	150,887	318,650	717,083
Worldwide users (number per 1,000 people)	6.9	25.4	52.5	110.5
North America Internet users (in thousands)	26,217	82,989	148,730	229,780
North America users (number per 1,000 people)	89.4	275.7	479.1	715.4
West Europe Internet users (in thousands)	8,528	34,741	86,577	202,201
West Europe users (number per 1,000 people)	21.7	87.5	217.5	501.4
East Europe Internet users (in thousands)	369	2,983	9,487	43,767
East Europe users (number per 1,000 people)	1.3	10.2	32.7	151.8
Asia-Pacific Internet users (in thousands)	3,628	24,559	57,607	171,098
Asia-Pacific users (number per 1,000 people)	1.1	7.2	16.6	45.9
South/Central America Internet users (in thousands)	293	2,722	10,766	43,529
South/Central America users (number per 1,000 people)	0.6	5.5	21.1	78.6
Middle East/Africa Internet users (in thousands)	444	2,893	7,482	26,708
Middle East/Africa users (number per 1,000 people)	0.5	2.9	7.2	23.6

Source: Computer Industry Almanac Inc., "North America Is the Leading Region for Internet Users According to the *Computer Industry Almanac*," August 18, 1999, <*http://www.c-i-a.com/199908iu.htm*>.

DIFFUSION AND the ADOPTION PROCESS IN THE FIRM

"I should change my title from CIO to technology personal trainer: I drag these guys kicking and screaming into the future and cause them a lot of agony along the way. But later on, when they look in the mirror, they like the results."
Ken Landis, CIO,
Strong Capital Management, at an *Information Week*
Conference in 1988[53]

In 1876, the Western Union Telegraph Company refused to purchase the rights to the telephone. It could justify this by presuming that it didn't make sense to replace a proven system with new technology. Western Union couldn't understand why telegraph operators would want to talk to each other to relay messages. Western Union didn't envision placing the telephone in an individual's home. Other managers were more innovative. A vice president of AT&T envisioned sending music over phone lines into people's homes; this idea was proposed in 1890.[54]

Businesses must evolve in order to adapt to changes in the environment. New ideas must be brought into an organization. These ideas could be for new products, new business models, or new workflow processes. The diffusion and adoption process outlined in this chapter is a model for the spread of new ideas and processes inside a firm. Just as individual consumers accept new products at differing rates, so do individuals inside a firm. When new business processes are introduced, they must offer substantial advantages in cost savings, time savings, or competitive advantages in order to revise fundamental business practices. Change is disruptive. This can be frustrating for individuals who want to introduce new ideas. These individuals are the innovators or intrapreneurs inside an organization. The diffusion of innovation theory is very helpful in understanding how these individuals can implement change in the organization. This section will outline the considerations involved in the diffusion process inside a firm, and will then discuss actions that change agents can take to implement new ideas and processes.

Intrapreneurs

Intrapreneurs are **change agents** with entrepreneurial and leadership traits who act within existing firms by building coalitions and managing workers in innovative tasks. Intrapreneurial behavior occurs in existing companies when someone introduces new products or new ideas that allow the company as a whole to grow.[55] Intrapreneurs work well in innovative organizational cultures, are willing to change, and are often willing to operate as product or idea champions. This means that they are willing to work with new ideas and to implement change.[56]

Intrapreneurial individuals are more likely to have outside contacts and an outward focus, and they bring outside ideas into the firm. They have personality traits such as innovativeness, risk-taking propensity, and proactive orientation.[57] Intrapreneurs may not attempt to act on new ideas unless there is a supporting atmosphere inside the firm. This can come both from a supportive management that stays out of the innovator's way and from the existence of a more

Hindsight Is 20/20

"This 'telephone' has too many shortcomings to be seriously considered as a means of communication. The device is inherently of no value to us."

Western Union internal memo, 1876

"Everything that can be invented has been invented."

Charles H. Duell, U.S. commissioner of patents, 1899

"The wireless music box has no imaginable commercial value. Who would pay for a message sent to nobody in particular?"

David Sarnoff's associates in response to his urgings for investments in the radio in the 1920s

"Who the . . . wants to hear actors talk?"

H. M. Warner, Warner Brothers, 1927

Figure 6.9 Interaction Between Innovator and Firm

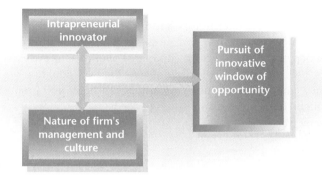

organic organizational culture that allows for the growth of new ideas. Figure 6.9 illustrates the interaction that must exist between the innovator and the firm in order for the individual to attempt to pursue a market opportunity.

Communication and Coalition Building

Innovators who attempt to introduce new ideas too quickly into a firm are likely to face rejection. This has a tendency to force innovative individuals out of more bureaucratic firms. In order to gain acceptance of new ideas, the innovator should follow the same type of influence process that occurs in the adoption process. As the **product champion,** the innovator should first communicate with the early adopters in the firm who would be supportive of a new idea. Once a coalition has developed, that core group can then expand the idea and gain support throughout the organization. The innovator acts as the change agent by developing a coalition of key participants who would be the early adopters of the idea. These key participants could be marketing managers, R&D managers, and other key management personnel. As these individuals refine and support the idea, they then can communicate to other managers and decision makers, spreading the idea throughout the organization.[58]

> A **product champion** is an individual inside an organization who acts as an advocate for an innovation.

The rate at which the communication spreads inside an organization is dependent on the culture of the business. Businesses that are more entrepreneurial than bureaucratic will have this process occur at a more rapid rate. A key to implementing change is support by top management. As leaders of an organization, management sets the strategic direction for the firm. These issues of leadership and culture will be explored more in Chapter 9.

Industry Leaders and Laggards

Consumers are learning to adopt Internet technologies by starting with Web-based research and e-mail and then moving toward making purchases online. As businesses transform through the use of technology, they are also moving from information-based Internet use to business process restructuring. A 1999 study of 1,000 business and IT managers, reported in *Information Week*, indicated that the e-business applications being used most often were intranets for internal communication (90%), Web sites for external communication (70%), extranets (30%), and e-commerce sites (25%). Future e-business applications being planned include extranets (19 percent of businesses); e-commerce applications are expected to grow by 21 percent.[59] Companies that lead in new technology adoption are more likely to see that they can gain competitive advantages through new products and have reported financial gains from using leading-edge technologies.[60]

KNOWLEDGE INTEGRATION TERMS AND CONCEPTS

Adoption curve *160*	Economic utility *156*	Netizen *165*
Change agent *174*	Hyperbolic tree *158*	Nonadopter *162*
Compatibility *156*	Innovation *151*	Observability *156*
Complexity *156*	Innovator *160*	Online community *164*
Continuous innovation 153	Instant messaging *156*	Opinion leader *161*
Diffusion of innovations process *151*	Interface *157*	Product life cycle *162*
	Intrapreneur *174*	Psychographics *165*
	Killer application (killer app) *156*	Relative advantage *156*
Discontinuous innovation *153*	Laggard *161*	Transparent technology *154*
Dynamically continuous innovation *153*	Late majority *161*	Trialability *156*
	Luddite *162*	Viral marketing *162*
Early adopter *161*	Mental model *157*	
Early majority *161*	Metaphor *157*	

CONCEPTS AND QUESTIONS FOR REVIEW

1. Describe how the diffusion of innovations model works.
2. Explain the major influences in the diffusion model.
3. Discuss the roles of behavioral and technical change in relation to how innovations are categorized.
4. Recommend how to increase the chances of acceptance for innovations. Relate this to the development of Web sites.
5. Justify the use of metaphors in the development of interfaces used on Web sites.
6. Describe how the product life cycle can be used to understand the surge and decline of innovations.
7. Explain the influences on individual adoption over time.
8. Define an electronic community and discuss which segmentation techniques are used to target markets with communities.

9. List some of the markets that are targeted by electronic communities.
10. Which countries are most accepting of Internet technologies and which are least accepting? Explain why those countries at the top of the list are more likely to accept than those at the bottom.
11. Describe how the diffusion process works within a firm.
12. Discuss the role of change agents in the diffusion process.
13. Recommend how a change agent could build a coalition within a firm.

ACTIVE LEARNING

Exercise 6.1: Innovation Typology

The Internet offers a number of innovations for individuals. Some of these will be discontinuous and some continuous innovations, depending on the markets served. Develop a chart like the one that follows for a number of technologies available on the Internet. Indicate where a target market would perceive a product to be and justify why it would be in that innovative space. Two examples are given. The senior market will probably have little experience with online downloads of music and would have to change their behavior to use an MP3 player. The youth market will need little training or behavior change to take advantage of buddy lists. For a list of the newest Web innovations, see Internet Product Watch at *http://ipw.internet.com.*

Innovation Typology

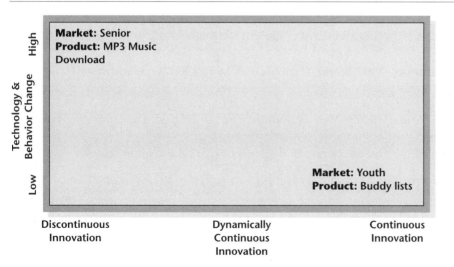

Exercise 6.2: Finding Your Community

There are a number of online communities available on the Internet. Make a list of your favorite activities, interests, and opinions. Choose the top two or three, and place those terms into a search engine with the search term "community." Explore a number of sites and see if these are designed to meet and hold your interest.

Exercise 6.3: Interface Design

Use the profile you developed in Exercise 6.2 to develop a Web page interface. Draw out the interface using a metaphor that the target market would understand. Justify that design given the experience of the target market. Why would that metaphor be beneficial to the target market?

Exercise 6.4: Intrafirm Diffusion

Consider yourself the designated change agent for introducing an e-business innovation within a firm. Using a business that you work in, or a group of friends or classmates you interact with, identify the key participants you would first contact. Then identify the other key players who would be necessary for getting an idea accepted. Determine which e-business innovation you would first like to introduce and which innovations would follow. What arguments would you use to help convince others to adopt the innovations?

WEB SEARCH — LOOKING ONLINE

| SEARCH TERM: | Internet Diffusion Statistics | First 7 out of 3,800 |

Commerce Net. Works with Nielson Media Research to provide statistics.
www.commerce.net

CyberAtlas. Updates Web use number and profiling data on segments. It also includes useful information on Web use and technology.
www.cyberatlas.com

Cyber Dialogue. Has limited statistics on Web use and commerce.
www.cyberdialogue.com

Georgia Tech University. Offers extensive information collected over time on Internet use.
www.gvu.gatech.edu/gvu/user_surveys

International Data Corporation. Sells research reports but also provides some statistics for free.
www.idcresearch.com

NUA Ltd. Provides international news and information about Web use and markets.
www.nua.ie/surveys

WorldOpinion. Provides news and information related to Web-based research. It also provides a list of major marketing research online sites.
www.worldopinion.com

SEARCH TERM:	Interface Design	First 3 out of 6,482

Reactiv: High Energy Web Interface. Is a business site with a tutorial on Web page interface design. It uses Flash and Java to make a highly active site.
http://pages.cthome.net/artman

Web Developer.com. Is a Web magazine offering articles on Web page design.
www.webdeveloper.com

Yale Web Style Guide. Is an online style guide for Web page development.
http://info.med.yale.edu/caim/manual/contents.html

SEARCH TERM:	Web Community Sites	First 6 out of 21,341,046

Geocities. Is one of the first free home page and community building sites, and is currently owned by Yahoo!
www.geocities.com

The Globe. Has a well-designed free home page and community building site.
www.theglobe.com

Microsoft Network. Offers free community development and access to a wide variety of communities.
http://communities.msn.com/people

Tripod. Is a well-designed site offering access to many community areas of interest and also offers free home pages and community building.
www.tripod.com

Xoom. Offers free home page development and support of community sites. It requires log-in to reach community pages.
www.xoom.com

Yahoo! Has a number of clubs or community sites and allows individuals to develop their own community site.
http://clubs.yahoo.com

R E F E R E N C E S

1. For more information on telecommunications history, see: Steven Lumbar, *InfoCulture,* Houghton Mifflin Company, New York, 1993.

2. Kevin Jones, "Buyer Behavior Is Key to Market Success," *Interactive Week,* September 7, 1998, p.37

3. David F. Midgley, "Patterns of Interpersonal Information Seeking for the Purchase of a Symbolic Product," *Journal of Marketing Research,* vol. 20, February 1983, pp. 74–83; and Everett M. Rogers, *Diffusion of Innovations,* 3rd ed., The Free Press, New York, 1983.

4. Hubert Gatignon and Thomas S. Robertson, "A Propositional Inventory for New Diffusion Research," *Journal of Consumer Research,* vol. 11, March 1985, pp. 849–867.

5. Data for the World Wide Web from NUA Analysis, "How Many Online Worldwide," NUA Internet Surveys, October 26, 1999, *<http://www.nua.ie/surveys/analysis/graphs_charts/ comparisons/how_many_online.html>*.

6. CIO Web Business, "And Still Growing," *CIO Web Business—Section 2,* October 1, 1998, p. 20.

7. For a multisource summary of worldwide Internet use, see: NUA Internet Surveys, "How Many Online," continuously updated, *<http://www.nua.ie/surveys/how_many_online/ index.html>*.

8. For more on this topic, see: Jeff Ubois, "Mass Appeal," *Internet World,* April 1997, pp. 62–70.

9. Everett M. Rogers, *Diffusion of Innovations,* 3rd ed., The Free Press, New York, 1983, pp. 281–284.

10. David Batstone and Eric Hellweg, "Cash on the Line, Introducing the Internet Consumer," *Business 2.0,* 1998 premiere issue, pp. 28–29.

11. NUA Internet Surveys, "Associated Press: End of an Era for the National Postal Service," October 21, 1999, *<http://www.nua.ie/surveys/index.cgi?f=VS&art_id=905355356& rel=true>;* and NUA Internet Surveys, "Reuters: Email Now Primary Reason People Go Online," October 1, 1999, *<http://www.nua.ie/surveys/index.cgi?f=VS&art_id= 905355315&rel=true>*.

12. Rany Barrett, "E-Mail Address Unknown," *Inter@ctive Week,* October 11, 1999, p. 64; and Sami Kuusela, "The Postman Always Clicks Twice," *Business 2.0,* September 1998, pp. 32–33.

13. Steven Vonder Haar, "Gooey Copycats Get the (Instant) Message," *Inter@ctive Week,* October 18, 1999, p. 19; and Steven Vonder Haar, "Interface of Things to Come," *Inter@ctive Week,* August 30, 1999, pp. 70–72.

14. Joseph C. Panettieri, "PCs Gain Social Skills," *Information Week,* July 3, 1995, pp. 32–42; and Edward C. Baig, "The Trouble with Bob," *Business Week,* January 30, 1995, p. 20.

15. Stephen H. Wildstrom, "Where Wintel Fears to Tread," *Business Week,* September 14, 1998, p. 19.

16. Andrew Marlatt, "When Imitation Works," *Internet World,* October 15, 1999, pp. 60–62; and Connie Guglielmo, "If Amazon Ruled the World," *Inter@ctive Week,* October 11, 1999, pp. 45–46.

17. Stephen H. Wildstrom, "A Computer User's Manifesto," *Business Week,* September 28, 1998, p. 18; and Peter Borrows, "Making Technology Idiot-Proof," *Business Week,* September 28, 1998, p. 6.

18. James C. Luh, "When Design Is All About the User," *Internet World,* September 28, 1998, pp. 23–25.

19 Nancy Dillon, "Can Games Be Training Tools?" *Computerworld,* September 28, 1998, pp. 39–40.

20 Gary H. Anthes, "Hyperbrowsing," *Computerworld,* May 18, 1998, p. 74; Rich Wiggins, "Flexible XML Redefines the Web," *NewMedia,* March 24, 1998, pp. 19–20; and Whit Andrews, "Search Engines Still Chasing Goal of Simplified Interface," *Web Week,* September 15, 1997, pp. 36–37.

21 Lee Mantelman, "Text Miners Face the Ultimate Test," *Knowledge Management,* December 1998, p. 82.

22 Ask Jeeves, "What Is Ask Jeeves," October 26, 1999, *<http://www.askjeeves.com/docs/about/ whatIsAskJeeves.html.>;* and Kimberly Weisul, "Ask Jeeves Serves Up Online Help for Corporate Customers," *Inter@ctive Week,* September 27, 1999, p. 54.

23 Paul Musich, Scot Petersen, and John Rendleman, "Rescuing Lost E-Dollars," *PC Week,* October 25, 1999, pp. 1, 20; and Zona Research, "Slow Download Time Will Cost Ecommerce," July 2, 1999, *<http://www.nua.ie/surveys/index.cgi?f=VS&art_id=905355001& rel=true>.*

24 Steven Vonder Haar, Connie Guglielmo, Kimberly Weisul, and Charlie Babcock, "Holiday Selling Season, High Hopes, High Stakes," *Inter@ctive Week,* September 27, 1999, pp. 72–73; and Connie Guglielmo, "Consumers Take Bad Shopping Trips," *Inter@ctive Week,* October 12, 1998, p. 38.

25 Kylen Campbell, "Use It or Lose It," *NewMedia,* July 1998, p. 72.

26 Information compiled from *GVU's 9th WWW User Survey,* Georgia Tech Research Corporation, 1996, *<http://www.cc.gatech.edu/gvu/user_surveys/survey-1998-04-Use.html/>* (note that Georgia Tech updates its survey data on a regular basis); and David Batstone and Eric Hellweg, "Cash on the Line, Introducing the Internet Consumer," *Business 2.0,* 1998 premiere issue, pp. 28–29.

27 William D. Friel, "Customer Confidence Is Key to E-Commerce," *Internet Week,* March 23, 1998, p. 37.

28 Leslie Marable, "Surfing for Points," *Web Week,* February 17, 1997, pp. 21, 25; and Deborah Branscum, "Click Your Way to Discounts," *Newsweek,* August 31, 1998, p. 60.

29 David F. Midgley, "A Meta-Analysis of the Diffusion of Innovations Literature," *Advances in Consumer Research,* vol. 14, 1987, pp. 204–207.

30 Leslie Gornstein, "Viral Marketing," *Sales & Marketing Automation,* November 1999, pp. 12–14; and Steve Jurvetson, "Turning Customers into a Sales Force," *Business 2.0,* November 1998, pp. 102–108.

31 Anne Stuart, "Something Old, Something New," *CIO Web Business—Section 2,* October 1, 1998, pp. 44–50.

32 Neil Gross, Richard Siklos, and Heidi Dawley, "HDTV: You're Not Going to Like This Picture," *Business Week,* October 25, 1999, p. 50.

33 Michael Meyer, "Ready for Prime Time?" *Newsweek,* September 28, 1998, pp. 83–85.

34 For more information, see: Catherine Yang, Neil Gross, Richard Siklos, and Steven V. Brull, "Digital D-Day," *Business Week,* October 26, 1998, pp. 144–158.

35 Jim Cashel, "Community Is a Commodity," *NewMedia,* August 1999, pp. 38–44.

36 For additional information, see: Mark Glaser, "Building Online Communities," *NewMedia,* March 3, 1997, pp. 36–46; and Robert D. Hof, Seanna Browder, and Peter Elstrom, "Internet Communities," *Business Week,* May 5, 1997, pp. 64–80.

37 *GVU's 9th WWW User Survey General Demographic Summary,* Georgia Tech Research Corporation, 1996, *<http://www.cc.gatech.edu/gvu/user_surveys/survey-1998-04-General.html/>.*

38 Karen Epper Hoffman, "Women's Sites Benefit as Face of Web Changes," *Internet World,* September 28, 1998, pp. 1, 49.

39 Kathleen Murphy, "Why Online Shops Need Women's Touch," *Web Week,* December 1995, p. 23; Kandy Arnold, "URLs for Girls," *AV Video & Multimedia Producer,* October 1997, pp. 31, 170; Gillian Newson and Gina Carfora, "Compelling Content for Wired Women," *NewMedia,* April 14, 1998, pp. 32, 34; Heather Green, "A Site of One's Own," *Business Week,* July 20, 1998, p. 62; and Karen Epper Hoffman, "AOL to Sell Three Women's Sites But Will Still Feature Them Online," *Internet World,* September 21, 1998, p. 5.

40 James C. Luh, "How Bloomingdale's Aims to Enrich Online Shopping," *Internet World,* August 24, 1998, pp. 27–29; Kathleen Murphy, "Undaunted by Obstacles, Cosmetics Firms Step into the Internet Fray," *Web Week,* February 1996, p. 20; and Maricris G. Briones, "On-Line Retailers Seek Ways to Close Shopping Gender Gap," *Marketing News,* vol. 32, no. 19, September 14, 1998, pp. 2, 10.

41 Susan Karlin, "It Takes an IVillage," *Upside,* January 1999, pp. 48–50.

42 NUA Internet Surveys, "Nua Ltd: Meeting Generation Y," July 19, 1999, *<http://www.nua.ie/surveys/index.cgi?f=VS&art_id=905355157&rel=true>;* and Barbara Grady, "Kid's Market Slow to Emerge as Safety Concerns Linger," *Web Week,* November 10, 1997, p. 4.

43 Paul M. Eng, "Cybergiants See the Future—And It's Jack and Jill," *Business Week,* April 14, 1997, p. 44; and Karen Epper Hoffman, "It's Fun, It's Flashy—But Can a Kid Site Make Money?" *Internet World,* September 7, 1998, p. 28.

44 Laura Koss-Feder, "Want to Catch Gen X? Try Looking on the Web," *Marketing News,* vol. 32, no. 12, June 8, 1998, p. 20; and Kathleen Murphy, "The Battle for Campus Cash," *Web Week,* March 31, 1997, pp. 16–18.

45 Karen Epper Hoffman, "Sports Sites Beef Up Content to Lure Fans," *Internet World,* September 14, 1998, p. 8.

46 Whit Andrews, "Sports Marketing Firm Targets Niches, Not Stadium Crowds," *Internet World,* May 4, 1998, p. 50; Elizabeth Gardner, "Joining Forces to Serve a Niche," *Internet World,* June 15, 1998, pp. 17, 20; and David R. Noack, "The Sporting World," *Internet World,* August 1996, pp. 48–52.

47 NUA Internet Surveys, "Greenfield Online: 78 Percent of Senior Users Buy Online," September 2, 1999, *<http://www.nua.ie/surveys/index.cgi?f=VS&art_id=905355250&rel=true>;* Barb Cole-Gomolski, "Selling to Seniors," *Computerworld,* May 24, 1999, pp. 58–59; NUA Internet Surveys, "PR Newswire: Rising Number of Over 50s Online," October 22, 1998, *<http://www.nua.ie/surveys/index.cgi?f=VS&art_id=905354444&rel=true>;* NUA Internet Surveys, "Activemedia: Older Netizens Say WWW Improves Relationships," March 26, 1998, *<http://www.nua.ie/surveys/index.cgi?f=VS&art_id=890934382&rel=true>;* and Susan Moran, "Baby Boomers Are the Target of a Different Kind of 'Adult' Site," *Web Week,* July 7, 1997, p. 16.

48 Daintry Duffy, "It Takes an E-Village," *CIO Enterprise—Section 2,* October 15, 1999, pp. 32–46.

49 Paul C. Judge, "Is the Net Redefining Our Identity?" *Business Week,* May 12, 1997, pp. 100–102.

50 Mitch Wagner, "Keeping the Human Touch on the Web," *Internet Week,* August 24, 1998, p. 21.

51 Lionel Dersot, "Letter from Japan, Where 'Net Adoption Lags," *Computerworld,* September 28, 1998, p. 33.

52 David Altig and Peter Rupert, "Growth and the Internet: Surfing to Prosperity?" *Economic Commentary: Federal Reserve Bank of Cleveland,* September 1, 1999.

53 "Quote of the Week," *Information Week,* September 21, 1998, p. 14.

[54] Steven Lumbar, *InfoCulture,* Houghton Mifflin Company, New York, 1993.

[55] For more information, see: Gifford Pinchott, *Intrapreneuring,* Harper & Row, New York, 1986; and Robert D. Hisrich and Michael P. Peters, "Establishing A New Business Venture Unit Within a Firm," *Journal of Business Venturing,* vol. 1, no. 3, 1986, pp. 307–322.

[56] Raymond E. Miles and Charles C. Snow, *Organizational Strategy, Structure, and Process,* McGraw-Hill Book Company, New York, 1978; and Michael D. Hutt, Peter H. Reingen, and John R. Ronchetto Jr., "Tracing Emergent Processes in Marketing Strategy Formation," *Journal of Marketing,* vol. 52, January 1988, pp. 4–19.

[57] Danny Miller, "The Correlates of Entrepreneurship in Three Types of Firms," *Management Science,* vol. 29, July 1983, pp. 770–791; and Michael Morris and Duane Davis, "Attitudes Toward Corporate Entrepreneurship: Marketers Versus Non-Marketers," in *Research at the Marketing/Entrepreneurship Interface,* eds. G. E. Hills, R. W. LaForge, and B. J. Parker, American Marketing Association, Chicago, 1989, pp. 33–45.

[58] For more on this process, see: Michael D. Hutt, Peter H. Reingen, and John R. Ronchetto Jr., "Tracing Emergent Processes in Marketing Strategy Formation," *Journal of Marketing,* vol. 52, January 1988, pp. 4–19.

[59] Rusty Weston, "From Here to Internet Transformation," *Information Week,* October 25, 1999, p. 147.

[60] Rusty Weston, "The Techno-Adoption Curve," *Information Week,* August 23, 1999, p. 109; and Rick Whiting and Beth Davis, "More on the Edge," *Information Week,* August 23, 1999, pp. 36–48.

Chapter 7

Information
Collection
and Use

In today's highly competitive environment, information has become a tool to gain competitive advantages. E-businesses are developing systematic means of collecting, storing, and analyzing data in order to better understand their customers, lower the costs of running the business, and create a base of organizational knowledge that can be used to develop strategies to enhance competitiveness.

What's Old Is New Again

The financial services industry, including banks and brokerage businesses, has been the focus of much consumer outrage. In 1999, laws were passed in some California cities making it illegal for banks to charge for ATM services. Bank customers were blocked from using automatic teller machines by banks where they were not members. In addition, some bank customers have been subject to additional charges if they want to use "live" tellers at their own banks. It almost seems that banks don't want customers.

The banking industry has been mining data on customers in an attempt to learn how to increase overall profits. Banks are using databases of customer information to determine how customers will react to changes in interest rates. They can pinpoint which customers are likely to accept new products, which are likely to default, and which are most profitable. The Bank of America's *(www.bankofamerica.com)* service center used its database to develop profiles of customers to cross-sell new products. The Bank of Montreal *(www.bmo.com)* mines a 1-terabyte customer knowledge database to determine the profitability of households and projects the lifetime value of customers. First Union Corp. *(www.firstunion.com)* plans to create a 27-terabyte database to analyze customer data for sales and marketing.[1]

In the search to identify profitable customers, one bank found that 10 percent of its customers incurred 90 percent of the ATM costs, and 80

Source: www.firstunion.com

percent of those customers were of low value to the bank. The bank did not drop these customers; instead, the data showed that 30 percent of the low-value customers were college students who could be turned into higher-value customers if they remained loyal to the bank.[2]

THINKING STRATEGICALLY

Determine the importance that the knowledge of customer data plays in increasing the profitability of banks. Justify why a bank should charge its own customers to use "live" tellers. Consider whether a bank should provide free customer service as a community service. Speculate on how customers would feel if they knew that their bank tracked individual behaviors. Determine how customers could benefit from the bank's knowledge of their behavior.

"One ignorant of the plans of neighboring states cannot prepare alliances in good time; if ignorant of the conditions of mountains, forests, dangerous defiles, swamps and marshes he cannot conduct the march of an army; if he fails to make use of native guides he cannot gain the advantages of the ground. A general ignorant of even one of these three matters is unfit to command the armies of a king."

Samuel B. Griffith

Sun Tzu, *The Art of War*, 500 B.C.[3]

"Close to 75% of CEOs use Internet technologies to scan business, economic, and industry news."

John Fontana,

Internet Week[4]

> Data is raw facts. Information is constructed from facts, gives meaning to phenomena, and allows managers to make decisions.

Managers use information to make decisions; the higher the quality of information a manager has, the better the decision. E-businesses are continuously collecting information from both external and internal sources. This information then becomes the collective knowledge of a company. E-businesses use a variety of techniques to enhance the process of knowledge creation, and then use this information to gain competitive advantages.[5]

Data (which is raw facts that become meaningful **information**) is collected from numerous sources such as daily transactions, Web-site usage, and third-party **databases.** Data stored in databases are mined to transform data into information for improving managerial decisions. For example, Yahoo! collects over 400 billion bytes of information on its users every day. Yahoo! uses this data to improve the targeting of customers with advertisements. This one-to-one marketing

FSITES

Data warehouses are computer systems (hardware and software) designed to process large amounts of data held in databases. Many databases carry tens of **terabytes** (trillions of bytes) or over 1,000,000,000,000 bytes. A terabyte of data would hold:

▶   A 100-byte record for every person on earth
▶   1 billion business letters
▶   10 million MPEG images, or enough video to run for 10 days and nights

Source: John Foley, "Towering Terabytes," *Information Week*, September 30, 1996, p. 48.

process is not the only goal of database marketing. Companies are also using knowledge gained to lower costs by targeting customers who have the highest profit potential. Database marketing is still in the early stages of its life cycle, and its full potential has yet not been reached.[6] A number of businesses are successfully using new techniques in **data warehousing** and **data mining** to gain insights and improve customer relations. Companies as varied as General Motors *(www.gm.com)*, Seagram *(www.seagram.com)*, Philip Morris *(www.philipmorris.com)*, and Harley Davidson *(www.harleydavidson.com)* are using database-marketing techniques to strengthen their relationships with customers and block out competitors.[7]

> Data mining is the process of using software to "drill" into a database to obtain meaningful information.

Databases act as repositories of organizational memory, allowing firms to engage in information-based competition and possibly to obtain substantial advantages over competitors. To gain these advantages, a business needs to structure a formal information-gathering system called a **marketing information system (MIS).** An MIS should be designed to collect data and provide meaningful information. There are three major categories of data that marketers collect: data related to marketing-mix elements (the effects of product, price, promotion, and place decisions), the behavior of individual buyers and prospects, and data from environmental scanning.[8]

Implementing an MIS requires obtaining data from internal as well as external sources. As the repository of organizational knowledge, databases become the hub of a business operation, providing information to managers, and controlling and coordinating business operations. Figure 7.1, on the following page, illustrates the major flows of data and information in a marketing information system.

Figure 7.1 shows that data for decision making comes from three major sources. The first is the firm's customers or market. This data can be gathered from customer transactions or can be purposefully collected through a marketing research process. Competitive intelligence comes from internal and external sources. A business's personnel, such as its sales force, can return information on the competitive environment. The process of environmental scanning allows managers to keep track of competitors and environmental trends to aid in strategic decision making. Environmental scanning can come from government sources, industry sources, or careful observations of media articles and competitive firm behavior. Third-party data can also be purchased from sources external to a business. Many companies and institutions collect information on their customers and then sell that data to firms that specialize in the collection and storage of data. These firms, in turn, sell the compiled data to interested parties.

NSITES

A **database** is a structured storage of data consisting of fields and records. A field is a column of data related to a single attribute or variable. A record is a collection of fields that represents a single case, such as the profile of an individual.

The table below represents fields of information for two records.

	Field 1 (Name)	Field 2 (Income)	Field 4 (Gender)	Field 5 . . . (Purchase behavior)	Field N (Psychographic)
Record 1	Jones	$50,000	Male	Product X Purchased 11/09/99	Tennis
Record 2	Smith	$54,000	Female	Product Z Purchased 09/16/98	Scuba diving

Figure 7.1 The Marketing Information System Flows

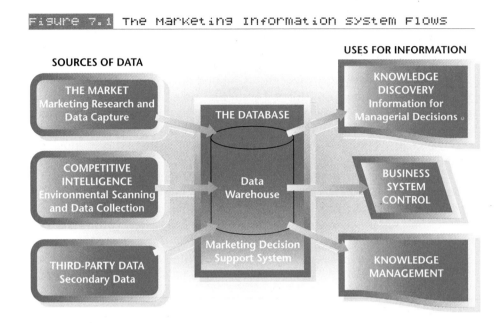

Data-mining techniques are used to extract information from data warehouses for managerial decisions. Specialized software is used to develop **marketing decision support systems (MDSS)** to provide information to aid in developing marketing strategies. A firm's database can also be used as a hub to control the business process by facilitating the mass customization process, aiding sales force automation, providing information for managers, and fostering knowledge organizations. The development of database warehouses is so vital to businesses that it is now considered to be the number one information technology priority for businesses.[9] This chapter will cover each aspect of the marketing information system and how it affects the marketing process.

SOURCES OF DATA

Data from the Market

The goal of data collection is to obtain the information necessary to develop and maintain relationships with customers. This can be achieved when marketers understand the wants and needs of their customers. There are three ways of obtaining that information from the market. The first is to collect data on the customer's behavior through the recording of transaction data taken from employees, data captured from point-of-sales scanners and/or electronic recording devices such as Web-tracking software. The data can be transaction-based data, customer-profile data, or more complex behavioral data. A second method of collecting data is to keep track of customers' complaints or questions. These can be used to spot product defects or improve communications. This type of information can be recorded from Web communications or logged in from telephone service operators. A third method is to collect primary data directly from the market through marketing research. We will explore each of these areas.

scanner and Tracking Data. Many retailers track customer activity by using **scanner data** to help determine shoppers' profiles, allowing for a market-of-one strategy. In 1998, close to 30 percent of grocery stores used card-based programs to track customers' purchases. When customers use a discount card, their identity is matched with a record of the products purchased from scanner data. This allows the grocer to target the needs of the heavy users. For some grocery stores, the highest-spending 50 percent of shoppers can account for 90 percent of sales. This data also allows the grocery store to save on costs. For example, advertisements do not need to be sent to the mass market; they can be targeted only to the store's users. The data these grocery stores collect allows them to target products to their customers and avoid engaging in direct competition with other grocers.[10]

The hospitality industry also tracks user information and collects it into databases to strengthen relationships with customers. The Ritz-Carlton Hotels collect information from all service employees to develop databases of customers' desires. If a maid notices that a client has tennis equipment in the room, a note is made to be sure to place tennis magazines in the room when that client visits again. This allows the hotel to offer personalized service even to the point of knowing who likes the bed turned down and who does not want a mint on the pillow.[11]

THINKING STRATEGICALLY

Describe how the casinos track customers. Determine what types of data the casinos would want to collect to identify high-value customers. Speculate on the use of that data. Should the casinos use gaming information to entice customers to return? Evaluate the competitive advantages that a casino would gain by having access to this behavioral data.

web-Based Tracking. Chapter 3 outlined the process of using databases to customize Web pages for customers. Cookies are used to identify Web users' behavior and generate pages on the fly. **Web tracking** also allows Web sites to monitor individual site use such as referral location (where the

CASE 7.1

Playing for Keeps
The gaming industry is very competitive because individuals can choose from numerous cities, riverboats, Indian gaming, or online gaming options. Casinos in Las Vegas are using information to gain competitive advantages. Research has shown that customers who return to a gambling resort will spend over 300 percent more than walk-in customers. To encourage return visits, casino hotels have customers fill out lengthy data forms when they check into the hotel or sign up for gaming cards. These customers are then given magnetic cards that can be used either to play slot machines or at gaming tables. Customer data is collected both electronically and by service personnel to develop customer profiles, allowing targeted marketing incentives. The more customers interact with the casino, the more incentives they receive. Customers also receive personalized newsletters sent to their homes, offering further incentives if they return to the casino.[12]

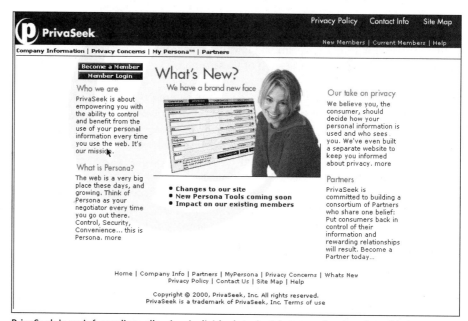

PrivaSeek is an infomediary allowing individuals to build personalized and permission marketing based relationships with businesses while protecting their individual identity.

individuals linked from), surfing paths, and duration within a site. This information can be made even more valuable when behavior is matched to **visitor registration information.** Businesses often give incentives to obtain information on names, e-mail addresses, demographics, vocations, hobbies, and psychographics. Business professionals often fill out in-depth data forms for free subscriptions to trade journals.

Information on Web users is a valuable asset. Hagel and Rayport proposed in a *Harvard Business Review* article a new type of information intermediary, or **infomediary,** that would become a repository of consumer information.[13] A number of companies are positioning themselves as infomediaries. "Green Stamp" companies such as CyberGold *(www.cybergold.com)* pay visitors to provide information. CyberGold charges advertisers for accessing highly targeted audiences. When individuals interact with an ad, play a game, or check out a Web site from CyberGold, they are rewarded with "CyberGold" which accrues in an account until it is spent. One dollar of CyberGold is equal to $1 of U.S. cash. Individuals can spend their CyberGold, transfer it to a Visa card or to a bank account, or they have other spending options.[14]

Engage Technologies *(www.engage.com)* has created a database of 30 million anonymous Web-user profiles. Engage does not capture the names and personal profiles of

An **infomediary** is a firm that specializes in the capture, collection, or analysis of data. This service can be marketed to other businesses and can protect individual's privacy.

Visitor registration information
Web developers suggest that visitors not be asked to register until they are ready to take some type of action, such as making a purchase. In addition, the more questions that are asked the less likely it is the questions will be answered.

the individual users; instead, it develops global cookies that are used to reference choices from a global database. The cookie, not the individual, has a profile. When an individual visits a Web site that participates in the global ID system, the cookie's code is sent to Engage's database where the profile of the cookie user is sent to the Web site for developing online advertising and customized marketing. This allows a participating business to customize Web-page development in a very short time.[15] These infomediaries are avoiding privacy concerns either by engaging in permission marketing and having individuals offer their own information, or by allowing the Web user to remain anonymous.

CUSTOMER INQUIRIES.   Many businesses use software to track consumers' complaints. Telephone service personnel can type consumers' concerns into computers where software then looks for patterns in the text. Information on patterns of inquiries can then be provided to management for action. Whirlpool Corporation *(www.whirlpool.com)* uses customer-tracking software to notify owners of its washing machines of potential problems. It also uses the data to identify defective parts, allowing Whirlpool to repair problems. Otis Elevator Company *(www.otis.com)* receives over 600,000 calls per year requesting unscheduled repair service. This information is used to develop repair histories of elevators and identify possible design problems.[16]

Marketing Research

Marketing research is the systematic and objective process of generating data for making marketing decisions. Using the Internet for **online research** offers many advantages over traditional methods; data can be collected in a much shorter time and at a lower cost. J.C. Penney had 417 women evaluate 60 swimsuits online and paid one-third the cost of regular survey-based research. Studies have found that using the Internet can cut research time in half and cut costs by as much as 80 percent. Errors from data collection can also be minimized. Avon found that its online research did a better job of predicting sales than traditional research methods.[17]

There are problems in using the Internet for data collection. The major limitation is that users do not represent a random sample of the overall population. If the research problem specifies individuals who match Web users' profiles, then the Web can be a very good research tool. Web users' profiles are attractive to some researchers because they represent the higher-income, heavy users of some product categories. The profile of Internet users will more closely match the general population as the price of computers drops and accessibility increases through Web-based TV.[18] Table 7.1 on the following page outlines the research process and indicates the advantages and disadvantages of using the Internet for data collection.

Online Research Design

▶   **Surveys.** A number of companies have developed software that enables them to place surveys online and then aids in the analysis of results. This software allows a researcher to develop questions using categorical (e.g., choose a, b, or c) or metric (e.g., choose anywhere between 1–7) measures. The questionnaire can then be sent out through e-mail systems or be placed on a Web site that returns CGI script. **Common gateway interface (CGI)** script is an Internet protocol that allows data to be sent back and forth between the Web user and Web server, allowing Web forms to return data to the Web server. As the data is returned to the server, statistical analysis is automatically performed, reports are generated, and charts are developed to aid in management decision making.[19]

Table 7.1 Marketing Research Steps

Step	Description	Application over the Internet
1. Problem definition	Identify problem and develop research objectives.	Requires that the research problem be related to a universe of Web users. The Web may represent a sample of heavy users.
2. Research design	Collect secondary research (previously collected data). Must determine use of qualitative data (such as focus groups) or quantitative data (such as surveys or experiments).	The Web offers easy access to secondary research. Web-based research allows both qualitative and quantitative data collection. Web-based research can show pictures, other Web sites, or interactivity (see Online Research Design section that follows).
3. Sample selection	Identify sample to be used. Determine if a random or nonrandom sample is to be used.	The Web allows the desired sample to find the site and answer questions at a low cost. This limits the randomness of the sample selection and may introduce a self-selection bias. Online panels can use databases to select qualified individuals for research subjects.
4. Data collection (primary)	Determine how the data will be collected—in person, over the phone, by mail, from panels, etc. Must try to control errors in data collection and data entry.	Web-based research can help limit interviewer errors. Logic checks can be built into the survey to limit contradictory or nonsensical answers. Randomizing presentation of items can eliminate order bias.
5. Data analysis	Must determine the analysis methods to be used. Data analysis is undertaken after data is collected.	Automated software can analyze the data directly from the Web, limiting data entry errors and providing continuous results.
6. Report preparation	Design the presentation of information derived from the data analysis.	Low cost and ease of use may lead researchers to minimize the problems of using a nonrandom sample. Charts and tables can easily be developed from software.

Sources: Dick McCullough, "Web-Based Market Research Ushers in New Age," *Marketing News,* vol. 32, no. 19, September 14, 1998, pp. 27–28; and Amy J. Yoffie, "The 'Sampling Dilemma' Is No Different On-Line," *Marketing News,* vol. 32, no. 8, April 13, 1998, p. 16.

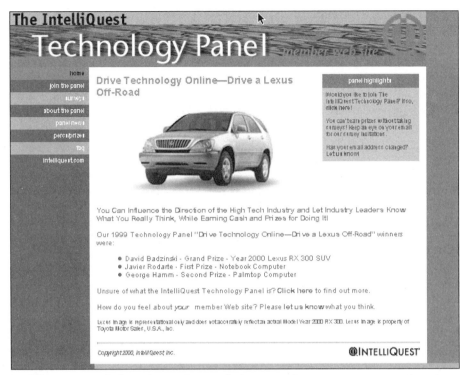

IntelliQuest uses online panels to collect marketing research.   Source: www.techpanel.com

▶   **Panels.** A panel allows researchers to pull respondents from a known pool. Panel members supply individual profile data and can then be selected as part of a sample pool for clients. This improves sample selection by allowing researchers to control who responds to the research.[20]

▶   **Online Focus Groups.** Traditional focus groups are a means of collecting a rich set of responses from a target audience. The focus group uses a moderator who works with 8 to 15 individuals discussing open-ended questions to investigate a topic of interest. The ability to have face-to-face interactions with focus-group participants allows a deeper understanding of consumers' thoughts and decision processes.

Two different types of focus groups can be used online: ongoing groups and real-time chat groups. **Ongoing groups** use forums or message boards to discuss the research topic. These can last for days or weeks, giving respondents time to think about their responses. The panel moderator posts questions to the focus group. The moderator or participants can post follow-up questions to obtain deeper levels of meaning.

Real-time chat groups allow several focus-group members to interact online at the same time and have real-time discussions. Moderators control the focus group by using password-protected rooms where they can "kick out" unruly respondents. Product information can be delivered online by using text, graphics, or multimedia files containing audio or video.[21] Real-time chats should be limited to 90 minutes to prevent fatigue. Online focus groups may also suffer from self-selection biases because they may not represent the population at large.[22]

IntelliQuest *(www.intelliquest.com)* is a leading online marketing research company. It uses panels of online respondents who answer questionnaires on technology-related products and services. This allows IntelliQuest to use a select group to respond to surveys and provides a rapid response time.

COMPETITIVE INTELLIGENCE

Gathering **competitive intelligence (CI)** is a continuous process involving the legal and ethical collection of information and the monitoring of the competitive environment, giving managers the ability to make strategic decisions. The Society for Competitive Intelligence Professionals *(www.scip.org)* views the collection of competitive intelligence as a way for managers to make informed decisions about marketing, R&D, and long-term business strategies.[23]

A 1998 survey of information technology managers indicated that nearly 75 percent of CEOs used the Internet to scan business, economic, and industry news.[24] Although the Internet offers low-cost access to a wide variety of information, marketing managers can become frustrated trying to find timely, accurate, and relevant information online. Companies that use CI collect data from customers, suppliers, trade publications, company employees, industry experts, the Internet, industry conferences, and commercial databases.[25]

The Internet allows marketing decision makers to develop virtual libraries of Internet-based sources to aid in decision making.[26] These libraries can either be used by managers to monitor their environment or be linked to an intranet for individuals to access inside an organization. Fuld & Company's com-petitive intelligence Web site is an example of a virtual library.

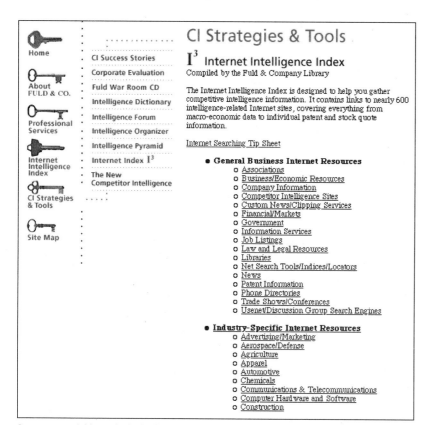

Source: www.fuld.com/i3/index.html

Fuld's Internet intelligence index *(http://www.fuld.com/i3/index.html)* contains close to 500 intelligence-related Internet sites that link on topics as varied as macroeconomic data, individual patents, and stock quote information.

Search engines can be used to find relevant sites, but the return information is often too general. Specialized search engines can narrow the number of hits to targeted areas. Table 7.2 outlines a number of free-access, specialized business search engines.

Ethical Snooping. When gathering competitive intelligence, it is important to maintain both ethical and legal boundaries. The CI trade industry gives eight recommendations to maintain **ethical snooping,** or fairness in the collection of data. These include[27]:

1. **Observe legal restrictions.** It is important to know and follow both the rules set up by the researcher's company and any applicable laws.
2. **Avoid misrepresentations.** Do not disguise the identities of the researcher and the researcher's company. State the clear reason for the data collection.
3. **Do not release misinformation.** Do not try to throw competitors off by releasing false information. This could backfire and erode the credibility of the firm.
4. **Never ask for or exchange price information with competitors.** This could directly violate antitrust laws.
5. **Don't steal trade secrets.** This could be cause for legal action.
6. **Do not offer bribes.** This is illegal!
7. **Do not hack other sites.** This is illegal!
8. **Protect information sources.** Do not forward e-mail from a source. This could jeopardize reputations and jobs.

Table 7.2 Free Business-Oriented Search Engines

Company or Journal	Site	Description
All-in-One Search Page	www.allonesearch.com	This site links to a variety of search engines that specialize in industry-specific search tools for the Internet.
ClickZ	www.searchz.com/index.shtml	This is a search and information page for decision makers interested in marketing related e-commerce issues.
Websitez	www.websitez.com/zhub.shtml	It searches for Web sites by the name of a business.
CompanyLink	www.companylink.com	It provides access to stock quotes, competitors, SEC filings, and publicly traded businesses.

Source: Information in this table is compiled from Jean L. Graef, "Piecing Together Client Information on the Web," *Sales & Field Force Automation,* May 1998, pp. 34–42.

The 1996 Economic Espionage Act that was passed by the U.S. Congress mandated that competitive intelligence should not be collected from rival companies' customer lists or e-mails, nor should deceit be used to obtain interviews from company employees. These actions could be seen as theft of trade secrets, resulting in fines of up to $500,000 and 10 years in jail.[28]

Third-Party Data Sources. Third-party data suppliers provide information for multiple uses. Almost any market-segment profile criteria can be purchased. This data can be obtained from companies that specialize in compiling data for mailings or e-mail lists, credit ratings, geodemographic information, etc. Data may also be purchased from the original source of the data collection. Retailers, hospitals, and other businesses sell data on their customers to interested parties.

Infomediaries use their expertise in data collection, data warehousing, and database mining to provide services to their clients. Catalina Marketing Corporation *(www.catmktg.com)* has developed a data warehouse of 2 trillion bytes of information collected from more than 143 million shoppers and 11,000 supermarkets nationwide. Using this data, Catalina Marketing is able to selectively target customers. This has allowed coupon responses for grocery stores to increase from 0.6 percent for magazines and newspapers to a redemption rate of over 8.9 percent.[29]

Source Informatics *(www.simatics.com)* purchases transaction data from 75 percent of U.S. pharmacies and produces monthly electronic data for its clients. This information includes a list of drugs doctors are prescribing for illnesses. Company-specific information is stored in **data marts** so a sales force can monitor how a doctor's prescription behavior changes after a sales call or a sales campaign.[30]

Data marts are small databases that serve a specific purpose in a firm. Metawarehouses are very large databases that centralize all data. Data marts can be linked together in a network to share information.

USES OF INFORMATION

Knowledge Discovery

Database-marketing techniques use computer data to aid in the process of making managerial decisions to reach marketing goals. Using databases for **knowledge discovery** typically follows two paths: The first is an **OnLine Analytical Processing (OLAP)** method that allows queries, or searches, of known variables such as asking how much of product A sold in district 1; the second approach is to use data-mining techniques. Properly used, database queries allow managers to determine the profitability of product lines and customers.

Strategic Value of Customers. A 1999 survey of 100 leading e-commerce companies indicated that 44 percent were determining the strategic value of customers. Determining the **strategic value of customer data** can increase the overall profits for a company by indicating which customers should receive specialized services and which customers should be dropped or prodded to increase their purchasing.[31] Database marketing allows businesses to limit nonproductive reach by limiting efforts to those individuals who are not likely to react to a marketing strategy.

The **Paretto Principle,** or 80/20 rule, dictates that 80 percent of profits may come from 20 percent of a business's customers. Although the percentages may not be exact, the idea that not all customers are profitable to a business is true. Databases are used to help determine the strategic value of all customers by running queries on their past and projecting their future behavior.[32] Data miners in the financial services industry have found that only 20 to 30 percent of customers are profitable. The First National Bank of North Dakota in Grand Forks *(www.fnbnd.com)* conducted a profitability analysis and found that only 10 percent of its customers were profitable. Once a bank identifies profitable and nonprofitable customers, it can develop strategies to turn potentially profitable customers into higher-level users. For those customers who are not profitable, fees can be increased.[33]

The value of the customer can be based upon a **recency, frequency, and monetary (RFM) measure.** A customer with a 1-1-1 would be the best customer because he or she would have made a number of purchases in the recent past for a high dollar value. Table 7.3 outlines how a business can determine the RFM measures for its customers. Relevant time periods are divided into five categories. The latest time period has the highest value and is given a rating of 1. The earliest period is of lowest value and is rated a 5. This procedure is repeated for frequency and the amount of money spent.[34]

Customer profiles can then be generated, as shown in Table 7.4 on the following page. Customer A would be the highest-value customer. Customer C would be of low value. Customer B, with a score of 2-3-1, may have potential as a valuable customer if frequency and recency could be increased.

The **majority fallacy** in marketing occurs when a business, focusing on just an RFM measure, serves only the heavy half and avoids the lower or nonuser segment.[35] This results in missing potential customers who could become profitable in the future.

Table 7.3 Determining a Customer's Strategic Value

Recency (time periods)	Rating	Frequency (how often)	Rating	Monetary (amount per order or purchase)	Rating
1/2000–6/2000	1	Over 10 times	1	$500 and over	1
7/1999–12/1999	2	8–9 times	2	$400–$499	2
1/1999–6/1999	3	6–7 times	3	$300–$399	3
1/1998–12/1998	4	3–5 times	4	$150–$299	4
1/1996–12/1997	5	1–2 times	5	Less than $150	5

Table 7.4   Customer Strategic Value

Customer	Last Purchase	Score	Frequency	Score	Average Purchase	Score	RFM Score
A	5/2000	1	12 times	1	$650	1	1-1-1
B	9/1999	2	6 times	3	$625	3	2-3-1
C	8/1997	5	2 times	5	$100	5	5-5-5

The second database technique used in knowledge discovery is data mining, which searches for unknown relationships. An example of a data-mining query would be to ask the database an open-ended question such as, What are indicators that are likely to lead our customers to purchase product A? The goal of data mining is to bypass the **normal science** method of data analysis wherein a hypothesis would be developed and then tested. Instead, data mining allows the software to generate a hypothesis by telling the marketer what patterns may exist. Used in combination, the two database knowledge-discovery techniques can locate patterns, suggest models, and then help to confirm relationships.[36] Figure 7.2 illustrates a possible model that could be developed from mined data. This model indicates that past behaviors and individual profiles may be related to future purchases. Data mining could detect which of those behaviors or profile characteristics are good predictors of future behavior.

The ability to mine data allows companies to identify and predict customer behaviors, allowing customized marketing. Table 7.5 outlines some of the major data-mining applications undertaken by Fortune 1000 companies.

Figure 7.2   Behavioral Model

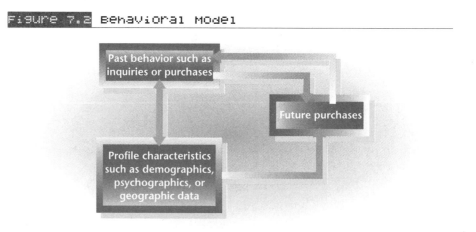

Table 7.5 Data-Mining Applications Undertaken by Companies

Application	Description
Market segmentation	Aids in indentifying common characteristics of customers who are likely to react to similar marketing strategies. Allows for one-to-one marketing practices.
Decision support	Provides data to guide and support management decisions.
Customer churn	Aids in the prediction of which customers are likely to switch to a competitor.
Fraud detection	Rates the likelihood that a transaction is fraudulent.
Customer service	Provide service to customers based on the customer's past experience and detects patterns of customer problems.
Interactive marketing	Identifies the prospects most likely to respond to direct marketing efforts. Predicts what each individual visitor to a Web site would be most interested in seeing (and then delivers that content).
Market-basket analysis	Groups products or services that are most likely to be purchased together.
Trend analysis	Aids in short, medium, and long term decisions by identifying differences and trends among groups of customers over a given period of time.

Sources: SPSS, "Data Mining Applications," January 14, 2000, <http://www.spss.com/datamine/applications.htm>; Synes, "Data Mining," January 14, 2000, <http://www.synes.com/p217.html>; Susan Osterfelt, "Searching for the Welcome Stranger," *DM Review,* July/August 1999, pp. 59–63; and Martin Marshall, "Data Mining: Rich Vein for Marketers," *Communications Week,* CMP Media, Inc., January 13, 1997, pp. 1, 69 (chart by Evelyn Bourdette, p. 69).

THINKING STRATEGICALLY

Determine how Capital One has gained a competitive advantage over other credit cards. List the factors that should be included in determining the value of a credit-card customer. Speculate on the source of the data that Capital One uses to choose its credit-card customers. Determine why it would be important that Capital One's employees be able to use and share information. Speculate on the importance of the collective organizational knowledge held by Capital One employees.

CASE 7.2

Giving Databases the Credit

Capital One *(www.capitalone.com)* used its terabyte database to identify how individuals used credit cards. This information leads users to choose from over 7,000 variations of credit cards from Capital One's Web site. Capital One offers credit cards to college and high school students. Its database indicated that college students were high-potential users. Capital One has been able to use information to avoid higher-risk credit-card users and to focus on more profitable segments. Capital One offers a superprime credit card with a low fixed interest rate and frequent-flyer miles. But the superprime cards go only to those identified as heavy chargers.

To compete against other credit-card companies, Capital One has linked its credit-card approval system directly to credit bureaus. Applicants can get credit approval in as little as 60 seconds. Capital One also hires employees based on how well they are able to use information. By fostering a sharing culture, Capital One has attained lower-than-industry-average employee turnover.[37]

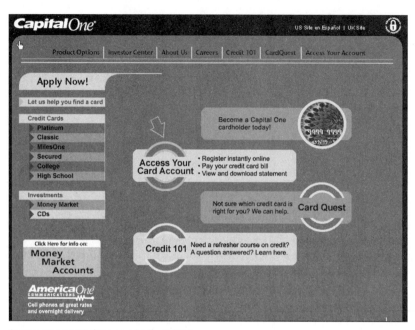

Source: www.capitalone.com/index4e.html

Database Development

The process of developing a database-marketing system starts with the collection of large amounts of data on the individual. This data is stored in a digital form in a data warehouse. The data in the warehouse is transformed into meaningful information through specialized software that "mines" the data, looking for patterns of behavior which enable the marketer to meet individualized needs.[38] Figure 7.3 illustrates the process of developing and using a data warehouse for database marketing.

Database-marketing techniques are expensive, but the benefits can outweigh the costs. A 1996 study by International Data Corp. indicated that the average cost for a data warehouse was $2.2 million. Evaluating 62 organizations with successful data warehouses, the average return on investment was close to 400 percent. The average payback on the investment was 2.3 years.[39] The benefits of data warehouses are not limited to large corporations. Small businesses are using desktop PC databases to collect data in order to develop and maintain relationships.[40]

The ideal outcome of database marketing is to tighten relationships with customers and to limit wasted marketing efforts, such as junk mail, by targeting only customers who would be interested in the offering. Data mining allows the marketer to identify those profiling characteristics that are related to the individual's actions and can result in personalized marketing and customer retention.

Data Warehouses. Data can be collected from a variety of sources, as outlined earlier in this chapter. In addition, customers may send in warranty cards, sweepstake applications, coupons, etc. This data can be combined with data purchased from third-party sources. For example, credit-card companies store virtually every customer transaction. This allows them to look at patterns and flag behavior that falls outside an individual's normal purchases. The credit-card company can then contact the individual or the store to verify the purchase.

In order to use the data, it must be scrubbed or cleansed. Data cleansing attempts to combine data from multiple sources, eliminate redundant data, and resolve conflicting data. This process can take as much as 75 percent of the information technologist's time. Once the data is cleansed, the data can be mined for meaning.

Figure 7.3 The Database-Marketing Process

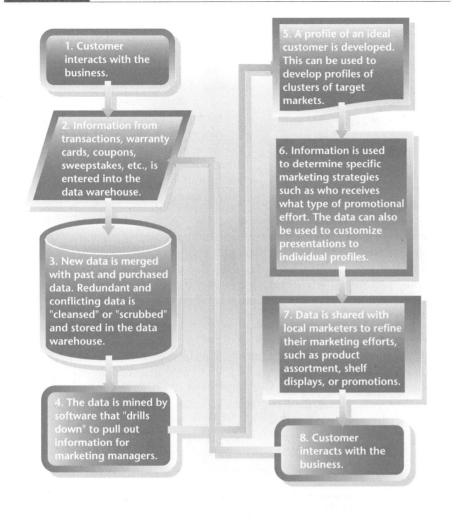

1. Customer interacts with the business.

2. Information from transactions, warranty cards, coupons, sweepstakes, etc., is entered into the data warehouse.

3. New data is merged with past and purchased data. Redundant and conflicting data is "cleansed" or "scrubbed" and stored in the data warehouse.

4. The data is mined by software that "drills down" to pull out information for marketing managers.

5. A profile of an ideal customer is developed. This can be used to develop profiles of clusters of target markets.

6. Information is used to determine specific marketing strategies such as who receives what type of promotional effort. The data can also be used to customize presentations to individual profiles.

7. Data is shared with local marketers to refine their marketing efforts, such as product assortment, shelf displays, or promotions.

8. Customer interacts with the business.

Data Mining. Sophisticated data-mining software can be used to turn the raw data into information for managerial decisions. Data mining reaches into data warehouses and extracts relationships using sophisticated statistical techniques. Computers use massive parallel processing with hundreds of microprocessors to analyze huge amounts of data. Neural-network software builds models by finding patterns of customer behavior.

MCI *(www.wcom.com)* used data mining to analyze 140 million households on as many as 10,000 attributes such as income, lifestyle, and past calling habits. MCI's data warehouse was based on an IBM SP/2 supercomputer. It developed a set of 22 statistical profiles of customers. These highly secret profiles allowed MCI

Caveat: Correlation Is Not Causation

Beer and diaper sales are correlated between 5 p.m. and 7 p.m. This bit of data-mined gold came from an analysis for Osco Drugs in 1992. Once this type of data is found, what should the company do with it? What was the reason for this correlation? Do men stop and buy beer and diapers on the way home from work? Should the store be redesigned to place beer next to diapers? Data mined from databases does not necessarily convey information; the marketing decision maker must understand the reasons behind the data. As a result of this finding, Osco did not rearrange its stores to place beer next to diapers.

to make promotional offers to clients before they engaged in switching behavior. This also allowed MCI to cut the cost of obtaining leads for new customers from about 65 cents down to about 4.5 cents per lead.[41]

Data mining should not be used as a substitute for managerial decisions; rather, managers should assess the information gleaned from databases.[42] Just because patterns emerge from data does not mean that those generalizations hold for a larger population. Four pitfalls that can occur using data-mining techniques are[43]:

1. **Using ad hoc theories.** When odd relationships are found, the researcher may develop a theory to fit the data.
2. **Not taking no for an answer.** If one has a preconception, it may be tempting to let the computer search to find it.
3. **Storytelling.** It may be tempting to develop a story to fit the data.
4. **Using too many variables.** The more variables, the more likely the computer is to find relationships regardless of what true relationships exist.

Researchers must learn to use data-mining techniques as a tool in model building.

The development, maintenance, and analysis required to successfully run a data warehouse and data-mining process can be very complex. Although large firms, such as banks, phone companies, and credit-card companies, have seen great benefits from data mining, small- and medium-sized enterprises can benefit as well. The Association for Computing Machinery Special Interest Group on Knowledge Discovery and Data Mining (SIGKDD) *(www.acm.org/sigkdd)* offers information and support. Additional information and lists of vendors of hardware and software can be found at the KDNuggets Web site *(www.kdnuggets.com)*.

BUSINESS SYSTEM CONTROL

Enterprisewide information technologies are being used to automate business systems and control process flows, allowing companies to cut costs and speed operations. Databases become the hubs of this control process, allowing customer support, sales for automation, links to inventory, and control over business processes. Figure 7.4 indicates the major business systems that can be enhanced through the database's ability to store, share, and control information.

Databases that control business systems are not always based on one large data metawarehouse; instead, many businesses use data marts, which are designed to control a single business operation but may be linked to other databases through a computer network. Sales force automation, linking extranets into the business, and customer relationship management have been covered in more

Figure 7.4 Database Business System Control

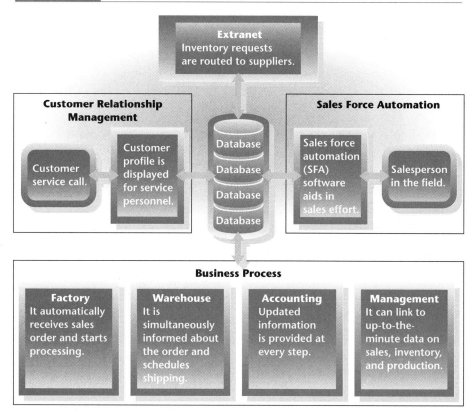

depth in Chapters 3 and 5. The following sections will summarize those processes, expand on business processes, and illustrate how database systems are being used to enhance the control of business processes.

Customer-Relationship Management Systems.   The Web is becoming the medium of choice for customers to use for sales support. The Web can cut the cost of service calls by allowing customers to use Web pages to obtain general information on a company and its products or to make queries about order status. Integrated database systems allow companies to develop close relationships with customers by customizing information. Digital Equipment Corporation *(www.digital.com)* has its extranet hooked into its database collection system. Customers can go in the system and look up parts, prices, marketing material, etc. This information is added to the database to design personalized Web pages for the customer.[44] Table 7.6 on the following page outlines five ways in which a business can provide customer support over the Web.

Table 7.6 Web-Based Customer Support Systems

Type of Web Site	Function	Technology Used
Content site	Offers product or company information	Web-authoring software
FAQ site	Organizes list of frequently asked questions with timely, accurate answers	Web-authoring software
Knowledge base site	Uses database to allow users to interact and ask questions	Web-authoring software with scripting, search engine, and relational database software
Trouble ticket site	Allows the customer to enter a "trouble ticket" using a Web form or e-mail report (good sites give customers case numbers and immediate acknowledgment, and they track customers' progress)	Same as above with additional e-mail, response management software, and knowledge management software
Interactive site	Will do almost everything a customer service rep would do (in addition to the above functions, customers can interact online)	Same as above with personalization, push, and security software

Source: Adapted from Sari Kalin, "Tales of a Web Customer," *CIO Web Business—Section 2,* September 1, 1998, p. 50.

Sales Force Automation. Sales force automation (SFA) systems are designed to be information support tools, with software to support the sales process. This can provide a salesperson with information on business contacts such as corporate relationships, notes, tasks, the sales influencers, order-fulfillment status, attachments, and sales opportunities. Structured selling methods can be retrieved to design sales approaches. SFA software can also act as a gateway to the business database, providing sales presentation information, contract fulfillment data, links to communications with service, and shipping.[45]

Control of Business Processes. The integration of database systems into organizational processes is cutting costs and time needed to complete tasks. Databases are being linked together to allow information to flow from functional areas and divisions. Warehouses have long used databases to control inventory. Grocery stores are linking together information on inventory with customer profile data to develop category management information, allowing the fine-tuning of inventory.

A business's database system is becoming the hub for controlling the reengineering process for organizations. **Enterprise software** systems, often called **ERP** (enterprise resource planning) software, from companies such as PeopleSoft *(www.peoplesoft.com)* and Germany's SAP *(www.sap.com)* are linking together the diverse aspects of a business through central database servers. Enterprise software supports a number of clients such as customers, the sales force, suppliers, and those involved in the business process (e.g., the factory floor, shipping, accounting, and management). The ability to have all the various parts of a business linked together is allowing businesses to service customers better.[46] Figure 7.5 illustrates how enterprise software systems control process flows. The illustration shows that when the sales order is entered into the enterprise system, the software checks inventory, schedules production, orders raw materials, notifies manpower to hire temporary employees, prepares the bill, schedules shipping, allows the buyer to track the purchase, and prepares reports for management on trends.

3M Company *(www.3m.com)* has plans to develop an enterprise system for its 500,000 variations of products sold around the world. Its enterprise system will be open to employees and business partners, allowing over 76,000 individuals to gain access to information. Eventually, customers will be able to go online to obtain brochures, pictures, presentations, etc.[47]

Figure 7.5 Enterprise Software and Database Business System Control

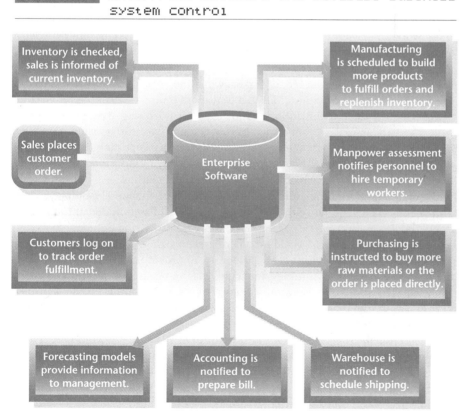

The development of centralized enterprise software systems can be very expensive and time-consuming for businesses to implement. The average total cost of implementing an ERP system (including hardware, software, services, staffing costs, and postimplementation costs) has been estimated at $15 million.[48] Many businesses are using databases to support individual processes, such as customer support, sales force automation, or inventories, without implementing a full ERP system. The advantage of having these diverse systems linked together is that management can access information in real time.

KNOWLEDGE MANAGEMENT

Knowledge management is the process of collecting corporate knowledge and developing a system to disseminate that knowledge throughout an organization. Managing knowledge is important for organizations. An *Information Week* survey indicated that 94 percent of companies considered knowledge management to be strategically important to their business. Knowledge management allows businesses to undertake day-to-day operations as well as become more innovative. In today's business environment, workers can be far from the center of the organization and the shared organizational knowledge. What one employee knows may be important to others, but without the ability to share that knowledge, the business is not working efficiently. In addition, when workers retire, quit, or otherwise leave an organization, the knowledge they possess can be lost.

Knowledge can reside in databases, on paper, and in workers' heads. This knowledge should be available to workers when they need it. A survey of U.S. and European business companies indicated that more than 94 percent felt they could better leverage their organizational knowledge. It is only in the past few years, with the introduction of the Internet, intranets, and data warehousing, that firms have had an effective and efficient means of knowledge collection and dissemination.[49] For businesses that have developed knowledge management systems, the top knowledge areas for which data is collected include business processes, sales and marketing information, and customer information, followed by employee data and product development data.[50] This knowledge is disseminated through relational databases, text search systems, groupware products, and database tools.[51]

Developing a knowledge management system can provide benefits to a firm by reducing the cost of information gathering, improving customer support, identifying new market opportunities, reducing cycle times, and retaining knowledge from workers who leave the organization.[52] A study evaluating firms that used knowledge management inside their organizations indicated that the average positive return-on-investment ratio was 12:1.[53] Andersen Consulting *(www.andersenconsulting.com)* built a worldwide intranet network allowing over 49,000 employees access to databases containing industry information, best-practices information, research, business approaches, and partnership information. Expertise developed for one project can be adapted to new projects.[54] Digital Equipment Corporation *(www.digital.com)* allows employees from around the world to access information from its intranet data warehouse. Digital's number one priority was to train employees to use organizational knowledge. Digital wants its employees to turn the data into information and the information into knowledge.[55] Levi Strauss *(www.levistrauss.com)* developed an intranet-based knowledge management system that allows employees around the world to share information and learn about products and strategies. Ideas generated in Europe, for example, can easily be transferred back to the United States. Employees can gain access to fact sheets, executive biographies, press releases, and advertisements. Levi Strauss also allows its employees to use the intranet to learn about cash flows or other business functions.[56]

Developing a system to manage knowledge requires more than just building a database; it requires a change in the culture of organizations to allow for trust and learning.[57] The development of an organizational culture that allows a business to compete in a virtual marketing age will be further evaluated in Chapter 9.

Privacy concerns

Privacy concerns have arisen because of the use of personal data collected in databases. In the United States, customer data belongs to the agency that collects it; in Europe, laws have been passed that govern the use of an individual's personal data. These issues will be further explored in Chapter 10.

KNOWLEDGE INTEGRATION

TERMS AND CONCEPTS

CONCEPTS AND QUESTIONS FOR REVIEW

1. Explain the relationship between data and information.
2. Describe the role of a marketing information system.
3. Outline the flows for sources of data and uses of data in a marketing information system.

4. Explain how databases are structured.
5. List the sources of data for marketing.
6. Describe how data is collected from customers.
7. Explain how Web-tracking data is collected.
8. Contrast the advantages and disadvantages between traditional marketing research and online marketing research.
9. Describe how competitive intelligence can be collected.
10. Explain how ethical snooping can be conducted.
11. Explain how knowledge discovery is undertaken using databases.
12. Contrast OLAP database searches with data mining.
13. Explain the dangers of using data-mining techniques.
14. Outline the roles databases play in controlling business systems.
15. Explain how a company can manage knowledge.

ACTIVE LEARNING

Exercise 7.1: Developing a Virtual Library

A virtual library can aid in the competitive intelligence-gathering process by developing a set of links to sources of information. This assignment requires developing a table that contains links to sites that provide information on an industry of interest, such as links to trade publications, competitors' sites, government sites, etc. The table should have the address linked to the site, the name of the site, and a description of the content that can be found at the site. After the table is created, develop a dated summary of the competitive intelligence found.

Industry or Business: Internet Marketing

Industry Environmental Scanning Sites (Example)

Site	Company or Journal	Description
www.internetwk.com	Internet Week	Articles related to technology trends and company practices
www.iw.com	Internet World	News journal covering a wider variety of topics related to the Internet

Summary of Competitive Intelligence for (date)

Write a brief summary of the information you find from these sites that can impact your business or industry.

Exercise 7.2: Database Field Exercises

Before a database can be developed, the field of information to be collected must be identified. For this exercise, pick an industry and list the fields that will help a business identify current customer behavior, project future customer behavior, or determine the value of its customers. Once those fields have been identified, determine the sources that would be used to gather that information.

Database Field of Exercise (Example)

Field	Source of Field Data
1. Age	Application forms, credit records, third-party data
2. Purchases	Credit card, check numbers, or shopping card link to register receipt

Exercise 7.3: Determining Your Strategic Value

As a customer, you have a strategic value to businesses. This value could be high or low. Using the following table, determine your strategic value for a number of businesses by rating yourself on recency, frequency, and monetary value. Use the five-point scale and compare yourself to other customers of the store.

Once you have identified your value, determine which types of incentives would be necessary to turn you into a high-value customer. Indicate the business strategy that should be undertaken (e.g., whether you should be given those incentives identified or dropped as a customer).

Determining Your Strategic Value

Business (name and type)	Recency High	Frequency 1-2-3-4	Monetary Low	Incentives	Business Strategy

WEB SEARCH — LOOKING ONLINE

SEARCH TERM:	Competitive Intelligence	First 5 out of 17,400

CIO Web Business. Is a journal site targeting chief information officers. It provides in-depth information on industry trends and practices.
http://webbusiness.cio.com

DM Review. Is a trade journal site with topics covering data warehousing and data mining. It contains searchable databases of trade articles.
www.datawarehouse.com

Inter@ctive Week. Is a journal targeting information on Internets, intranets, and infrastructure.
www.interactive-week.com

Internet Week. Has articles related to technology trends and company practices.
www.internetwk.com

Internet World. Is a news journal covering a wide variety of topics related to the Internet.
www.iw.com

SEARCH TERM:	Online Libraries	First 3 out of 2,468,420

CEO Express. Is an online library with links to newspapers, trade magazines, news feeds, and topic searches.
www.ceoexpress.com

CorporateInformation.com. Provides information on public and private companies from around the world.
www.corporateinformation.com

Fuld & Company. Includes over 500 intelligence-related Internet sites that contain varying information.
www.fuld.com/i3/index.html

SEARCH TERM:	Marketing Research	First 5 out of 63,879

Focusgrps.com. Is a qualitative market research company that does in-depth research to ensure that you are getting the best value for your dollar.
www.focusgrps.com

Isurveys.com. Allows companies to build surveys online. A link is made from the company's home page to the survey at the iSurvey site. The developer can then look at data summaries.
www.isurveys.com

MarketTools. Is a marketing research firm offering online survey development, survey hosting, and panel services.
www.markettools.com

Perseus Development Corp. Sells software for marketing research and market polling. It also offers research design consulting.
www.perseus.com

Speedback. Is a marketing research agency that provides both qualitative and quantitative results for your inquiries.
www.speedback.com

SEARCH TERM: Infomediaries	First 2 out of 4,768

CyberGold. Is an online company that rewards customers for checking out a certain Web site through advertisement links.
www.cybergold.com

Engage Technologies. Gathers information from "cookies" that are captured from pages and finds ways to limit the ads on a Web page.
www.engage.com

SEARCH TERM: Database Management	First 3 out of 195,450

ACM SIGKDD. Is an ACM special-interest group on knowledge discovery in data and data mining.
www.acm.org/sigkdd

Data Warehousing Information Center. Is a library of data warehousing and decision support system sites.
http://pwp.starnetinc.com/larryg/index.html

Primary Knowledge. Is a database service company providing online data warehousing to aid marketing campaign development.
www.primaryknowledge.com

SEARCH TERM: Knowledge Management	First 2 out of 95,270

Hyperion. Is a site dedicated to helping improve efficiency, gain knowledge, and achieve wisdom through the process of turning information into success.
www.hyperion.com

KDNuggets. Is a site that lists additional information on hardware and software.
www.kdnuggets.com/index.html

R E F E R E N C E S

[1] Rick Whiting, "Mega Data Warehouse," *Information Week,* April 19, 1999, p. 31; and Peter Fabris, "Advanced Navigation," *CIO—Section 1*, May 15, 1998, pp. 50–55.

[2] Linda McHugh, "Who's Doing What With Data Mining?" *Teradatareview,* Summer 1999, pp. 23–31.

[3] Adapted from Samuel B. Griffith, *Sun Tzu, The Art of War,* Oxford University Press, Oxford, England, 1971, p. 138.

[4] John Fontana, "Businesses Gear Up for Web Expansion," *Internet Week,* September 14, 1998, pp. 16–19.

[5] For more on the theory behind information as a competitive advantage, see: Rashi Glazer, "Marketing in an Information-Intensive Environment: Strategic Implications of Knowledge as an Asset," *Journal of Marketing,* October 1991, pp. 1–19.

[6] Heather Green, "The Information Gold Mine," *Business Week E.Biz,* July 26, 1999, pp. 16–30; and Tom Davenport, "From Data to Knowledge," *CIO—Section 1,* April 1, 1999, pp. 26–28.

[7] Jonathan Berry, John Verity, Kathleen Kerwin, and Gail DeGeorge, "Database Marketing," *Business Week,* September 5, 1994, pp. 56–62.

[8] Robert Shaw and Merlin Stone, *Database Marketing Strategy & Implementation,* John Wiley & Sons, New York, 1990, p. 88.

[9] Marianne Kolbasuk McGee, "IT Renaissance?" *Information Week,* August 17, 1998, pp. 36–41.

[10] B. G. Yovovich, "Scanners Reshape Grocery Business," *Marketing News,* vol. 32, no. 4, February 16, 1998, pp. 1, 11.

[11] Mike Fillon, "Ritz-Carlton Gets Personnel," *Sales & Field Force Automation,* May 1998, p. 16.

[12] Edward Cone, "Taking No Chances," *Information Week,* December 12, 1994, pp. 30–40.

[13] John Hagel and Jeffrey Rayport, "The Coming Battle for Customer Information," *Harvard Business Review,* January–February 1997, pp. 53–61; and Scott Kirsner, "To Know Me Is to Pay Me," *WebMaster,* May 1997, pp. 52–56.

[14] Elizabeth Gardner, "Two New Incentive Programs Merge," *Internet World,* November 16, 1998, p. 8; Jim Carr, "Enough About Us, Let's Talk About You," *NewMedia,* November 24, 1997, p. 75; and Get Paid to Surf the Net, CyberGold, Inc., October 1, 1998, *<http://www.cybergold.com>*.

[15] Thomas J. Deloughry and Kathleen Murphy, "Marketer Offers Sites a Database of Customer Preferences," *Internet World,* March 2, 1998, p. 5; and *Engage Technologies'* Profile-Enabled Targeting Becomes New Standard for Precision Online Marketing, Engage Technologies news release, August 17, 1998, *<http://www.engagetech.com/press/releases/081798.htm>*.

[16] John W. Virity, "The Gold Mine of Data in Customer Service," *Business Week,* March 21, 1994, pp. 113–114.

[17] Leslie Marable, "Online Market Research Begins to Catch On," *Web Week,* March 31, 1997, pp. 16–18; and Roy Furchgott, "If You Like the Suit, Click Here," *Business Week,* November 17, 1998, p. 8.

[18] Maricris G. Briones, "Cheaper Desktops Will Help Net Researchers Corral Clients," *Marketing News,* vol. 32, no. 23, November 9, 1998, pp. 1, 17.

[19] For a review of four survey software packages, see: Esther Schindler, "Ask Anything," *Sm@rt Reseller,* July 20, 1998, pp. 88–91.

[20] J. D. Mosley-Matchett, "Leverage the Web's Research Capabilities," *Marketing News,* vol. 32, no. 8, April 13, 1998, p. 6; and Rudy Nadilo, "On-Line Research Taps Consumers Who Spend," *Marketing News,* vol. 32, no. 12, June 8, 1998, p. 12.

[21] !Research, Online Focus Groups, November 10, 1998, *<http://www.iresearch.com/pages/focus.html>*.

[22] Aileen Crowley, "Looking for Data in All the Right Places," *PC Week,* October 21, 1996, pp. 51, 56.

[23] Society for Competitive Intelligence Professionals, "What Is CI?" November 9, 1999, *<http://www.scip.org/ci>*.

24 John Fontana, "Businesses Gear Up for Web Expansion," *Internet Week,* September 14, 1998, pp. 16–17.

25 Chris Nerney, "The Competitive Intelligence Edge," *Network World,* November 9, 1998, p. 42; and Ann Harrison, "Why IS Must Go Spying," *Software Magazine,* May 1998, pp. 30–44.

26 Society of Competitive Intelligence Professionals, *SCIP Frequently Asked Questions,* October 26, 1998, <http://www.scip.org/faq.html>; and Jennifer Bresnahan, "Legal Esp," *CIO Enterprise—Section 2,* July 15, 1998, pp. 56–63.

27 For more information on this topic, see: Leonard M. Fuld, *The New Competitor Intelligence,* John Wiley & Sons, New York, 1994; Anne Stuart, "Click and Dagger," *WebMaster,* July/August 1996, pp. 38–43; and Society of Competitive Intelligence Professionals, *SCIP Code of Ethics for CI Professionals,* October 26, 1998, <http://www.scip.org/ethics.html>.

28 Leonard M. Fuld, "Spyer Beware," *CIO Web Business—Section 2,* August 1, 1998, pp. 26–28.

29 Nick Wreden, "Get to Know Your Customer," *Information Week Solution Series* insert, July 13, 1998, pp. 8SS–12SS.

30 Aileen Crowley, "Delivering a Healthy Dose of Sales Data," *PC Week,* November 24, 1997, p. 53.

31 Don Peppers and Martha Rogers, "Customer Strategic Value," *DM Review,* November 1998, p. 20; Paul C. Judge, "What've You Done for Us Lately?" *Business Week,* September 14, 1998, pp. 140–144; Mel Duvall, "Winery Juices Up Database Link," *Inter@active Week,* November 2, 1998, p. 43; and Dennis A Pitta, "Marketing One-to-One and Its Dependence on Knowledge Discovery in Databases," *Journal of Consumer Marketing,* vol. 15, no. 5, 1998, pp. 468–480.

32 For more information on this topic, see: Don Peppers and Martha Rogers, "Customer Strategic Value," *DM Review,* November 1998, p. 20; and Don Peppers and Martha Rogers, *The One to One Future,* Doubleday, New York, 1996.

33 Rick Whiting and Jeff Sweat, "Profitable Customers," *Information Week,* March 29, 1999, pp. 44–56.

34 For more on RFM measurement, see: Ron Kahan, "Using Database Marketing Techniques to Enhance Your One-to-One Marketing Initiatives," *Journal of Consumer Marketing,* vol. 15, no. 5, 1998, pp. 491–493.

35 Jim Laiderman, "Developing Retention, Acquisition and Loyalty Programs," *Business Geographics,* November 1998, pp. 24–27.

36 Steve Alexander, "Users Find Tangible Rewards Digging into Data Mines," *InfoWorld,* July 7, 1997, pp. 61–62; Robert D. Small, "Debunking Data-Mining Myths," *Information Week,* January 20, 1997, pp. 55–60; and Martin Marshall, "Data Mining: Rich Vein for Marketers," *Communications Week,* January 13, 1997, pp. 1, 69.

37 Mike McNamee, "Isn't There More to Life Than Plastic?" *Business Week,* November 22, 1999, pp. 173–176.

38 Information for this section is in part drawn from Jonathan Berry, John Verity, Kathleen Kerwin, and Gail DeGeorge, "Database Marketing," *Business Week,* September 5, 1994, pp. 56–62; Herman Holtz, *Databased Marketing,* John Wiley & Sons, New York, 1992; and Robert Shaw and Merlin Stone, *Database Marketing & Strategy Implementation,* John Wiley & Sons, New York, 1990.

39 Nick Wreden, "The Mother Load," *Communications Week,* February 17, 1997, pp. 43–47.

40 For more information, see: Gary McWilliams, "Small Fry Go Online," *Business Week,* November 20, 1995, pp. 158–162.

41 John Foley, "Towering Terabytes," *Information Week,* September 30, 1996, pp. 34–48; and John W. Verity, "Coaxing Meaning Out of Raw Data," *Business Week,* February 3, 1997, pp. 134–138.

[42] Srikumar S. Rao, "Birth of a legend," *Forbes,* April 6, 1998, p. 128.

[43] Peter Coy, "He Who Mines Data May Strike Fool's Gold," *Business Week,* June 16, 1997, p. 40.

[44] Christopher Elliott, "Give Your Data a Workout," *Internet Week,* June 1, 1998, pp. 32–34.

[45] Rich Bohn, "Aurum Customer Enterprise," *Sales & Field Force Automation,* August 1998, pp. 92–94; Sean Dugan, "Mining the Benefits of SFA," *InfoWorld,* October 5, 1998, p. 74; and Shep Parke, "Gotcha! Avoiding the Unseen Perils of Sales Technology," *Sales & Field Force Automation,* November 1998, pp. 30–38.

[46] Ronald B. Lieber, "Here Comes SAP," *Fortune,* October 2, 1995, pp. 122–124.

[47] Bob Francis, "Open Door Policy," *PC Week,* May 35, 1998, pp. 87–88, 103.

[48] Christopher Koch, "The Most Important Team in History," *CIO—Section 1,* October 15, 1999, pp. 41–52.

[49] For more on this topic, see: Justin Hibbard, "Knowing What We Know," *Information Week,* October 20, 1997, pp. 46–64; or visit KM World Magazine Web site, *<http://www.kmonline. com/>* for online access to knowledge management topics.

[50] Connie Moore, "KM Meets BP," *CIO—Section 1,* November 15, 1998, pp. 64–68.

[51] Beth Davis and Brian Riggs, "Knowledge Management Get Smart," *Information Week,* April 5, 1999, pp. 40–50.

[52] Paul Penny, "Knowledge Management, Maximizing the Return on Your Intellectual Assets," *DM Review,* November 1998, pp. 36–39, 64.

[53] Gary Abramson, "Measuring Up," *CIO Enterprise—Section 2,* May 15, 1998, pp. 28–32.

[54] Mary Ryan Garcia, "Knowledge Central," *Information Week,* September 22, 1997, pp. 252–256.

[55] Erin Callaway, "Digital Spins Training Web," *PC Week,* November 24, 1997, pp. 62, 70.

[56] Lauren Gibbons Paul, "Eureka! Levi Finds Gold Mine of Data," *PC Week,* May 13, 1996, pp. 53–56.

[57] Tom Davenport, "Knowledge Management, Round Two," *CIO Enterprise—Section 1,* November 1, 1999, pp. 30–33; Wendi R. Bukowitz and Ruth L. Williams, "Looking Through the Knowledge Glass," *CIO Enterprise—Section 2,* October 15, 1999, pp. 76–85; and Susan S. Hanley, "A Culture Built on Sharing," *Information Week,* April 26, 1999, pp. 16ER–17ER.

Chapter 8
E-Business Strategy

This chapter explores the dynamics of developing strategies in an e-business environment. A number of environmental drivers are forcing businesses to develop effective strategies. E-businesses are attempting to react quickly and fill market niches before competitive firms are able to do this. E-businesses are using their economic resources to develop brand names, differentiate themselves from competitors, and strengthen customer relationships. As e-businesses find ways to compete, their strategies are being evaluated by the stock market, which is placing value on these new business models.

1. Outline the steps involved in strategy development.
2. List the major drivers of e-business strategy and their impact.
3. Explain the importance of an e-business value chain.
4. Discuss how the roles of alliances and acquisitions relate to strategy development.
5. Identify the major strategies e-businesses use to differentiate themselves.
6. List the advantages that a pioneering firm can gain.
7. Explain the importance of brand names for e-businesses.
8. Describe the strategic role of portals.
9. Identify the alternative competitive arenas where e-businesses can find opportunities.
10. Describe the measures that businesses can use to judge e-business success.

Microsoft vs. the World

In the early 1990s, Microsoft had near monopoly power in a number of software areas including operating systems, spreadsheets, and word processing. Microsoft was a very powerful supplier of software to computer manufacturers, able to dictate prices and products on the Windows desktop. Microsoft's dominance in the market made it very difficult for buyers to switch to new products. Corporate computer systems buyers felt safe purchasing Microsoft's industry-standard products. Very few companies attempted to compete against Microsoft. If Microsoft announced that it would produce a product, software companies would stay away from that product category. Microsoft seemed to be safe and in control of the microcomputer industry.

Then came the rise of the Internet and the growth of the Web through the use of graphical browsers. In 1994 Microsoft's chairman, Bill Gates, realized Microsoft was not the first to move into this new Internet industry and had to play catch-up. Gates mustered his forces to have Microsoft's software retooled for the Internet. Microsoft may have been heading in the wrong direction, but within eight months it was able to change direction and become a dominant Internet player. Software or services that Microsoft could not produce itself it purchased, licensed, or formed an alliance to obtain.[1]

Microsoft's Internet Software
Strategic Actions: Purchases/Licenses/Alliances

1994	Licenses Spyglass browser technology: Helps develop Internet Explorer Web browser.
1995	Invests in UUNET Internet access provider for Microsoft Network.
1995	Alliance with AOL: Places AOL icon on Windows desktop, Internet explorer becomes AOL browser.
1996	Purchases Vermeer Technology: Obtains FrontPage Web design software.
1996	Purchases Colusa Software Inc.: Gets Web-based object-oriented software.
1996	Purchases eShop, Inc.: Gains Internet commerce software.
1996	Purchases Electric Gravity, Inc.: Obtains an Internet multiplayer game company.
1996	Licenses Sun Microsystems: Gains Java programming language.
1996	Forms AT&T, Netcom, MCI, CompuServe alliances: Places Internet Explorer as the default browser.
1997	Invests in RealNetworks: Gives access to video- and sound-streaming technology.
1997	Purchases Hotmail for $400 million: Gains access to millions of e-mail users.
1997	Purchases WebTV for $425,000: Gains access to television-based Web technology.
1999	Invests in Nextel: Gains access to cellular customers.
1999	Invests in AT&T: Allows Windows CE and network software to be used for television-based Web access.

Source code is the original building blocks of a program. **Open source** code allows anyone to gain access to the inner workings of a software package and revise the software. These revisions are often posted on the Internet.

Microsoft's Internet Explorer began to take market share away from Netscape. In 1996, Netscape's share of the browser market shrunk from nearly 80 percent to only around 50 percent. Netscape fought back by picking another market in which to compete, the corporate Internet and server market. It formed alliances with Sun, Sprint, Hewlett-Packard, and IBM. Microsoft was able to increase its market share of the browser market because it gave away Internet Explorer for free. This was, in part, the impetus for antitrust action taken against Microsoft. Keeping up with the legion of Microsoft programmers was a large task for Netscape. Dominance on the desktop was Netscape's and Microsoft's ultimate goal. In 1998, Netscape decided to release its **source code** for the Netscape browser. This allows programmers from around the world to understand how the Netscape software operates, and to enhance and customize the software. In one move, Netscape enlisted a world's supply of additional creativity and innovation.[2]

Meanwhile, Linux entered the market. Linus Torvalds, a Finnish graduate student, developed an alternative operating system and released the source code on the Internet. Programmers from around the world were free to add to, improve, and customize the software. After a slow start, Linux has been gaining support. The installed base of Linux users grew from 100,000 in 1993 to an estimated 12 million by 1998. Linux has received support from companies such as IBM, Dell Computer, Intel, Netscape, Hewlett-Packard, Compaq, and Corel. Corel developed a free downloadable version of WordPerfect for the Linux operating system.[3] Microsoft sees Linux as a strong potential threat and reported to the Justice Department that freeware programs such as Linux prove that Microsoft does not have a monopoly in the marketplace.

Back at the Redmond ranch, Microsoft has been positioning itself for a much wider competitive environment. Microsoft has been moving to develop an Internet media- and commerce-based business. WebTV, MSNBC, and alliances with cable companies give Microsoft access to the television market. Expedia allows customers to purchase travel services, and CarPoint offers car sales; Microsoft Network is the second most popular online portal.[4]

Microsoft is evolving from a company that supplies software to a company that plans to link customers to goods and services. Microsoft's electronic commerce mission

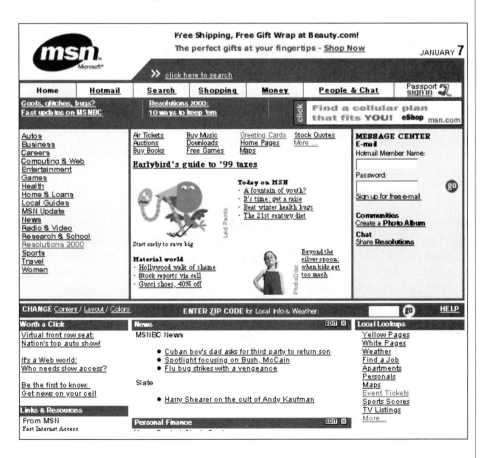

is: *Making the Internet indispensable and relevant to every person and every business, every day.* To achieve this mission, Microsoft has determined that its main core competency is recruitment of the best high-technology workers. Microsoft attempts to hire the very smart and reorganize to become more efficient.[5]

THINKING STRATEGICALLY

Determine what environmental factors are influencing Microsoft. Contrast Microsoft's strengths and weaknesses. Decide which of Microsoft's strengths allow it to gain an advantage over its competitors. List environmental threats that Microsoft currently faces and could encounter in the future. Determine what steps Microsoft could take to lower those threats. Speculate on the future opportunities that Microsoft may have. List the different competitive arenas in which Microsoft is competing. Determine what steps Microsoft would need to take to pursue those opportunities.

The vignette illustrates a number of issues found in this chapter and Chapter 9. Businesses must develop strategies that allow them to compete if they are to survive. The full process of strategy development and implementation is beyond the scope of this text. Instead, this chapter will look at the broad process of strategy development for e-businesses by considering the current drivers of strategy and the major strategies undertaken in the e-business marketplace. Chapter 9 will investigate how management practice is changing to allow firms to compete and implement e-business strategies.

WHAT IS STRATEGY?

A **strategy** consists of a pattern of decisions that set the goals and objectives that lead to long-run competitive advantages for a firm.[6] E-businesses must develop strategies to survive in their competitive environments. The tools and techniques outlined in this text are being used by e-businesses to gain competitive advantages. These include not only pure-play Internet companies but brick and mortar–based e-businesses as well. These advantages come from gaining efficiencies in logistics and production, meeting customers' needs better than the competition, and being able to respond to a changing environment. A rapidly evolving and highly competitive environment is forcing businesses to reassess current strategies and develop new strategies to ensure long-term survival. The essence of strategy development for businesses involves four basic steps:

1. **Undertake a SWOT (strengths, weaknesses, opportunities, threats) analysis.** This requires investigating the strengths and weaknesses of the business

Figure 8.1 Model of Strategy

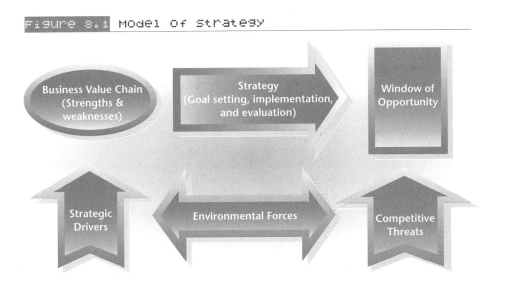

and analyzing new opportunities as well as threats from competitors and the environment.

2. **Determine distinctive competencies.** After performing a SWOT analysis, a business must determine where it has advantages over competitors or how it can achieve distinctive competencies. This process requires an analysis of a business's **value chain** to identify internal strengths and weaknesses that can help determine how a business can compete. Determining distinctive competencies and maintaining these over a long time period can be very difficult for a business.

3. **Determine the competitive arena.** Performing a SWOT analysis and identifying distinctive competencies allow a business to determine its competitive arena. This helps establish the mission for the business by indicating the windows of opportunity to be pursued and the nature of the competitive environment in which a business can and wants to compete. Gaining an advantage often requires finding a fit between a firm's distinctive competencies and the nature of the competitive environment.

4. **Develop a plan to reach the business goals.** The strategic planning process outlines the actions and tactics a business must use to move from where and how it currently competes to where and how it needs to compete given its distinctive competencies. The planning process sets targets, maintains feedback, and implements control to aid in reaching strategic goals.

This strategy process is illustrated in Figure 8.1. In this figure, environmental **strategic drivers** force a business to evaluate and strengthen its value chain in order to undertake strategic actions both to pursue opportunities and to avoid or limit competitive threats.

Distinctive competencies are unique areas of advantage in which a firm can differentiate itself from competitors.

A value chain is a way of envisioning the collection of activities that a business undertakes to design, produce, market, deliver, and support products or services.

The competitive arena is the competitive environment in which a business operates.

DRIVERS OF STRATEGY

Businesses need to be able to respond to changes in turbulent environments. **Environmental turbulence** means that the environment is changing both rapidly and unpredictably and is often characterized by rapid change both in competitors' products and in customers' needs.[7] Environmental turbulence forces change in business strategies and in the distinctive competencies needed to compete. Some of the environmental drivers leading to environmental turbulence are included in Table 8.1.

These drivers can present both opportunities and threats to an e-business. E-businesses that understand these chances and can leverage the technology necessary to serve customers have the opportunity to capture market share. Those that do not respond to these drivers will face competitive threats from faster, more nimble competitors. E-businesses are responding to this turbulence by leveraging assets and deploying technology. Businesses must be willing to take **proactive** steps to maintain current and future competitiveness.

Before a business undertakes a strategy, it should first undertake a SWOT analysis to help determine internal strengths and weaknesses and assess external opportunities and threats. An analysis of an e-business value chain can help a

Proactive implies acting in anticipation of future problems or opportunities, rather than being reactive, waiting and reacting to the environment.

Table 8.1 Drivers of Environmental Turbulence

Environmental Drivers	Description
Technological change	**Moore's law,** which states that the density of microprocessors doubles every two years while costs decrease, seems to be holding. This is allowing technology to be applied across a broader spectrum of products and uses.
Changing customers	Customers around the globe are rapidly accepting Internet use and online purchasing. Most individuals are facing time compression in that there is not enough time for them to do everything they would like; technology is being used as an enabler, allowing individuals to accomplish more. Customers have more power due to an increase in access to information and negotiating power.
Shorter product life cycles	Product life cycles are getting shorter due to the rapid development of new technology, aggressive marketing, and buyers' willingness to try new products.
Number of competitors	Distance between competitors is vanishing. Online competition allows sellers from many different locations to sell anywhere. This is causing an increase in the intensity of competition and allowing international competitors to enter new markets.
Need for speed	Time is collapsing across business applications. Instant connectivity is becoming the norm in business-to-business applications as well as in the way consumers shop.

Sources: *Business 2.0,* "10 Driving Principles of the New Economy," Premier Issue; William Qualls, Richard W. Olshavsky, and Ronald E. Michaels "Shortening of the PLC—An Empirical Test," *Journal of Marketing,* vol. 45, Fall 1981, pp. 76–80; and Milton D. Rosenau Jr., *Faster New Product Development,* AMACOM, New York, 1990.

business identify its strengths and weaknesses. When taken into consideration along with opportunities and competitive threats, a business can identify areas of distinctive competencies and the competitive arenas in which to operate.

E-BUSINESS VALUE CHAIN

Identifying the individual activities that a business undertakes to design, produce, market, deliver, and support products or services is the first step in determining how to deliver value to customers. An e-business value chain considers the inbound logistical process (obtaining raw materials, logistical procedures, and production) and the outbound logistical process (outbound logistical procedures, marketing, sales, support). To gain a distinctive competency, a business must be able to perform some function in its value chain better than its competitors. This could mean providing a function at a lower cost or in a unique way. Businesses that compete in similar industries serving similar markets may have value chains that differ from other industries.[8] With the growth of e-business tools and techniques, a new perspective has been added to the value chain. The **e-business value chain** views information technology as part of a business's overall value chain and adds to the competitive advantages of a business.[9] A survey of over 400 information technology managers indicated that 96 percent believe that electronic sales and purchasing applications were very (61 percent) or somewhat (35 percent) important to their businesses.[10] According to the trade journal *Information Week,* the number one priority for businesses in the *Information Week 500* (a list of the most innovative users of technology) is implementing e-business strategies and, specifically, improving supply chains and electronic data interchange.[11] This text has

Figure 8.2 The E-Business Value Chain

Inbound Logistics	Production	Management	Marketing/Sales	Customer Support	
Extranets: Lower costs, increase speed.	*ERP software:* Lowers costs. *Customized production:* Provides differential advantage.	*Leadership:* Focuses direction. *Intranets:* Lower costs, facilitate better communications. *Innovativeness:* Generates speed, flexibility, new product ideas.	*E-commerce:* Lowers costs, allows new market entry. *Databases:* Meet market needs better, facilitate better decisions.	*Internet:* Lowers costs, speeds service.	Competitive Advantage Through Stronger Customer Relationships

outlined a number of techniques that an e-business can use to gain advantages throughout its value chain. Figure 8.2 illustrates how these technologies impact the components of an e-business value chain.

As shown in Figure 8.2, a firm can gain cost advantages through the use of extranets, enterprise resource planning software, and e-commerce. Although a survey of chief executive officers indicated that 78 percent viewed information technology as a source of competitive advantage, cost advantages may only give firms industry parity or short-term advantages, not long-term differential advantages. Chief financial officers have indicated that the most important criterion for evaluating technology investments is whether or not IT helps reduce operating expenses (71 percent of respondents). The next four most important criteria were related to gaining distinctive advantages: Technology would enable the business to stay ahead of competition (62 percent), provide an opportunity to enhance operating revenue (44 percent), position the company to increase market share (40 percent), and help reduce lead times (39 percent).[12] Improvement of any component in the value chain can result in an overall improvement in customer satisfaction.

Identification Of a Distinctive Advantage

A distinctive advantage must come from some area in which a business can gain a long-term advantage over competitors. Technology by itself may not impart a competitive advantage; it must be leveraged to be responsive to the needs of the company and its customers. By lowering costs, improving responsiveness to customers, and improving businesses' ability to respond to environmental change, technology is already having an impact on the logistical and supply-chain processes across a large number of industries. Companies are learning how to use technology to impact sales and customer support. But as these processes become more widely accepted in both business-to-business markets and business-to-consumer markets, they may not impart long-term advantages. Instead, they may only be the basis for competition in a market. For example, if a business was not able to leverage a technology such as e-mail, it may not be able to compete because it would not be able to respond rapidly enough to external customers and internal communications needs.[13]

Coca-Cola is attempting to link together its production with 11 anchor bottling partners in an attempt to stay ahead of its global competitors and a changing market. This will link together 43 percent of Coke's production. Databases will be used to provide information on store sales and customer use around the world. Coke bottlers in Australia and New Zealand have vending machines that are linked through cellular systems; they can report on the sales in each machine. Coca-Cola is hoping that this technology implementation will allow it to become a more efficient operation around the world. Figure 8.3 illustrates the e-business value chain being developed for Coca-Cola.[14]

The Coca-Cola example illustrates that Coke is increasing the efficiency of its operations, but it still needs to be able to maintain its brand name and product quality to keep its competitive position.

Figure 8.3 Coca-Cola E-Business Value Chain

A key to implementing e-business technology is having a management team and employees who are willing and able to restructure organizations. This is part of the reason that Microsoft has stated that its distinctive competence is rooted in its hiring policy. Management and employees must be able to capitalize on the advantages that can be found in customer databases, online access to information between buyers and sellers, rapid responses to environmental change, and proactive innovation.[15]

Chapter 9 discusses the management aspects of the e-business value chain, including managing e-businesses, hiring individuals who are comfortable with the current rate of change, and using intranets that allow faster communications inside a business. Not all the components of the e-business value chain must come from within the organization itself; many e-businesses outsource key components or form alliances with other businesses.

Alliances and Acquisitions

The creation of an e-business value chain may come from the formation of **alliances** or through the **acquisition** of other firms. Online-only firms have a number of advantages over brick and mortar businesses including established online brand names and a mastering of the technology needed to contact customers at low cost. They may also have weaknesses in the ability to provide service and logistical delivery components of the value chain. Without a physical location for customers to touch, feel, and return products, sales of some product categories may be limited. E-businesses without warehouses have encountered problems with

Alliances are formal or informal relationships between independent companies that work together for a common purpose.

An **acquisition** exists when one corporation purchases all or a controlling part of another company.

controlling the delivery of products, resulting in untimely delivery to customers. Brick and mortar stores that are able to leverage the Internet as an alternative selling channel can obtain advantages over online-only sellers. For example, Charles Schwab *(www.schwab.com)* leveraged its online system with its brick and mortar and service support system to become the number one online brokerage business.[16]

Alliances allow partnering companies to pool expertise, enter new markets, share financial risks, and get products and services to markets faster. Alliances have been growing worldwide and have increased in the United States by 25 percent each year since 1987.[17] A number of companies are positioning themselves to be competitive in the e-business arena. Communications companies such as AT&T are purchasing cable TV companies. Alliances are being used to build Internet **portals** because they allow content, expertise, and money to be pooled to develop sites that attract viewers. Television and media companies have developed a number of alliances with Internet companies. This is in part because homes with Internet access watch up to 15 percent less television than non-Internet homes. In 1998, the Walt Disney Company partnered with Infoseek to help develop the GO Network portal site. Infoseek's search engine was combined with Disney resources, allowing both access to content from Disney-owned companies (such as ABCNews.com, ESPN.com, and Mr. Showbiz) and alliances with NFL.com and NASCAR.com. GO Network is designing its site to be attractive to new Internet users. A $165 million advertising budget heavily backed this strategy.[18]

In the high-tech industry, **co-opetition** is developing as a new competitive model in which businesses that are competitors in some areas cooperate with each other in noncompetitive areas. The Java software platform is an example of co-opetition. When Sun Microsystems introduced the programming language in 1995, it sought out partners to ensure that it would be accepted by the industry. Sun even partnered with companies with which it competes in other software or hardware areas.[19]

A **portal** is an entranceway onto the Internet. It is often the preferred starting point for searches, entertainment, information, e-mail, or other Internet-based products.

E-BUSINESS STRATEGY

Firms have traditionally taken two paths to gain distinctive advantages. The first is to attempt to be the **low-cost** (and therefore low-price) **competitor.** The second is to attempt a **differentiation strategy** by finding a unique market position against competitors. Information technology is allowing businesses to become more efficient through decreased costs in sales and marketing. In addition, improvement in internal and external communications is speeding manufacturing, R&D, and purchasing, resulting in cost savings.[20] Being the low-cost producer may not be enough to gain a long-term advantage because competitors can gain the same efficiencies. E-business technology can be both a blessing and a curse for businesses. A **frictionless market** implies that customers have almost perfect information and can compare prices around the world, and using intelligence agents to search out the best prices enhances this process. This forces businesses

Table 8.2 Methods of Differentiation

Differentiation Strategy	Advantages	Disadvantages
Gain speed and first-mover advantages	Provides a number of first-mover advantages including cutting costs, meeting needs, decreasing risk, and lowering prices.	Requires being flexible to be fast. Increases risks and may require a large amount of capital to maintain advantages of being first.
Build brand name	Gives buyers assurance when interacting with a site. Allows for easy name recognition.	Requires a large amount of capital to obtain and maintain a brand name.
Use portal development	Allows for economies of scale. Builds barriers to entry.	Requires a large amount of capital, pushing off profitability.
Pursue niche strategies	Allows a business to focus and become an expert in one competitive arena (very good strategy for smaller or weaker businesses).	Can be risky having only one niche because all the "eggs" could be in one basket (with one customer).
Enhance customer relationships	Allows businesses to build barriers to entry. Can meet needs better by staying close to customers.	Could result in a loss of power by the business supplying the product or service.

selling over the Internet, and those that compete against Internet sales, to lower prices or differentiate.[21] Table 8.2 outlines a number of strategies e-businesses are currently using to differentiate themselves.

THINKING STRATEGICALLY

Consider how a business that sells CDs could differentiate itself from other CD-selling businesses. Determine which components of the e-business value chain could be used to create value. Visit the CDNOW Web site *(www.cdnow.com)*. Determine how this site is differentiated from other CD-selling sites. List a number of competitive threats that could impact CDNOW's competitive position. Suggest strategic actions that CDNOW can take to remain competitive into the future.

CASE 8.1

CDNOW—Here for Now

CDNOW was founded in 1994 in a basement. By the beginning of 1998, CDNOW was the market leader in online CD music sales with an inventory of 200,000 CDs and sales of $17.4 million for 1997. In 1998, CDNOW faced increased competition from other online-only CD sellers such as N2K, music clubs that moved their inventory access online, and Amazon.com. N2K attempted to differentiate itself by combining entertainment with CD sales. Amazon.com differentiated by giving buyers a one-stop shop where they can purchase books, CDs, and other products. To respond to these challenges, CDNOW has developed alliances with Yahoo!, GeoCities, and Excite's WebCrawler, and it purchased N2K. To survive, CDNOW cofounder Jason Olim set two strategic goals: "Get Big Fast" and "Speed Is God."[22] Musicland, on the other hand, decided to forgo an Internet presence until it could see a profitable Internet business model. Musicland has an information-based Web site *(www.musicland.com)* but does not want to compete with the over 3,500 Web sites that sell music.[23] All of these sales channels could be threatened by the delivery of music online through MP3 and other formats.

CDNOW

And the Winner is...You!
30% Off GRAMMY and AMA Awards Music

Now Showing at the Video Store...
Great Savings on DVD and VHS Titles.

MUSIC   VIDEO   GIFTS   MY CDNOW   HELP   COSMIC Music Network

News & Reviews   Sales & Specials   Top 100   Downloads   Custom CDs

Shopping Cart
contains 0 items

Artist   Find It   Search Classical

Welcome   VISA CDNOW prefers Visa

CDNOW is more than a music store! It's your connection to music, with news, reviews, downloads and much more!

- New Visitors Guide
- Shopping at CDNOW is Secure
- Create an Account
- Earn FREE music! Join Fast Forward

Browse
- Rock
- Alternative/Indie
- Pop/R&B
- Hip-Hop
- Electronic/Dance
- Jazz
- Country
- Folk/Blues
- World
- Classical
- New Age
- Christian/Gospel
- Vocal/Theatrical
- Soundtracks
- Comedy/Spoken
- Kids/Family

Departments
- MTV CD Lounge
- VH1 Music Shop
- Billboard Charts
- Imports
- Greatest Hits
- Music Accessories

Gift Certificates
- Buy Gift Certificates
- Redeem Gift Certificates

Link to CDNOW
- Sell Music
Earn commissions on sales made through

Center Stage

CDNOW WebSessions: Wilco
You're invited to the world premiere of CDNOW's WebSessions. Go behind the scenes to watch -- on streaming video -- an intimate studio performance with Wilco.

Cosmic Music Network
A community created for music enthusiasts like you. Chat with fans... post messages... download music... find new artists... and more.

What's Hot

Featured Album 30% Off
Celine Dion
All The Way-A Decade Of Song
List $16.97
Add to Cart $13.28

Just in time for the holidays! All of the award-winning diva's best, including a heartwarming version of "The First Time Ever I Saw Your Face."

Listen   The Power Of Love

Featured Album 30% Off

Sales & Special Offers

And the winner is...You at
AWARDS CENTRAL
All GRAMMY and AMA award music 30% off

Hot Sony Latin Music On Sale!
Jaci Velasquez, Elvis Crespo, And More

Make Your Own Beastie Boys 2-CD Set
YOU choose the songs. YOU pick the order. YOU give it a title. We'll do the rest!

FREE Downloads Are Here!
Sixpence None The Richer, Q-Tip, Smashing Pumpkins...

Autographed Books from the Music Bookmobile!
Signed by Aretha Franklin, T-Boz, Meat Loaf and more...

More Sales & Specials...

allstar.
CDNOW'S DAILY MUSIC NEWS
Moby To Contribute To John Waters Film
Bone Thugs-N-Harmony's Flesh-N-Bone Arrested On Weapons Charges
Sixpence None The Richer, Buckcherry Speak Out On Grammy Noms

Case 8.1, CDNOW, illustrates a number of different strategic approaches. For online sellers, speed and flexibility allow quick response to environmental change, size permits economies of scale, brand names give assurance to the buyer, and close customer relationships entice customers to return to a site. These do not guarantee long-term advantages. Severe price competition may hurt all but the most efficient businesses or those with a differentiated niche. The following sections will expand on the strategies outlined in Table 8.2.

Speed and First-Mover Advantages

"We'll sacrifice almost anything for speed."
Peter L. S. Currie
Chief Financial Officer for Netscape, 1997[24]

Time-based competition implies that businesses are flexible enough to respond quickly to the environment, allowing advantages to be gained over slower businesses.[25] This is especially true for first movers or pioneering firms. A **pioneering firm** has, by definition, differentiated itself from the competition because it is the first to enter a competitive arena or is able to help define the competitive arena, giving it a **first-mover advantage.** For example, Microsoft was not the first company to develop an operating system, but its alliance with IBM allowed its operating system to grow to dominate the PC industry. Pioneering with new business

Souce: www.etoys.com

models has opened the competitive window of opportunity to new, and often smaller, businesses.

THINKING STRATEGICALLY

Speculate on the importance of the first-mover advantage for eToys. List some of the advantages that eToys may have gained because it beat Toys 'R' Us to the market. Consider whether, if the order of entry was reversed, eToys would have been able to gain market share. Recommend a strategy that eToys could follow to maintain its competitive advantage.

Speed has become a major method of competing in a turbulent environment, and businesses are attempting to act as quickly as possible.[28] Being fast or a

eToys—First on the Block

eToys *(www.etoys.com)* was founded in 1997 with just over 100 employees. This upstart competed online directly against major toy companies such as Toys 'R' Us *(www.toysrus.com)*, which had $11 billion in sales and over 25,000 employees. Toys 'R' Us started to move its Web site from brochureware to e-commerce in February 1997 but did not launch the site until June 1998. eToys was ready to launch its site in October 1997. The eight-month difference was due to the chosen strategy. eToys moved much more quickly, outsourcing jobs and dedicating its employees to the Web. By August 1998, Toys 'R' Us was visited by 0.5 percent of Internet users while eToys was visited by 1.2 percent. In 1998, eToys was the top online toy store, selling $23 million during the Christmas holiday season.[26]

By 1999, eToys was competing in a $300 online toy market against other online-only sellers, such as Amazon.com, and established brick and mortar toy sellers, such as Kbkids *(www.kbkids.com)*, Wal-Mart *(www.wal-mart.com)*, and Target *(www.target.com)*. Of the predicted 28.8 million online Christmas shoppers in 1999, 10 million were expected to be first-time purchasers. These new shoppers were expected to shop for brand names they recognize and at sites where they can easily exchange products. eToys sees its mission as becoming a resource for parents who need help buying presents for their children.[27]

A comparison standard is what the customer uses to judge a product. For example, if a customer had first gained online search experience with Yahoo!, he or she will evaluate all other search engines against Yahoo!. This gives Yahoo! an advantage because experience with other sites must be compared to the habits gained from using Yahoo!.

pioneer has a number of advantages. These include lower costs, meeting current needs, lower consumer risk perceptions, and higher prices. Being first to market can also increase risk if a firm tries to lead a market that is unwilling to follow. Some firms act as second movers or fast followers, relying on size or some other distinctive advantage to gain market share. Each of these first-mover advantages works as follows[29]:

- **Lower costs.** Shortening the development time for new products or business processes may reduce costs. Being fast or a pioneer can increase the business's or product's time in a life cycle, spreading development costs both over time and among the number of products produced. In addition, an early-entry firm can gain cost advantages through experience curves; when greater market shares are obtained, they obtain greater economies of scale. Firms that follow have less time in the life cycle to recover all costs.[30]

Preview travel *(www.previewtravel.com)*, an online travel agency, was able to lower the cost of issuing tickets from $28 in 1996 to $12 by the end of 1997 because of its growth in size and the experience it gained. The industry average for conventional agents was $15 to $18. Preview's size, with 4 million visits per month, allowed advertisers to use the site to reach an audience. This provided a secondary revenue stream from advertising monies for Preview.[31]

- **Meeting current needs.** A fast firm can gain distinctive advantages by meeting current market needs. The faster a business can respond to the market, the more likely that information from areas such as marketing research will be valid, resulting in actions that could lead to higher market share. First movers have a substantially higher market share than later entrants. A product that is six months' late to market may miss out on one-third of the potential profit over the product's lifetime.[32] Market share is an important consideration because of its impact on reducing per-transaction costs.

- **Lower consumer risk perceptions.** In circumstances in which the consumer lacks knowledge about a product (or product category) but also realizes that the product can offer benefits, the consumer may lower the risk involved in purchasing by choosing a product with an established image or brand name. This gives a strong advantage to the first mover, as it may become the **comparison standard** for all rival products by setting the standard for performance. The first mover also is likely to be the product that consumer innovators and early adopters try first; therefore, the product is likely to be recommended through word of mouth in the diffusion process.

Advertising and publicity for new products can aid in consumer search, but given the lack of alternative products in many innovative markets, advertising may have the effect of setting the relevant product attributes the consumer uses in the evaluation process. The first mover becomes the industry standard by which all entrants will be compared. Advertising can help hold customers to the first mover's products, allowing a higher price to be charged.[33]

The first mover gains **switching-cost** advantages by having firms invest in its technology. For customers, there are additional information advantages gained through brand-name familiarity and the risk involved in switching between products. In the software industry, companies have used strategic tactics such as announcing new product variations to preempt competitors' market entry with new products.

▶ **Higher prices.** The first mover has an advantage in the price it can charge to the consumer and in the maintenance of that price when new competitors enter the market. Consumers will try a new product when the price charged is justified given the benefits of the product and the perceived risks in purchasing the product. The first mover can set a higher introductory price for an innovative buyer who is often more risk-tolerant and who may have higher disposable income. Upon trying the product, the consumer gains additional information on the product benefits. With greater amounts of information available to the later adopting consumer, backed by possible word of mouth about benefits, a higher price can be maintained. Because consumers lack information on their products, later-entering firms are forced to charge lower prices. In addition, the only remaining customers may be those who were more risk-averse and do not want to purchase from the first mover, thus driving the later entrants' price even lower.

A switching cost is the additional cost involved in learning something new. For example, for a business, the costs involved in adopting a new software package would include the software expense, support expense, training costs, decreased productivity costs. The largest of these expenses could come from training, support, and decreased productivity.

Second Movers

Amazon.com was not the first bookstore on the Internet. BookStacks was started in 1992 as a dial-up bulletin board service on the Internet.[34] Obviously, it is not enough for a firm to be the first entrant into the market because this does not guarantee a long-term competitive advantage. A firm must have the expertise, resources, and creativity necessary to exploit first-mover opportunities. Pioneers must also find ways to forestall or neutralize the efforts of later entrants, or they will not gain the distinctive advantages outlined earlier.[35] The forestalling or neutralizing of later entrants can be even more important if there is easy entry into an industry because this can decrease the lead time needed by followers. **Second movers** (also called fast followers) can mitigate the advantages of first movers and help build barriers to any other firms that lag behind; second movers must close the distance between themselves and the first mover in order to limit the first mover's advantage and to obtain as many of the benefits as possible. The entry order of products has a direct effect on the expected market share, with later entrants gaining smaller market shares and diminished profits.

It is sometimes dangerous for firms to be pioneers. The Web has seen a large number of businesses develop and fade over the past few years. Some companies decide to wait on the sidelines until they see business models that look successful. Pioneers can use a great deal of resources educating the market to get it ready to buy; once the market is developed, firms may follow and take advantage of a more educated market. Firms that wait can also gain advantages by observing the competitive mistakes of pioneers. This may work for firms with established brand names, but for smaller start-up firms, entering late can increase costs considerably. These firms will have to spend heavily on advertising, finding new niches, and gaining distinctive advantages.[36]

Building of Barriers

Fruit of the Loom, Inc., developed a Web site that offered ordering and inventory capabilities free to its distributors. Fruit of the Loom set up a separate division, FTL, to build Web sites for its distributors at no cost. Its distributors were free to offer competitive products and to order competitive products online. More than 30,000 screen-printing shops could use the distributors' Web sites for ordering inventory. If a competitive manufacturer, such as Hanes, did not have the inventory to meet the distributors' needs, the system defaulted and offered Fruit of the Loom products. This saved the distributors the production costs of creating a Web site and offered advantages to all involved. Fruit of the Loom was the first to offer this type of service to its distributors. For other companies to follow, they would need to have the distributors switch from a free Web development and management company. Fruit of the Loom has, in effect, built barriers to other firms following its model; it has locked its distributors in and locked its competition out.[37]

The advantages held by pioneering firms can be built into barriers to entry for later followers or potential new entrants. A firm can build barriers by limiting entry into an industry through economies of scale, cost advantages, or high switching costs. These have already been outlined as advantages gained by fast firms and first movers. The Internet does offer relatively low barriers to entry. The technology is widely available and low in cost. In the virtual marketplace, gaining economic power from a large resource base can be a means of obtaining these advantages and limiting the number of substitutes available.[38]

Developing loyalty through brand names or strong customer relationships also acts as a barrier. The more the supplier can lock a user into a relationship, the larger the barrier to entry and the lower the power of the buyer. For consumers, this could be due to assurance in a brand name; for industrial customers, this could include links to supply, JIT inventory systems, or strong dependency locks in a customer.[39] Buyers, on the other hand, do not want to be locked in to a single supplier. With the information advantages offered through the Internet, a larger number of suppliers and substitutes may be available.

Brand Names

A **brand** is a sign, symbol, design, term, name, or combination that allows for easy recognition of a product or company. Products with well-recognized brand names often give assurance to purchasers because purchasers believe that the risk of using a brand-name product is lower. At the end of 1998, the top Internet brand names were America Online, Yahoo!, Netscape, Amazon.com, Priceline, Infoseek, and Excite.[40] Of the companies on this list, the e-commerce sites that customers trusted most included Amazon.com, Yahoo!, Netscape, and Infoseek.[41]

To achieve a recognized brand name, companies have been advertising offline. In 1997, Auto-By-Tel ran an advertisement during the Super Bowl. Other online companies have spent large percentages of their capital on advertising to achieve brand-name recognition. From April to September 1998, Priceline spent $20 million to achieve its brand-name recognition.[42] E*Trade was able to establish its brand name by spending 75 percent of its advertising budget in traditional media.[43] For 1999, Internet companies were projected to spend close to $1.7 billion on advertising to help create brand image.[44]

Building online brand names requires more than simply placing a name in front of the public. The ease of navigation and the user's overall experience influence the individual's attitude toward the Internet brand. Brands and businesses that exist offline can create brand image through the consumer's interface with packaging, stores, and salespeople, as well as advertising. Online branding comes from advertising and the individual's experience with the Web site. Web sites such as AOL, Yahoo!, Netscape, and Amazon.com not only had first-mover advantages; they also

Source: AOL.com screenshot © 2000 America Online, Inc. Used with permission.

developed interfaces that were easy to use and provided services that were benefi-cial to the user. Without providing substantial benefits to consumers, brand-name recognition will not result in loyal customer use.[45]

Portals

Web sites that are able to generate high levels of traffic can gain advantages. Like any medium that sells advertising, the higher the number of viewers, the higher the price a Web site can charge for an ad placement. In addition, an e-business's ability to gain sponsorships and alliances can depend on the number and quality of users. AOL, Yahoo!, and Microsoft Network have become portals to the Internet. A portal is more than just the first site that individuals see when they go online; it is the site that users depend on to access other Internet services. The difference between portals and **online services** such as AOL is that the online service offers both Internet access and content for a fee. The online service billing process gives companies a more loyal set of viewers and a larger database of information on the viewers, allowing for more targeted advertising.[46] As less technologically savvy Internet users go online, they may look for brand names with perceived easy

Table 8.3 TOP Web Domains

From Homes (66.7 million Web users)	%	From Businesses (24.3 million Web users)	%
AOL Network Proprietary & WWW	74.8	AOL Network Proprietary & WWW	66.6
Yahoo! Sites	53.4	Microsoft Sites	60.7
Microsoft Sites	49.9	Yahoo! Sites	60.3
Lycos	35.0	Lycos	40.5
GO Network	27.0	GO Network	32.2
Excite@Home	18.0	Amazon.com	22.2
Amazon.com	17.1	Excite@Home	21.5
Bluemountainarts.com	15.1	Time Warner Online	18.4
Time Warner Online	13.8	ZDNet Sites	16.0
Go2Net Network	13.7	Bluemountainarts.com	15.0

Source: Media Metrix Press Release, "Media Metrix Releases the Top 50 at Home and at Work Digital Media and Web Audience Ratings in the U.S. for November 1999," December 21, 1999, <http://www.mediametrix.com/PressRoom/Press_Releases/12_21_99b.html>.

access to a confusing technology. Portals are attempting to offer an easy-to-use, all-in-one starting point for Web access. From homes, the largest online service is AOL; the largest home portal is Yahoo!. For businesses, the largest portal is Yahoo!, followed by Netscape (purchased by AOL). Table 8.3 outlines the top domains for 1999 traffic sites as measured by percent of users who visit the sites (a single individual can visit more than one site).

Portals structure their sites as one-stop Internet access. By providing a number of services, such as search, shopping, e-mail, and games, individuals do not need to spend time browsing the Web but can rely on one Web host or portal. Since this drives eyeballs, it also drives advertising revenue and alliances. In 1998, Citicorp paid Netscape $40 million to become the exclusive sponsor for the financial channel on Netscape's Netcenter. This allows Citicorp to be the exclusive provider of bank services. For another $40 million, Barnesandnoble.com became the exclusive bookseller for AOL. Portal sites have been projected to be the conduit for over 40 percent of all commerce revenue and to gain up to 67 percent of advertising dollars.[47]

Companies are attempting to become major portal brand names for the Web. In the battle to become mega-portals, a number of alliances were formed, and large amounts of advertising dollars were spent in 1998. In June 1998, Walt Disney purchased 43 percent of Infoseek and NBC purchased 19 percent of Snap.[48] Both companies spent heavily on brand-name development to capture shares of specific target markets. As the Internet industry consolidates, the number of general-use portals may shrink to just a few survivors.

THINKING STRATEGICALLY

Speculate on the reasons for AOL's portal success. Determine why AOL was able to grow to dominate Internet access. List some advantages that AOL's size gives it in the competitive portal arena. Compare and contrast AOL *(www.aol.com)* with other portal sites such as Yahoo! *(www.yahoo.com)*, the GO Network *(www.go.com)*, or Excite *(www.excite.com)*. Determine how differentiated these sites are from each other. Justify AOL's use of strategic alliances to maintain its advantages.

CASE 8.3

Nobody's Laughing Now

AOL has made a number of purchases to establish itself as the preeminent online portal site. In 1998, AOL purchased its competitor CompuServe and formed an alliance with China Internet Corp. (an Internet service in Hong Kong).[49] One of the largest Internet-related acquisitions was America Online's $4.2 billion purchase of Netscape in an alliance with Sun Microsystems. AOL was able to increase the total number of users it services on the Internet by controlling two of the largest portals, AOL and NetCenter. It also took control of the Netscape browser and gained programming expertise from Sun. Netscape, in turn, received financial stability; Sun received the suite of Netscape e-commerce applications, Internet server software, and a partnership with the largest portals. This new alliance allowed Microsoft to claim in court that it did not have monopolistic control over the Internet, even though Microsoft was found in federal court to have engaged in monopolistic practices.

In the face of these two large competitors, search engines have taken on partners to maintain their portal status. AOL/Netscape could gain control of up to 35 percent of Internet advertising revenue. AOL/Netscape, along with the other large Internet players, is placing a large amount of pressure on smaller companies.[50]

AOL has continued to increase its reach by forming alliances. In 1999, AOL made an $800 million purchase of Gateway stock, allowing AOL to become the default portal for Gateway computers. AOL formed an alliance with Wal-Mart: Wal-Mart stores will promote AOL services, and AOL will drive traffic to Wal-Mart's e-commerce site.[51] AOL has also formed an alliance with DirectTV *(www.directtv.com)* to allow AOL to be the access point for satellite television–based browsing.[52] In the beginning of 2000, AOL announced the largest merger in history when they proposed purchasing Time-Warner for $163 billion in stock.

AOL gained market share by sending out millions of free disks, allowing individuals to load software and use AOL's services.

Large general-use portals are very good at obtaining a great number of visitors, but these visits have not necessarily resulted in increased sales for advertisers. To capture higher-quality audiences, some advertisers are using traditional media or more specialized portals.[53]

Specialized Portals

Niche portals are being developed to target specific markets. The number one sport site on the Web is ESPN *(www.espn.com)*. This site is targeted toward males ages 18 to 34. Ivillage *(www.ivillage.com)* is a site targeted toward women. E*Trade *(www.etrade.com)* targets individuals interested in receiving financial information. Snap *(www.snap.com)* is attempting to differentiate itself by offering a rich-media portal, which will allow individuals with high-speed Internet access to obtain streamed video, audio, and animation. Snap sees this move as a way to position itself for digital television convergence.[54] Disney's GO Network is positioning itself as family-friendly; this site offers a GOguardian service to filter adult content.[55]

International portals are being designed for international markets. Web sites that are dominant in the United States are often the top Web sites for other countries. Yahoo!, AOL, and Microsoft are all in the top five domains for the United Kingdom, Germany, and France.[56] Portal sites such as Yahoo! have services for European, Asian, and other country-specific markets. *Yahoo! en Español* is designed for a Hispanic market. These general-service portals may not meet the market's needs as well as narrowly targeted portals. StarMedia *(www.starmedia.*

com) is a portal site specifically designed to serve the Spanish-speaking markets of Central and South America as well as those in the United States.[57] SurfChina.com *(www.surfchina.com)* is a search engine for Chinese Web sites.

In 1998, Yahoo!, Excite, and Netscape were all attempting to set up Web guides for the Chinese markets. The Chinese government fostered competition between two ISPs, bringing down prices for access in China. English-based Web guides do not work well in China because of language differences and the difference in character sets used to generate onscreen characters. Offering content is further complicated by the Chinese government's censuring of certain types of content available from anti-China sites or pornography sites.[58]

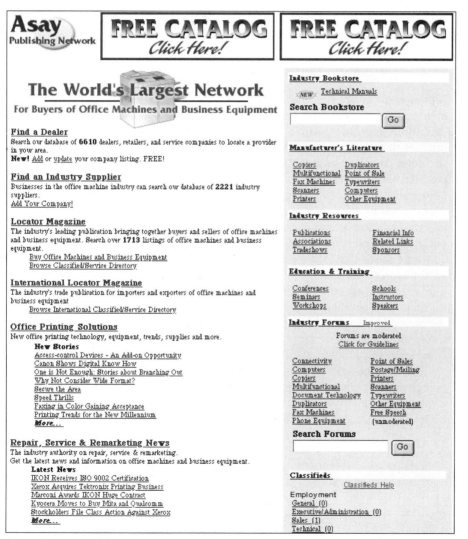

AsayPub.com is a niche strategy vertical portal.

Vertical portals are designed to serve narrow niches within specific industries.

Vertical portals are being designed to offer business users a one-stop site for all information and purchase needs, allowing businesses to access industry or trade information and to buy and sell online. Established portal sites are developing vertical portals for individual companies' internal intranet use and for use by trade and industry groups. For example, Netscape's NetCenter offers customized portal design and hosting for businesses. Outsourcing these services allows firms that specialize in information categorization to organize and maintain data.[59]

VerticalNet *(www.verticalnet.com)* is a portal site linking to other narrow-niche vertical portal sites. Hosted sites include technology, communications, food service, health care, and others. These vertical portals compete with trade magazine sites.[60] Asay Publishing *(www.asaypub.com)* leveraged its trade magazines into a portal site supporting the used office equipment aftermarket. The site provides information to sellers, buyers, and service repair personnel in the print-on-paper office equipment aftermarket.

Customer Relationships and Niche Strategies

Although all businesses need to develop and maintain strong relationships with their customers, businesses that have not gained first-mover advantages and that lack the economic resources to develop strong online brand names or become Internet portals must be able to closely focus on customers and search for niche strategies. **Small- and medium-sized enterprises (SMEs)** differ from large corporations in that they do not have the capital and human resources of larger corporations. To compete, SMEs have traditionally used niche strategies to gain distinctive advantages over their larger competitors. A **niche strategy** requires that the SME find a competitive arena in which larger businesses, with their greater resources, are not competing. SMEs are currently using information technology to gain distinctive advantages. Companies with 500 or fewer employees spent over $200 billion on technology products and services in 1998, more than five times as many dollars as larger companies.[61] Small businesses are using Web sites, intranets, and e-mail at close to the same percentages as larger businesses.[62] E-commerce applications have been slower to be accepted; this could be due to the relatively high cost of setting up and maintaining e-commerce applications. Outsourcing e-commerce to other e-business companies can lower these costs.[63]

Table 8.4 outlines the results of a survey of more than 400 information technology managers worldwide and shows the main strategies that SMEs should use to compete in a global arena. In addition to these competitive strategies, smaller businesses are often more innovative, faster to respond to environmental demands, and willing to change business models in order to gain distinctive advantages.

The recommendations given to SMEs are centered on their ability to focus on the customer. SMEs do have an opportunity to hold their current customers if they can leverage e-business tools and techniques before their larger competitors enter their market.

SMEs

Definitions of **SMEs** differ. Some consider small businesses to have less than 100 employees and medium-sized businesses to have 101 to 500 employees. Others consider SMEs to be less than 200 employees.

Table 8.4 TOP WEB DOMAINS

Strategy	Percent of Respondents	Advantages
Improved customer service	Over 80%	Online systems allow channel members and consumers to gain access to product and inventory information.
Electronic commerce	Over 60%	E-commerce offers SMEs access to larger markets without the cost of setting up new distribution systems. It also allows SMEs to target narrow markets faster than larger competitors. Lower overhead costs can be passed on as lower prices to customers.
Customer relationship management applications	Over 50%	Online connections between the SME and its customers increase the speed of response and allow for close to instant communications. Linked extranets allow SMEs to act as virtual partners with other businesses.
Increased business-to-business connections (extranets)	Over 40%	SMEs can act as an e-business intermediary linking larger businesses with very small suppliers. Online access to inventory and supplies helps control costs.

Source: Natalie Engler, "Small But Nimble," *Information Week,* January 18, 1999, pp. 57–62.

CHOOSING THE OPPORTUNITY

To be successful, businesses must find a competitive arena in which to compete where they will have an advantage. A business will set a mission to define how it will serve a specific market with a specific product. Table 8.5 on the following page is a matrix of competitive arenas in which e-businesses can compete. One axis is based on the amount of resources a business can apply toward pursuing its opportunity. Businesses that are resource-rich are much more likely to gain brand-name recognition, if they do not already have it. Businesses can also differentiate themselves from larger competitors by pursuing niche markets or developing closer relationships with customers.

Once a business chooses its competitive arena, it must develop a strategic plan to reach its goals. This process will be further explored in Chapter 9.

EVALUATION OF STRATEGY

Questions have arisen over whether or not the Internet stock market is another **investment bubble.** Investors have bid the price of Internet stocks to extremely high levels. Internet stocks have confounded many stock analysts. In 1998, it seemed that any

nSITES

The tulip craze of the seventeenth century was an **investment bubble.** A bubble occurs when the price of a commodity or product is bid beyond any rational level. Growers, dealers, and speculators traded tulip options, causing prices to skyrocket. In 1636, the bubble burst and almost brought the Dutch economy down.

Table 8.5 E-Business Strategy Matrix

	Low Differentiation	High Differentiation
High Resource	**Characterized by:** High brand-name recognition. Large portals and general e-commerce sites. **Keys to success:** Heavy brand name advertising. **Examples:** Yahoo!, Amazon.com, Disney, Wal-Mart, Schwab.com.	**Characterized by:** High brand name recognition with niche markets. **Keys to success:** Develop vertical portals. Serve niche community. **Examples:** iVillage, VerticalNet, ESPN.com.
Low Resource	**Characterized by:** Low brand name recognition. **Keys to success:** First mover advantages. Enhance customer relationships. **Examples:** CDNOW, E-Toys, SMEs with Web site support.	**Characterized by:** Low brand name recognition outside of niche market. **Keys to success:** Use first mover advantages. Serve niche markets. Enhance customer relationships. **Examples:** Asay Publishing.

Market capitalization is the value of the company on the stock market. It is the number of shares outstanding times the value of those shares.

company attached to the Internet saw its **market capitalization** reach unprecedented levels. While many traditional companies have valuations set at 7 to 20 times their earnings, in 1998 eBay had a valuation of 773 times its expected 1999 earnings.[64]

Investors may be making rational evaluations of a firm's e-business strategy. Amazon.com has achieved a market capitalization that is larger than its two major brick and mortar competitors, Barnes & Noble and Borders. Unlike Amazon.com, Barnes & Noble has $2 billion in leases, pays for inventory, moves inventory to all of its stores, stacks it on shelves, and has staff in over 1,000 locations. Amazon.com has one location, owns one main warehouse, and collects money from its customers before it pays for merchandise. In addition, Amazon.com can easily expand its business model into other product lines. Other online businesses such as Yahoo! incur little additional cost to obtain additional revenue. The addition of banners, positioning fees, and revenue sharing provides revenue streams with little additional costs.

First movers into markets and those firms that are able to develop brands and build barriers to entry should be more highly rewarded than weaker, later-entry firms. The investing market has taken into consideration the e-business strategies firms are adopting. To keep these high valuations, e-businesses will have to prove that their plans will provide adequate returns over the long term.[65]

Terms and concepts

Acquisition *225*
Alliance *225*
Brand *233*
Comparison
  standard *230*
Competitive arena *221*
Co-opetition *226*
Differentiation
  strategy *226*
Distinctive
  competency *221*
Environmental
  turbulence *222*

First-mover
  advantage *228*
Frictionless market *226*
Investment bubble *239*
Market
  capitalization *240*
Moore's law *222*
Niche portal *236*
Niche strategy *238*
Online service *234*
Pioneering firm *228*
Portal *226*
Proactive *222*

Reactive *222*
Second mover *231*
Small- and medium-
  sized enterprises
  (SMEs) *238*
Strategic driver *221*
Strategy *220*
Switching cost *231*
SWOT *220*
Value chain *221*
Vertical portal *238*

Concepts and questions for review

1. Describe the steps included in the process of strategy development.
2. Explain the importance of undertaking a SWOT analysis.
3. List the current drivers of strategy.
4. Explain how a value chain analysis helps a business develop strategies.
5. List the strategic alternatives e-businesses are using.
6. Describe the advantages that pioneering firms can gain.
7. Recommend how an e-business can build barriers to other businesses.
8. List some of the advantages of having a brand name.
9. Describe the advantages of having large amounts of resources for competing on the Internet.
10. Describe the different types of Internet portals and whom they target.
11. Explain how firms use alliances and acquisitions to gain advantages.
12. Recommend how small- and medium-sized enterprises can compete.

A C T I V E   L E A R N I N G

Exercise 8.1: Evaluating an E-Business Value Chain

Develop a value chain model for an industry or business. Using a model like the one shown in the figure, identify the key e-business technologies needed to compete in the chosen industry. Identify which of the value chain components would give a business in that industry a distinctive advantage. Determine if it is possible to hold that advantage over time.

Model Of E-Business Value Chain

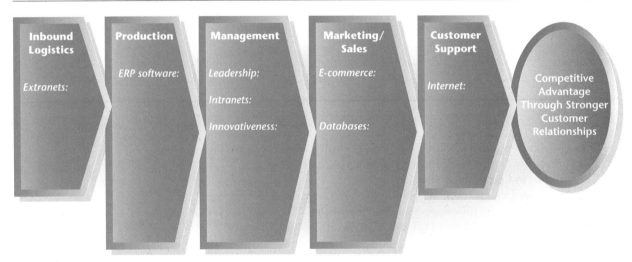

Inbound Logistics *Extranets:*	**Production** *ERP software:*	**Management** *Leadership:* *Intranets:* *Innovativeness:*	**Marketing/ Sales** *E-commerce:* *Databases:*	**Customer Support** *Internet:*	**Competitive Advantage Through Stronger Customer Relationships**

Exercise 8.2: SWOT Box

Use the following matrix to undertake a SWOT analysis by identifying the strengths, weaknesses, opportunities, and threats faced by a business or industry.

Given this SWOT analysis, propose a recommended e-business strategy that could be pursued to reach the opportunity and limit future threats.

Strengths:	Opportunities:
Weaknesses:	Threats:

Exercise 8.3: Evaluating Differential Advantages

Use the table provided to indicate the types of services offered by portal sites. America Online is given as an example. Each check represents an available service. After investigating all these sites, determine what allows each one to differentiate itself from the others. If you cannot find any differences, determine what that means for the long-term survival for some of these portal sites.

Portal Site Content

Major Portal Sites	Free E-Mail	News	Sports	Games	Chat	Shopping	Personalization	Weather	Finance	Free Home Pages	Other
AOL.com	✓	✓	✓	✓	✓	✓	✓	✓	✓	✓	✓
Yahoo.com											
Netscape.com											
Excite.com											
Infoseek.com											
GO Network											
Yahoo! GeoCities.com											
Microsoft's MSN.com											
Snap											

Exercise 8.4: Strategy Analysis Matrix

Use the Internet to identify strategic positions for a number of e-businesses. Try to find at least one business for each cell in the matrix. Identify which strategies these businesses are pursuing and what the keys to their long-term success will be.

E-Business Strategy Analysis Matrix

High	Characterized by:	Characterized by:
Resource	Keys to success:	Keys to success:
Low	Characterized by:	Characterized by:
Resource	Keys to success:	Keys to success:
	Low Differentiation	**High Differentiation**

W E B   S E A R C H   —
L O O K I N G   O N L I N E

SEARCH TERM: E-Business Strategy Support	First 4 out of 17,400

Business 2.0. Is a business strategy magazine site. It provides information and articles on cutting-edge business strategy.
http://www.business2.com

CIO Web Business. Is a journal site targeted toward chief information officers. It provides in-depth information on industry trends and practices.
http://webbusiness.cio.com

IBM. Provides information on major e-business strategies with case studies.
http://www.ibm.com/e-business

Red Herring. Is a business strategy magazine site. It provides information and articles on cutting-edge business strategy.
http://www.redherring.com

SEARCH TERM: Internet Portals	First 3 out of 440,213

Europe Online. Is a portal site for Western Europe. It provides links to different countries and topics related to Europe.
http://www.europeonline.com

Media Metrix. Lists the top-ranking Web sites by category.
http://www.relevantknowledge.com/TopRankings/TopRankings.html

SearchEngineGuide.com. Lists over 2,500 search engines and portal sites by category.
http://www.searchengineguide.com

SEARCH TERM: SMEs Online	First 4 out of 2,442,924

GO Network. Provides information and help on developing business plans for small businesses.
http://www.go.com/Center/Business/Small_business?svx=CTOC_Business_Advice

SCORE. Is the Service Core of Retired Executives site that provides information on how to obtain free consulting.
http://www.score.org

Small Business Administration. Is a U.S. government site that provides information to small businesses.
http://classroom.sba.gov

TechWeb. Provides advice for small businesses in areas related to technology.
http://www.techweb.com/smallbiz

R E F E R E N C E S

[1] Cheryl J. Myers, "M&A Insight," *Red Herring,* August 1999, p. 156; Brent Schlender, "Whose Internet Is It, Anyway?" *Fortune,* December 11, 1995, pp. 120–142; Michael Neubarth, "Microsoft Declares War," *Internet World,* March 1996, pp. 36–42; Kathy Rebello, "Inside Microsoft," *Business Week,* July 15, 1996, pp. 56–67; and Brent Schlender, "Software Hardball," *Fortune,* September 30, 1996, pp. 107–116.

[2] Robert Hof, Kathy Rebello, and Amy Cortese, "Cyberspace Showdown," *Business Week,* October 7, 1996, pp. 34–36; Randall Stross, "Netscape: Inside the Big Software Giveaway," *Fortune,* March 30, 1998, pp. 150–152; Jason Levitt, "Netscape Releases the Source," *Information Week,* April 20, 1998, pp. 85–90; and Sean Gallagher, "Netscape: Crazy Like a Fox," *Information Week,* April 20, 1998, p. 94.

[3] David Orenstein, "Corel to Give Out Free Linux WordPerfect," *Computerworld,* November 2, 1998, p. 105; Sandy Reed, "Linux Is Making the Transition from Bit Player to Overnight Sensation," *InfoWorld,* January 11, 1999, p. 69; Steven Levy, "Code Warriors," *Newsweek,* January 18, 1999, pp. 60–62; and Steve Hamm, Ira Sager, and Peter Burrows, "It Might Not Break Windows, But . . ." *Business Week,* February 1, 1999, p. 36.

[4] Steve Hamm, Amy Cortese, and Susan B. Garland, "Microsoft's Future," *Business Week,* January 19, 1998, pp. 58–68; and Steven Vonder Haar, "Microsoft Rethinks the Online Road Ahead," *Inter@ctive Week,* January 4, 1999, pp. 38–40.

[5] Sandy Reed, "From .com Fever to New Technospeak, Microsoft Is a Company in Evolution," *InfoWorld,* June 28, 1999, p. 59.

[6] For more on strategy and strategy definitions, see: Paul F. Anderson, "Marketing, Strategic Planning and the Theory of the Firm," *Journal of Marketing,* Spring 1982, vol. 46, pp. 15–26; Yoram Wind and Thomas S. Robertson, "Marketing Strategy: New Directions for Theory and Research," *Journal of Marketing,* Spring 1983, vol. 47, pp. 12–25; and Henry Mintzberg and James A. Waters, "Of Strategies, Deliberate and Emergent," *Strategic Management Journal,* 1985, vol. 6, pp. 257–272.

[7] Danny Miller and Peter H. Friesen, "Innovation in Conservative and Entrepreneurial Firms: Two Models of Strategic Momentum," *Strategic Management Journal,* vol. 3, 1982, pp. 1–25.

[8] For more on value chains, see: Michael E. Porter, *Competitive Advantage,* The Free Press, New York, 1980.

[9] Jeffrey F. Rayport and John J. Sviokla, "Exploiting the Virtual Value Chain," *Harvard Business Review,* November–December 1995, pp. 75–85.

[10] Rusty Weston, "Value Chains Go Global," *Information Week,* January 18, 1999, pp. 125–126.

[11] Rusty Weston, "What's Driving the E-Frenzy?" *Information Week,* September 27, 1999, p. 482.

[12] Carol Hildebrand, "IT and the Bottom Line," *CIO Enterprise—Section 2,* June 15, 1998, pp. 70–76.

[13] For more on the relationship between IT and distinctive competencies, see: Don Tapscott, David Ticoll, and Alex Lowy, "The Rise of the Business Web," *Business 2.0,* November 1999, pp. 198–208; Howard A. Rubin, "The Millennium IT Manifesto," *Information Week,* September 27, 1999, pp. 310–313; Bob Violino, "Customer at the Core," *Information Week,* September 27, 1999, pp. 302–308; Gary H. Anthes, "Drucker: IT Hasn't Done Job," *Computerworld,* April 26, 1999, p. 51; Adrian Slywotzky, "How Digital Is Your Company?" *Fast Company,* February–March 1999, pp. 94–112; and Jeanne W. Ross, Cynthia Mathis Beath, and Dale L. Coodhue, "Develop Long-Term Competitiveness Through IT Assets," *Sloan Management Review,* Fall 1996, pp. 31–41.

[14] Bob Violino, "Extended Enterprise," *Information Week,* March 22, 1999, pp. 46–63.

[15] For more on this, see: Derek Slater, "The Corporate Skeleton," *CIO,* December 15, 1998–January 1, 1999, pp. 100–106; and Larry Downes and Chunka Mui, *Unleashing the Killer App: Digital Strategies for Market Dominance,* Harvard Business School Press, Boston, MA, 1998, Doubleday, New York, 1996.

[16] Luc Hatslestad, "Brick-and-Mortar and Online Retailers Come Together," *Red Herring,* December 1999, pp. 127–130; Geoffrey James, "Clicks and Mortar," *Upside,* November 1999, pp. 209–214; and Bill Roberts, "Why Click Is Marrying Mortar," *Internet World,* November 15, 1999, pp. 32–48.

[17] Peter Fabris, "Getting Together," *CIO,* December 15, 1998–January 1, 1999, pp. 92–98.

[18] Jim Kerstetter, "New Portal Player Set to Go," *PC Week,* December 7, 1998, p. 22; and Jeffrey Davis, "Ready. Set. Go?" *Business 2.0,* February 1999, pp. 56–60.

[19] For more information on this topic, see: Alex Frankel, "Mutual Aid," *CIO Web Business—Section 2,* February 1, 1998, pp. 48–52; and Adam M. Bradenburger and Barry J. Nalebuff, *Co-Opetition: A Revolutionary Mindset That Combines Competition and Cooperation,* Doubleday, New York, 1996.

[20] Amy K. Larson, "Manufacturing Retools," *Internet Week,* September 14, 1998, p. 44; and Chuck Moozakis, "Survey Tracks IT Strides," *Internet Week,* September 14, 1998, p. 13.

21 For more on this topic, see: Robert Kuttner, "The Net: A Market Too Perfect for Profits," *Business Week,* May 11, 1998, p. 20.

22 Nelson Wang, "CDNOW's Mantras 'Get Big Fast,' and 'Speed Is God,'" *Internet World,* March 30, 1998, pp. 42–44.

23 Karren Mills, "Musicland to Forgo Internet Market," *Marketing News,* vol. 32, no. 12, June 8, 1998, p. 23.

24 Robert D. Hof, "Netspeed at Netscape," *Business Week,* February 10, 1997, p. 79.

25 For more on this topic, see: George Stalk Jr. and Thomas M. Hout, *Competing Against Time,* The Free Press, New York, 1990; and Richard D. Stewart, "Speed Kills Competition," *Chief Executive,* vol. 54, November/December 1989, pp. 46–49.

26 Jeff Sengstack, "EToys Plays Against a Giant," *NewMedia,* November 1998, pp. 60–61; and Gene Koprowski, "Santa's New Helpers," *Business 2.0,* December 1998, pp. 34–37.

27 Connie Guglielmo, "Online Toys Get Serious," *Upside,* December 1999, pp. 62–74; and Connie Guglielmo, "A Babbour Tries to Save Geoffrey the Giraffe," *Inter@ctive Week,* November 1, 1999, pp. 80–82.

28 Clinton Wilder and Jeff Angus, "Faster Than the Speed of Data," *Information Week,* July 21, 1997, pp. 36–54.

29 Brad Kleindl, "Accelerating New Product Development Speed," *Southern Business & Economic Review,* vol. 14, no. 4, Winter 1994, pp. 12–15.

30 Milton D. Rosenau Jr., *Faster New Product Development,* AMACOM, New York, 1990.

31 Lenny Liebmann, "E-Commerce: The Payoffs of Faith," *Network Magazine,* May 1998, pp. 34–38.

32 William T. Robinson, "Sources of Market Pioneer Advantages: The Case of Industrial Goods Industries," *Journal of Marketing Research,* vol. 25, February 1988, pp. 87–94; William T. Robinson and Claes Fornell, "Sources of Market Pioneer Advantages in Consumer Goods Industries," *Journal of Marketing Research,* vol. 22, August 1988, pp. 305–317; and Joseph T. Vesey, "The New Competitors Think in Term of 'Speed-to-Market,'" *SAM Advanced Management Journal,* vol. 56, Autumn 1991, pp. 26–33.

33 F. M. Scherer and David Ross, *Industrial Market Structure and Economic Performance,* Houghton Mifflin Company, Boston, 1992.

34 Elizabeth Gardner, "Early Adopters," *Internet World,* March 9, 1998, pp. 76–78.

35 Roger A. Kerin, P. Rajan Varadarajan, and Robert A. Peterson, "First-Mover Advantage: A Synthesis, Conceptual Framework, and Research Propositions," *Journal of Marketing,* vol. 56, October 1992, pp. 33–52.

36 Sharon Machlis, "E-Commerce: Late Is Relative," *Computerworld,* May 18, 1998, vol. 32, no. 20, pp. 1, 16; and Cheryl Currid, "The Perils of Pioneering," *Information Week,* August 11, 1997, p. 138.

37 Aileen Crowley, "Underwear, Activewear, Now Web-ware," *PC Week,* February 10, 1997, pp. 111, 114–116; John Robinson, "Fruit of the Loom Stitches Web Service for Distributors," *Network World,* June 3, 1996, p. 33.

38 Fahri Karakaya and Michael J. Stahl, "Barriers to Entry and Market Entry Decisions in Consumer and Industrial Goods Markets," *Journal of Marketing,* vol. 53, April 1989, pp. 80–91; and Michael Porter, *Competitive Strategy,* The Free Press, New York, 1980.

39 Carl Shapiro and Hal R. Varian, "Lock 'em Up!" *CIO,* October 15, 1998, pp. 72–76.

40 "Brand-New Bag," *CIO Web Business—Section 2,* December 1, 1998, p. 18.

41 Justin Hibbard, "E-Commerce: It's a Matter of Trust," *Information Week,* January 18, 1999, p. 14; and Jeffrey Davis, "A New Way of Branding," *Business 2.0,* November 1998, pp. 76–86.

[42] David Noonan, "The Priceline.com Is Right," *The Industry Standard,* December 28, 1998–January 4, 1999, pp. 60–64.

[43] Karen Epper Hoffman, "Net Firms Spending Millions to Build Brands Offline," *Internet World,* April 27, 1998, pp. 1, 45. For more on branding, see: Jeffrey Davis, "A New Way of Branding," *Business 2.0,* November 1998, pp. 76–86.

[44] Paul Judge, Heather Green, Amy Barrett, and Catherine Yang, "The Name's the Thing," *Business Week,* November 15, 1999, pp. 36–39.

[45] Michael Grebb, "Spend It or Lose It," *Business 2.0,* November 1999, pp. 113–114; Evan I. Schwartz, "Brands Aren't Everything," *The Standard,* April 30, 1999, *<http://www.thestandard.com/article/display/0,1151,4421,00.html>;* Scott Kirsner, "Branding Tall," *CIO Web Business,* December 1, 1998, *<http://www.cio.com/archive/webbusiness/120198_main.html>;* and Jeffrey Davis, "A New Way of Branding," *Business 2.0,* November 1998, pp. 76–86.

[46] Steven Vonder Haar, "Disney, Infoseek Make a Go of Online Service," *Inter@ctive Week,* October 5, 1998, p. 9.

[47] Jim Kerstetter, "Will Portals Pay Off?" *PC Week,* August 31, 1998, pp. 1, 14–15; and Heather Green, "The Skinny on Niche Portals," *Business Week,* October 26, 1998, pp. 66–68.

[48] Ann Stuart, "Something Old, Something New," *CIO Web Business—Section 2,* October 1, 1998, pp. 44–50.

[49] Elizabeth Gardner, "AOL Ups Rates, Cuts Staff As It Absorbs CompuServe," *Internet Week,* February 16, 1998, p. 9.

[50] For more information, see: Jared Sandberg, "Net Gain," *Business Week,* December 7, 1998, pp. 46–49; Susan Moran, "After Megadeal, Whither AOL-Netscape?" *Internet World,* December 7, 1998, pp. 1, 4–5; Clinton Wilder, Justin Hibbard, and Jennifer Mateyaschuk, "Three-Part Harmony?" *Information Week,* November 30, 1998, pp. 18–19; Charles Babcock, "Sun: Out of the Shadows," *Inter@ctive Week,* December 14, 1998, pp. 62–63; and Michael Moeller, "Microsoft to File for Dismissal," *PC Week,* November 30, 1998, p. 18.

[51] Steven Vonder Haar, "AOL, Wal-Mart Work on Mass Marketing Pact," *Inter@ctive Week,* December 6, 1999, p. 9; and Steven Vonder Haar, "Gateway May Open Doors for AOL," *Inter@ctive Week,* October 25, 1999, p. 10.

[52] Catherine Yang, Richard Siklos, Steve Brull, and Larry Armstrong, "America Online—And on the Air," *Business Week,* May 24, 1999, p. 33.

[53] Mark Halper, "Portal Pretense," *Business 2.0,* September 1999, pp. 43–49; Heather Green and Linda Himelstein, "Portals Are Mortal After All," *Business Week,* June 21, 1999, p. 144; and Connie Guglielmo, "Thumbs Down on Portal-Play Deals," *Inter@ctive Week,* May 3, 1999, p. 40.

[54] Steven Vonder Haar, "Snap! To Take Wraps off Rich-Media Portal," *Inter@ctive Week,* January 18, 1999, p. 10.

[55] Jeffrey Davis, "Ready. Set. Go?" *Business 2.0,* February 1999, pp. 56–60; and Brad Stone, "Disney Says Let's Go," *Newsweek,* January 11, 1999, p. 61.

[56] Stacy Lawrence, "U.S. Sites Top European Charts," *The Standard,* December 7, 1999, *<http://thestandard.com/article/display/0,1151,8127,00.html>.*

[57] For more information, see: Nelson Wang, "Planting a Flag in Latin America," *Internet World,* December 14, 1998, p. 54; and Lee M. Tablewski, "Rising Star," *Business 2.0,* February 1999, pp. 22–24.

[58] David Batstone, "Billion Man Market," *Business 2.0,* November 1998, pp. 30–32.

[59] For more information, see: Deborah Gage and Mary Jo Foley, "Portals: Not Just for Consumers Anymore," *Sm@rt Reseller*, December 7, 1998, pp. 25–26; Benjamin Keyser, "Portal Power," *InfoWorld*, October 5, 1998, pp. 1, 46–48; Lauren Gibbons Paul, "Using Portals to Find Needles in Haystacks," *PC Week*, November 16, 1998, pp. 113, 120; and Kevin Jones, "Business Services Moving Online, "*Inter@ctive Week*, January 18, 1999, p. 30.

[60] Andrew Marlatt, "Creating Vertical Marketplaces," *Internet World*, February 8, 1999, pp. 38–39; and Jonathan Littman, "Vertical Reality," *Upside*, October 1999, pp. 61–66.

[61] Bruce Caldwell and Candee Wilde, "Emerging Enterprises," *Information Week*, June 29, 1998, pp. 53–60; and Candee Wilde, "Internet Levels the Field," *Information Week*, June 29, 1998, pp. 64–66.

[62] Clinton Wilder, "E-Business Work Status," *Information Week*, January 4, 1999, pp. 53–54.

[63] Richard De Soto, "Creating an Active Internet Presence: A New Alternative," *Telecommunication Magazine*, December 1998, pp. 73–75.

[64] Natalie Engler, "Small But Nimble," *Information Week*, January 18, 1999, pp. 57-62.

[65] Linda Himelstein, Robert D. Hof, and Geoffrey Smith, "Why They're Nuts About the Net," *Business Week*, November 23, 1998, p. 52.

[66] Mark Veverka, "Get Ready for Dow.com," *Barrons*, December 20, 1999, pp. 31–34; Andrew Bary, "Net Worth," *Barrons*, December 20, 1999, pp. 36–41; and David Batstone, "What's It Worth?" *Business 2.0*, November 1998, pp. 58–68.

10001000010010111111
1111111000000000001
000011110000110000
111111111   1111
000000000   10000
10101010101010
1110001110   00110100111001010011
10101010   00110011000000
10101010   10100

Chapter 9
E-Business Management

E-businesses are finding competitive advantages by developing innovative management systems necessary to implement e-business strategies. An e-business needs to facilitate entrepreneurial leadership and be innovative in order to be adaptive to its rapidly changing environment. Intranets, extranets, and the Internet are being used as the technology base, speeding and improving communications flows inside the organization and acting as the hub for organizational knowledge. E-businesses are focusing on their core values and restructuring their businesses to gain competitive advantages and efficiencies. Information management inside organizations is becoming so important that chief knowledge officers (CKOs), chief information officers (CIOs), and Webmasters are beginning to play roles in preparing e-businesses to compete strategically.

1. List the pillars of success for innovative businesses.
2. Explain how management systems can create value for a business.
3. Discuss the interplay between the management components of the e-business value chain.
4. Describe the role that leadership and organizational culture play in giving an e-business its unique advantages.
5. Outline the role that organizational learning plays in giving an e-business a definite advantage.
6. Discuss how e-businesses are organizing themselves to compete.
7. Recommend the steps that a business would need to take to restructure in order to be competitive in an e-business environment.
8. Identify which new management positions and duties are used to meet e-business needs.

AT&T

". . . this elephant is beginning to dance."

C. Michael Armstrong
CEO of AT&T[1]

In 1907, AT&T was taken over by a group of New York bankers led by J. P. Morgan. AT&T then engaged in monopolistic practices by locking out smaller phone companies until they almost failed and then bought them at discounted prices. In 1913, strong public feeling about monopolies led the Justice Department to form an agreement with AT&T, giving it a near monopoly in telephone services in exchange for operating under government oversight. AT&T held this monopoly until January 1, 1984, when (after antitrust action) AT&T broke up its telecommunications monopoly in the United States.[2] This did not immediately change AT&T's monopolistic corporate culture.

Lack of leadership, vision, and innovation allowed AT&T to miss the Internet boom because it failed to capitalize on its advantages. In 1997, C. Michael Armstrong took over as CEO. Armstrong has attempted to speed decision making by changing AT&T's culture. He put in place an aggressive management team, collapsed the management structure, encouraged innovation, bought out 18,000 employees, sold off business units, and formed relationships with Internet and cable companies.[3] To aid in this transformation, AT&T uses an intranet to disseminate knowledge about the company. AT&T's 135,000 employees use the intranet to obtain information on stock data, audio and video clips of executive presentations, human resources information, e-mail addresses, and other information of interest.[4]

Armstrong's vision is for AT&T to be a one-source company for all telecommunications needs, including telephone, cellular, Internet, and content. To reach this, AT&T has formed alliances with Time Warner and has purchased a number of cable companies. AT&T has positioned itself to offer telephone, cable television, and broadband Internet access to about 40 percent of the customers in the United States. This may once again give AT&T a strong advantage in the competition against ISPs, Internet portals, and other phone service companies.[5]

THINKING STRATEGICALLY

Speculate on why AT&T was a late mover into the Internet industry. List the types of skills AT&T's management and employees will need to demonstrate to be competitive in the online marketplace. Determine if AT&T is too large to respond quickly to market changes. Explain the importance of a transformational leader in an organization like AT&T.

....

"The digital economy is revolutionizing how we think about the traditional corporate value chain, and it's also redefining relationships between manufacturers, suppliers, distributors, and consumers.

The value chain is in fact a value network, or web, in which companies engage in multiple two-way relationships to bring increasingly complex products and services to market."

Doug Aldrich
VP and Managing Director of
Strategic Information Technology Practice
at A.T. Kearney[6]

Businesses are gaining distinctive advantages by developing new e-business models to deliver goods and services and to enhance relationships with customers. One of the keys to achieving these advantages is the ability to develop management systems that are flexible enough to respond to a rapidly changing environment. Newly formed e-businesses may have advantages because they constructed value chains that fit the demands of current competitive environments. Brick and mortar businesses that want to take advantage of e-business efficiencies face a more difficult challenge because they must be willing to break old value chains and develop e-business value chains to maintain competitiveness.

Over time, businesses develop systems of operation, form a culture that fits their operational system, adopt strategic plans that reduce risk, and set financial targets for divisions. In an e-business environment where businesses are forced to be innovative in business models, new products, new business processes, and management practices, they must be able to overcome past **momentum** and find ways in which to compete. **Restructuring** businesses and adopting e-business

Momentum refers to the general tendency for businesses to keep moving in the same direction. Like big ships, the larger the business, the longer it takes to change direction.

Table 9.1 Pillars of Success for Innovative Businesses

Pillars of Success	Description	Value Chain Implication
Business focus	Businesses stay within a highly focused product line. The company stays focused on its mission.	A business should determine what it does well and focus on those priorities. A business may want to outsource nonessential business functions.
Hands-on management	Top management must become involved in the innovation process. It must support new ideas and processes and gain an understanding of the relevant technology.	Managers must develop cultures that allow for innovation and flexibility. Managers must also become technologically savvy to understand the issues related to organizing an e-business.
Entrepreneurial culture	Internal change agents must be fostered. Risk taking must be encouraged, and failure must be tolerated.	An innovative culture must be promoted in the firm. Innovative employees must be allowed to introduce new practices and be allowed to fail.
Adaptability	A business must be able to undertake major and rapid change when needed.	A firm must develop a culture that allows flexibility and adaptability. Intranets can foster the free flow of communication, speeding change.
Organizational cohesion (a sense of community)	The organization must have everyone working toward the organizational goal. Ideas must flow freely and quickly.	Less attention should be paid to rank and seniority. Idea sharing and teamwork are important. Collecting and using organizational knowledge becomes a priority. Intranets can facilitate this process.
Sense of integrity	A business must establish long-term relationships with all its constituencies.	Employees must feel empowered to make decisions at lower levels in the organization. E-business techniques can link e-business partners together.

Source: Modesto A. Maidique and Robert H. Hayes, "The Art of High-Technology Management," *Sloan Management Review,* Winter 1984, pp. 17–31, in *Readings in the Management of Innovation,* ed. Michael L. Tushman and William L. Moore, Ballinger Publishing Company, Cambridge, Massachusetts, 1988.

techniques may require changes in business processes, moves into risky new venture areas, and uncertain returns.[7] Pursuing new business models requires an innovative orientation. Maidique and Hayes have outlined six pillars of success for innovative businesses. Even though their study interviewed managers involved in high-technology companies and firms that engaged in research and development, these six pillars are very important for all organizations looking to structure themselves for innovative and highly competitive environments. Table 9.1, on the previous page, indicates these pillars of success and their implications for developing e-business value chains.

MANAGEMENT AND THE VALUE CHAIN

Intranets, extranets, and the Internet are allowing new business models to form and are forcing others to reevaluate how they are providing value to the customer. In order to seize new market opportunities and gain competitive advantages in an e-business environment, businesses must evaluate the strengths and weaknesses of their current value chain and then devise business systems that are flexible and

Figure 9.1 Management Components Of the E-Business Value Chain

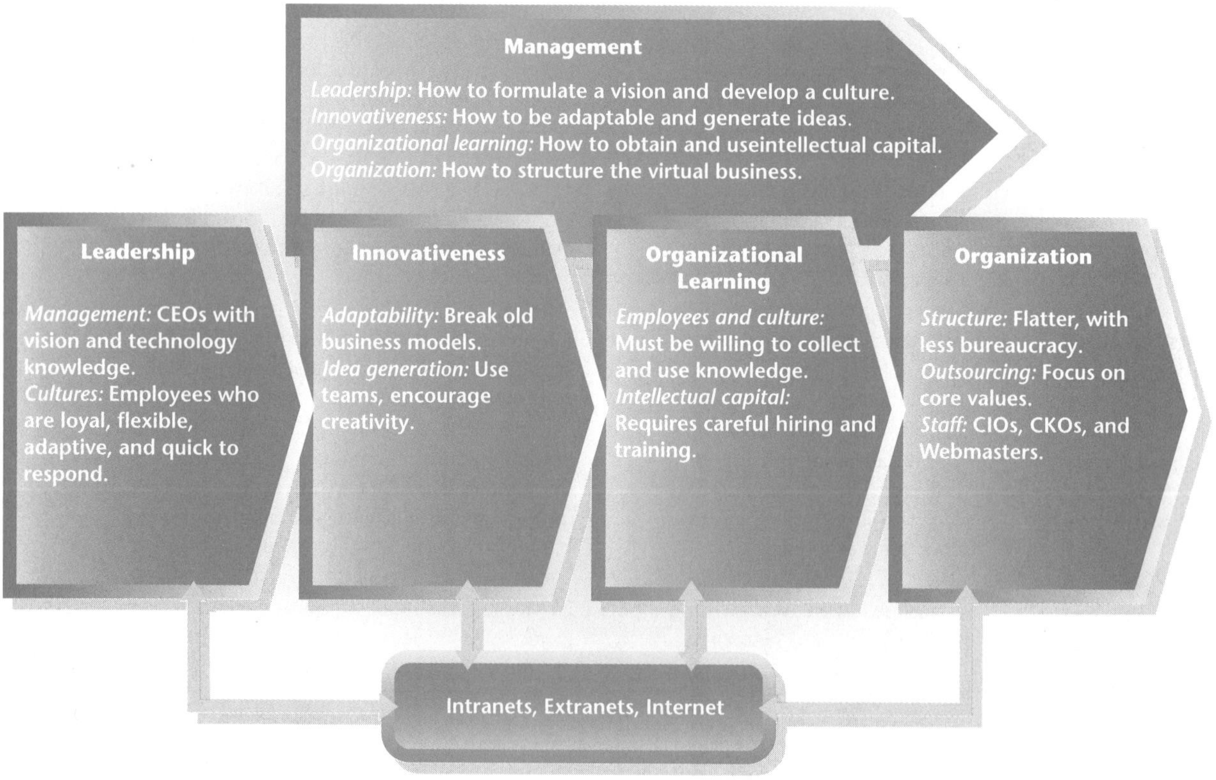

Management
Leadership: How to formulate a vision and develop a culture.
Innovativeness: How to be adaptable and generate ideas.
Organizational learning: How to obtain and use intellectual capital.
Organization: How to structure the virtual business.

Leadership

Management: CEOs with vision and technology knowledge.
Cultures: Employees who are loyal, flexible, adaptive, and quick to respond.

Innovativeness

Adaptability: Break old business models.
Idea generation: Use teams, encourage creativity.

Organizational Learning

Employees and culture: Must be willing to collect and use knowledge.
Intellectual capital: Requires careful hiring and training.

Organization

Structure: Flatter, with less bureaucracy.
Outsourcing: Focus on core values.
Staff: CIOs, CKOs, and Webmasters.

Intranets, Extranets, Internet

innovative.[8] Figure 9.1 outlines the management components of the e-business value chain currently being used to gain advantages. These consist of the leadership process within an organization that helps set the direction and the tone for the culture of a business. [9]

Information technology is used to enhance the e-business value chain and is aiding in the development of closer relationships with customers by speeding up ordering and delivering of products, improving customer service, and lowering costs.[10] The impact of intranets will be intertwined with the larger organizational changes outlined in this chapter.

LEADERSHIP

"Top management no longer runs the company. It's the young people who run the company; top management runs relationships."
Peter Drucker[11]
Twenty-three percent of Fortune 1000 senior executives can explain what a modem does. Ninety-three percent of sixth graders can.[12]

Traditionally, the top management of an organization sets the vision for the company, oversees the development of strategy, and is in charge of delegating responsibility to be sure that plans and strategies are carried out. With the advent of new competitive paradigms, top-level executives are changing their view of the management process, but not all executives are willing to embrace new business practices. There are a number of reasons leaders of businesses ignore e-business techniques. Some executives see these as unproven technologies that may go the way of other failed fads. Other executives may see the changes in technology and management practices coming but fear their disconnection from those changes.[13] New technology requires a relearning process, and new business practices can mean a shift in leadership power.

Forward-looking CEOs are learning to love the Net. A survey of 303 IT managers indicated that 61.7 percent saw their CEOs as advocates of Internet-based technologies, 36 percent were neutral, and only 2.3 percent were technology blockers.[14] Leaders of organizations are beginning to realize that information technology is a means of gaining competitive advantages. These CEOs see the use of information technology, the management of data, the impact of new technology, and reengineering as the most important business issues they are facing. One of the main motivating factors for CEOs is the fear of losing their competitive edge if they do not keep up with technological change.[15]

To manage these newly evolving organizations, top executives in successful firms are learning to enable their employees to help run the business. These leaders are creating innovative cultures, fostering organizational learning, promoting teamwork, and creating a new generation of leaders, thereby encouraging loyalty to the organizations.[16] Each of the following sections will explain how successful leaders are building competitive organizations.

nSITES   organizational culture

Organic cultures have decentralized control and nonformal relationships. Their organizational structures are often flatter, and more
responsibility is given to individuals at the bottom of the organizational
hierarchy. The opposite of an organic culture is a **bureaucratic culture.** Hierarchies, rules and regulations, and strong management oversight characterize bureaucracies.

An organization's **culture** includes the shared values, beliefs, behaviors, and norms that are generally accepted and practiced by group members. The founder of the organization often sets the tone for an organization's culture. As the organization develops over time, the organizational culture must adapt to its competitive situation. Cultures can become self-selective and self-reinforcing. Organizations that have developed cultures that fit a competitive environment may look to hire only individuals who fit the current culture. Individuals who rise up through organizational ranks may be very good at operating within that culture; they, in turn, reinforce that culture. This can be very problematic when a changing competitive environment threatens the organization. In this case, there may be a misfit between the organization and its culture.[17] Businesses that attempt to develop cultures that result in satisfied and engaged employees can substantially reduce turnover, preserve intellectual capital, and lower hiring and retraining costs.[18]

A variety of cultural typologies have been developed, the full scope of which is beyond this text. But one cultural form, organic, has been recommended for environments that are highly uncertain and that do not hold for traditional marketing systems.[19] **Organic culture** provides greater flexibility and responsiveness to environmental change. **Innovative organizations** often have organic forms of culture.[20] Organic organizations often encourage change agents, discussed in the diffusion of innovations process investigated in Chapter 6. In order for these change agents to work effectively, there must be a culture of innovation in an organization in which new ideas can be developed, brought forward, nurtured, and implemented without fear of failure.

E-businesses are preparing their management systems for an environment of continuous change. Innovative enterprises are pushing responsibility toward the bottom of the organization, placing an additional burden on the organization to develop the conditions where employees can act for the good of the business. Leaders of innovative e-businesses are using the following five strategies to develop responsive management systems[21]:

1. **Organizational learning.** E-businesses are developing learning organizations or business systems that can learn from their environment and experience.
2. **Talent.** E-businesses are attempting to hire employees who will fit flexible work situations.
3. **Cross-functional teams.** Teamwork facilitates input from multiple constituencies within an organization.
4. **Sense of community.** Individuals must feel loyal to an organization and its organizational goal.
5. **Intranets.** A major tool that aids in the development of e-businesses is the use of intranets that can link all internal constituencies within a business.

Organizational Learning

Organizational learning implies that a business system is able to develop insights, knowledge, and associations between the actions taken and the effectiveness of those actions. This should allow the organization to adapt by making incremental adjustments to the environment. Learning occurs at the individual level, but a business can help to spread knowledge throughout the organization. Once a widely accepted view of the world is developed, it can become part of the organization's culture. This can have advantages but also strong disadvantages if the culture does not change. A learning organization must renew itself.[22]

Although the importance of organizational knowledge is well known, the creation of learning organizations is just getting under way. A 1997 study indicated that of 431 European and American companies, 94 percent thought they could do a better job of leveraging their business knowledge. The top three reasons that companies implement knowledge management systems is to transfer best-practices information (89 percent of company responses), increase employee capabilities (83 percent), and provide customer and market information (77 percent).[23] Using knowledge management can result in increased revenue by fostering best practices across frontline employees, improving team collaboration, and leveraging expertise.[24]

Creating learning organizations requires devising a knowledge culture where individuals have a shared belief in the importance of knowledge and its use. The following seven suggestions are for setting the foundation of a learning organization:

1. **Create a knowledge culture.** This is seen as the number one obstacle to knowledge creation in firms. It is important to make acquiring data part of the job description. Copying ideas from other firms can be a way to bring knowledge into a company. British Petroleum gives a "Thief of the Year" award to employees who bring in the best ideas in applications development. Texas Instruments has a "Not Invented Here, But I Did It Anyway Award" for those who borrow ideas. Employees and management need to talk about the knowledge creation process.
2. **Set a value on the knowledge created.** Organizations and individuals are more likely to set priorities to collect and use knowledge if they can see returns from their efforts.
3. **Democratize knowledge.** A firm must allow individuals in the organization to collect and use the acquired knowledge.
4. **Use knowledge tools.** Tools such as e-mail, intranets, databases, guides, templates, and questionnaires can be used to obtain knowledge. Knowledge management tools such as Lotus Notes provide search engines for data repositories, organize and categorize data, allow collaboration, and provide links to other data topics.[25]

5. **Understand what the organization knows and does not know.** Organizations should undertake knowledge audits to assess how knowledge can better be collected and utilized.
6. **Act on the knowledge.** Access to organizational knowledge should be easy and encouraged. Intranets can facilitate this process.
7. **Train workers.** Workers need to be able to access and use the knowledge created.[26]

Intranets can act as a **hub** for collecting and structuring organizational learning. Companies are using their intranets to allow employees to enter best-practices information into databases. When other employees have questions, they can query the database for examples of how to handle a problem. This process collects, stores, and disseminates knowledge. Maritz *(www.maritz.com)*, a $2 billion sales incentive company, uses its intranet to organize sales pitches. Background on different product categories is provided along with customers' FAQs (frequently asked questions) and recommended sales presentations.[27] Bay Networks, a computer networks hardware and software firm, used its intranet to structure organizational knowledge. Obtaining needed knowledge faster resulted in a $10 million savings for the company.[28]

It is important that organizational knowledge is categorized so that employees can use the information to serve the organization and its customers. Employees are becoming overwhelmed by the amount of messages sent and received every day. Some workers can send or receive up to 200 messages a day over the telephone, e-mail, voice mail, postal mail, interoffice mail, fax, and other media.[29]

Talent

Human capital is the skill that individuals gain through education, training, and experience.

E-businesses have recognized that **human capital**, or **talent**, is a key area of competitive advantage; in a **knowledge economy**, employees must have the capacity to learn and relearn new tasks. Employees who have technical skills and the ability to work with others to achieve organizational goals are highly sought after in the e-business industry.[30]

A **knowledge economy** gains wealth based on what individuals can create from knowledge rather than what they can create from physical labor alone.

E-businesses are attempting to recruit technologically savvy employees from a limited pool. Internet start-ups and high-technology companies have been pulling employees from traditional businesses.[31] The demand for technology workers in the United States has been so high that, in 1999, between 400,000 and 500,000 technical jobs went unfilled; in 2000, there is expected to be a shortage of over 500,000 technical workers. U.S. companies that have not been able to meet their employee needs in the United States have sought to hire from overseas.[32] The technical skill shortage in Europe is expected to be even higher; in 2000, there may be 1.3 million more technical jobs than there are trained employees. IBM Germany paid employees up to $4,200 for finding qualified candidates for the company to hire.[33]

THINKING STRATEGICALLY

List some of the advantages and disadvantages that employees may see in working for Microsoft and Netscape. Determine how different generations of workers may feel about each of these companies. Explain why an employee would want to leave Microsoft. Determine if Microsoft should worry about the brain-drain problem. List some of the advantages and disadvantages employees would have in working for a start-up like Netscape. Speculate on whether Microsoft and Netscape would attract different types of employees.

ORGANIZATION

Community vs. Hierarchy

Developing e-business applications cuts across a large number of functional areas

CASE 9.1

Pooling Talent

Two companies characterize the highly dynamic and competitive e-business environment. In 1996, Microsoft Corporation received more than 120,000 resumes. This allowed Microsoft to hire only the super smart, or the top, candidates. Microsoft looked for individuals who are pragmatic, verbally agile, and able to respond when challenged with new ideas. Microsoft realized that its products were based on knowledge that had about a four-year shelf life. Microsoft's employees had to grasp and use new knowledge very quickly.[34] By 1999, Microsoft was facing a brain drain. Many of the younger employees saw Microsoft as a large company with less opportunity for cutting-edge growth. These talented employees were pursuing Internet start-ups as an area for future opportunity.[35]

When Netscape stood as a separate company, it was able to attract high-quality employees. Netscape's culture was highly organic; it did not have rigid schedules and policies. Employees were allowed to come and go as they wished and work from home. They were encouraged to have a voice in the organization and shift to new, challenging jobs. The company attempted to provide personal services to make the employees' lives easier. The top reason Netscape's employees gave for staying with the company was that they like to work with really smart people.[36]

Source: Netscape screenshot © 2000 Netscape Communications Corporation. Used with permission.

The gap in technical skills between older generations and the Net generation may be very large. **Net generation (N-Gen)** refers to those individuals born after 1977. This is the largest generation that has ever existed. These individuals often understand and have grown up with digital technology. The Internet has already played a role in the development of their lives. They are comfortable with technology, and the youngest segment of this generation will not have known a world without the Internet.

These individuals prefer collaboration to working alone and do not like the idea of having a traditional boss. Technologically savvy N-Gens have the ability to shift easily between jobs; when they invest their intellectual capital into organizations, they expect to be compensated for it.[37] The N-Gen attitude has become a point of contention between older managers and younger employees. In 1998, the 46-year-old chairwoman of iVillage, Candice Carpenter, saw her younger employees leaving to obtain higher pay. She saw this as a danger to her company. Whereas she and her senior managers have learned how to run companies over time, her younger employees were pursuing paychecks. Many of the younger employees lacked the ability to work with others, and their judgment was not mature. Carpenter restructured the company. She replaced younger employees with older executives and implemented a radical mentoring program in which employees were pushed to develop as executives faster than they would normally. This has helped to develop a loyalty culture where younger employees see reward in staying for the long term.[38]

within organizations. Electronic communications enhances the ability of organizations to link marketing, production, accounting, and management to pursue strategic goals. These projects are often worked on in teams and require managers who have both technology and business backgrounds. Collaboration between functional groups can help change the culture of organizations and make them more customer-focused.[39]

The use of corporate intranets is allowing businesses to form **teams,** communities of workers who work on problems rather than rely on typical organizational hierarchies. Technology permits communities to have participants from around the world work on projects. Xerox uses a community approach to projects, allowing individuals from different departments to share ideas, best practices, and other types of information. However, developing a culture of collaboration is not without problems. Individuals who are leaders or experts may be unwilling to share what they know because it is their source of power within an organization.[40]

Communities of workers represent social networks as opposed to organizational **hierarchies.** Social networks map how people in organizations actually communicate. This structure includes individuals, hubs, and gatekeepers.[41] Figure 9.2 illustrates the difference between traditional hierarchies and social network structures.

Figure 9.2 illustrates the social network hubs of highly connected individuals within functional areas who carry on high levels of face-to-face communications (no arrows are shown within a hub). These hubs may be connected through gatekeepers, such as individual **A,** in the marketing hub. This can increase the power of the **gatekeeper,** who controls the flow of information. All employees should be encouraged to engage in communication to lessen gatekeepers' power and speed communication.

> A **gatekeeper** is an individual who controls the flow of information in a communication system.

Business-based electronic communities can permit individuals inside organizations to tap knowledge resources through local intranet home pages.[42] E-mail allows each member of a hub to contact all other members; collaboration software permits individuals from around the world to work together on projects. General Electric Capital used an intranet to link 52,000 people in 27 different business units in more than 57 countries. These different groups were not immediately willing to share all their knowledge, so the intranet was designed to allow different divisions to hide data behind firewalls. To overcome the fear of information sharing, GE Capital devised a promotion system based on how well employees shared their knowledge.[43]

Figure 9.2 Hierarchies and social networks

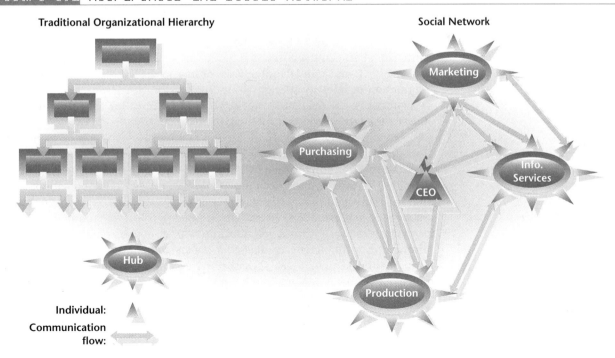

The traditional role of the **marketing core** (those directly involved in the marketing process) is to stay close to the customers and act as the interface between the company and its customers.

Combining intranets and extranets allows individuals outside the organization, such as suppliers and customers, to interact with an organization. This communications system facilitates the growth of distance workers and helps build e-business corporations. Each of these will be discussed below.

Teams

Developing successful e-business systems that focus on the needs of customers requires blending talent from different constituencies within a business. Marketers must work together with technology specialists, designers, and other individuals with specialized skills in order to create Web sites, e-commerce applications, and database management, as well as to utilize other technology-based tools.[44] Bringing together individuals from the marketing core and the technology core does not always work smoothly. These two groups often have different views of the world and how businesses should be conducted. Marketers often see the technical core as lacking a customer orientation. The technical core sees marketers as reacting too quickly in response to short-term market demands. When these two groups act as a team—sharing their individual skills, perspectives, and alternative approaches to new product development—they are more likely to come up with decisions that result in gaining competitive advantages.[45]

A five-year study of executives from more than 800 businesses in 15 different industries found that the most important factors for aligning information technology with business practices were senior executive support for IT, IT management's involvement in strategy development, IT's understanding of the business, and a partnership between the business core and the IT core. The biggest inhibitors were the lack of IT and non-IT individuals' ability to develop relationships.[46] Just as information technology specialists are learning that they must understand business practices, so, too, must marketers understand that they must learn and embrace the technology that will help them accomplish their jobs.

Technology-based tools are becoming more widely available to the marketer. Marketing automation software is being designed to help with campaign management, sales lead management, database mining, and business-to-business relationships.[47] A lack of understanding of what technology can and cannot do may limit the marketer's ability to make sound design decisions as to how to use technology to meet the market's needs. The marketing core is beginning to realize that its goal of developing strong relationships with customers requires the support of information technology specialists. Marketers want to use database marketing techniques but require a technologist to set up and maintain databases. The ultimate goal of one-to-one marketing requires that marketers and information technologists work together to develop strategic approaches and enable the technological solutions.[48]

Collaboration software allows team members to work together across distances. The collaboration process has been enhanced through the development of intranets. By allowing rapid development of teams in distant locations, e-business teams can work together on projects, solve customers' problems, and then move on to other projects. The biggest problem in using collaboration software is creating a culture where individuals work well in teams and work well online.[49]

Collaboration software, or groupware, permits individuals to use e-mail and message lists, share files, or open file archives. The goal is to have individuals collaborating on projects.

Virtual Corporations

Virtual corporations evolved through the 1990s. A **virtual corporation** business model allows a business to focus on its core competency by developing a temporary network of value chain components brought together to take advantage of market opportunities. For example, a business may see the possibility of a new product in the market. The company may hire a design firm, license with a separate manufacturer, use independent agents to help sell, and use an ISP to develop and maintain a Web site for marketing and support. These temporary partnerships may last only as long as the market opportunity, or the business may wish to continue this for the long term. The advantage of using a virtual corporation is that it brings together the best components in developing a value chain.[50] Virtual companies can create new ideas for products and services, position them in the marketplace, and develop a team of partners who can successfully get the product to market.[51]

The movement toward virtual corporations is being accelerated by the standardized interfaces used in extranets, intranets, and the Internet. This allows all the components of the virtual corporation to use simplified linkages.[52] Not all companies have the human and mechanical or technical resources for developing and maintaining networked communications. Skills such as coding and scripting, site design, and systems management often need to be brought in from outside an organization.[53] To meet these needs, companies are outsourcing information technology services. This saves on costs, enhances the technology that can be accessed, and facilitates more market agility. The e-business system outlined in Chapter 4 typifies this partnership process. Marketing services are also being outsourced, allowing small specialty companies to emerge. The market value for outsourcing Web development services, such as marketing expertise, ad agencies, Web developers, consultants, and systems integrators, is expected to reach close to $16 billion by the year 2002.[54]

Distance Workers

Telecommuting allows **distance workers** to interface with their job and work groups online from their homes. This trend is accelerating. In 1998, an estimated 52.1 million workers did all or part of their job by telecommuting from home. Some companies, such as AT&T and CISCO Systems, allow more than 50 percent of their workforce to telecommute. The average age of telecommuters is about 41 years; 48 percent are knowledge workers. One study indicated that more than 60

Hoteling is the sharing of a physical office space such as a desk, cubicle, or actual office.

percent of these employees saw telecommuting as having a positive effect on their careers. Telecommuters save companies money by lowering office space requirements. Many employees can occupy the same office or cubicle by **hoteling** in the office. Distance workers proclaim higher levels of work satisfaction, but they express concerns about being out of the political office loop. Distance workers have less ability to form relationships with other employees and are less likely to be seen by those who can aid in advancement and promotion.[55]

To successfully implement telecommuting, businesses should[56]:

1. **Carefully select employees who telecommute.** Not all jobs or employees are likely to fit a telecommuting model. Employees who don't work well at a business are not likely to work well at home.

2. **Provide training.** It may take distance workers up to 18 months to adjust to working at home. Managers also need to be trained on how to feel comfortable supervising employees they can't see.

3. **Support telecommuters with technology.** Distance workers need equipment that is as good as, or better than, what can be found in the office. A technology staff must also support them.

4. **Facilitate face-to-face contact.** Contact between employees and supervisors must be encouraged to develop relationships. Distance workers may feel alienated from the organizational culture.

5. **Ensure management support.** Most resistance comes from mid-level managers, so organizations must be sure that telecommuters receive top management support.

One of the ways that e-businesses are controlling information flows for team collaboration, distance workers, and virtual corporations is through restructuring intranets into corporate portals. **Corporate portals,** like public access portals, are centralized intranet Web sites that businesses use to permit access to e-mail, databases, and document management, as well as access to news services and other Web sites. Portal sites are being used to manage knowledge for businesses, provide competitive intelligence, and support field sales forces.[57]

RESTRUCTURING

"Destroy-your-business.com"

General Electric CEO Jack Welch's name
for General Electric's Internet business unit[58]

Becoming competitive in an e-business environment requires restructuring the value chain.[59] In 1994, the number one priority for senior information systems executives (up from number 11 in 1989) was reengineering business processes through information technology.[60] By 1999, 86 percent of 399 businesses surveyed by *Information Week* saw IT as contributing to or leading in business and marketing transformation. The primary technology used in this transformation was the Internet, due to its ability to rapidly transfer information.[61]

Changing from one business model to another is a very difficult process for any business. It may take five or more years for an organization to change cultural practices. In a highly turbulent environment, organizations do not have the luxury of evolutionary change; revolutionary change is more often the norm.[62] Businesses can take a number of approaches to become successful players in an e-business environment. It is possible for some organizations to implement change from the top leadership down. Organizations that are highly flexible and organic may respond well to change, and individual employees who are flexible may be able to break old patterns and retrain themselves. To avoid cultural conflict between existing entrenched cultures that may not be technologically inclined and the new knowledge workers necessary to operate e-businesses, some businesses opt to spin off new e-business divisions. These can act as separate units that are able to develop their own unique cultures, hire new talent, and operate without the bureaucracy of a larger entrenched organization.

A May 1993 *Fortune* magazine article designated General Motors and IBM as corporate dinosaurs. The reason cited for their decline was the lack of ability to adapt to new market conditions due to fixed bureaucratic cultures.[63] In 1993, new CEO Lou Gerstner helped IBM reorient itself toward the Internet by empowering a number of change agents. John Partick, a senior strategy executive, wrote a white paper on how IBM should get connected. A group of individuals from around the world discussed the idea via Internet discussion groups. This allowed interested individuals to coalesce around the idea of developing Internet strategies. IBM also formed new divisions such as alphaworks *(www.alphaworks.ibm.com)*, an online laboratory designed to develop new ideas on how to commercialize products and collaborate with customers. New people were hired to staff this division. Part of their job was to shake up the status quo and make IBM a cool place to work for the N-generation.[64]

CASE 9.2

Buying into BuyPower

In May 1997, GM gave Ann Pattyn, director of GM's Consumer Marketing Initiative, 90 days to develop a way to sell cars over the Internet. With 21 percent of car buyers using the Internet for information and with the emergence of new online car sellers such as Auto-By-Tel and Microsoft, GM realized it had a problem. Pattyn's solution was the GM Buypower site that rolled out in a four-state area. Shoppers were able to configure a desired car, compare it to the competition, and conduct a search of dealer inventory to find a model. Buyers could contact the dealers, who were required to respond within 24 hours with their best price. To obtain buy-in, a salesperson at each dealership was trained on how to make e-mail contacts. Yet, only 60 percent of the dealer networks signed up for the program.

To develop this program, Pattyn put together a six-person team and outsourced hosting and design to other firms. Rather than spend a lot of time researching, the goal was to get to market as fast as possible and learn from the market's interaction with the site. Providing more information online creates a problem for the traditional car sales business model. Dealers like to be able to switch customers between products to reduce their own inventory. GM has made an effort to sell online, but Auto-By-Tel was projected to sell up to 10 times as many GM cars as GM does from its site.[65]

THINKING STRATEGICALLY

Determine who would be hurt in the new business model proposed by GM. List the key people who would need to buy into the new selling process. Contrast the incentives and disincentives that salespeople would have in adopting this model. Speculate on GM's top management support for this new business model. Determine what key areas could be leveraged to speed adoption of this new business model.

Business Process Reengineering

Changing from one business process to another requires a reengineering of procedures, processes, and standards, which is called **business process reengineering (BPR).** BPR does not have a high success rate. It is estimated that up to 70 percent of BPR projects fail. To increase the odds, the following five BPR steps are recommended[66]:

1. **Require top management commitment.** Top management must support the change process, and a clear leader of the change team must be designated.
2. **Understand the current business model.** This process entails modeling how the current business operates. To be sure current processes are understood, the business model may be required to work with only small sections of large complicated businesses.
3. **Identify key players in the organization.** Organization knowledge is most likely held by key individuals in the firm. These individuals must be allowed to become part of the change process.

4. **Develop a communications plan.** Constant communication permits individuals to become part of the change process.

5. **Design an implementation plan.** It is important to decide how change will be undertaken for the firm. The following steps can aid in implementing a reengineering process:

   a. **Analyze leverage points.** A business needs to look for critical areas where change can be made.

   b. **Identify process breakthroughs.** Areas of possible business success need to be identified and goals must be set. This is where change will have a positive impact on the organization.

   c. **Design business processes.**

   d. **Implement the business process.** If the new process results in positive change, further reprocessing is more likely to be accepted.

   e. **Institutionalize continuous improvement.** This facilitates continuous reengineering and change in an organization.

Intranets can act as leverage points for change. As employees become familiar and comfortable with Web browsing, additional layers of functionality can be added. Intranets also facilitate rapid deployment of information and the collaboration necessary to achieve mission-critical goals.

Spin-Offs

A **spin-off** occurs when a parent company creates an independent division. This could entail a distribution of shares of stock in the new division to owners of the parent company.

Pure-play Internet companies are able to develop new e-business models, hire technologically savvy employees, move quickly to serve new markets, and set strategic goals that fit their competitive environment. Traditional businesses have attempted to achieve these objectives by spinning off divisions.

E-business **spin-offs** from larger companies gain the freedom to act as entrepreneurial ventures. A number of businesses have recognized that e-business management requires a different set of skills than brick and mortar business. Retailers such as Macy's, Office Depot, Barnes & Noble, and Toys 'R' Us have spun off e-commerce divisions. AltaVista and Snap were spun off from Compaq Computer and General Electric. These spin-offs have not performed as well as their pure-play Internet rivals, possibly because the spin-offs were late movers, or because they have not fully broken off from their parent divisions.[67]

CASE 9.3

An Old Player in a New Gamble
Procter & Gamble has implemented a change program called Organization 2005 that will incorporate collaborative technology, business-to-consumer e-commerce, extranet-based supply chains, and database management systems. Top executives of P&G realize that they have a business with a 160-year history and an entrenched culture. One of the new ventures that P&G is pursuing is a Web-based direct-selling venture that will sell cosmetics and hair products customized to individual buyers. The new venture is called reflect.com and was spun off from P&G's Cincinnati corporate headquarters; it is located in San Francisco. The employees who left P&G were forced to resign so they would dedicate themselves to the online venture. P&G's lawyers reviewed contracts for reflect.com, and 50 percent of the board of directors were from P&G.[68]

© REFLECT.com LLC

THINKING STRATEGICALLY

Speculate on the reasons why P&G would want to start a Web-based venture. Determine why P&G would spin off this venture rather than have it in-house. List some reasons why the venture would be located in San Francisco. Contrast the advantages and disadvantages of having a corporate board tied to P&G. Visit the *www.reflect.com* Web site. Evaluate reflect.com against other customizable cosmetic Web sites. Speculate on the future of reflect.com and P&G's ability to compete online with this current strategy.

ORGANIZATIONAL POSITIONS

The importance of using information to aid in the development of business value is well recognized. When asked to offer input to organizations, many individuals will provide knowledge for others to share. Someone must be in charge of organizing and controlling the dissemination of the information coming from hundreds or thousands of different sources. This has led to the rise of new organizational positions, outlined below.[69]

Chief Information Officers

Chief information officers (CIOs) are senior executives who are in charge of a company's information technology and systems and who help direct the use of information technology to support a company's goals. The CIO needs to understand both technology and business processes and should have a cross-functional perspective. CIOs often take a leadership role in reengineering business processes to utilize IT. CIOs are also taking leadership roles in implementing knowledge management systems. They help in the development of an organization's Internet, intranet, and Web site development.[70] CIOs do not necessarily have the skills required to become CEOs. A cross-cultural study of CIOs indicated that they were seen as lacking adequate business and functional experience, as well as the CEO skills of revenue generating and marketing, and were seen as too technical in their orientation.[71] A more direct-line position is the vice president for e-commerce.

Vice Presidents of Electronic Commerce

New positions are being created in a number of organizations that are responsible for the creation and execution of e-commerce business practices; the title being used is vice president for e-commerce. Skills required include MBA degrees, with technical training in undergraduate degrees, and a number of years of business and electronic commerce experience.[72]

Chief Knowledge Officers

Chief knowledge officers (CKOs) are individuals whose responsibilities are to work with CIOs to oversee organizational knowledge management; they must act as knowledge champions to encourage individuals to add to the organization's knowledge and to use that knowledge.[73] CKOs need to have a unique combination of skills. They need to have a strong comprehension of business practices in order to understand what type of knowledge is useful to the organization. They also need to know technology in order to collect and disseminate that information. In addition, they need an entrepreneurial spirit in order to be champions and to get involved in restructuring how businesses operate.[74]

Webmasters

The position of Webmaster has recently evolved in organizations. **Webmasters** are often involved in designing Web pages and graphics, coding and maintaining pages, answering users' questions, aiding in Web strategic planning, compiling statistics, and making purchasing decisions. Webmasters must often be cross-functional experts, able to understand the marketing and media aspects of a company and the technological requirements of developing and maintaining Web sites. Intranets have more specialized requirements because they are involved in the management of an organization. Indi-

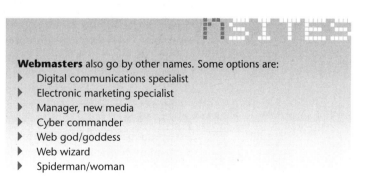

Webmasters also go by other names. Some options are:
- Digital communications specialist
- Electronic marketing specialist
- Manager, new media
- Cyber commander
- Web god/goddess
- Web wizard
- Spiderman/woman

viduals who oversee intranets often come from marketing and management fields. Most Web sites are maintained by small cross-functional teams that often outsource specialized skills such as design and coding.[75]

KNOWLEDGE INTEGRATION   TERMS AND CONCEPTS

Bureaucratic culture *256*	Distance worker *263*	Net generation
Business process	Gatekeeper *261*	(N-Gen) *260*
reengineering (BPR) *266*	Hierarchy *261*	Organic culture *256*
Chief information	Hoteling *264*	Organizational
officer (CIO) *268*	Hub *258*	learning *256*
Chief knowledge	Human capital *258*	Restructuring *253*
officer (CKO) *269*	Innovative	Spin-off *267*
Collaboration	organization *256*	Talent *256*
software *263*	Knowledge economy *258*	Team *260*
Community *261*	Marketing core *262*	Telecommuting *263*
Corporate portal *264*	Momentum *253*	Virtual corporation *263*
Culture *256*		Webmaster *269*

CONCEPTS AND QUESTIONS FOR REVIEW

1. List the pillars of success for innovative companies.
2. Explain the components of the management value chain.
3. Describe the technology used to help provide value in the e-business management value chain.
4. State the role that leadership plays in the e-business management value chain.
5. Explain the role that organizational culture plays in an organization.
6. List some of the advantages of having an organic culture.
7. Recommend how an organic culture can be developed in an organization.
8. Explain the role organizational learning plays in adding value to an e-business.
9. Recommend how to develop a learning organization.
10. Explain how employee talent adds value to an organization.
11. List ways in which N-Gen employees are different from older employees.
12. Explain the role that teams play in adding value to an organization.
13. Compare and contrast the marketing core's beliefs and the technical core's beliefs.
14. Explain the role that collaboration software plays in the team process.
15. Compare and contrast communities and hierarchies.
16. Explain how communities play a role in adding value to an e-business.
17. Explain how virtual companies differ from traditional ones.

18. Explain the role of distance workers and how they fit in with the organizational community.

19. List some steps that can be taken to improve the chances for business process reengineering success.

ACTIVE LEARNING

Exercise 9.1: Identifying Components of the Management Value Chain

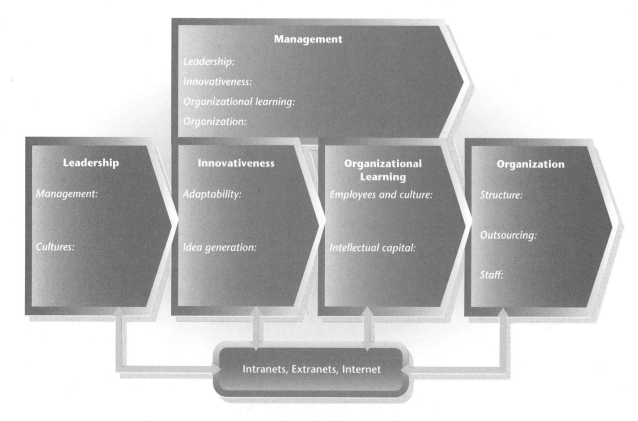

Using the figure above, outline the management value chain for a business with which you are familiar, and indicate areas that can be improved by applying any e-business techniques outlined in this text.

Exercise 9.2: Message Count

Develop a log to keep track of the number of messages you receive in one day. Place the messages into categories that include phone calls, e-mail, voice mail, postal mail, interoffice mail, faxes, Post-it notes, message slips, and any other message sources. Rate the messages in terms of immediate action needed, information to remember for future actions, organizational knowledge, and social information.

Compare and contrast your list with others. Determine if it is possible to remember all the messages received. Recommend a Web-based strategy that would help you receive, organize, and use the information that you must work with every day.

Exercise 9.3: Mapping Social Networks

Develop a map of the social networks you are involved with. This could include networks in business, at school, or with friends. Draw out any communications links between individuals that would link these networks together. Determine the role you play in each of the hubs.

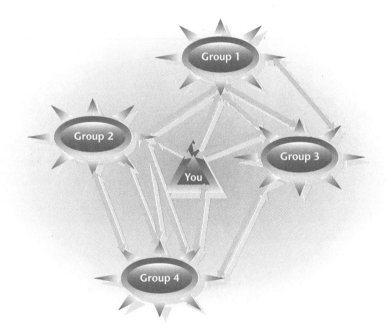

Exercise 9.4: Design a Corporate Portal

Put yourself in the role of a chief information officer. Design a corporate portal for a business. Set up links to the types of information that are needed by each constituency inside the business. Determine how the Web site would foster social networks. List the types of information that should be used to increase organizational knowledge. Justify the design of the Web site for the business's culture.

Exercise 9.5: Business Process Reengineering

Choose a business that you believe needs restructuring to compete in an e-business environment. Answer the following five questions relating to the reengineering process for this business:

1. How does the business model need to change?
2. How can top management's commitment be secured?
3. Which key players in the organization need to back the change?
4. What are some key leverage points that can be addressed?
5. What process breakthrough can be achieved with success?

WEB SEARCH — LOOKING ONLINE

SEARCH TERM: Innovation	First 3 out of 665,520

Bill and Melinda Gates Foundation. Is a grant site with information on how to increase innovations in education, technology, and global health.
http://www.gatesfoundations.org

The Ernst & Young Center for Business Innovation. Is a source of new knowledge, insights, and frameworks for management.
http://www.businessinnovation.ey.com

Small Business Innovation Research (SBIR). Is a U.S. government site offering opportunities and incentives for small businesses to engage in innovative research that has a possibility of commercialization and public benefit.
http://www.eng.nsf.gov/sbir/about_sbir.htm

SEARCH TERM: E-Business Management	First 7 out of 750,588

Business Process Reengineering & Innovation. Has links to topics related to business process reengineering and innovation.
http://www.brint.com/BPR.htm

The Conference Board. Is a site where visitors can gain cross-industry knowledge and share experiences and best practices with executives from more than 3,000 organizations in 67 countries.
http://www.conference-board.org

Hatch Organizational Consulting, Inc. Consults in the culture change field. This Web site outlines culture change strategies.
http://www.hocinc.com

Healthyculture.com. Has a mission to empower people to create cultures that support health and productivity at home, at work, and in the community.
http://www.healthyculture.com

Knowledge Management & Organizational Learning. Is a Web site with links to topics related to knowledge management and organizational learning.
http://www.brint.com/OrgLrng.htm

National Science Foundation. Is a workshop report on the methodological advances in measuring human capital.
http://www.nsf.gov/pubs/1997/nsf9797/nsf9797.htm

Virtual Corporations & Outsourcing. Has links to topics related to virtual corporations and outsourcing.
http://www.brint.com/EmergOrg.htm

REFERENCES

1. Louis Trager, "AT&T Corp.'s Armstrong Righting a Sinking Ship—Year 1," *Inter@ctive Week,* November 2, 1998, p. 62.
2. Steve Lubar, *Info Culture,* Houghton Mifflin Company, New York, 1994.
3. Jared Sandberg, "She's Baaack!" *Newsweek,* February 15, 1999, pp. 44–46; and Louis Trager, "AT&T Corp.'s Armstrong Righting a Sinking Ship—Year 1," *Inter@ctive Week,* November 2, 1998, pp. 62–63.
4. Debby Young, "AT&T's Intranet Reaches Out to Touch Everyone," *CIO Web Business—Section 2,* October 1, 1997, p. 78.
5. Allan Sloan, "AT&T's Golden Boy," *Newsweek,* May 10, 1999, pp. 69–71; and Nate Zelnick, "ISPs Fear AT&T Will Corner Market," *Internet World,* February 8, 1999, pp. 1, 7.
6. Doug Aldrich, "The New Value Chain," *Information Week,* September 14, 1998, p. 280.
7. Mel Duvall, "To Spin Off or Not to Spin Off?" *Inter@ctive Week,* October 28, 1999, pp. 28–29.
8. Doug Aldrich, "The New Value Chain," *Information Week,* September 14, 1998, pp. 278–280.
9. For more on this topic, see: *Corporate Internet Planning Guide: Aligning Internet Strategy with Business Goals,* Van Nostrand Reinhold, New York; Richard J. Gascoyne and Koray Ozcubucvu, *Corporate Internet Planning Guide: Aligning Internet Strategy With Business Goals,* John Wiley & Sons, New York, 1997; and Richard J. Gascoyne, "Adapt to the Internet," *Information Week,* May 5, 1997, pp. 89–100.
10. Bruce Caldwell, "Time and Money Pay Off," *Information Week,* February 8, 1999, p. 16ER; and Ralph Szygenda, "Information's Competitive Edge," *Information Week,* February 8, 1999, pp. 4ER–10ER.
11. *Information Week,* "Quote of the Week," February 13, 1998, p. 14.
12. *Newsweek,* "Clueless in the Suites," April 20, 1997, p. 8.
13. Joel Maloff, "Do Execs Get the Net?" *Internet World,* November 1996, pp. 64–68.

[14] Tim Wilson, "Cautiously, CEOs Lead the Way," *Internet Week*, September 14, 1998, pp. 11–12.

[15] Bruce Caldwell, Marianne Kolbasuk McGee, and Clinton Wilder, "CEOs Turn to IT," *Information Week*, June 22, 1998, pp. 18–20.

[16] Don Tapscott, "Leadership for the Internetworked Business," *Information Week*, November 13, 1995, pp. 65–72; and Thomas A. Stewart, "Managing in a Wired World," *Fortune*, July 11, 1994, pp. 44–56.

[17] For more on the development of organizational cultures and strategic fit, see: Henry Mintzberg, "Organizational Design: Fashion or Fit?" *Harvard Business Review*, January–February 1981, pp. 103–116; Rohit Deshpande and Frederick E. Webster Jr., "Organizing Culture and Marketing: Defining the Research Agenda," *Journal of Marketing*, vol. 53, January 1989, pp. 3–15; Danny Miller, "Environmental Fit Versus Internal Fit," *Organizational Science*, vol. 3, no. 2, May 1992, pp. 159–178; and Rohit Deshpande, John U. Farley, and Frederick E. Webster Jr., "Corporate Culture, Customer Orientation, and Innovativeness in Japanese Firms: A Quadrad Analysis," *Journal of Marketing*, vol. 57, January 1993, pp. 23–27.

[18] Daintry Duffy, "Cultural Evolution," *CIO Enterprise—Section 2*, January 15, 1999, pp. 44–50.

[19] Barb Cole-Gomolski, "Unwary CIOs Can Walk into Business Disasters," *Computerworld*, April 19, 1999, p. 24; and Larry English, "DQ Point 13: Education and Self-Improvement," *DM Review*, March 1999, pp. 32–33.

[20] Robert W. Ruekert, Orville C. Walker Jr., and Kenneth J. Roering, "The Organization of Marketing Activities: A Contingency Theory of Structure and Performance," *Journal of Marketing*, vol. 49, Winter 1985, pp. 13–25.

[21] Megan Santosus, "The Organic Root System," *CIO*, December 15, 1998–January 1, 1999, pp. 38–45; Megan Santosus, "Pop Quiz," *CIO*, December 15, 1998–January 1, 1999, pp. 48–55; and Justin Hibbard, "Cultural Breakthrough," *Information Week*, September 21, 1998, pp. 44–55.

[22] Daniel H. Kim, "The Link Between Individual and Organizational Learning," *Sloan Management Review*, Fall 1993, pp. 37–50; Mark Dodgson, "Organizational Learning: A Review of Some Literatures," *Organizational Studies*, vol. 14, no. 3, 1993, pp. 375–394; and C. Marline Fiol and Marjorie A. Lyles, "Organizational Learning," *Academy of Management Review*, vol. 10, no. 4, 1985, pp. 803–813.

[23] Julekha Dash, "Knowledge Power," *Software Magazine*, January 1998, pp. 46–56.

[24] Carol Hindebrand, "Making KM Pay Off," *CIO Enterprise—Section 2*, February 15, 1999, pp. 64–66.

[25] Judy DeMocker, "Knowledge-Management Tools Billed as Key to Accessing Data on Intranets," *Internet World*, April 6, 1998, p. 18.

[26] This section compiled from Perry Glasser, "The Knowledge Factor," *CIO*, December 15, 1998–January 1, 1999, pp. 108–118; Tom Davenport and Larry Prusak, "Know What You Know," *CIO*, February 15, 1998, pp. 59–63; Michele S. Darling, "Building the Knowledge Organization," *Business Quarterly*, Winter 1996, pp. 61–67; and Jim Bair, "Knowledge Management: The Era of Shared Ideas," *Forbes*, September 22, 1997, p. 28.

[27] Cheryl Dahle, "Fast Pitch," *Webmaster*, August 1997, pp. 50–51.

[28] Peter Fabris, "You Think Tomaytoes, I Think Tomahtoes," *CIO Web Business—Section 2*, April 1, 1999, pp. 46–52.

[29] Working Knowledge, "Message Overload," *Knowledge Management*, November 1999, p. 34; and Tom Davenport, "Overload Redux," *CIO—Section 1*, October 1, 1999, pp. 32–34.

[30] Daintry Duffy, "A Capital Idea," *CIO Enterprise—Section 2,* November 15, 1999, pp. 54–62; Mark Swanson, "Net Employees in the Driver's Seat," *NewMedia,* August 1999, p. 22; Mindy Blodgett, "Fast Forward," *CIO,* August 15, 1999, pp. 46–58; J. Neil Weintraut and Jeffrey Davis, "The Startup Economy," *Business 2.0,* July 1999, pp. 61–68; and Don Tapscott, "Minds Over Matter," *Business 2.0,* January 1999, pp. 89–97.

[31] Louis Trager, Randy Barrett, Kathleen Cholewka, Connie Guglielmo, and Steven Vonder Haar, "Nothing But Net: The Scarcity Syndrome," *Inter@ctive Week,* June 7, 1999, pp. 70–71; and Barb Cole-Gomolski, "IT Labor Issues Add to Retailers' Woes," *Computerworld,* March 15, 1999, p. 4.

[32] Charles Babcock, "Webnations: Filling the High-Tech Void," *Inter@ctive Week,* November 22, 1999, pp. 68–69.

[33] Jack Ewing and Heidi Dawley, "The Missing Worker," *Business Week,* December 27, 1999, pp. 70–71.

[34] Randall E. Stross, "Microsoft's Big Advantage—Hiring Only the Supersmart," *Fortune,* November 25, 1996, pp. 159–162.

[35] Michael Moeller, "Outta Here at Microsoft," *Business Week,* November 29, 1999, pp. 156–160.

[36] Polly Schneider, "The Renaissance Company," *CIO,* December 15, 1998–January 1, 1999, pp. 66–76.

[37] Don Tapscott, "Growing Up Digital," *Information Week,* November 3, 1997, pp. 64–73; and Don Tapscott, "Minds Over Matter," *Business 2.0,* January 1999, pp. 89–97.

[38] Pamela Kruger and Katharine Mieszkowski, "Stop the Fight," *Fast Company,* September 1998, pp. 93–111.

[39] Gregory Dalton, "Web-Organized," *Information Week,* January 25, 1999, pp. 71–76; Tom Stein and Jeff Sweat, "Customer Culture," *Information Week,* January 25, 1999, pp. 49–55; and Lauren Gibbons Paul, "Over the Line," *CIO Web Business—Section 2,* March 1, 1998, pp. 54–59.

[40] Noah Shachtman, "Group Think," *Information Week,* June 1, 1998, pp. 77–84.

[41] Dawne Shand, "Making Community," *Knowledge Management,* June 1999, pp. 64–70; and Carol Hildebrand, "Mapping the Invisible Workspace" *CIO Enterprise—Section 2,* July 15, 1998, pp. 18–20.

[42] Mary Johnston Turner, "Electronic Communities Will Lead the Way for Corporations," *Communications Week,* May 26, 1997, p. 37.

[43] Jennifer Bresnahan, "Capital Gains," *Webmaster,* August 1997, pp. 36–40.

[44] Ellis Booker, "Marketing Seizes Big E-Business Role," *Internet Week,* September 6, 1999, p. 12; Martin LaMonica, "Learning to Play Nice," *InfoWorld,* June 28, 1999, p. 69; and Jim Sterne, "Building Bridges," *CIO Web Business—Section 2,* June 1, 1998, pp. 58–60.

[45] For more background on marketing interactions in teams, see: Richard T. Hise, Larry O'Neal, A. Parasuraman, and James U. McNeal, "Marketing/R&D Interaction in New Product Development: Implications for New Product Success Rates," *Journal of Product Innovation Management,* vol. 7, June 1990, pp. 142–155; Robert W. Reukert and Orville C. Walker Jr., "Interactions Between Marketing and R&D Departments in Implementing Different Business Strategies," *Strategic Management Journal,* vol. 8, 1987, pp. 233–248; Robert W. Reukert and Orville C. Walker Jr., "Marketing's Interaction with Other Functional Units: A Conceptual Framework and Empirical Evidence," *Journal of Marketing,* vol. 51, January 1987, pp. 1–19; and Ashok K. Gupta and Everett M. Rogers, "Internal Marketing: Integrating R&D and Marketing Within the Organization," *Journal of Services Marketing,* vol. 5, Spring 1991, pp. 55–68.

[46] Jerry Luftman, "Enablers & Inhibitors," *Information Week,* September 14, 1998, pp. 283–286.

[47] John Moore, "Untapped Market," *Sm@rt Reseller,* January 25, 1999, pp. 44–46.

[48] Jennifer Bresnahan, "Improving the Odds," *CIO—Section 2,* November 15, 1998, pp. 36–48; and Jason Busch, "How to Get the Most Out of Your Web Marketing Efforts," *Internet Week,* July 13, 1998, p. 29.

[49] For more on collaboration software use, see: Richard Adhikari, "Groupware to the Next Level," *Information Week,* May 4, 1998, pp. 106–111; Justin Hibbard, "Virtual Teams Improve Customer Service," *Information Week,* October 5, 1998, p. 30; and Fred Hapgood, "Tools for Teamwork," *CIO Web Business—Section 2,* November 1, 1998, pp. 68–74.

[50] For more on this topic, see: John A. Byrne, Richard Brandt, and Otis Port, "The Virtual Corporation," *Business Week,* February 8, 1993, pp. 98–103; Shawn Tully, "The Modular Corporation," *Fortune,* February 8, 1993, pp. 106–113; and William H. Davidow and Michael S. Malone, *The Virtual Corporation,* HarperBusiness, New York, 1993.

[51] Joyce Chutchian-Ferranti, "Virtual Corporation," *Computerworld,* September 13, 1999, p. 64; Steven Bell, "Ready, Set, Go Virtual," *CIO,* October 15, 1998, pp. 86–90; and David Joachim, "The Virtual Corporation: It's Closer Than You Think," *Internet Week,* April 6, 1998, p. S3.

[52] David Joachim, "The Virtual Corporation: It's Closer Than You Think," *Internet Week,* April 6, 1998, p. S3; and Linda Musthaler, "Virtual Corporations," *LAN Times,* August 18, 1997, p. 90.

[53] Sari Kalin, "Good Help Is Hard to Find," *CIO Web Business—Section 2,* June 1, 1998, pp. 38–43.

[54] Maryann Jones Thompson, "Market Spotlight: Internet Professional Services," *The Industry Standard,* November 16, 1998, p. 42.

[55] Kathleen Murphy, "Web Fosters Telecommuting Boom, and Many in the Industry Take Part," *Internet World,* February 9, 1998, p. 38; Anne Tergesen, "Making Stay-At-Homes Feel Welcome," *Business Week,* October 12, 1998, pp. 155–156; Edward C. Baig, "Saying Adios to the Office," *Business Week,* October 12, 1998, pp. 152–153; and Melanie Warner, "Working at Home—the Right Way to Be a Star in Your Bunny Slippers," *Fortune,* March 3, 1997, pp. 165–166.

[56] Bruce Caldwell and Jill Gambon, "The Virtual Office Gets Real," *Information Week,* January 22, 1996, pp. 32–40; Jennifer Bresnahan, "Why Telework?" *CIO Enterprise—Section 2,* January 15, 1998, pp. 28–34; and Todd Spangler, "Serving the 30-Second Commuter," *Inter@ctive Week,* December 14, 1998, p. 30.

[57] For more on corporate portals, see: Sarah L. Roberts-Witt, "Making Sense of Portal Pandemonium," *Knowledge Management,* July 1999, pp. 37–48; Emily Fitzloff, "Portal Patrol," *InfoWorld,* May 17, 1999, pp. 1, 32–33; Rick Overton, "Take the Vertical Challenge," *Business 2.0,* May 1999, p. 128; Beth Bacheldor, "Portals Make Business Sense," *Information Week,* October 18, 1999, pp. 81–90; Jason Meserve, "Preparing Your Firm for Corporate Portals," *Network World,* October 4, 1999, p. 49; and David Orenstein, "Corporate Portals," *Computerworld,* June 28, 1999, p. 73.

[58] Jerry Useem, "Internet Defense Strategy: Cannibalize Yourself," *Fortune,* September 6, 1999, pp. 121–134.

[59] Paula Klein, "E-Business: No Quick Fix," *Information Week,* June 21, 1999, p. 5SS; Teri Robinson, "Reinventing the Business Wheel," *Information Week,* June 21, 1999, pp. 6SS–10SS.

[60] Ira Sager, "The Great Equalizer," *Business Week/The Information Revolution,* 1994, pp. 100–107.

[61] Clinton Wilder, "E-Transformation," *Information Week,* September 13, 1999, pp. 44–62.

[62] Charles Fishman, "Change," *Fast Company,* April–May 1997, pp. 64–75.

63 Carol J. Loomis, "Dinosaurs?" *Fortune,* May 3, 1993, pp. 36–42.

64 Luc Hatlestad, "New Shades of Blue," *Red Herring,* November 1999, pp. 118–128; and Eric Ransdell, "IBM's Grassroots Revival," *Fast Company,* October–November 1997, pp. 182–199.

65 David Diamond, "Can General Motors Learn to Love the Net?" *Business 2.0,* September 1998, pp. 46–54.

66 Burnes P. Hollyman and Robert L. Howie Jr., "Mastering Change: Information Technology Integration in Successful Enterprises," *Business Week,* December 19, 1994, Special Advertising Section; and John H. Mayer, "Avoiding a Fool's Mission," *Software Magazine,* February 1998, pp. 43–48.

67 Julia King, "Web Start-Ups Need to Leave to Succeed," *Computerworld,* May 24, 1999, p. 41; and Brian E. Taptich, "spin-off.com," *Red Herring,* April 1999, pp. 40–46.

68 Marianne Kolbasuk McGee, "P&G Jump-Starts Corporate Change," *Internet Week,* November 1, 1999, pp. 30–31; Marianne Kolbasuk McGee, "Lessons from a Cultural Revolution," *Information Week,* October 25, 1999, pp. 46–62; and Linda Himelstein and Peter Galuszka, "P&G Gives Birth to a Web Baby," *Business Week,* September 27, 1999, pp. 87–88.

69 Christopher Koch, "Authors, Authors Everywhere," *Webmaster,* January 1997, pp. 36–40.

70 CIO, "What is a CIO?" *CIO Executive Research Center,* December 17, 1998, <http://www.cio.com/forums/executive/description.html>.

71 Mindy Blodgett, "The CIO Starter Kit," *CIO—Section 1,* May 15, 1999, pp. 38–50; and David Pearson, "National Insecurities," *CIO—Section 1,* February 1, 1999, p. 24.

72 Robert Preston, "New Breed of Internet Exec Is Born," *Internet Week,* October 25, 1999, pp. 54–55; and Sari Kalin, "Title Search," *CIO Web Business—Section 2,* February 1, 1999, pp. 42–47.

73 Justin Hibbard, "Knowledge and Learning Officers Find Big Paydays," *Information Week,* June 15, 1998, p. 170; Julekha Dash, "Turning Technology into TechKnowledgey," *Software Magazine,* February 2, 1998, pp. 64–73; and J. Michael Pemberton, "Chief Knowledge Officer: The Climax to Your Career?" *Records Management Quarterly,* April 1997, pp. 66–70.

74 Michael M. Earl and Ian A. Scott, "What Is a Chief Knowledge Officer?" *Sloan Management Review,* Winter 1999, pp. 29–38; Daintry Duffy, "Knowledge Champions," *CIO Enterprise—Section 2,* November 15, 1998, pp. 66–71; and Barb Cole-Gomolski, "Knowledge Managers Need Business Savvy," *Computerworld,* January 25, 1999, p. 40.

75 Andrew Marlatt, "Running a Big Site? Better Be Good at Juggling," *Internet World,* March 29, 1999, p. 30; James C. Luh, "Intranet Webmasters Must Do It All," *Internet World,* December 7, 1998, p. 40; Elizabeth Gardner, "More Work—But More Money," *Internet World,* October 5, 1998, pp. 8–10; and Elizabeth Gardner, "Backlash Against Title of Webmaster," *Internet World,* September 15, 1997, pp. 1, 38–39.

10001000010010111111
111111110000000000001
000011111...0000
1111111111...1111
0000000000...0000
101010101...010
11100011101...00110100111001010011
101010101010...0110011000000
101010101010...0100

Chapter 10

The Political, Legal, and Ethical Environments

Are the overall benefits of the Internet worth the costs? It seems clear that the new e-business systems are having a major impact on the way that business is conducted. Just as the television and telephone changed society, the new telecommunications age will change how individuals interact with businesses, governments, and each other. Governments around the world are fostering the growth of Internet services in order to obtain the benefits outlined in this text. To receive these benefits, a new level of responsibility needs to be pursued by both businesses and individuals. Businesses must learn to gain customers' trust, governments must ensure a safe Internet environment, and individuals must become Net savvy in order for the Internet to remain a truly free and dynamic system of communication, commerce, and efficiency.

1. Explain the role that some governments are taking to foster the growth of the Internet and e-business.
2. List and describe the major legal issues related to e-business.
3. Outline the major types of fraud committed online and what is being done to limit fraud.
4. Discuss how each of the intellectual property areas is impacting e-business.
5. Explain why jurisdiction is a problem for legal authorities.
6. List and describe the ethical considerations impacting the Internet.
7. Discuss why privacy is an issue in Internet use and what e-businesses can do about it.
8. Compare and contrast the economic welfare concerns related to the Internet.

eBay

In 1995, Pierre Omidyar designed a Web site called Web Auction to allow his girlfriend to sell Pez dispensers. Demand was so strong for the service that Omidyar began charging sellers. This initial idea turned into the online auction business eBay (www.ebay.com). By 1998, the founder had become a billionaire and eBay was valued at $7 billion, a valuation higher than Kmart's. By 1999, eBay accounted for the largest dollar volume of consumer sales on the Internet.

However, running an online auction is not without problems. eBay attempted to auction a jacket autographed by members of the *Today Show* for charity. *Today Show's* Katie Couric announced that the bids had reached $200,000. Unfortunately, pranksters had escalated the bids. The highest legitimate bid was only $11,400. Not only can sales be subject to pranks, but scam artists use online auction sites to bilk bidders. One scam artist developed a positive reputation at eBay's auction site. The scammer then offered additional products online, received payments, and never sent the products. eBay does not give rebates, and the customers lost their money. To overcome the problem of fraud, eBay has offered customer service support and educational resources including a feedback forum, third-party escrow accounts, verification of eBay users' personal information, insurance, and expert opinions for authentication and grading.

Another problem occurred when eBay's server crashed and it received a number of complaints on its discussion list. When eBay attempted to control the listing of complaints, it was accused of censuring free speech.[1]

Auction fraud is the number one complaint in e-commerce. Auction sites are attempting to deal with this problem by allowing discussion lists to rate buyers and sellers. The industry is also using escrow services, digital certificates, and insurance systems.[2] The industry knows that if it does not take care of this problem, it may face federal regulations.

eBay is only one example of the creative new business models that governments would like to see develop on the information superhighway. It is expected that the value of goods and services sold through online auctions will be $129 billion by the year 2002.[3] These new sales systems are bringing efficiency to the market by increasing competition, lowering costs, and expanding customer bases. In 1999, U.S. President Bill Clinton acted as an advocate of the Internet by proposing opening world trade and limiting restrictions for online sales.

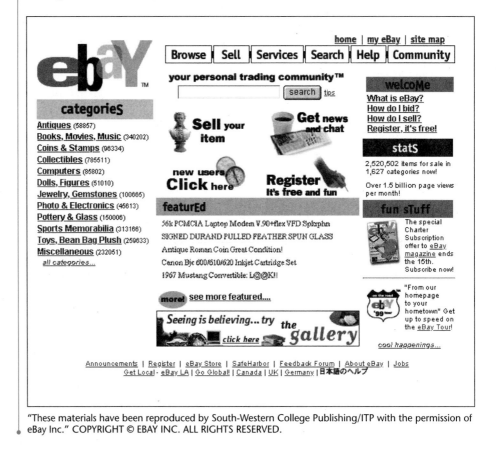

THINKING STRATEGICALLY

Consider whether or not society is better off because of the introduction of eBay. Discuss both sides of this economic welfare question. Consider why a government would be interested in fostering the growth of a business like eBay. Decide what types of government actions would benefit e-businesses like eBay, and what government actions would limit e-businesses. Discuss whether it is proper for e-businesses to collect data on their customers' shopping behaviors and personal profiles. Determine how a customer could benefit and how a customer could be damaged if an e-business uses this data.

"Internet commerce is going to profoundly change our economy for the better. It may well have the same impact that the Industrial Revolution had a couple of centuries ago: to improve productivity across all sectors of the economy as well as to provide significant economic growth in many sectors. So we believe that laying the proper foundation for electronic commerce to flourish globally is one of our most important economic tasks."

Ira Magaziner,
Internet Commerce Advisor to President Clinton[4]

This chapter will investigate the emerging political, legal, and ethical environments facing e-businesses and the public. The political and legal environments represent the rules by which businesses and society operate. Although the imposed rules may attempt to increase the overall **economic welfare** of a society, not everyone plays by the rules. Another social concern is that not everyone in society will benefit from the e-business revolution. Some individuals and businesses may be left out of the connected world.

Economic welfare is the net benefit an economic system provides to a society.

The development of an e-business–based competitive arena has given rise to a number of unique political, legal, and ethical considerations, and the rules of the game of business are being reshaped to fit these new realities. As a truly global medium, the Internet allows businesses to operate across borders. The rules that govern business practice in one location or state may not pertain in other areas. Governments around the world are seeing their business constituencies facing competition from global competitors. These governments are working to set regulations that foster the growth of their own virtual business systems.

As has been discussed throughout this text, consumers can benefit from using e-business systems, but only if they have access to the Internet and the information, goods, and services offered. Without access, individuals may not benefit. This may leave a portion of society relatively worse off. In addition, the global nature of the Internet makes it hard to regulate. This has allowed some unscrupulous individuals to take advantage of others by running scams, offering access to pornography, or otherwise exploiting the customer.

This chapter will explore the role governments play in fostering the growth of information superhighways. It will look at the rules and regulations imposed on Netizens and how these rules are broken. The chapter will conclude with a consideration of the ethical impact of this revolution.

Private sector businesses provide access in Copenhagen when national infrastructures limit access.

POLITICAL ENVIRONMENT

The U.S. government is the grandfather of the Internet. It sponsored and provided the funding for the early versions of the ARPAnet, NSFnet, and the Internet. Once the Internet had grown to a sustainable level, the U.S. government turned it over to the private sector. This process is being followed around the world as governments deregulate the telecommunications industry. One of the roles that governments take is the fostering of business opportunities. The U.S. federal government is currently funding the development of a **Next-Generation Internet (NGI);** the federal government invested more than $300 million to fund pure research on increasing the speed of the Internet by up to 1,000 times.[5] Governments around the world are also facing a dilemma in imposing order to the current Internet. They do not want to hinder the growth of the Internet, but they often protect a number of **constituencies.** To avoid regulation, the Internet industry is in favor of self-regulation and software solutions rather than government intervention.

Constituencies are those people who are involved with or served by an organization. Internet constituencies include governments, businesses, customers, ISPs, schools, families, children, or just about anyone impacted by changes in telecommunications.

In 1996, the Clinton administration attempted to control the Internet with the Communications Decency Act. This authorized criminal fines of $250,000 and a two-year jail sentence for those who intentionally transmitted indecent material or made it available online. The Internet community vehemently opposed this action. ISPs did not want to be responsible for what their customers posted on ISP sites. The U.S. federal courts ruled that ISPs were like bookstores in that they held material but were not responsible for what is made available for others to view. This is not necessarily true in other countries. An ISP in France was held liable for allowing a subscriber to place nude and seminude pictures of a model on a Web page. The French judge ruled that the ISP must monitor the content of its Web pages to ensure that no third party would be hurt.[6]

After its initial attempt at control, the Clinton administration moved to foster a laissez-faire policy for the Internet. The U.S. federal government believes that Internet commerce will have a major impact on the U.S. and world economies and has developed a **National Telecommunications and Information Administration (NTIA)** *(www.ntia.doc.gov)* to work with other countries to make the Internet a tariff-free zone and to keep government regulations out of Internet commerce. The NTIA set forth five primary principles for global electronic commerce[7]:

1. The private sector should take the lead in developing Internet-based commerce.
2. Governments should avoid undue restrictions on Internet-based commerce.
3. Government intervention should be focused on ensuring competition, protecting intellectual property and privacy, preventing fraud, fostering transparency, supporting commercial transactions, and facilitating dispute resolution.
4. Governments should recognize that the Internet is a unique medium and that it should not have the same regulations as other media.
5. Electronic commerce should be facilitated on a global basis.

Intensified competition is forcing new infrastructures, lower prices, and more Internet services. In response, governments in Canada and the European Community are deregulating their telecommunications systems.[8] The World Bank has taken an active role in helping to wire developing countries to the Internet as a means of fostering business growth.[9] Table 10.1 outlines laws passed by the U.S. Congress in 1998 to help set the rules for e-businesses in the United States.

LEGAL ENVIRONMENT

The United States has been using established rules and regulations to control behavior in the cyberworld. This has proven to be effective in cases of cybercrime such as fraud and hacking, but the **case law** system in the United States has yet to develop rulings on the application of laws to many online activities. The ease of copying data, files, or images forces firms to develop policies for copyright and trademark use and violations. Flaming and spamming are new areas of concern for businesses and the Internet community. Although the Internet community itself has developed a series of standards that users are expected to follow, the free-

Case law is based on English common law. Case law is used in the United States to determine how laws should apply to specific situations.

Table 10.1 U.S. Laws Governing the Internet

Law	Description
Internet Tax Freedom Act	This sets a national policy against interfering with interstate commerce over the Internet and imposes a three-year moratorium on taxes for online services.
Child Online Protection Act	Online distributors of material harmful to minors must restrict access to minors. Web site operators must check visitors' IDs or face $50,000 in fines and six months in prison for each access by a minor.
Child Protection and Sexual Predator Punishment Act	This imposes penalties for using the Internet to send obscene material to a person underage 16 or to sexually solicit minors. ISPs must report child pornography as soon as they are made aware of it.
Children's Online Privacy Protection Act of 1998	This act establishes a framework for regulating the unfair collection of personal information from children over the Internet.
Government Paperwork Elimination Act	This makes it possible to use electronic signatures for forms submitted to federal agencies.
Digital Millennium Copyright Act	This sets rules for copyrighted material online. It helps limit ISPs' liability for copyright infringements by their customers and outlaws technology that can crack copyright protection devices.

Source: Kathleen Murphy, "Congress Shows Interest in Playing Active Internet Role," *Internet World,* November 9, 1998, p. 46.

wheeling world of the Internet is causing governing bodies to impose new laws and regulations. Table 10.2 outlines the major legal topics covered in this chapter.

Cybercrime

For e-commerce to grow, consumers and businesses need to feel safe to surf. The ease of engaging in Web transactions, the low cost of entry, and the ability to do business across borders make the Internet a prime venue for **cybercrime,** or criminal activity on the Internet.

Hackers are individuals who attempt to break through online firewalls for pleasure or profit. They hack their way into computer networks.

Hacking.   In May 1998, seven **hackers,** members of the independent watchdog group L0pht *(www.l0pht.com),* told the U.S. Senate Committee on Government Affairs that they could bring the Internet down in 30 minutes and could disrupt communications between the United States and other countries.[10] This never happened. Hacking includes at least three types of offenses: infrastructure attack, economic espionage, and theft. Losses due to hacking in 1997 were estimated to be more than $136 million. The largest loss was due to the theft of proprietary information.[11]

Table 10.2 Summary of Legal Issues

Legal Topic	Problem	Legal Solution	Industry Solution
Hackers (people illegally breaking into computer systems)	This can result in theft or damage of information.	Use existing laws to pursue hackers.	Use hackers-for-hire and firewall protection.
Fraud (deception by online scammers to gain others' assets)	Scammers can operate offshore or outside of one country's jurisdiction.	Use existing laws to pursue scammers.	Coordinate with governments. Provide information on scammers and types of fraud.
Intellectual property (copyrights, trademarks, trade secrets, patents) **and its protection**	Digital information can be easily copied, reproduced, and sent to others.	Make everything sent online copyrighted.	Use encryption software to protect valuable copyrighted material such as music, videos, books, etc. Use watermarks and other techniques to protect images. Use search systems to locate copyrighted material on Web sites.
Censorship (limiting communications considered to be sensitive or harmful)	Laws in one country don't apply in other countries.	In some countries, the ISP is responsible.	Rating systems help users block information. Software filters can control access to Web sites.

Infrastructure attack occurs when an individual interferes with the operations of a computer system. This could involve something as prankish as changing the CIA's or the *New York Time's* home page or much more serious violations such as rerouting Web traffic. In 1997, an alternative domain name registration service AlterNIC rerouted Web users who were trying to reach the InterNIC domain registration service. This attack disrupted service for thousands of Web users and resulted in the arrest of the AlterNIC founder.

Economic espionage occurs when individuals steal intellectual property. The most likely sources of this type of theft are disgruntled employees, employees about to be laid off, and recently fired employees.[12] Companies defend against hacking by using firewalls and **ethical hackers,** individuals hired to find ways around a company's firewall, to identify security problems. The U.S. federal gov-

> A *shill* is an individual who takes the place of a real bidder by inflating the bids for an object, forcing other bidders to increase their offers.

Table 10.3 The Top Ten Internet Fraud Areas for 1998

Web auction scams	Items are bid for but are never delivered by the sellers. Values of items are inflated. **Shills** are suspected of being used to drive up bids.
General merchandise fraud	Products are advertised and sold but are never delivered or are not as advertised.
Internet services fraud	Individuals are charged for services that were supposedly free. Customers pay for online and Internet services that are never provided or are falsely represented.
Hardware/ software fraud	Customers purchase computer products that are never delivered or are misrepresented.
Pyramids or multi-level marketing scams	These are schemes in which profits are made from recruiting others, not from sales of goods to end users.
Business opportunities/ franchise scams	Customers are promised big profits with little or no work by investing in prepackaged businesses or franchise opportunities.
Work-at-home scams	Customers buy materials and equipment that are sold with false promises of payment for piecework performed at home.
Advance fee loans fraud	Individuals are promised loans contingent on their paying a large fee in advance. Once the fee is paid, the loans are never disbursed.
Credit repair fraud	Individuals are promised that accurate negative information will be removed from their credit report.
Credit-card issuing scams	Individuals with bad credit histories are promised credit cards upon payment of upfront fees.

Source: *Internet Fraud Watch,* remarks to the Consumer Protection in Electronic Commerce Panel at the Public Voice in the Development of Internet Policy Conference of the Global Internet Liberty Campaign by Phillip C. McKee III, Internet Fraud Watch Coordinator, on October 7, 1998, and November 25, 1998, <*http://www.fraud.org/internet/9810stat.htm*>.

ernment takes the threat of hacker attacks so seriously that it has developed a cyberdefense structure with a national coordinator for security, infrastructure protection, and counterterrorism. This coordinator works with the FBI and other agencies to protect against attacks to the information infrastructure from other countries, terrorists, and cyberpunks.[13]

Scams and fraud are two ways of indicating an act of deception or misrepresentation.

Scams and Fraud. The National Consumers League *(www.nclnet.org)* has developed a Web site to act as a global reporting venue for Internet fraud *(www.fraud.org/internet/intstat.htm).* The top 10 areas for **fraud,** as reported by the Internet Fraud Watch for 1998, are shown in Table 10.3 on the previous page.

Stock **scams** can be facilitated on the Internet because it is relatively easy to promote a company through a **pump-and-dump** scheme: A stock is promoted and hyped through telemarketing or using online chat groups, news releases, spam e-mails, or advertisements; when investors buy stock in the company, the

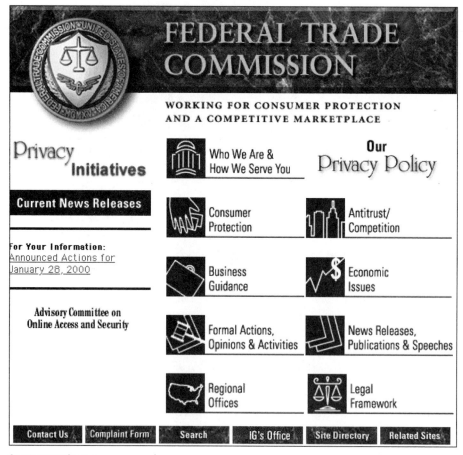

Source: www.ftc.gov.

owners sell at a high stock price or take the money and run. One individual designed a Web page to present information as if it came from the finance information company Bloomberg's Web site *(www.bloomberg.com)*. The fictitious information stated that the company the individual worked for was going to be purchased. The stock of the company rose 31 percent at the news. Bloomberg fought back by issuing subpoenas to the search engines Yahoo! and Lycos, a number of stock discussion sites, and the ISP that hosted the site, leading to the arrest of the individual for securities fraud.[14] It is vital that all online investors thoroughly investigate an investment offer before sending money.[15]

The Internet also acts as a venue for scam and fraud protection. A number of Web sites are available for consumers to obtain information on legitimate as well as illegitimate firms. As a government watchdog, the FTC *(www.ftc.gov)* has sent notifications about deceptive practices to more than 500 Web sites that used the words "no risk" or "get rich."[16] Some sites provide a broad set of information whereas others are more narrowly targeted.

THINKING STRATEGICALLY

Describe some of the damage that could result from the creation of the Melissa virus. Explain why an individual would want to create a virus and release it on the Internet. Describe the damage that resulted from the threatening e-mail messages sent to the high school. Discuss why an individual would want to send such an e-mail. Explain how the publicity on the rapid capture of these individuals may affect future attacks over the Internet.

Intellectual Capital

The Internet is moving from a freewheeling, lightly scrutinized communications medium to a more mainstream business system. The importance that businesses are placing on the Internet is forcing compliance to the same laws and regulations that pertain to all other businesses. This is especially true for the rules governing intellectual property or a firm's intellectual capital. **Intellectual capital** refers to the ownership of a company's knowledge, the results of ideas and creativity, and the symbols that represent products, companies, or brands.[18] Ownership of intellectual capital is covered by copyrights, trademarks, trade secrets, and patents. Each of these will be discussed in this section.

CASE 10.1

Fingered on the Net

The Melissa virus was one of the fastest-spreading viruses to ever move around the Internet. The virus would show up as an e-mail with an attachment. If the recipient opened the attached file, it displayed a list of pornography sites. The virus then replicated itself by hijacking the individual's address book and sending a copy of itself to the top 50 names. Some business Internet servers were crashed because of the amount of e-mail that was generated. As each new recipient opened the file, the virus spread. David L. Smith, the virus creator, spent less than 3 minutes to modify an earlier virus to create Melissa. Smith's actions were tracked by a number of virus hunters, and in 1 week he was caught. Smith faced a penalty of 40 years in prison and a $480,000 fine.[17]

In 2000, a high school student received an e-mail message threatening his school. This message was shown to school administrators, and the threatened school went on winter break early. The sender of the e-mail was tracked and arrested. The message sender, another high school student in a different part of the country, faced a possibility of 5 years in prison and a $250,000 fine.

COPYrightS   A **copyright** protects original works of authorship, which include literary, dramatic, musical, artistic, and certain other intellectual works, both published and unpublished. Under current U.S. copyright laws, protection exists from the time the work is created in fixed form. The copyright immediately becomes the property of the author who created the work, and only the author or those assigned rights from the author can rightfully claim copyright. No publication or registration with the Copyright Office is required to secure a copyright. A copyright notice is no longer required under U.S. law, but it can act as a signal to others that the author is interested in protecting the work. Older copyright laws did contain a notification requirement so the use of notice is still relevant to the copyright status of older works.

Copyright registration with the Copyright Office establishes a public record of the copyright claim. If registration is made within three months after publication of the work or prior to an infringement of the work, the copyright owner can collect statutory damages and attorney's fees in court actions; otherwise, only an award of actual damages and profits is available to the copyright owner. Registration also allows the owner of the copyright to record the work with the U.S. Customs Service for protection against the importation of infringing copies.[19] The 1971 Berne Convention allows copyrights granted in one country to automatically be upheld in all other member countries.

Many of the elements that are used to create content for the Internet, such as pictures and graphic files, sound files, text, or programs, are copyrighted by other companies or individuals. The ability to copy and transfer digital information makes copyright violations relatively simple. This has alarmed a number of

The Copyright Clearance Center (CCC) at copyright.com allows individuals and organizations to obtain permissions online for the use of copyrighted material.

industries. For example, the music industry is concerned about unauthorized copying of its material. Newly released albums are being copied to unauthorized Web sites for downloading. Individuals then take this music and record it to CDs. This is a clear violation of copyright restrictions. Individuals can also violate copyright restrictions by using sound clips in a Web site. BMI (Broadcast Music, Inc.), a media licensing firm, looks for unauthorized use of copyrighted material and then forces compliance through the payment of royalties. BMI has developed a Web bot, or spider, that searches the Web looking for unauthorized use of sound clips.[20]

The music industry is being directly attacked on college campuses throughout the world. MP3 compression standard is being used across the world to compress CD music files. On some college campuses, the largest use of the Internet by students is the downloading of illegally recorded and forwarded music files.

There are numerous sources of copyright-free material on the Internet, or material can be purchased on CDs. Businesses that develop Web sites must be sure they are not violating copyrights when they develop content. They should also ascertain that they do not develop links to third-party sites that engage in copyright violations.

Software and Technology Protections. Software theft has been a problem for a considerable time. Worldwide losses due to theft from illegal copying were close to $15 billion in 1994. It was projected that the piracy rate for software in the United States was 35 percent; in China 98 percent and in Japan 67 percent of software were illegally copied.[21]

This copyright problem is hindering the ability to sell many products over the Internet. Book publishers do not want to sell digital books if they could be freely copied and dispersed. Music companies do not want to lose control of their products. Television and movie producers do not want to have their products distributed without compensation.

The Copyright Archive *(www.copyrightarchive.com)* is a firm that allows individuals to register their Web sites for a $10 yearly fee. This places the Web site in a database of copyright works. Copyright Archive uses Web crawlers and robots to search for copyright violations in order to provide copyright protection for electronic works worldwide.[22]

Other software protection systems are being developed for images, sound files, DVD files, and video files. A number of protection routines are outlined in Table 10.4, on the following page.

Trademarks

A **trademark** or service mark refers to any word, name, symbol, or device that is used to indicate the source or origin of goods or services and that distinguishes one company's goods or services from others'. Trademark rights cover such practices as preventing others from using a confusingly similar mark, dilution of the trademark, and unfair use of the trademark.

® is the symbol used to indicate a registered trademark; otherwise, notice is given as: Dr. Brad Kleindl^(TM).

Table 10.4 Technological Copyright Protections

Technology	Description
Digital watermarks	This technology allows images to be sent over the Internet with visible watermarks over a page or with watermarks that will show up only after an image is copied.
Secure containers	The publisher can encrypt a file, stipulate conditions for use, and then send the content to a user. The user can then send payment and receive a key to unlock the product. If the data is sent on to others, they must also have a key to unlock the file.
Information metering	This provides an auditing trail, allowing determination of who forwarded the protected material.

Sources: Alan Zeichick, "Digital Watermarks Explained," *Red Herring,* December 1999, pp. 270–272; Richard Wiggins, "Corralling Your Content," *NewMedia,* October 13, 1997, pp. 40–45; and Otis Port, "Copyrights New Digital Guardians," *Business Week,* May 6, 1996, p. 62.

Owners of registered trademarks can challenge the ownership of domain names registered through Network Solutions, Inc. (NSI). This prevents individuals from using a domain name such as *www.Pepsi.com* for a privately owned Web site. The owner of a trademark must protect its use or face the possibility of losing that ownership because the trademark can become a generic reference. A trademark could be considered abandoned if the trademark owner allows a Web site to display the trademark without permission. Billy Joel® has registered his name as a trademark to prevent unauthorized use of his name.

Because the trademark represents the image of the firm, the firm may want to determine who can set up automatic links to its site. Disreputable firms could hurt another firm's positive image. When developing a Web site, the designer should not use copyrighted material or trademarks without permission. When building a link to another site, it is advisable to notify that site's Webmaster.[23] Some Web site designers have attempted to increase the number of hits obtained in Web searches by using trademarked names in meta tags. This is a trademark violation and could result in a cease-and-desist order or a lawsuit.[24]

Companies have filed suit against search engines for trademark violations due to the use of targeted advertising. For example, an individual who wants to run a search on AT&T may see ads paid for by rival telecommunications companies or ads that could hurt AT&T's image. The courts may find that it is unfair competition when competitors pay to have their ads displayed on a search based on a company's trademarked name.[25]

Trade Secrets. There are laws to protect **trade secrets,** which are non-publicly disclosed inventions, ideas, or information held in a firm that make it unique or give it an advantage over other firms. If trade secrets are placed on a Web site, they may no longer be considered trade secrets.

Firms can protect themselves by having employees sign nondisclosure and noncompete agreements, which prevent individuals from using information or working for rival firms. Nondisclosure agreements prevent employees from spreading trade secrets. Noncompetitive agreements prevent employees from moving on to or working at competitive firms within a stated period of time.

Patents **Patents** allow individuals or firms to monopolize or gain exclusive rights to the use of an invention; the term of a patent is 20 years from the date of the application. There are different types of patents. A utility patent includes machines, industrial processes, compositions of matter, and articles of manufacture. A design patent protects the appearance or shape of a product instead of the function. Plant patents are granted for biological species. **Software patents** have grown considerably, from 1,300 issued in 1990 to almost 12,000 by 1997.[26]

In January 1999, the Supreme Court of the United States let stand a lower court's decision in *State Street Bank & Trust Co. vs. Signature Financial Group,* upholding the patenting of business methods. This has allowed the Internet business community to patent a number of business processes.[27] Excite *(www.excite.com)* has a patent on its search engine and has asserted that other search engines may be infringing. Priceline *(www.priceline.com)* holds a number of patents on its business model in an attempt to control the process whereby consumers submit prices they are willing to pay to a business, and the business can then accept or reject online bids. Priceline's claim for a patent was based on using a computer to facilitate payment between a buyer and a seller when the buyer inputs the conditions for the sale. CyberGold *(www.cybergold.com)* was awarded a patent for pay-per-view ads. If these patents on business models are upheld in court, it could force firms to pay royalties for the use of technology or business models. While it is possible to fight patents in court, it is expensive to try to overturn a patent and to defend a patent. Many businesses have opted to pay royalty fees for business process use instead.[28]

Intellectual Property Protection

The following is a list of five suggestions* to limit Web site problems with intellectual property laws[29]:

1. Independent contractors should release to the business all copyrights related to the creation of the Web page. The independent contractor should also obtain copyright releases from all subcontractors.
2. Place a copyright notice on the Web page, such as © 2001, South-Western Publishing. This serves as notice.
3. For extra protection, register the site with the Copyright Office.
4. The Web site should have a legal page so people see the rules for using the site. This should include notices about downloading material from the site, especially material owned by third parties.
5. To protect from being sued for copyright infringement, obtain written permission before using any other Web site's material or when developing links to other sites.

*This list is for informational purposes only; it is not meant to be legal advice. It is always advisable to obtain legal advice from a lawyer. (This is an example of a legal disclaimer.)

Legal Jurisdiction

The United States operates under three levels of laws: the federal level, the state level, and the local level. Federal laws and regulations cross state borders, state laws and regulations govern the actions within the state's borders, and local laws and ordinances allow communities to govern themselves. Enforcement of those laws and regulations occurs within each jurisdiction. In some states, for example, it is legal to gamble. This allows an individual to visit Las Vegas and tempt the fates in a variety of games of chance that may be illegal in his or her home state. To engage in the same behavior online from that individual's home state may be illegal and could get the gambler fined or imprisoned. This process becomes even more complicated when the gambling venue is outside U.S. jurisdiction altogether. The United States has attempted to fine both Internet gambling companies and Internet gamblers, but the Australian government is attempting to allow legalized online gambling sites.[30]

THINKING STRATEGICALLY

Compare and contrast the ability of U.S. businesses and European businesses to engage in e-business. Explain why a standardized set of regulations for all nations engaging in e-business is important. List some of the problems facing nations that try to limit e-business. Speculate on the economic welfare implications for each economy.

CASE 10.2

A Tale of Too Many Nations

National governments are adopting different strategies to control the growth of the Internet, e-commerce, and e-business development. The United States has been pushing for low or no import tariffs or taxes on goods purchased online.[31] At the end of 1999, the Clinton administration started a federal, state, and local government initiative to evaluate how laws and regulations could be revised to lower barriers to the growth of electronic commerce. The administration was also concerned about promoting consumer protection online.[32]

Europeans are faced with a tougher regulatory problem. For example, if a British-based e-business sells across Europe, it must conform to all member countries' regulations on defamation, advertising, and unfair competition. If even one European country does not conform to a Pan-European set of e-business regulations, e-commerce growth can be hindered.[33] The European Community Parliament has considered legislation that would allow consumers to sue e-businesses from the consumers' home country. The European Internet industry sees this as a barrier to e-commerce development, especially for smaller businesses that would have to defend against lawsuits across European countries. The European Parliament believes this would encourage e-commerce because consumers would have greater confidence in purchasing online.[34]

The United States has attempted to regulate the rapid growth of the Internet by adapting older laws and regulations. In many cases, laws that pertain to broadcasting and advertising are being adapted to the Internet. This does not necessarily work with this new communications venue. In a many-to-many Internet world, everyone with a Web page becomes a broadcaster. An ISP does not want to be held responsible for the content of each and every one of these nonlicensed broadcasters. Under old laws, the ISP could be held responsible for libel, pornography, copyright violations, or fraud. Yet an ISP that attempts to limit content on its site could be accused of censuring Web page content, which could be an infringement of free speech.[35]

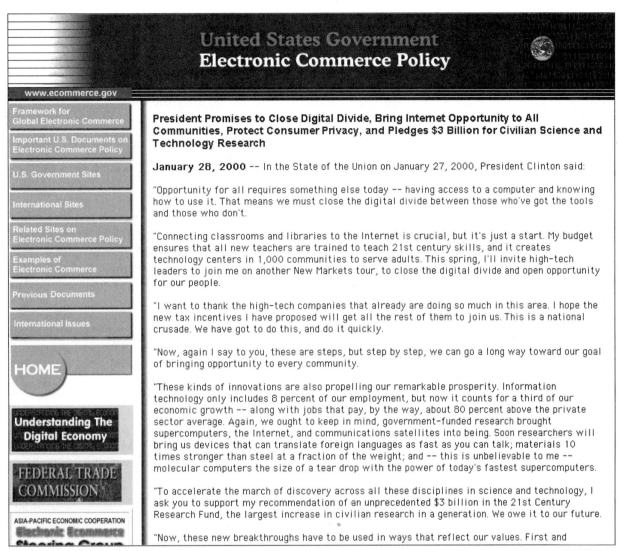

United States Government
Electronic Commerce Policy

www.ecommerce.gov

- Framework for Global Electronic Commerce
- Important U.S. Documents on Electronic Commerce Policy
- U.S. Government Sites
- International Sites
- Related Sites on Electronic Commerce Policy
- Examples of Electronic Commerce
- Previous Documents
- International Issues

HOME

Understanding The Digital Economy

FEDERAL TRADE COMMISSION

ASIA-PACIFIC ECONOMIC COOPERATION
Electronic Commerce
Steering Group

President Promises to Close Digital Divide, Bring Internet Opportunity to All Communities, Protect Consumer Privacy, and Pledges $3 Billion for Civilian Science and Technology Research

January 28, 2000 -- In the State of the Union on January 27, 2000, President Clinton said:

"Opportunity for all requires something else today -- having access to a computer and knowing how to use it. That means we must close the digital divide between those who've got the tools and those who don't.

"Connecting classrooms and libraries to the Internet is crucial, but it's just a start. My budget ensures that all new teachers are trained to teach 21st century skills, and it creates technology centers in 1,000 communities to serve adults. This spring, I'll invite high-tech leaders to join me on another New Markets tour, to close the digital divide and open opportunity for our people.

"I want to thank the high-tech companies that already are doing so much in this area. I hope the new tax incentives I have proposed will get all the rest of them to join us. This is a national crusade. We have got to do this, and do it quickly.

"Now, again I say to you, these are steps, but step by step, we can go a long way toward our goal of bringing opportunity to every community.

"These kinds of innovations are also propelling our remarkable prosperity. Information technology only includes 8 percent of our employment, but now it counts for a third of our economic growth -- along with jobs that pay, by the way, about 80 percent above the private sector average. Again, we ought to keep in mind, government-funded research brought supercomputers, the Internet, and communications satellites into being. Soon researchers will bring us devices that can translate foreign languages as fast as you can talk; materials 10 times stronger than steel at a fraction of the weight; and -- this is unbelievable to me -- molecular computers the size of a tear drop with the power of today's fastest supercomputers.

"To accelerate the march of discovery across all these disciplines in science and technology, I ask you to support my recommendation of an unprecedented $3 billion in the 21st Century Research Fund, the largest increase in civilian research in a generation. We owe it to our future.

"Now, these new breakthroughs have to be used in ways that reflect our values. First and

Source: www.ecommerce.gov

This jurisdictional dilemma exists even for rights that many countries hold very dear, such as free speech. What might be considered free speech in the United States, for example, may be seen as libelous in other countries. In Saudi Arabia, sex, religion, and politics are typically controlled in the media. The Internet allows access to sites, discussion groups, and information that would otherwise be outlawed.[36]

Jurisdiction can be a problem for businesses. If a business is sued, it may need to fight the case in the jurisdiction of the plaintiff.[37] A business can limit its liability by restricting where it does business. Enforcement of any laws passed is also a problem. Part of the Internet's design was to prevent blocking by allowing information to be rerouted through a number of different systems. Many wineries in the United States have been selling wine online. Their ability to sell in every state is limited. Local and state laws control the sale of alcoholic beverages. Shipments to some states are blocked.

Netiquette

Netiquette refers to proper etiquette over networks and includes the rules for common courtesy online and the informal rules of the road for cyberspace. Virginia Shea has written a book called *Netiquette* outlining these rules. An online version is available on the Web at the Netiquette home page site: *www.albion.com/netiquette.*[38] Some of the basic considerations when going online with e-mail are[39]:

▶ Be respectful of others online. Behave as if you were having a conversation with someone in person.
▶ Remember that the Internet is a global medium; others online may have a culture, language, or humor that is different from yours. Jokes and sarcasm may not travel well.
▶ Respect the copyright on reproduced material.
▶ Don't send chain letters through e-mail. Chain letters are forbidden on the Internet.
▶ When in a chat group, observe the discussion to get a feel for the group culture before making comments.
▶ Use mixed case. UPPER CASE LOOKS AS IF YOU'RE SHOUTING.
▶ Keep file sizes small.
▶ Don't send large amounts of unsolicited information to people.

Rumors   In the beginning of 1995, an e-mail message reported to be from the Associated Press was sent around the Internet; it stated that Microsoft Corporation had purchased the Vatican. This fraudulent AP news release should have been seen as an obvious hoax, but Microsoft received a number of complaints.[40] What is truth on the Internet? Can all Web sites be trusted? These questions are important considerations for the legitimacy of the Internet as a communications medium. Web sites from recognized brand-name news sources may be seen as equally trustworthy as newspapers, magazines, or television. Yet the Web allows easy access to all types of information in a many-to-many communications system, and all of that information may not be true.

The ease of posting information over the Internet allows the dissemination of rumors. This could be due to the lack of research undertaken by the sender of information, or it could be the purposeful sending of misinformation. It is vital for Internet users to learn to use a critical eye for information sent over the Internet.

Spam, Spam, Spam, Spam . . .
Internet spam received its name from a Monty Python ditty. The song refers to the canned ham product that was popular in England during World War II.

Spam   **Spam** is the practice of sending unwanted e-mail to a large number of

1-800-876-7060

"Consumer Protection in Electronic Commerce" Panel
at The Public Voice in the Development of Internet Policy Conference
of the Global Internet Liberty Campaign
by Phillip C. McKee, III
Internet Fraud Watch Coordinator

One hundred years ago next year, the National Consumers League was formed as America's first nonprofit consumer group. At that time, the League was at the forefront of the consumer movement battling overcrowded working conditions, unsanitary food handling procedures, and other market and workplace abuses. NCL is still leading the fight to protect the American consumer. One of the many threats facing consumers today is fraud. Criminals attempt to raid the pockets of consumers over the phone, through the mail, in person or over the Internet.

To fight this growing threat, the National Consumers League founded the National Fraud Information Center in 1992. NFIC was designed to fight telemarketing fraud through prevention and by improving the enforcement capabilities of federal and state agencies. We run a national 800# hotline where consumers can call to ask questions and report cases of fraud. That number is 1-800-876-7060. Consumers from all across the US and Canada now know to call NFIC before sending their money. We handle on average 350 calls a day at the NFIC phone center. Of these, approximately 35% are consumers who have already lost money to scam artists. But we can still help them. Our telephone counselors can assist English and Spanish speaking consumers by taking a full report of what happened, including all the information a law enforcement agency would need. This report is entered into our computer system and shared with the Federal Trade Commission. It is also faxed out on a real time basis to any of more than 160 law enforcement agencies whose interests match the report. NFIC works closely with authorities in both the US and Canada to ensure that all cases of fraud reported to us are referred to the appropriate agents.

In early 1996, the National Consumers League decided to expand its efforts to cover scams in cyberspace. Thus was born the NFIC website and the Internet Fraud Watch project. With the creation of www.fraud.org, consumers from all across the globe can get tips on how to avoid scams or can report fraud through our online forms 24 hours a day, 7 days a week. Fraud.org receives over 70,000 visits and over 1300 e-mails per week from consumers all across the globe. Internet Fraud Watch compliments the efforts of the National Fraud Information Center by performing the same prevention and reporting functions for Internet based fraud that NFIC does for telemarketing. IFW uses the same 800# and website as NFIC, allowing consumers and law enforcement one call or URL for all the information they need on telemarketing and Internet fraud.

And what are the most common frauds online?

Top Ten Subjects of Reports to Internet Fraud Watch for January - June 1998

1. Web Auctions - items bid for but never delivered by the sellers, value of items inflated, shills suspected of driving up bids;

2. General Merchandise - sales of everything from T-shirts to toys, calendars and collectibles, goods never delivered or not as advertised;

3. Internet Services - charges for services that were supposedly free, payment for online and Internet services that were never provided or falsely represented;

4. Hardware/Software - sales of computer products that were never delivered or misrepresented;

5. Pyramids/MLM's - schemes in which any profits were made from recruiting others, not from sales of goods or services to end-users;

6. Business Opportunities/Franchises - empty promises of big profits with little or no work by investing in pre-packaged businesses or franchise opportunities;

individuals.[41] This is usually direct solicitation but could include other types of e-mail. Unlike the sending of junk mail through the postal system, e-mail spammers do not need to purchase postage for every message sent and therefore can greatly increase the number of people they can reach. Unlike legitimate marketers who target messages and worry about hurting their image if their messages reach unintended audiences, spammers believe that the more e-mail sent, the better their chances.

E-mail would seem ideal for marketers. It is a very-low-cost medium, is easy to use, has a global reach to individuals who do not have World Wide Web access, and provides quick turnaround. Yet because e-mail is abused by spammers, legitimate marketers are hesitant to use e-mail because they do not want their image tarnished.[42] Some companies use e-mail to nudge past purchasers with targeted sales. Once a customer initiates a relationship with Amazon.com, Amazon.com uses e-mail to notify customers of related books, shipping dates, or other information its databases dictate as relevant. As much as 60 percent of Amazon's customers are repeat buyers.[43]

Spam is a problem for the Internet. It shifts the cost of mail from sender to the intermediaries and the receiver. The total amount of spam sent over the Internet is increasing. Some ISPs have had more than half their e-mail load accounted for by spam. When spam is sent to a business, the cost can be more than $100 per employee per year in wasted time. Although this may not seem high, with 5,000 employees, this could cost a business one half million dollars per year.[44]

Flaming is the process of sending angry e-mail messages, often characterized BY USING ALL CAPITAL LETTERS.

Some spammers forge the online identity of the sender. The spammer's e-mail is routed through a third-party server, changing the sending address. This can cause the recipients to flame the victimized sender; this **flaming** is also a violation of the server's trademark. Lawsuits have resulted in large judgments against spammers, forcing some to withdraw from spamming.[45] The state of Washington has enacted an antispam statute allowing individuals who receive spam to sue for monetary damages. Under this statute, a California marketer had to pay $200 to an individual after being threatened with a lawsuit.[46]

The Internet community has developed a number of software tools to control the receiving of spam. These tools filter incoming e-mail by domain names and by content such as "XXX" or "earn money fast." In 1999, 25 percent of spam e-mail was adult content–oriented, and 37 percent contained get-rich-quick proposals.[47] There are also organizations that are attempting to control spammers by setting up reporting agencies. The Mail Abuse Prevention System (MAPS) *(http://maps. vix.com)* project allows complaints to be registered. MAPS volunteers evaluate the questionable site; if the site does not agree to stop spamming, its IP address is placed into a Realtime Blackhole List (RBL). When a spam sender on the RBL attempts to send mail to a receiver who refers to the list, the spam is blocked.[48] If the Internet community does not take action to limit the sending of spam, governments might. At least three bills have been brought before the U.S. Congress, and more than 12 states have adopted or considered legislation designed to limit the sending of unsolicited e-mail.[49]

Self-regulation is when an industry imposes its own voluntary standard on members.

Internet Self-Regulation The Internet has operated under **self-regulation** for much of its short life. In the past few years, the government has attempted to implement control in certain areas, such as the use of privacy information related to children. In the United States, the basic view of government and the population at large is that the industry should regulate itself; if it does not, then the government should step in.[50]

ETHICAL ENVIRONMENT

An **ethical dilemma** exists when a proposed action benefits an individual, business, or society but at the same time has negative consequences for others.

Ethics is the study of how individuals or businesses make decisions given the consequences of those decisions. It helps to answer the questions, What should I do? and What should my business do? When contemplating ethical considerations, an individual or business must ask, What will be the consequences of my actions? Often an **ethical dilemma** may arise. This is when conflicting concerns may surface, i.e.: the action undertaken may increase the overall returns to a business but hurt some other constituency in the process.

Many businesses realize the benefits of being ethical. Individuals want to be employed with and customers prefer to buy from companies that uphold ethical standards. Chief ethics officers for Sears must develop policies that balance the needs of three main constituencies: customers, employees, and shareholders. To achieve this, Sears developed a 15-page code of conduct guide. It also has a telephone hotline employees can use to call and receive help when faced with ethical dilemmas. Other companies, such as Columbia/HCA and United Technologies, put similar programs in place.[51]

Business decisions typically impact a number of ethical concerns across a spectrum of constituencies. Ethical concerns related to property rights, honesty and deception, and the use of technology (Netiquette) were discussed in the first section of this chapter. This section of the chapter will cover the topics of privacy, economic welfare, and access and equity. It is important that e-business decision makers understand each of these areas of concern and are able to articulate the pros and cons of individual and business actions as well as the possible outcomes of those actions. This process can aid in the development of corporate policies.[52]

Privacy

The right to privacy has become a central issue in e-business. E-businesses see benefits in using information on individuals to enhance the marketing process. Individuals, on the other hand, want control over their private information. Polls by Forrester Research and *Business Week*/Harris have indicated that as many as 78 percent of individuals would use the Web more if their privacy was protected, and close to 50 percent indicate that the government should pass laws protecting privacy.[53] A major concern for U.S. citizens is not the collection of data but what that data will be used for. U.S. consumers are willing to provide data for customizable services and other uses for which they see benefits.[54]

On October 24, 1998, the European Union initiated a regulation that stipulated that data on EU citizens cannot be sent to countries that do not provide the same level of protection as do EU member countries. U.S. privacy laws do not meet these criteria; therefore, data can only be transferred when that individual agrees to have the information sent or when an approved contract exists.[55]

Web sites collect data in two ways: voluntarily and involuntarily. When an individual voluntarily gives information to a site for a specific purpose, there may not be a privacy issue, but when that information is used for other purposes, privacy concerns are raised. Data can also be collected on an involuntary basis. For example, newsgroups' or discussion groups' postings can be combed to find information. When individuals log on to sites, they may fill in forms providing personal and demographic data. Cookies on browsers can provide information on an individual's surfing behavior. In most cases, the cookie only identifies the computer, not the user, unless the individual has registered from that computer to a Web site.[56]

Current technologies' ability to easily collect and track individual profile data and behaviors is bringing privacy concerns to the forefront of ethical concerns.

Home: Help: Topics: Snap Privacy Policy

- Snap's Privacy Philosophy
- Information that Snap Gathers
- How Snap Uses Information
- Snap Content Providers, Advertisers and Partners
- Kids and Privacy
- Changes to Policy
- Opt-Out Policy
- Correct/Update Policy
- Delete/Deactivate Policy

Help Topics ◔

Snap is TRUSTe Certified

This Overall Privacy Statement verifies that Snap is a member of the TRUSTe Program and is in compliance with the TRUSTe privacy principles. This statement discloses the privacy practices for the entire Web Site.

About TRUSTe
When you visit a Web site displaying the TRUSTe trustmark, you can expect to be notified of what personally identifiable information of yours is collected; the organization collecting the information; how the information is used, with whom the information may be shared; what choices are available to you regarding collection, use and distribution of the information; the kind of security procedures that are in place to protect the loss, misuse or alteration of information under Snap's control; and how you can correct any inaccuracies in the information.

Questions regarding this statement should be directed to Snap support services by e-mail at support@snap.com or by mail at One Beach St., San Francisco, CA 94133. If the Web site has not responded to your inquiry within five business days or your inquiry has not been satisfactorily addressed please contact TRUSTe (http://www.truste.org/users/watchdog.html). To return to the site, please use the "Back" button on your browser.

Snap's Privacy Philosophy

Your privacy on the Internet is important to us. Because we gather certain types of information about Snap users, we want you to understand the terms and conditions surrounding the capture and use of that information. This privacy statement discloses what information we gather, how we use it, and how t correct or change it.

Information that Snap Gathers

Snap gathers two types of information about users:

1) Personal data, provided through voluntary registration.
2) Aggregated data, which tracks users as a whole.

Personal data may be requested when you sign up for Snap's personalized services or register for contests, sweepstakes or other promotional programs offered on our service. We ask for this in order to provide you with the best Web experience possible. This information might include member name, password, age, gender, ZIP code and/or country information. Except as described below, it is not disclosed to parties other than Snap and its parent companies in any way that personally identifies you

Snap's search engine posts its privacy policy.   Source: www.truste.org.

The ability to acquire personal information and the use of databases give companies a powerful tool to target promotions and develop products. Laws vary from country to country on who controls personal information. In the United States, when an adult engages in a transaction with a business, in most cases that business is free to use the information, sell it, or pass it on to others. In other countries, data pertaining to an individual is owned by that individual and can only be released by consent.

The Federal Trade Commission (FTC) has intervened in e-business by issuing policies that require online businesses that ask for data to post a privacy policy outlining how the information will be used. If the company then uses that data in ways other than are indicated in the policy, it can be sued for damages.

In the United States, the Children's Advertising Review Unit (CARU) and the Federal Trade Commission have made recommendations and regulations to govern the collection and use of children's private information. CARU's Web site

Table 10.5 Recommendations on Developing Privacy Policies

Adopt and Implement a Privacy Policy Including	Description
Notice and disclosure	Explain to the public the company's policy on personal information. For children's sites, this should be directed toward parents and disclose: 1. Who is collecting the data. 2. What information is to be collected. 3. How this data will be disclosed to any third parties (for children's sites, the parents' permission must be obtained). 4. How the user can control the use of that information. 5. Whether they are links to other Web sites that do not comply with FTC's or CARU's guidelines.
Choice and consent	Ask permission to compile information: 1. When the information will be used for other than the original purpose, individuals should be allowed to opt out. 2. Consent should be obtained before sending the information to a third party. 3. Ask permission before sending targeted e-mail.
Data security	Organizations need to take measures to: 1. Ensure that data is accurate. 2. Prevent loss, misuse, or alteration of data. 3. Be sure data is transferred to third parties who will also take appropriate precautions.
Data quality and access	Organizations should: 1. Ensure that the data is accurate, complete, and timely. 2. Set up procedures to allow data to be corrected.

Sources: For more information, see: "Privacy Policy Guidelines," *Online Privacy Guidelines,* December 10, 1998, <*http://www.privacyalliance. com/resources/enforcement.shtml>*; Gregory Dalton, "Pressure for Better Privacy," *Information Week,* June 22, 1998, pp. 36–38; Linda A. Goldstein, "Child Care," *CIO Web Business—Section 2*, June 1, 1998, pp. 32–34; and Hanna Hurley, "Online Privacy Policies: Be Aware," *Network Magazine,* November 1998, pp. 72–76.

(http://www.bbb.org/advertising/caruguid.html) offers extensive advice on children's privacy issues.

The Internet industry is aware that if it does not regulate itself, it may face regulation from the federal government. In a 1998 survey, the FTC found that close to 90 percent of 1,400 commercial Web sites collected personal information, but only 14 percent of commercial Web sites disclosed their privacy policies, and only 2 percent offered a comprehensive privacy policy.[57] IBM has threatened to withhold advertising from sites that do not post privacy policies.[58] Industry groups have organized to develop policies. One group, the Online Privacy Alliance

E-mail can be monitored and stored. This has allowed e-mail messages to be used in numerous lawsuits as representing internal memos.

(www.privacyalliance.com), has brought together businesses and associations to help businesses create an environment of trust by fostering the protection of individual privacy rights. Their guidelines are summarized in Table 10.5, on the previous page.

Employee Privacy

The privacy rights that an individual may enjoy in the public domain do not necessarily apply when that individual is employed at a job. The Electronic Communications Privacy Act gave U.S. employers the right to monitor and control what employees do with private property such as computers and telephones. An employee's Web surfing and e-mail can be monitored by a business. Businesses should post a policy of this practice to avoid possible liability.

Employees have been known to use organizational resources for other than business purposes. Compaq Computer dismissed 20 employees who logged on to sexually explicit sites more than 1,000 times. Salomon Smith Barney dismissed two top executives who downloaded pornographic images and sent them to others in their office. Smut surfing not only uses resources of a business for nonbusiness purposes, it could also put the business in jeopardy for sexual harassment lawsuits.[59]

Companies have options other than just posting notices of proper surfing. Monitoring and filtering software can be used to track and block Web users in a business. A business must balance its desire to conserve resources with its need to treat employees as adults and with its need to have employees learn to use the Internet as an information-gathering tool. While employees may be cyberloitering or surfing the Net without a specific business purpose, they may also be gathering information on competitors, site designs, or other information that has practical use for a business.[60]

ECONOMIC WELFARE

Is society better off with an interconnected world? This is an economic welfare question. Although some may argue that there are problems with the Internet's ability to foster fraud, theft, pornography, invasion of privacy, or other ills, there are also social benefits. Benefits to both businesses and individuals have been outlined throughout this text, but perhaps the greatest social benefit is the Internet's ability to act as a free speech venue. This section will investigate two major issues related to the economic welfare aspects of the Internet: pornography and freedom of speech.

Pornography. On September 11, 1998, 22.4 million users accessed the Starr Report on the Internet. The Starr Report included descriptive information on sexual behavior, something that may have received an X rating at other sites. Yet because this information was considered to be of social value, it was freely available on the Internet. This problem of social value versus prurient interest is an ethical dilemma.

Many sites on the Internet are considered to contain **pornography.** This is a concern for many individuals, families, and civil libertarians. The Communications Decency Act made it illegal to knowingly transmit electronically to a minor under the age of 18 any comment, request, suggestion, proposal, image, or other communication that is obscene or indecent. The fines were to be $200,000 with jail terms of two years for violators. Within hours of the bill being signed, the American Civil Liberties Union and 16 other organizations filed a lawsuit to fight the bill. A three-judge panel struck down the bill as unconstitutionally vague. The U.S. government's attempt to censor the flow of information over the Internet ran head-on into the First Amendment of the U.S. Constitution. It also had a practical problem as well: It would have been very difficult to enforce across national boundaries. A number of countries have shifted the burden of censoring the Internet to the local ISPs. Even in the United States, two ISPs have had their news servers seized by state police because hosted news groups were sending pictures of child pornography.[61] This shifts the burden of information access from the individual or family to a third party. **Filters** can be used on a PC or server to block access to sites considered to be pornographic. One type of filtering software uses a database of sites considered to be unacceptable; these could be sites considered to be pornographic or sites deemed by a parent or business to be off-limits. Other software filters use rating systems to allow acceptable pages to pass through. This can be a problem because only a small percentage of all Web pages have been rated.[62]

Pornography exists online when material depicts erotic behavior intended to cause sexual excitement.

A software filter blocks unwanted material, such as pornography, from being downloaded from the Internet.

Free Speech. There is a fundamental shift in power that occurs due to the use of the Internet. Large media companies no longer control widely broadcast public speech. Small independent communications systems can grow online. Two online magazines have had considerable impact on the larger media environment. *Slate (www.slate.com),* part of Microsoft's network, has broken news stories. The *Drudge Report (www.drudgereport.com)* also broke news stories that the larger media would not report, including the Clinton/Monica affair. The Internet allows online news to be reported very quickly, but these sources do not have the editorial control of larger media outlets. It is important that consumers of Internet information learn **Net literacy** or how to evaluate information that they find online.[63] A survey of 2,000 users indicated that 80 percent viewed online news sources as trustworthy as other media sources, and 7 percent saw them as even more believable.[64] A review by *Brill's Content* of the *Drudge Report* indicated that of 51 stories claimed as exclusive by the *Drudge Report*, 32 percent of the stories were untrue and/or never happened, 36 percent were true, and 32 percent were debatable or unverifiable.[65]

Rogue sites allow individuals to express their feelings about companies, products, or organizations. Rogue sites have targeted Wal-Mart, America Online, Kmart, Packard Bell, Chase Bank, and many others.[66] The information on these sites could be factual or fiction. There is no overreaching monitor of truth on the Internet. This leaves it up to individual companies to take action. Itex Corporation

NSITES

The FTC does act as an **overreaching monitor,** or controlling body, of Web advertising. Truth-in-advertising laws apply to Web sites just as they apply to any other promotional medium.

(www.itex.com), an online trading company, filed suit against 100 "John Does" who made defamatory statements about Itex on one of Yahoo!'s message boards. The John Does were used because Itex couldn't identify the individuals who made the comments.[67]

In the United States, the First Amendment to the Constitution guarantees freedom of speech. The **free speech** right is seen as fundamental and protects most forms of expression. This can lead to ethical dilemmas. Regulations against pornography are sometimes seen as encroaching on free speech rights. In the United States, libraries often provide Internet access. A Virginia library attempted to limit its patrons' access to certain sites. The U.S. District Court ruled that libraries do not need to provide Internet access, but if they do, they must not censure what adults may view.[68] Pornography can flow across borders and violate laws in other countries. China attempted to control the flow of information to its citizens by having all Internet access traveling through one gateway. The Chinese system was designed to operate like America Online, with the power to control access to content, both pornographic and political.[69]

For some individuals, the Web is a free speech forum for political information. Political elections around the world have demonstrated that candidates are able to use the Internet to spread information at a fairly low cost. Political thoughts can also travel across borders, allowing dissidents, human rights advocates, and alternative political parties to provide information to those who gain access to the Web. China has regulations that prohibit its citizens from using the Internet to defame the government, promote separatist movements, or divulge state secrets. Taiwanese citizens are free to develop Web pages that criticize China, but this cyberactivism may not get through China's filters.[70]

Access and Equity

Computers are the main interface to the Internet, but access will remain limited. Those who have higher incomes will be able to afford computers and line connection fees. This inequity can result in an ethical dilemma, with disparity between the information rich and the information poor. Lower computer prices and Web-based television may mitigate this problem somewhat but will not eliminate it.

Disparity of access exists along racial lines. White households have greater access to phone service (96 percent for whites and 86 percent for nonwhites) and have a 21 percent higher PC ownership than nonwhites. Grade-school whites may be up to three times more likely to have Internet access at home than minority students.[71] More disparity exists between those with higher incomes using the Internet more often. The greatest disparity, however, is age-based. Only 5 percent of Americans between the ages of 55 and 64 have online services; for those over age 65, less than 3 percent have access.[72]

The U.S. federal government has attempted to address this problem by implementing the E-rate program. This was part of the 1996 Telecommunications Act and was designed to provide funding for universal service for schools and libraries. The E-rate program provides a lower educational rate and is funded by an additional charge to telephone long-distance services.[73]

KNOWLEDGE INTEGRATION

T E R M S   A N D   C O N C E P T S

Case law *285*

Constituencies *284*

Copyright *290*

Cybercrime *286*

Economic espionage *287*

Economic welfare *283*

Ethical dilemma *298*

Ethical hackers *287*

Ethics *298*

Filters *303*

Flaming *298*

Fraud *288*

Free speech *304*

Hacker 286

Infrastructure attack *287*

Intellectual capital *289*

    National Telecommunications and Information Administration (NTIA) *284*

Net literacy *303*

Netiquette *296*

Next-Generation Internet (NGI) *284*

Patent *293*

Pornography *303*

Pump-and-dump *288*

Scam *288*

Self-regulation *298*

Shill *287*

Software patent *293*

Spam *296*

Trade secret *292*

Trademark *291*

C O N C E P T S   A N D   Q U E S T I O N S   F O R   R E V I E W

1. Explain the role that governments play in e-business.
2. Describe the role of the NTIA in the United States.
3. List and explain the laws in the United States that have been passed to regulate the Internet.
4. Define the major types of hacking and why these are a problem.
5. Describe the major types of scams on the Internet and the actions being taken to limit fraud.
6. Define each of the major types of intellectual property.
7. Explain how copyright laws affect the creation of Web pages.
8. Explain how trademark laws affect the creation of Web pages.
9. Describe the software solutions that are being used to protect intellectual property.
10. Explain the impact of patent laws on e-business.
11. Define Netiquette and list the rules of behavior.
12. Define spam and how it affects the Internet and its users.
13. List the ethical considerations that apply to cyberspace.
14. Compare and contrast the concerns related to privacy and the Internet.
15. Explain how the Internet plays a role in maintaining free speech.

ACTIVE   LEARNING

Exercise 10.1: Ethical Analysis

Use the following table to evaluate the ethical implications of e-business practices. List both advantages and disadvantages in each cell. Identify the ethical dilemmas that can surface when the advantages in some cells conflict with the disadvantages in others.[74]

Constituencies	Privacy	Access & Equity	Social Welfare
Customers			
Employees			
Stakeholders (owners)			
Community			

Exercise 10.2: Web Site Analysis

1. Visit a Web site and identify all the components that have some legal aspect. For example, are there links to other sites? Are there images that may be copyrighted? Does the site use trade names? Does the site collect information on individuals?
2. Visit a Web site that has a terms-of-use section. Explain how these statements protect the Web site.

Exercise 10.3: Privacy Policies

Visit a Web site with a privacy statement. Determine if the policy complies with the suggestions outlined in the table that follows (taken from Table 10.5).

Privacy Policy Analysis

Policy	How Site Complies
1. Who is collecting the data.	
2. What information is to be collected.	
3. How this data will be disclosed to any third parties (for children's sites, the parents' permission must be obtained).	
4. How the user can control the use of that information.	
5. Whether there are links to other Web sites that do not comply with FTC's or CARU's guidelines.	
6. When the information will be used for other than the original purpose, individuals should be allowed to opt out.	
7. Consent should be obtained before sending the information to a third party.	
8. Ask permission before sending targeted e-mail.	
9. Prevent loss, misuse, or alteration of data.	
10. Be sure data is transferred to third parties who will also take appropriate precautions.	
11. Ensure that the data is accurate, complete, and timely.	
12. Set up procedures to allow data to be corrected.	

WEB SEARCH —
LOOKING ONLINE

Americans for Computer Privacy. Is an online organization that is trying to keep privacy a huge issue in the world today.
www.computerprivacy.org

Cyberlaw. Has articles pertaining to legal matters.
www.cyberlaw.com

Cyberspace Law Center. Has articles and searchable database on legal topics, including citations for legal cases.
http://cyber.findlaw.com/

Legalethics.com. Is a site for legal professionals to help them understand the unique ethical issues related to the Internet and Internet technology.
www.legalethics.com

NewLaw Web site. Offers information to Web site builders on U.S. laws and U.K. laws.
www.netlaw.com

United States Department of Justice's Web. Has information on cybercrimes related to computer crimes and intellectual property.
www.usdoj.gov/criminal/cybercrime/index.html#nifpa

U.S. Government Copyright Office. Provides extensive links to advice on copyright information.
lcweb.loc.gov/copyright

U.S. Patent and Trademark Office. Provides information pertaining to trademarks and patents and includes a patent search system.
www.uspto.gov

Better Business Bureau Online. Provides advice to online shoppers, information on companies, and a reliability seal for businesses that adhere to the BBB guidelines.
www.bbbonline.org

Consumer World. Is a noncommercial site that has collected and categorized over 1,700 consumer resources on the Internet, from buying advice and product reviews to comparison shopping. It also allows the filing of consumer complaints and provides news of the latest scams.

www.consumerworld.com

National Consumers League. Reports on the most common fraudulent acts for online and offline commerce.

www.fraud.org/internet/intstat.htm

PublicEye. Is a testing, certifying, and Internet business monitoring site. It gives a reliability seal to participating businesses.

www.thepubliceye.com

SEARCH TERM:	Internet Self-Regulation	First 5 out of 253,020

Direct Marketing Association. Provides information on direct-marketing issues and privacy issues.

www.the-dma.org

Netiquette Home Page. Provides information on network and Internet etiquette.

www.albion.com/netiquette/index.html

Network Abuse Clearinghouse. Helps the Internet community report network abuse and abusive users.

www.abuse.net

RFC 1855 Netiquette Guidelines. Contains a memo from Sally Hambridge of Intel Corporation outlining the basic rules of Netiquette.

www.dtcc.edu/cs/rfc1855.html

TRUSTe. Is an independent, nonprofit privacy initiative. It has a protection seal program designed to alleviate users' concerns about online privacy to build users' trust and confidence for the Internet industry.

www.truste.org

SEARCH TERM:	Web Site Evaluation	First 3 out of 28,523

The Recreational Software Advisory Council. Provides a rating service for evaluating Web pages and lists its rating system.

www.rsac.org

zSafeSurf. Provides a rating service for evaluating Web pages and lists its rating system.
www.safesurf.com

World Wide Web Consortium. Is a platform for Internet Content Selection (PICS) standard and allows ratings to be placed in the meta tag of a Web page. These are read by filtering software.
www.w3.org/PICS

R E F E R E N C E S

1 Jennifer Tanaka and Beth Kwon, "Risky Business," *Newsweek,* December 21, 1998, pp. 72–74.

2 Whit Andrews, "Auction Sites Seek Ways to Build Trust Between Buyers, Sellers," *Internet World,* October 5, 1998, p. 24.

3 Mathew Nelson, "Going Once, Going Twice . . . " *InfoWorld,* November 9, 1998, pp. 1, 64–65.

4 Anne Stuart, "Uncle Sam Wants You," *CIO Web Business—Section 2,* April 1, 1998, pp. 36–41.

5 Scott Berinato, "The Net's Next Frontiers," *PC Week,* March 2, 1998, p. 21.

6 Jeffrey D. Neuburger and Jill Westmoreland, "Legal Link," *Silicon Alley Report,* September 1998, pp. 76–78.

7 Anne Stuart, "Uncle Sam Wants You," *CIO Web Business—Section 2,* April 1, 1998, pp. 36–41.

8 Steven Baker, Joan Warner, and Heidi Dawley, "Finally, Europeans Are Storming the Net," *Business Week,* May 11, 1998, pp. 48–49; and Curt Harler, "Picking Apart Europe in Age of Deregulation," *Inter@ctive Week,* November 30, 1998, p. 19.

9 Christopher Kock, "It's a Wired Wired World," *Webmaster,* March 1997, pp. 50–55.

10 Rutrell Yasin, "Hackers: Users, Feds Vulnerable," *Internet Week,* May 25, 1998, pp. 1, 49.

11 Tim Wilson, "Profits Embolden Hackers," *Internet Week,* March 23, 1998, pp. 1, 10–12.

12 The following information is compiled from: Richard Power and Rik Farrow, "Crime and Punishment in Cyberspace," *Network Magazine,* November 1998, pp. 84–85.

13 Will Rodger, "Cyberwar: Proper Vigilance or Paranoia?" *Inter@ctive Week,* October 5, 1998, pp. 54–56; and Tom Field, "Sweat About the Threat," *CIO—Section 1,* December 1, 1998, pp. 34–43.

14 Ann Harrison, "Arrest Made in Net Stock Fraud Case," *Computer World,* April 19, 1999, p. 12.

15 Geoffrey James, "Stock Scams and Spams on the Internet," *Upside,* November 1998, pp. 77–86.

16 Kathleen Murphy, "Fraud Follows Buyers onto Web," *Web Week,* October 20, 1997, pp. 15, 19; and David Zgodzinski, "Buyer Beware," *Internet World,* March 1997, pp. 42–46.

17 Steven Levy, "Biting Back at the Wily Melissa," *Newsweek,* April 12, 1999, pp. 62–64.

18 Derek Slater, "Storing the Mind, Minding the Store," *CIO Web Business—Section 2,* February 15, 1998, pp. 46–51.

19 *Copyright Basics,* U.S. Copyright Office, September 1, 1998, <*http://lcweb.loc.gov/copyright/circs/circ1.html#cr*>.

[20] Kathleen Murphy, "Roving Robot Will Unmask Online Music Pirates," *Web Week,* October 20, 1997, p. 7.

[21] Joseph C. Panettieri, "The Software Mobsters," *Sm@rt Reseller,* September 6, 1999, pp. 38–42; and "The World's Top Pirates," *Business Week,* June 5, 1995, p. 4.

[22] James Evans, "Copyright Protection at a Discount," *Internet World,* July 1997, pp. 38–39; and *The Copyright Archive,* December 1, 1998, *<http://www.copyrightarchive.com>.*

[23] James Evans, "Whose Web Site Is It Anyway?" *Internet World,* September 1997, pp. 46–50.

[24] Elizabeth Gardner, "Trademark Battles Simmer Behind Sites," *Web Week,* August 25, 1997, pp. 1, 45; and John Fontana, "Trademark Trickery," *Internet Week,* September 29, 1997, pp. 1, 124.

[25] Eileen Glanton, "Firms Claim Search Engines Abuse Their Names," *Marketing News,* March 15, 1999, vol. 33, no. 6, p. 16.

[26] Paul C. Judge, "From the Patent Wars, a Patent Medicine," *Business Week,* May 25, 1998, p. 111.

[27] James Heckman, "Marketers Can Say 'Mine!' " *Marketing News,* February 15, 1999, vol. 33, no. 4, pp. 1–2; and Bradley C. Wright and Gregory J. Carlin, "Patenting Methods of Doing Business," *Knowledge Management World,* March 1999, pp. 42–43.

[28] Mel Duvall, "Patents Hook Start-Ups," *Inter@ctive Week,* August 16, 1999, pp. 72–74; Brett N. Dorny, "Stop, Pay Toll," *CIO Web Business—Section 2,* November 1, 1998, pp. 64–66; and Becky Waring, "Patently Obvious," *NewMedia,* October 1998, p. 6.

[29] This information is compiled from: Maxine Lans Retsky, "On-Line Work Needs Copyright Protection, Too," *Marketing News,* December 7, 1998, vol. 32, no. 25, p. 21; and Sara Shay, "Stealing Beauty," *CIO Web Business—Section 2,* September 1, 1998, pp. 22–25.

[30] Edward C. Baig, Tracey Aubin, and Amy Borrus, "Outlaw Online Betting? Don't Bet on It," *Business Week,* December 15, 1997, p. 44; and Steward Taggart, "Aussies Jump for Net Gambling," *Business 2.0,* January 1999, p. 26.

[31] Patrick Thibodeau, "Europe Wants U.S. Firms to Pay E-Commerce Taxes," *Computerworld,* August 30, 1999, p. 41.

[32] Mary Hillebrand and Paul A. Greenberg, "Clinton Directs Government to Evaluate E-Commerce Laws," *E-Commerce Times,* November 30, 1999, *<http://www.ecommercetimes.com/news/articles/991130-3.shtml>.*

[33] Paul A. Greenberg, "Europe Struggles to Standardize E-Commerce Laws," *E-Commerce Times,* November 1, 1999, *<http://www.ecommercetimes.com/news/articles/991101-2.shtml>.*

[34] "Business: The Economy EU Threat to E-Commerce," *BBC Online Network,* November 4, 1999, *<http://news.bbc.co.uk/hi/english/business/the_economy/newsid_505000/505237.stm>.*

[35] For more information, see: Catherine Yang, "Flamed with a Lawsuit," *Business Week,* February 6, 1995, p. 75; and Catherine Yang, "Law Creeps onto the Lawless Net," *Business Week,* May 6, 1996, pp. 58–60.

[36] Faiza S. Ambah, "An Intruder in the Kingdom," *Business Week,* August 21, 1995, p. 40.

[37] Ellen Messmer, "It's E-Comm vs. the Law," *Network World,* October 12, 1998, p. 39.

[38] Netiquette Home Page, *Netiquette,* December 8, 1998, *<http://www.albion.com/netiquette/index.html>.*

[39] Adapted from: Sally Hambridge, "RFC 1855 Netiquette Guidelines," October 24, 1995, *www.dtcc.edu/cs/rfc1855.html*; and Netiquette Home Page, *Netiquette,* December 8, 1998, *<http://www.albion.com/netiquette/index.html>.*

[40] "Stop the Presses! Microsoft Has NOT Bought the Vatican," *Open Systems Today,* January 9, 1995, p. 54.

[41] "Spam Spam Spam . . ." *Newsweek,* March 30, 1998, p. 10.

42 Al Bredenberg, "Online Marketing—Hold the Spam," *Sales & Field Force Automation,* May 1998, pp. 116–120.

43 Nicole Harris and Rob Hoff, "Spam That You Might Not Delete," *Business Week,* June 15, 1998, pp. 115–118.

44 Kimberly Patch and Eric Smalley, "E-Mail Overload," *Network World,* October 26, 1998, pp. 1, 45–48.

45 Anna Maria Virzi, "Spammer Must Pay Hosting Company $173,000 After Sending E-Mail Ads," *Internet World,* April 20, 1998, p. 8.

46 Jeffrey D. Neuburger and Jill Westmoreland, "Legal Link" *Silicon Alley Report,* September 1998, pp. 76–78.

47 "How Much Spam Can You Stand?" *Newsweek,* June 21, 1999, p. 16; and Lee Chae, "Tools That Help You Can Spam," *Network Magazine,* November 1998, pp. 68–71.

48 Todd Spangler, "Anti-Spam Crew Carries Big Stick," *Inter@ctive Week,* November 16, 1998, p. 40.

49 Suzanne A. Smith and Emily Woodson Davis, "Is Spam Edible?" *CIO Web Business—Section 2,* December 1, 1998, pp. 32–36.

50 For more discussion on this topic, see: Robert Ellis Smith and H. Robert Wientzen, "Privacy Sound Off: Regulation vs. Self-Regulation," *Internet Week,* September 21, 1998, pp. 35–40.

51 Jennifer Bresnahan, "For Goodness Sake," *CIO Enterprise—Section 2,* June 15, 1999, pp. 54–62.

52 For more on teaching ethics and ethical frameworks, see: James Linderman, "Top Management's Role in Business Ethics," *Beyond Computing,* May 1999, pp. 16–17; and Chuck Huff and C. Dianne Martin, "Computing Consequences: A Framework for Teaching Ethical Computing," *Communications of the ACM,* vol. 38, no. 12, December 1995, pp. 75–84.

53 "Forrester Technographics® Finds Online Consumers Fearful of Privacy Violations," *Forrester,* October 27, 1999, <http://www.forrester.com/ER/Press/Release/0,1769,177,FF.html>; and Heather Green, Catherine Yang, and Paul C. Judge, "A Little Privacy Please," *Business Week,* March 16, 1998, pp. 98–102.

54 Brett Mendel, "Online i.d.entity Crisis," *InfoWorld,* October 18, 1999, pp. 36–37; Kenneth Neil Cukier, "Is There a Privacy Time Bomb?" *Red Herring,* September 1999, pp. 90–98; Edward C. Baig, Marcia Stepanek, and Neil Gross, "Privacy," *Business Week,* April 5, 1999, pp. 84–90; and Nate Zelnick, "Is IT Privacy That Users Want, or Does Everyone Have a Price?" *Internet World,* March 15, 1999, pp. 1, 45.

55 Gregory Dalton, "Privacy Law Worries U.S. Businesses," *Information Week,* October 26, 1998, p. 26; and Peter P. Swire, "The Great Wall of Europe," *CIO Enterprise—Section 2,* February 15, 1998, pp. 26–30.

56 Bill Mann, "Stopping You Watching Me," *Internet World,* April 1997, pp. 42–46.

57 Jim Kerstetter, "'Fessing Up to Data Deeds," *PC Week,* July 13, 1998, pp. 1, 14.

58 Nelson Wang, "IBM to Spurn Sites That Lack Privacy Policies," *Internet World,* pp. 17, 25.

59 Tom Field, "Web Cops," *CIO—Section 1,* November 15, 1997, pp. 51–58; and Art Jahnke, "Unsafe Sex," *CIO Web Business—Section 2,* June 1, 1998, p. 18.

60 Kathryn F. Munro, "Hands Off," *Small Business Computing & Communication,* June 1999, pp. 82–84; Peter Cassidy, "Beaching Surfers," *CIO Web Business—Section 2,* February 1, 1999; and Charles Waltner, "Web Watchers," *Information Week,* April 27, 1998, pp. 121–126.

61 Randy Barrett, "Porn Raid Leaves ISPs in Bind," *Inter@ctive Week,* November 9, 1998, p. 38.

[62] For more information, see: Kevin Reichard, "Is Your Web Site PG—or X?" *Internet World,* November 1997, pp. 108–110; and Gus Venditto, "Safe Computing," *Internet World,* September 1996, pp. 48–58.

[63] For more on this topic, see: Esther Dyson, "The End of the Official Story," *Brill's Content,* July/August 1998, pp. 50–51.

[64] Eileen Colkin, "If It's Online, Then It Must Be True, Right?" *Information Week,* November 30, 1998, p. 14.

[65] For more information on these sites, see: D.M. Osborne, "Ahead of the News," *Brill's Content,* September 1998, pp. 52–56; and David McClintick, "Towncrier for the New Age," *Brill's Content,* November 1998, pp. 112–127.

[66] Mike France and Joann Muller, "A Site for Soreheads," *Business Week,* April 12, 1999, pp. 86–90; and Charles Bermant, "Pest Control," *Business 2.0,* January 1999, pp. 24–25.

[67] Robert Hertzberg, "The Limits of Free Speech," *Internet World,* September 21, 1998, p. 10.

[68] Todd Spangler, "Court Rules Against Library Filters," *Inter@ctive Week,* December 7, 1998, p. 58.

[69] Amy Cortese, John Carey, and David Woodruff, "Alt.Sex.Bondage Is Closed. Should We Be Scared?" *Business Week,* January 15, 1996, p. 39; and Kathleen Murphy and Ellis Booker, "China Builds an Internet, But Limits the Access," *Web Week,* February 3, 1997, pp. 40–43.

[70] John Dodge, "The Internet Is on a Slow Boat to China," *PC Week,* May 10, 1999, p. 3; and Joyce Barnathan and Margaret Dawson, "The Taiwanese Fight Fire with Wire," *Business Week,* April 1, 1996, p. 48.

[71] Victor Rivero, "William E. Kennard: Bridging the Digital Divide," *Converge,* January 1999, pp. 54–55.

[72] Christopher Harper, "The Haves and Have Nots, Some Surprising Cyber Demographics," *Editor and Publisher Interactive,* May 16, 1997, <*http://www.mediainfor.com/ephome/news/newshtm/recent/051697/n2.htm*>.

[73] For more information on this topic, see: Federal Communications Commission, "Welcome to LearnNet," November 19, 1998, <*http://www.fcc.gov/learnet/*>; and E-rate Hotline, "Welcome to the E-rate Hotline," January 13, 1999, <*http:www.eratehotline.org/*>.

[74] For a more in-depth look at ethical analysis, see: Chuck Huff and C. Dianne Martin, "Computing Consequences: A Framework for Teaching Ethical Computing," *Communications of the ACM,* vol. 38, no. 12, December 1995, pp. 75–84.

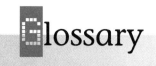lossary

© is the symbol used to indicate a registered copyright.

® is the symbol used to indicate a registered trademark; otherwise, notice is given as: Dr. Brad Kleindl(TM).

24/7/52 or 24/7 indicates that the business is open 24 hours a day, 7 days a week, 52 weeks a year.

A

Acquisition exists when one corporation purchases all or a controlling part of another company.

AIDA process indicates that the audience's attention must first be gained, interest created in the product or service, desire generated, and finally some action taken by the targeted audience.

Alliances are formal or informal relationships between independent companies that work together for a common purpose.

B

Bandwidth indicates the amount of digital information that can be carried over a line. The basic rule in developing multimedia (combined text, images, sound) is that the richer the media, the larger the file, and therefore the higher the bandwidth needed to deliver the content in a given amount of time.

Banner ads a common way to advertise on an internet site.

Brick and mortar refers to tangible physical assets such as a factory, office building, or warehouse.

Brochure sites are designed to make visitors aware of and informed about a business's image or products.

Browser is the interface between the Web content and the user.

Business model (or commerce model) is the basic process flow indicating how a business operates. It shows how business functions are linked together.

C

Case law is based on English common law. Case law is used in the United States to determine how laws should apply to specific situations.

Channel conflict exists when a company sells products to the same market through more than one distribution system.

Chat involves a number of individuals who send messages over the Internet into a repository or chat room for viewing in real time or "live" or chats can be viewed at a later time.

Click-through is having an individual click on a linked banner to link to other sites.

Collaborative software (or groupware) permits individuals to use e-mail and message lists, share files, or open file archives. The goal is to have individuals collaborating on projects.

Commerce (or business) model is the basic process by which a business obtains its inventory, produces its good or service, and delivers to its customer.

Commerce service providers are companies that facilitate commerce for other businesses.

Company image is how a company's is viewed by the public.

Comparison standard is a standard the customer uses to judge a product. For example, if a customer had first gained online search experience using Yahoo!, he or she will evaluate all other search engines against Yahoo!

Competitive arena is the competitive environment in which a business competes.

Competitive intelligence is gathered using a continuous process involving the legal and ethical collection of information and the monitoring of the competitive environment, giving managers the ability to make strategic decisions.

Computer network consists of a number of computers linked through a network server. The server controls the flow of information between the users.

Constituencies are those people who are involved with or served by an organization. Internet constituencies include governments, businesses, customers, ISPs, schools, families, children, or just about anyone impacted by changes in telecommunications.

Cookie is a small bit of code left on a user's computer that is used by an e-business's database to look up information. This code retrieves information such as past actions, search interests, or past purchases, which can be used to personalize the site.

Customer relationship management systems combine software and management practices to serve the customer from order through delivery and after-sales service.

Cybermediaries are organizations that operate in electronic markets to facilitate the exchange process.

D

Data are raw facts.

Data marts are small databases that serve a specific purpose in a firm. Metawarehouses are very large databases that centralize all data. Data marts can be linked together in a network to share information.

Data mining is the process of using software to "drill" into a database to obtain meaningful information.

Database a compilation of information.

Daughter window pop up and freely float to display ad content

Destination site is a Web site that is designed to have the visitor return over and over. This requires including extras, such as games, chats, contents, or new information, as well as other content that the targeted audience may desire.

Diffusion of innovation is the process by which an innovation spreads over time through a series of adopters.

Digital convergence implies that multiple technologies will be used to access the Internet.

Disintermediation is the process of eliminating the middleman from the exchange process.

Distance workers complete all or part of their job by telecommuting from home.

Distinctive competencies are unique areas of advantage in which a firm can differentiate itself from competitors.

Domain name the name that is used to access an internet site.

Drop-ship to drop-ship means a manufacturer or wholesaler ships directly to the customer at the request of the seller (retailer or broker).

Dutch auction works by having the seller lower the price continuously until a buyer decides to purchase at the stated price.

E

E-business value chain views information technology as part of a business's overall value chain and adds to the competitive advantages of a business.

E-business, or electronic business are systems that use a number of information technology–based business practices to enhance relationships between the business and the customer.

E-cash (or electronic cash) allows individuals to purchase without paper dollars.

E-commerce is the practice of engaging in business transactions online.

Economic welfare is the net benefit an economic system provides to a society.

E-mail (or electronic mail) allows for the transfer of text-based content over the Internet.

Enduring involvement exists when an individual has a high-level interest in a topic over an extended time period.

Ethical dilemma exists when a proposed action benefits an individual, business, or society, but at the same time has negative consequences for others.

Ethical snooping is fairness in the collection of data.

Extranets are Internet links between business suppliers and purchasers.

F

Filter a software filter blocks unwanted material, such as pornography, from being downloaded from the Internet.

Firewalls are security measures designed to prevent hackers from gaining access through a server to a Web site.

Flaming is the process of sending angry e-mail messages, often characterized BY USING ALL CAPITAL LETTERS.

Flash and Shockwave are platforms that allow multimedia (sound, videos, animation, etc.) to be played on Web pages.

Frequently Asked Questions (FAQ) are commonly asked question and related answers, often ordered by topic and posted on a Web site.

G

Gatekeeper is an individual who controls the flow of information in a communication system.

H

Hackers are individuals who attempt to break through online firewalls for pleasure or profit by "hacking" their way into computer networks.

High involvement exits when individuals consider the purchase or topic to be interesting or important resulting in the individual attending more closely to information, attempting to comprehend complex messages, and be more willing to spend time with a Web site.

Home page the main page (commonly the first page) that a visitor sees at a Web site often linking to more pages.

Host each server that is hooked up to the Internet is a host.

Hoteling is the sharing of a physical office space such as a desk, cubicle, or actual office.

Human capital is the skill that individuals gain through education, training, and experience.

Hyperbolic tree allows users to visually navigate hierarchies of hundreds or thousands of objects. Each level of the hierarchical structure is linked to other subcategories.

I

Infomediary is a firm that specializes in the capture, collection, or analysis of data. This service can be marketed to other businesses and can protect individual privacy.

Information is constructed from facts, gives meaning to phenomena, and allows managers to make decisions.

Infrastructure is the basic structure that allows a system to operate. For the Internet, this includes lines, browsers, computers, servers, etc.

Infrastructure attack occurs when an individual interferes with the operations of a computer system.

Innovation a new product or process or the act of creating a new product or process.

Interface links the user to the technology. An ideal interface does not require any behavioral change on the part of the user.

Intermediaries are wholesalers and retailers that facilitate exchange between producers and consumers (both business and end users).

International portals are portals designed for international markets.

Internet is a global network of computer networks that use a common interface for communication.

Internet Service Provider is the means of going online or linking to the Internet backbone that Internet users must have.

Intranet are internets that operate inside a business.

IPO (initial public offering) a company has an IPO of stock when it first offers shares to the public.

K

Killer application (killer app) is the software product that entices a user to adopt a larger technology.

Knowledge economy gains wealth based on what individuals can create from knowledge, rather than what they can create from physical labor alone.

L

Last mile represents the narrowest access to the user, which is usually the link from an exchange to an home or business.

Lifetime value of a customer (LVC) is the sum of expected lifetime earnings minus the lifetime costs (acquisition costs, operating expenses, customer service) of a customer.

Linear communication communication that follows a scripted flow.

Low-cost competitor one of two broad strategies that can be used to gain a distinctive advantages.

M

Market capitalization is the value of the company on the stock market. It is the number of shares outstanding times the value of those shares.

Marketing decision support system (MDSS) provides information to aid in developing marketing strategies.

Mass customization is the process of producing individualized products at mass-production speeds and efficiencies.

Mental model is a set of relationships kept in one's mind used to understand how the world, or a piece of it, operates.

Metaphors language tools that allow a person to understand a new idea by relating it to previously understood concepts. "Surfing the net" is an example of a metaphor.

Micropayments are a means of paying for small Web transactions often set up with digital wallets or charged to an individual's credit card.

Mirrored site allows a Web site to be placed on more than one ISP, allowing less congestion and faster delivery of content.

Momentum refers to the general tendency for businesses to keep moving in the same strategic direction.

Moore's law states that the density of microprocessors doubles every two years while costs decrease.

N

Net generation (N-Gen) refers to those individuals born after 1977.

Netiquette refers to proper etiquette over networks and includes the rules for common courtesy online and the informal rules of the road for cyberspace.

Niche sites are designed to target a market's psychographics by focusing on narrow activities and interests.

Nonlinear communication allows a free flow and exchange of information as with conversations between individuals.

O

Online communities are groups of individuals who share common interests and use the Internet to foster their communities by accessing the same Web sites for communication, commerce, or support.

Open source code allows software to be improved through public collaboration by allowing access to the inner workings of a software code.

Open standards are basic sets of instructions, such as programs or programming methods, that are not owned by a single company and are free for others to use.

Operating system is the program that controls the computer. Windows 95/98 is an operating system, as are Linux, OS2, Windows NT, and DOS.

P

Paretto Principle (or 80/20 rule) dictates that 80 percent of profits may come from 20 percent of a business's customers.

Permission marketing is when the customer ops in, or signs in, at a Web site and agrees to receive e-mail based on direct marketing.

Plug-ins allow rich content files such as video, radio programs, and other multimedia content to play through browsers.

Pornography exists online when material depicts erotic behavior intended to cause sexual excitement.

Portal is an entranceway onto the Internet. It is often the preferred starting point for searches, entertainment, information, e-mail, or any other Internet-based product.

Proactive implies acting in anticipation of future problems or opportunities, rather than being reactive, waiting and reacting to the environment.

Product champion is an individual inside an organization who acts as an advocate for an innovation.

Promotional mix includes the use of public relations and publicity, advertising, personal selling, sales promotions, and hypermedia such as Web sites.

Psychographics (lifestyle criteria) generally profile individuals based on their preferred activities, interests, and opinions.

R

Reactive waiting and reacting to the environment.

Real-time chat groups allow several focus-group members to interact online at the same time and have real-time discussions.

Relationship marketing refers to the strategies a business must undertake to hold desirable customers over a long time period.

S

Sales auction sites allow individuals and businesses to sell products online and have potential customers bid for the price of the product.

Sales channels are the models that businesses use to sell to their customers. These could include brick and mortar outlets, catalogs, direct marketing, or e-commerce.

Scams and fraud are two ways of indicating an act of deception or misrepresentation.

Self-regulation is when an industry imposes its own voluntary standard on members.

Shill is an individual who takes the place of a real bidder by inflating the bids for an object, forcing other bidders to increase their offers.

Snail mail is mail delivered through a postal service.

Software wallet requires that a buyer set up an online account so that when a microtransaction is undertaken, the wallet is debited or has money taken out. This system works much the same way as a smart card.

Source code is the original building blocks of a program.

Spam is the process of broadcasting unsolicited content to a large number of individuals over the Internet.

Spin-off occurs when a parent company creates an independent division. This could entail a distribution of shares of stock in the new division to owners of the parent company.

Sponsorship (or co-branded ads) integrates a company's brand to the editorial content of the Web site.

Streaming allows digital information to be sent in packets, or small units. These packets can be played as they stream in. This allows large multimedia files to play without downloading the entire file at once.

Streaming brings in a number of smaller packets of information to load and play.

Stretch goals are goals that may seem impossible to reach. A stretch goal focuses a business on what it would like to be able to achieve and motivates employees to be creative.

Supply chain is the network of suppliers and customers for goods, services, or information used from the point of origin to final consumption.

Supply chains are the suppliers, warehouses, shippers, distributors, and anyone else who may be involved in providing materials to a company.

Switching cost is the additional cost involved in learning something new. For example, for a business, the costs involved in adopting a new software package would include the software expense, support expense, training costs, and slowed productivity costs. The largest of these expenses could come from training, support, and slowed productivity.

Systems approach helps decision makers look at how all aspects of a strategic business unit (SBU) interact with each other. Systems are also seen as being organic in that they must change in response to their environment or face the possibility of becoming extinct.

T

Targeted e-mail an effective means of directing users to an internet site.

Threaded discussion lists allow individuals to add to an initial message with successive messages. This allows a newsgroup user to add to a thread, or single conversation, by indicating a response to the prior message.

Thumbnail is a quick sketch of a communications concept. This allows the developer to create a large number of ideas in a short time period.

Transaction cost analysis is the process of assessing the overall cost of maintaining and finding new relationships. A firm will stay with a current partner if the cost of finding a new partner outweighs the benefits that can be obtained.

U

Upstream traffic is communication from the browser to the provider. This usually requires small amounts of data to be sent back to the provider, which may then send large files downstream to the browser.

V

Value chain is a way of envisioning the collection of activities that a business undertakes to design, produce, market, deliver, and support products or services.

Vertical portals are designed to serve narrow niches within specific industries.

Viral marketing occurs when a customer promotes something through use of a product or service such as a Web site or e-mail.

Virtual private network (VPN) A VPN can connect two businesses, such as a franchise and its headquarters, by using dedicated lines (communications lines that are not open to outside users) that are connected to ISPs. The ISPs then use the Internet for long-distance communication.

W

Web spiders are bots, or software robots, that "crawl" through the Internet looking at Web sites. They collect information and send it back to the search engine database, allowing the information on sites to be retrieved.

Webcast video allows for streaming of video signals to an individual's Web-accessing device.

Webcasting allows users to have information delivered to their "doorway" or browser without requesting or searching for information.

World Wide Web uses graphically based Internet standards and has allowed easy access to information and communication around the world.

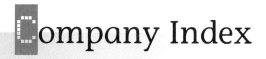

Company Index

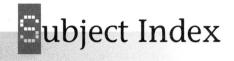ubject Index

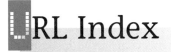

URL Index